The Oxford Book of Australian Travel Writing

THE OXFORD BOOK OF AUSTRALIAN TRAVEL WRITING

Edited by

ROS PESMAN

DAVID WALKER

RICHARD WHITE

Melbourne
OXFORD UNIVERSITY PRESS
Oxford   Auckland   New York

OXFORD UNIVERSITY PRESS AUSTRALIA

Oxford   New York
Athens   Auckland   Bangkok   Bombay
Calcutta   Cape Town   Dar es Salaam   Delhi
Florence   Hong Kong   Istanbul   Karachi
Kuala Lumpur   Madras   Madrid   Melbourne
Mexico City   Nairobi   Paris   Singapore
Taipei   Tokyo   Toronto

and associated companies in
Berlin   Ibadan

OXFORD is a trade mark of Oxford University Press

Introduction, selection, biographical information and notes
© Ros Pesman, David Walker, Richard White 1996
First published 1996

National Library of Australia
Cataloguing-in-Publication data:

The Oxford Book of Australian Travel Writing
    Bibliography.
    Includes index.
    ISBN 0 19 553640 1.

    1. Australian literature. 2. Travelers' writings, Australian. 3. Australians - Travel - Foreign countries—
History. I. Pesman, Ros, 1948– . II. White, Richard, 1951– . III. Walker, David (David Robert),
1945– . IV. Title: Australian travel writing.

    A820.80355

Edited by Katherine Steward
Text design by Cora Lansdell
Cover illustration: Horizon Photo Library
Typeset by Desktop Concepts P/L, Melbourne
Printed by OUP Hong Kong
Published by Oxford University Press,
253 Normanby Road, South Melbourne, Australia

CONTENTS

CONTENTS

EDITORS'
ACKNOWLEDGMENTS

The editors would like to thank Geoffrey Serle, Stuart Macintyre and Penny Russell for generously sharing their knowledge of people, books and places in Australian history; Katherine Steward and Peter Rose of Oxford University Press for their sympathetic editing and astute advice; Ann Chandler, Terri McCormack, Catherine Dick, Melissa Harper and Karen Hutchings for diligent and good-humoured assistance; the students of 452S in the Department of History, University of Sydney for the inspiration and enthusiasm that makes the relationship between teaching and research so productive; as always the staff at the Mitchell Library, the National Library of Australia and the La Trobe Library for their expertise and forbearance; and finally the Australian Research Council, Deakin University and the University of Sydney for financial support for this and related projects.

INTRODUCTION

Travel has always been central to the experience of living in Australia and to giving that life a meaning. For Aboriginal Australians, identity was — for many still is — bound up in the travelling of the land; possession was confirmed not by a title deed but in the very movement from place to place.[1] Some travelled 'overseas' too, to Papua and Sulawesi, well before 1788.[2] Non-Aboriginal Australians defined themselves through a different form of travel, an experience or folk memory of migration. All migrant societies necessarily develop a keen — if ambiguous — sense of place. Wealthy and mobile, European Australians travelled the continent, creating a relatively uniform culture that spanned vast distances. Some have argued the distinctive Australian was to be found among the greatest travellers, the nomad tribe of drovers, shearers, bullockies and swagmen. Their travelling, in distancing them from their European roots, helped forge a nation.[3] Others have stressed the impact of migration and the displacement at the core of the migrant experience. The sense of being Australian for non-Aboriginal Australians has involved a comparison with somewhere else a world away — most often England or a generalised Europe, but also frequently Asia or the United States.

Making those comparisons at first hand, and making imaginary places real, became a confirmation of identity and so travel abroad became a central ritual for the European Australian élite. Ironically though, the distinction of taking the first recorded overseas trips by Australians belongs to two Aborigines, Bennelong and Yemmerrawannie, who accompanied Governor Phillip when he returned to London in 1792. Yemmerrawannie died there, buried at Eltham in Kent, the first of many Australians to find the separation from home unbearable. Bennelong returned home in 1795 to regale his community with the sights he had seen. From then on, ships on the return voyage to England would carry a contingent of travellers seeking to measure themselves against the Old World. Europe would always be the great measuring rod of civilisation. From this European outpost in the

Pacific Australians would conquer new worlds with remarkable thoroughness as well. Asia particularly would attract attention, as the great mystery;[4] the Americas would be their future;[5] the Pacific, their colonial domain.[6] They would become among the world's most enthusiastic travellers, with 800 000 passports being issued annually and two million overseas trips by Australians each year. The statistics are particularly remarkable when we consider how distance ensured that any foreign travel was expensive and time-consuming, and that the favoured destination, for most of the past two hundred years, was as far away from Australia as it was possible to go.[7]

They would return to tell their friends their travel stories; flaunt their souvenirs, paintings, sketches, postcards, photographs, slides and videos. Most interestingly, this supposedly anti-intellectual, insular, provincial society would write about travel, in diaries, letters, newspapers, magazines and books. In the relatively small Australian market, travel books alone would number almost 1000 by 1970.[8] It would seem to be a genre that found a ready readership, judging by the number of rapid reprints and the number of Australians who produced multiple travel books. Despite their popularity when first published, most are no longer in print. This anthology is a selection of what Australians have published about their travel overseas, a skimming of a vast national travel diary which has for the most part lain forgotten.

Given the importance of travel for Australians, it may seem surprising that no previous attempt has been made at a comprehensive selection of that genre of Australian overseas travel writing. There have been attempts to go some of the way — shorter anthologies of the travel writing of respectable literary figures, of Australians in the United States, of Australian women at home and abroad, of Australian poets in Europe and writers in Asia, of particularly prolific individuals, of recent Australian writers in Europe, of contemporary travel stories.[9] But none have recognised Australian travel writing as a category in itself, as something to write home about. Elsewhere the genre has been ignored. There is no entry for travel writing in the *Oxford Companion to Australian Literature* (second edition, 1994); nor does it feature in the *Penguin New Literary History of Australia* (1988). There have been no significant critical studies of Australian travel writing, and historians have paid it little attention despite the rich history of travel, its culturally revealing customs and conventions and the value of travel writing as source material.[10]

The reasons for this apparent lack of interest are not hard to find. Conceiving the subject itself is difficult for Australians. When we think of English travel writing we think readily enough of what the English have written about the world.[11] When we think of Australian travel writing, we are more likely to think of what the world has written about Australia. 'Australian travel' in library catalogues tends to bring together the works of visitors travelling in Australia; what Australians have had to say about the outside world is dispersed throughout a collection. The immediate interest has been in what outsiders have said about us, not what we have said about them.[12] This anthology breaks that habit in asserting that 'Australian travel writing' ought to be concerned with Australians' perceptions of the rest of the world.

These attitudes are part of the colonial condition. Colonialism implies a one-way gaze, the imperial power gazing over the colonised territory, its people and resources: few have bothered about the gaze in the other direction. We too readily accept that provincials on the periphery of the centres of power, cringing or strutting their way round the world, cannot possibly have anything useful to say. This anthology has been put together in the conviction that not only might the peculiarity of Australians' peripheral vision on the world offer fresh and useful insights into what they have seen, but it also speaks volumes about the ways in which Australians have seen themselves.

Other explanations may originate in the élitism and escapism of travel abroad. For most of Australia's history, travel has been the preserve of the middle class, a middle class often seen as not being particularly relevant to the creation of Australian culture or society, least of all when enjoying the frivolity of leisurely overseas travel. Furthermore, Australian history and cultural criticism has tended towards navel gazing, regarding Australia as the object of attention, and seeing those identified with the outside world as remote and even irrelevant. When literary studies insisted upon an Australian-focused canon, they not only marginalised a great tradition of Australian writing — Martin Boyd, Henry Handel Richardson, Christina Stead — in which travel and overseas experience were central, but also failed to recognise how important overseas experience could be even to many writers associated with the staunchly nationalistic *Bulletin*, of whom Henry Lawson, Randolph Bedford, Louis Becke and Nathan Spielvogel are represented in this anthology. Even in 1994 Frank Moorhouse's *Grand Days* could still be excluded from the Miles Franklin Award on the grounds that its setting in Geneva in the 1920s did not fit the condition that a book deal with 'Australian life in any of its phases', despite the novel's protagonist being remarkably similar to Miles Franklin herself. Similarly in art history, an emphasis on the Australian landscape as the defining element in Australian painting meant the exclusion of expatriates from the national canon, as well as devaluing a considerable body of work by artists such as Arthur Streeton on the grounds that it was painted overseas.

The need to correct these tendencies is now widely recognised. There have been major biographies of Richardson, Boyd, Stead and

George Johnston,[13] along with exhibitions of expatriate artists. Donald Denoon has asked that we shift the focus of historical enquiry from Australia to Australians, wherever they may be.[14] And many historians are turning their attention to the values and experiences of the Australian middle classes. This anthology is part of that revisionism, recognising that the overseas experience is critical in Australian culture and that the rituals of the middle class are important in Australia's history.

A final explanation for the neglect of Australian travel writing lies in the fact that the Australian travel experience is very hard to pin down. Travel is so pervasive as a theme in Australian literature that we take it for granted, yet at the same time the range of travel experiences Australians have written about is particularly diverse, so we do not always recognise it as travel. Australian travel writing straddles, for example, the conventional though suspect hierarchy of explorer–traveller–tourist. Australians have been in the forefront of opening up the last frontiers of Western exploration in the twentieth century: Douglas Mawson in the Antarctic and Jack Hides in Papua New Guinea are both represented here. Mary Gaunt, alone in Africa in 1910, and George Morrison's remarkable journey through China must rate close to exploration too. Explorers can return with stories of the 'unknown' that verge on fiction. In documenting the 'unknown', they are also, as Rana Kabbani and Edward Said have made clear, involved in a colonising project: 'The claim is that one travels to learn, but really, one travels to exercise power over land, women, peoples'.[16] Others — Alexander Morrison in Russia, Malcolm and Anna Oram motor-scootering through Asia — did not think of themselves as explorers but still saw themselves as travellers, distinct from and rather superior to mere tourists.

At the other extreme 'mere tourism' has also established its legitimacy in Australian travel writings, and not just as an object of satire. As Ethel Turner pointed out, it is all very well for superior English acquaintances to suggest getting off the beaten track, but for the untravelled Australian, like a blind man 'only just possessed of the priceless treasure of sight', exploration can often take place in a world that is very *well* known.[17] It is a paradox that Randolph Bedford exploits in the title of his travel book, *Explorations in Civilization*.[18] All-too-familiar Europe leaves the poet John Forbes perplexed: 'what do you make of a landscape that/ reminds you of itself?'.[19] And what can be more familiar than Clive James flying into Los Angeles? No chance of tall stories or explorer's fictions here, for the destination is itself a fiction that Hollywood has ensured everyone knows better than their own backyard. So Australian travel writing can readily encompass both the centre's journey to the periphery — as a modern western traveller explores the 'unknown' — and the periphery's journey to the centre —

as the provincial explores the metropolis. The Australian traveller can be both coloniser and colonised.

The literary range is wide too, and the boundaries between travel writing and other literary genres quickly become blurred. In most national literatures, for example, the difference between travel writing and autobiography is reasonably clear-cut, but in Australia the border is not policed. In the typical autobiography of a bourgeois Australian — and autobiography is a supremely bourgeois form — overseas travel not only takes up a lot of space but often represents a crucial turning point in the narrative.[20] The critical rite of passage, the supreme test of one's courage or identity, the moment of epiphany or the occasion that the veil falls from one's eyes so very often happens overseas. It was in Alexandria that Patrick White found Manoly Lascaris, 'the central mandala in my life's hitherto messy design', and on the Acropolis that he found 'the symbol of everything I or any other solitary artist aspired to before we were brought down into the sewage and plastic of the late Twentieth Century'.[21] It was at Oxford that Manning Clark recognised himself as an Australian and later began to write his monumental history;[22] it was at Pisa that Martin Boyd found 'something towards which I had always been groping … a homecoming of the spirit'.[23] It was in London, after only two nights, that Christina Stead's semi-autobiographical Teresa was turned from a 'foolish, romantic girl' into a woman;[24] in Leipzig that Henry Handel Richardson 'became a person in my own right' and discovered her creative talent lay in writing.[25] Arriving in Naples 'was like going to heaven' for Shirley Hazzard; 'really for the first time I knew what joy was'.[26] For Clive James, merely passing through Sydney Heads 'was like being born again'[27] and Peter Conrad was not born at all until he stood on Waterloo Bridge, aged 20.[28]

Many of the cultural élite return to Australia, as if to normality, but many others travel on for a lifetime, or they settle elsewhere. Where are the boundaries then? Is the autobiography of an expatriate anything other than an extended travel story? When do the autobiographical writings of Jill Ker Conway, or Henry Handel Richardson, or Clive James, or Donald Horne, or Barry Humphries stop being travel writing and become something else? Similarly other genres — the social commentary of C. P. Fitzgerald in China or Geoffrey Blainey in the Soviet Union, the journalism of Alister Kershaw in Paris or Richard Hughes in Hong Kong, even the war correspondence of 'Banjo' Paterson in South Africa or Alan Moorehead in North Africa — regularly spill over into a literature of travel, in narrative structure as well as in positioning the author as the wide-eyed, the curious, the accidental but always attentive tourist. Even at war, it has been argued, the Australian soldier was half a tourist.[29]

All these forms need to be included in a definition of Australian travel writing and represented in an anthology. It would have been easy to fill several volumes from conventional travel writing alone; indeed our related project, *An Annotated Bibliography of Australian Overseas Travel*, specifically excludes journalism, autobiography, varieties of war literature and fiction. But given the pivotal role of travel in Australian life, it would have been perverse to exclude related genres that have sometimes taken on the form of a travel narrative. We have, however, restricted our selection to published work.

Definitions and hard-and-fast boundaries are just as problematic when it comes to the relationship between fiction and travel writing. Because of the traveller's long-established reputation as a fabulist whose tales of monsters and curiosities defy belief, the traditional traveller's tale falls into a crevasse of ambiguity. Lady Mary Wortley Montagu lamented the plight of the modern eighteenth-century traveller who was resigned to not being believed:

> We travellers are in very hard circumstances: if we say nothing but what has been said before us, we are dull, and we have observed nothing. If we tell anything new, we are laughed at as fabulous and romantic ... For my part, if I live to return amongst you, I am so well acquainted with the morals of all my dear friends and acquaintances that I am resolved to tell them nothing at all.[30]

Indeed Eric Leed suggests that it is in the traveller's tale that we may find the origins of fiction, 'a story or an image that, assumed to be neither true nor false, functions in a climate of suspended belief'.[31] In that context conventions of empirical non-fiction emerge to assert the 'truthfulness' of the narrator. But those conventions can only ever be conventions, and they can be adopted at will. Who is to know? Does it really matter in a travel book if something really happened? In bringing back news of the unknown, who will ever know anyway if the truth is embellished? The first travel articles describing Yellowstone in the USA were rejected by publishers on the grounds they were unbelievable.[32] The challenge for the travel writer on the unknown frontier, where tales of the extraordinary are to be expected, is to be believable, not to tell the truth. The two writers in this collection who came closest to the unknown both had their veracity questioned: critics insinuated that Mawson, with the only account of the deaths of two comrades, and Jack Hides, whose explorations in Papua New Guinea left many dead in their wake, could have had reason to bend the truth. It is only a short step to dispense with any obligation to fit conventions of truth and simply create an entirely fictional world — and Australian literature has its examples, from Norman Lindsay's *Hyperborea* and Lemurian fantasies through to a strong tradition of science fiction.[33] We have resisted including examples here, more for lack of space than a conviction that such writing must by definition be excluded from the literature of travel.

On the other hand, the dilemma for travellers to the centre is to say something new and fresh about worlds that are extremely well known, where the scope for surprising the reader is so much less. Not only are these worlds known in a factual sense, studied at school, read about in newspapers; they are also intensely familiar as imaginative constructions. Indeed the knowledge, even the fully elaborated imaginative construction, precedes the experience of travel, and particularly of Australian travel to Europe. Time and time again travellers write of how a heritage of European literature had created their experience for them before they had even arrived, or had created the desire to travel in the first place. The most common Australian metaphor for the experience of travel to the Old World was that it was like entering some sort of pre-existing imaginative world, a dream, a painting, a novel, a film.[34]

While not a peculiarly Australian dilemma, it is a problem that characterises a great deal of Australian travel writing. How can yet another description of familiar sights, yet another discovery of familiar places, be justified? The solution in Australia has been to emphasise one of the two extremes of the spectrum from the social to the personal. The first response is to reject what Roland Barthes has seen as the Blue Guide tourist tradition, which separates the tourist site from the uninteresting and inconvenient society surrounding it.[35] Many quite ordinary Australian tourists engage in the very social analysis that Barthes sees as normally being precluded by tourism. It is striking how often social structures rather than sights engage the interest of these travellers, coming from a society often convinced of the superiority and modernity of its own social arrangements. They can then look back on the centre, as to the past, with some disdain. A great deal of Australian travel writing derives from a journalistic fascination with slum life — consider the examples of Holman and Bedford in this collection.

At its best, social criticism was the product of a deeply offended sense of social justice reacting to the hypocrisy and oppressions of old regimes at home and in their far-flung empires. At its worst and most basic, it sprang from an obsession with dirt as a supreme test of social efficiency, the traveller a disdainful visitor running a superior finger through the dust on a foreign window sill.[36] Australian travel narratives are full of comments on exotic diseases, dodgy plumbing, dubious food, undrinkable water, disabling climates, smelly foreigners, grinding poverty, and dirt. Patrick White's melancholy scrutiny of Greek cisterns is a vivid reminder of the Australian abroad. Cleanliness was the supreme test of civilisation, and coming from this cleanest of all possible worlds,

Australians often considered themselves more vulnerable to disease and more sensitive to dirt than travellers from grimmer, less-favoured regions. The tropics were particularly menacing. 'To walk about your bedroom or bathroom with bare feet is unsafe', warned Ambrose Pratt in 1931: 'The germs of poisonous tropical diseases are lurking everywhere, ready to attack any abrasion of the skin'.[37] C. E. W. Bean's tourist guide for Australian troops in Egypt advised extreme caution: 'never dream of taking your meals in a native restaurant' where the colour of some aperitifs was 'obtained in ways too disgusting to be described'.[38] Even in London Ada Holman could be revolted by the smells and squalor of the East End. They blamed, variously, the ignorance of natives, the peculiarities of foreigners, the complacency of Empire. Yet even on this most fundamental measure of barbarism, there could be tolerance and self-criticism. Mr Dobbie, a staunch Methodist, had heard Naples described as a filthy city, but after thorough investigation concluded that 'its dirt and filth is somewhat exaggerated. It can hardly be called a clean city, but it is nothing like so bad as it is sometimes painted'.[39] The 'Vagabond', Australia's most famous slummer journalist, smelt nothing in China half so bad as the banks of the Yarra.[40]

If some travellers justify themselves with social commentary, others escape into the personal, with a more romantic focus on the subjective response of the writer, on the experience of stepping into a landscape of one's own imaginative making, or on travel as rite of passage. It is at this point that travel writing so readily merges into fiction. In the novels of Henry Handel Richardson, Christina Stead or Martin Boyd, the experience of travel, so central to the narrative structure, is clearly autobiographical. A travel sketch by Henry Lawson or Frank Moorhouse might end up as either travel writing or a short story. Moorhouse, himself one of the most astute commentators on the experience of travel — his *Room Service* (1985) is among the most penetrating analyses of the psychology of postmodern travel available — argues that in the 1980s, the travel-based short story was 'the most successfully practised short story genre in Australia', accounting for about 20 per cent of the best.[41] With no clear boundary between travel and fiction, Charles Higham and Michael Wilding included fiction, as well as personal letters by literary figures, in their anthology *Australians Abroad* (1967). We have not been so promiscuous, drawing a line, arbitrary as it is, between writing that saw its final published form *as* travel writing, and writing that is traditionally fictional or was never meant for publication. Even so, our distinction is loose enough to include autobiography and, in our penultimate section, some contemporary writing where the lines between fiction and non-fiction seem to dissolve completely. We have included extracts from what Suzanne Falkiner called a 'novel' and from what Gerard Lee called a story on the grounds that they are almost untouched travel experiences, the 'I' at the centre of these examples being no more (and no less) a fictional persona than the putative author of any piece of travel writing.

These ambiguities help explain why literary critics held the genre in low esteem for so long. Those same ambiguities explain the upsurge of interest internationally in recent years, not only in travel writing, but in the meaning of the travel experience.[42] Travel is a supremely ambiguous or liminal experience — in Victor Turner's analysis — where identities can be played with, where one is by definition betwixt and between, where new possibilities emerge, where cultures collide, and where play is sanctioned. That travel lends itself to postmodern analysis — the traveller's playfulness, marginality and loss of identity epitomising the postmodern condition — helps explain the upsurge of recent interest, yet it is surprising nevertheless that travel and travel writing have not attracted more attention. The journey is both the richest and most banal of all metaphors. The narratives through which we construct our lives are those of journeys, of rites of passage from childhood to maturity, from innocence to experience, from birth to death. Travel is loaded with inherited meanings and associated with central myths and sacred journeys — the expulsion from Eden, the journey from paradise lost to paradise regained, the wanderings of Ulysses, the journeying of the people of Israel to the promised land — with archetypes of eternal return — to a golden age, to Eden, to Ithaca, to childhood, to the womb.[43]

This is clearly an international discourse, but it is one in which the Australian experience arguably looms as more significant than the usual footnote, given Australians' propensity to travel and to write about it. Certainly Australian travellers saw themselves fitting into an international context. Many of them responded to the echoes of previous travellers, gaining a sense of historical depth from the multiple journeyings that had gone before. 'Now I knew perfectly well why I was going away', one traveller admitted. 'To sail the Eastern Seas in the wake of Drake and Tasman … to walk the streets of Peking once walked by Messer Marco Polo; to stand on the Great Wall of China where Khubla Khan may once have stood.'[44] It connected the traveller to an ancient lineage of human journeyings. Australian travellers had no hesitation placing themselves within this universal experience. The two most common models Australians have used to describe their travel experiences, particularly of Europe, are two older forms of travel: the pilgrimage and the Grand Tour.

Australians have long construed their travels as pilgrimage.[45] In many cultures pilgrims are encouraged — often required — to travel, once in a lifetime, to the religious centre: Muslims to Mecca, Buddhists to Benares, Christians to Jerusalem. What they find varies: a temporal equivalent to paradise, spiritual fulfilment, an ecstatic rite of passage, propitiation for their sins. We have included here examples of journeys that can well be regarded as pilgrimages. Marie Byles followed a well-worn pilgrim route in search of spiritual enlightenment, but hers was a Buddhist pilgrimage, not a Christian one, and so implied rebellion rather than the fulfilment of a socially sanctioned religious quest. The Nolans, searching for traces of Rimbaud in Africa, did it with all the gusto and disappointments of a medieval pilgrim looking for a minor saint. Katharine Susannah Prichard's journey through the Soviet Union followed a convention of political pilgrimage, even down to her insistence that she had seen the real thing, and not a version staged for tourists.[46] There were individual pilgrimages by Australians to the Holy Land, to Rome, and to other traditional pilgrimage sites.

These, however, were all individual quests: none, not even those to the Holy Land, implied the fulfilment of a duty, or an acknowledgment by the wider Australian society that the pilgrims had become better people. To the extent that there was a single socially sanctioned spiritual centre for Australians, that spiritual centre was 'Home'. The voyage Home acquired the rich associations of a mythic journey for Australians. Many travellers selfconsciously wrote of their approach to Europe as of a pilgrimage. When Robert Menzies had his first sight of England at the age of 40, by which time he had already created a world view whose spiritual centre was London, he wrote 'Our journey to Mecca has ended', while Nancy Phelan's father put her on the ship to England saying 'There she goes. To Mecca'.[47] Particularly for those whom Peter Cochrane has called 'the very best people' — the Anglocentric élite — the approach to London could be an intensely emotional experience.[48] By 1950, George Johnston could satirise the ecstasy of 'Bert Bloxham', a fellow passenger, as he neared London. He

> had been saving for years for his trip Home ... He wept when we raised the Lizard and saw the Cornish folds beyond, and wept again for the Isle of Wight and the Dover cliffs, and he has much weeping yet to do.[49]

England for the Bloxhams, a more amorphous Europe for others, could well be considered a spiritual centre with distinct religious overtones. Ethel Turner's lifelong ambition was 'To go to Italy' and there she could claim:

> We have walked with the Gods!
> We have been to Rome.[50]

The romance writer Louise Mack commented upon what she considered the peculiar intensity of Australian travel at the beginning of the century:

> I wonder are we more than a little hysterical as travellers, we Australians, packed away there at the other end of the world, shut off from all that is great in art and music, but born with a passionate craving to see, and hear, and come close to these great things and their homes ... Twelve thousand miles removes Australians into a realm of such ardent hero-worship as no peoples living nearer the world's centre could ever understand.[51]

The gushing of a Nina Murdoch, included here, has something of the ecstatic religious about it, highly charged, erotic even. Complete spiritual fulfilment could only occur on the other side of the world. There was also, perhaps, a literalness in colonial culture which required tangible demonstration that these old worlds really existed, and also thought of the spiritual as being impossible in a mundane place like Australia. In 1955, a year after his graduation, Chrisopher Koch set out for England with a friend: 'It was still the traditional pilgrimage for young Australians. We were returning to a home we had never seen: to the cultural Blessed Isles'. This was a voyage that mattered.[52]

In his very next sentence, Koch slid easily into the other popular model for Australian travel: the Grand Tour. As with pilgrimage, it became a favourite throwaway line for travellers themselves, and a great cliché for tour promoters. The Grand Tour is a surprisingly fitting metaphor for a great deal of Australian travel, at least in Europe, despite being identified with young gentlemen of the eighteenth century, and functioning to secure the boundaries of the aristocracy. Young men and their tutors took an extended tour of the continent along a well-defined route — Paris, Florence and Rome were essentials — in order to complete the education and refine the manners (and usually sow the wild oats) of the young aristocrat before he returned with his diary and sketches to 'settle down'. It was most commonly an aristocratic rite of passage in Britain and Germany, where Protestantism by the seventeenth century had meant pilgrimage was no longer an appropriate form of travel, but where the sophistication of older societies was still recognised as desirable by the thrusting élites of the new capitalism. By the nineteenth century it was in decline, challenged by new forms of travel. The railways and Thomas Cook allowed middle-class families and middle-aged women to cover the same route on short holidays rather than Grand Tours. Mass tourism had begun. At the same time travel further afield — to the Middle East, Africa, Asia — came to be embroiled in the imperialist adventure. These new frontiers were still dominated by young men, not only aristocrats but the new aristocracy of romantic male heroes. The distinction between 'travellers' and 'tourists' was born.[53] The critical difference from the old Grand Tour was that both the traveller and the tourist understood their own society to be more sophisticated than the societies they visited. They no longer imagined they would be improved by living elsewhere.

For Australians foreign travel could not undergo the same transformation until the arrival of the jumbo jet in 1970, and even then a kind of Grand Tour remained a dominant strand in the history of Australian travel. Young Australians continued to purposefully plod the same well-worn track through Europe, of necessity taking a long time over it, often experiencing their first break with the moral constraints of home, imagining it as a rite of passage that was doing them good, and always, religiously, keeping their diary. Only then would they return to 'settle down', confident they had acquired a sophistication and knowledge that only an overseas trip could bestow on a provincial Australian. As Kevin Murray's study of the middle-class dinner parties of Melbourne reveals, travel talk for Australians remains a thoroughly negotiable form of cultural capital; it positions us, defines our access to the world and provides stories that enable the teller to weave variations on the theme of worldly knowledge.[54]

If we are to accept the Grand Tour as a model for Australian travel, two qualifications need to be made relating to the ways in which travel is bound up with hierarchies of gender and class. As the Grand Tour declined and the distinction between travellers and tourists emerged, Western culture associated travel with masculinity and imperial expansion while tourism, conceived as the inferior and more popular form, was seen as feminine.[55] This distinction carried to Australian travel, with men being seen as the adventurers in Asia or the Pacific while women dominated European travel; there are, however, important qualifications to be made.

Women were numerically the more enthusiastic travellers to Europe[56] and indeed the notion of England as Home drew heavily on Victorian notions of separate spheres for men and women, picturing England as domestic and feminine and the rest of the world, including Australia, as 'the outside world' and hence the preserve of men. Within separate spheres ideology, the activities of men were seen as more significant than (although not necessarily morally superior to) those of women. Certainly there was much in Australian culture that valued the practical, democratic, money-making, physical aspects of Australian life over the 'civilising' influences of education, high culture and femininity. Nevertheless within strands of bourgeois Australian culture, travel to Europe was highly valued, and indeed women's role as nurturers included responsibility for maintaining European manners and 'civilised' values in Australia. If anything women were more active in the pursuit of high culture in Australia, and for much of Australia's history that pursuit ended in Europe.[57] Whereas the sister of a British Grand Tourist might be sent to a continental finishing school, representing refinement, confinement and protection, the young Australian woman in Europe often had a reputation for precocity and independence. Europe offered her possibilities of escape from conventional routines, moralities and responsibilities in Australia, from prying eyes and local gossip, and such things weighed more heavily on women (variations of these oppressions were also felt more keenly by intellectually oriented and/or homosexual men). Clearly then, any definition of Australian travel as Grand Tour would have to allow for the participation of women. While women were the more active travellers, and probably the more assiduous recorders of their travels, men were still more likely to have their accounts of travelling published.

When we turn from abstract discourses to what people were actually doing, we have to recognise that Australian women as elsewhere have also been active as adventurers testing themselves against a hostile world: Mary Gaunt in Africa, Freda du Faur on Mount Cook, Kay Cottee on the ocean, Robyn Davidson in the desert. They have often been as ready as men to take up 'the White Man's burden', finding that imperialism gave them more authority and independence in Africa or Asia than they could ever have at home. And certainly women as often as men have engaged in sexual conquest while overseas — consider how often Australian women ended up married to men met on their travels. Only recently, however, has it been possible for a Suzanne Falkiner to write of such matters with the confidence, predatoriness even, of a Peter Pinney or Eric Muspratt.

The second qualification to the Australian version of the Grand Tour concerns its identification with the aristocracy. Those who, in the nineteenth century, aspired to be an Australian aristocracy regarded a conventional Grand Tour, collecting *objets d'art*, agricultural hints and sophisticated manners along the way, as essential.[58] But in an Australia where class boundaries were insecure and status depended on adopted customs, behaviour and wealth more than breeding,[59] the habit was soon taken up by the middle class, many of whom could do it in style. In 1906 Eliza Mitchell, wife of a wealthy Melbourne barrister, took her four daughters and a nurse to spend eighteen months in Europe:

> We had long had in mind the possibility of my taking our daughters abroad — not to finish, but in a sense to begin their education. My own early experiences had shown me the value of impressions made by foreign travel on receptive young minds.[60]

And even before the 1950s the ethic of the Grand Tour, as an extended improving exercise for young people, was spreading beyond the middle class. The First World War saw working-class men enthusiastically participating in European tourism,[61] and many of the itinerants, drifters and ambitious adventurers began their 'Grand Tour' by running away from poverty. Frank Clune was born into the poor Irish-Australian inner-Sydney working class, but managed to become one of Australia's most prolific and popular travel writers. Sport, soldiering, seafaring, circuses, vaudeville and the international activities of feminists, trade unionists, politicians, temperance advocates and religious organisations, all offered travel opportunities to Australians who otherwise could not afford to go.

Nevertheless the vast majority of Australian travellers came and still come from the middle class, as a class the most likely to want to tell their stories in print, despite the common disingenuous disclaimer that publication came only because friends insisted. Like traditional Grand Tourists they believed that travel was a serious business. Although many accounts are very funny, usually though not always intentionally funny, there is an earnest belief in travel as improving the mind, as conferring status or now as a simulacrum of the postmodern condition. Enormous value was placed on having firsthand experience of the world, though many travellers could have learnt as much from a few hours in a good library. This earnest approach to the acquisition of knowledge contrasts with the casual manner in which they told their tales. They often chose titles, from Sir William à Beckett's *Out of Harness* (1854) to Robyn Davidson's *Travelling Light* (1989), which suggested that both their travel and travel writing were informal and immediate, or were being made to appear so. There are any number of rambles, wanderings, tramps and a certain amount of drifting, mainly in the South Seas. Impressions, glimpses, jottings, sketches, snapshots, notes, diaries and letters recur in various combinations in the titles, implying writing that was done on the spot, in haste, with a certain improvisation.

Casualness is also suggested by the faith in the importance of the first impression. In 1885, James Hingston boasted that he had avoided guide books altogether and that his weighty travel writings 'recorded the impressions made upon his mind by what he saw and heard while such were still fresh'.[62] From London, Henry Lawson told 'Jack Cornstalk' and his *Bulletin* readers:

> You know I always had a great idea of the value of first impressions —
> an exaggerated idea, you used to say. I have it stronger than ever
> — indeed, I sometimes fear that the eagerness to seize first impressions,
> and write them down before they become blurred and lost, is becoming

a mania with me. If I had to write up a big city I'd rather be there a month than a year. We Australians seem to adapt ourselves so quickly to strange places and upside-down conditions.[63]

Florence Taylor agreed: 'Personally, I think the time to write a book is before one has become acclimatised in a country and accustomed to the habits of the people, when scenery that is different can be admired and when everything is unexpected and curious'.[64] A cynic may see this as proof of the adage that Australia produces journalists rather than writers, may conclude that the local market requires the flashy dashed-off first impression more than it does the sustained consideration, may imagine that the writer only has time for a first impression because of the need to press on to the next item on the itinerary. But that would ignore the fact that many autobiographies, sometimes written long after, strain to recapture the first impression. It would ignore the fact that some first impressions proved consistently dramatic: we could have devoted a whole anthology to first impressions of Colombo, the first exotic port, or of Naples, the first taste of Europe, or of the coast of England, the first experience of 'Home'. In such contexts it could almost be said that gushing became a national style for the travel writer. First impressions were emphasised not because they were easy but because they were so potent. They were the moment imagination met reality.[65] In describing their first impressions, Australian travellers could combine the moral seriousness of a cultural élite with the casualness of a democrat. Ultimately the paradox of a casual seriousness springs from a conviction that the real meaning of life is somewhere 'out there', but Australians, uncertain of their social and geographical status, could not possibly be the primary interpreters of it.

For every attempt to generalise there are enough exceptions to break the rule. Neither pilgrimage nor the Grand Tour can account for all Australian overseas travel, or travel writing. Some travels may be spiritual pilgrimages; some are simply rational explorations; others are pure escape. Some travellers have their eyes opened; some have their very worst prejudices confirmed. Some return insistently to Australia as a point of comparison; some lose themselves in the experience. Some like Nina Murdoch are ecstatic; some like Gerard Lee hate it. Some write for an Australian audience but a good many, from Catherine Spence to Clive James, do not. Some explore the unknown while others discover the most intensely familiar landscapes; still others find themselves. They represent almost every social stratum, use almost every means of transport, travel every continent. It comes as no surprise that in 1892, a thousand miles up the Yangtze, 'Chinese' Morrison should run into an Australian working with the Chinese customs service who knew him from Ballarat.[66]

When it comes to Australians' experience of overseas travel, any attempt at reductionism is doomed. Even the one thing that we can be sure is common to these extracts, that they all happen to be written by Australians, ends up as a sleight of hand, disguising great diversity and considerable ambiguity. 'Australian' needs to be defined widely enough to include both immigrants and expatriates. For the purposes of this anthology, we have defined travellers as Australian if Australia provided the stable reference — the home or the sense of origins that underpins identity — against which their other experience, of travel, was defined. Germaine Greer, who grew up in Australia but has lived the rest of her life elsewhere, fits that definition as readily as Sir William à Beckett, who migrated to Australia as an adult, did some travelling in later life, but intended returning to Australia as home. Even Clive James, whose piece reflects a career in England, a reputation as a postmodern media junkie, a need to appeal to the audience of an English newspaper, saw himself as ultimately Australian.[67] All, if pressed, would accept that Australia provided the well-spring for their personal understanding of the experience of travel.

But which Australia? Frank Moorhouse has said travel is 'an encounter with one's nationality'.[68] But nationality is constantly being renegotiated, especially by those separated from their roots. This anthology is arranged in chronological order because the experience of travel is as much about history as geography. The arrangement demonstrates that neither the Australia nor the travelled world was the same for Sir William à Beckett in 1854 as it is for us today. Even within any one period, there are many very different Australias that were referred back to; if the places they travelled were always fictions, then the Australias they remembered were figments of their imagination too. We learn much from these extracts about the worlds they travelled; we learn still more about the Australias they came from; but most of all we learn about that most vital aspect of modern life, the experience of travel itself.

Ros Pesman
David Walker
Richard White

NOTE TO READERS

Original spellings and punctuation have been retained in these extracts, although minor typographical errors have been corrected. Ellipses in square brackets [...] indicate a cut that has been made by the editors. These are situated within the text for smaller cuts, and on a separate line for larger ones.

1

To 1889

The colonial abroad

Throughout the nineteenth century, most Australians overseas saw themselves simply as British travellers, making no great distinction between their reactions and what they imagined were those of the British abroad. If they did think of themselves as diverging from that norm, it was in being a colonial variant rather than being distinctively Australian. Catherine Helen Spence in England found a polite interest in the colonial viewpoint, while Alexander Morrison found the Russians most interested in his possum coat. Most of the writing in this period can be regarded as merely a sub-branch of English travel literature, with some colonial resonances.

As economic prosperity expanded the ranks and power of the colonial bourgeoisie from the 1850s, the old squattocracy were joined on the homeward-bound ships by an increasing number of their fellow colonists. By the 1870s Australia had formed a substantial travelling class, one that was probably larger in proportion to total population than that of the United States. Already sport was beginning to provide occasional opportunities for a wider social range of Australian travellers: an Aboriginal cricket team in 1868, champion scullers and, represented here by Captain Blannin, a shooting team. More usual travellers were youths being sent off for education and a Grand Tour, the pastoral élite stitching up business deals and maintaining family connections, and bourgeois success stories taking an overseas trip as one of their life's rewards. The coming of the steamship and the opening of the Suez canal in 1869, with the subsequent reduction in the duration of the voyage from three months to little more than one, also brought the trip Home within range of a greater number of colonists, as well as making ocean voyages safer, more reliable and even pleasurable. Moreover, Australians were an unusually literate people served by some some unusually good newspapers. They knew that the world would offer more experiences and challenges than Australia ever could.

1854

William à Beckett in Italy

Born in London, Sir William à Beckett (1806–69) had already established a career in law and literature before he arrived in Australia in 1837. Trained as a lawyer at Lincoln's Inn, he made rapid progress at the New South Wales Bar and was appointed as New South Wales solicitor-general in 1841. He moved to Port Phillip as resident judge in 1846 and became the first chief justice of Victoria in 1852. As befits a progenitor of the Boyd family, à Beckett maintained strong literary interests and wrote poetry which included travel themes. Suffering from a form of paralysis in the legs, à Beckett was granted two years leave of absence in 1853 and went to England with his wife and sons for medical treatment. His account of his travels focuses on the three-month tour that the family made on the Continent and particularly on their time in Italy where à Beckett had lived for nine months before coming to Australia. Out of Harness *(1854) was intended 'to convey an idea of my own impressions and feelings during my rapid tour, rather than to afford information or instruction to intending readers'. À Beckett expresses forthright opinions on a wide variety of subjects. He found much to criticise in Italy, from 'intolerably ugly' women, to the 'screaming opera of Verdi', to scandalous mythological paintings. Offensive above all were the denizens of tourist land — customs officials, porters, waiters, beggars, touts of all kinds. Though resented for obstructing the Grand Tourist's gaze on the vestiges of Ancient Rome, they ended up being à Beckett's real subject. His opinions were unremarkable, being common to his class and time. More distinctive is the confidence and decisiveness with which the Victorian Chief Justice delivered his verdicts. Continued ill-health led to à Beckett's early retirement from the bench in 1857, but he remained in Melbourne until 1863, actively committed to promoting the cultural life of the young colony.*

From Rome we made arrangements to proceed to Naples, which we reached on the third day from that of our departure. A vetturino took us as far as Capua, whence we continued the rest of our journey by railway. Our sleeping-places on the road were Cisterna and Molo di Gaeta; at the latter, in the hotel supposed to be built on the identical spot of Cicero's villa. A charming view of the shore and sea of the Mediterranean is to be had from its windows; but unless the villa of the orator was more comfortably appointed than we found the hotel which bears his name, it must have afforded sorry accommodation to the 'distinguished circles' which he is said to have gathered there in his intervals of leisure. The country between Rome and Naples is more interesting from its historical associations and monumental vestiges of the classic past, than from the beauty of its scenery. It has, for the most part, a wild, desolate appearance; and if the realities of brigandage had not existed there, the imagination would have readily suggested them. The high road is tolerably secure; but I would not advise the traveller to wander far off it alone, in the neighbourhood of Terracina or Fondi, or even Albano; at the lake called after the latter place, I read that an English gentleman was stopped the other day (I write this in April 1854) by a brigand, who, after presenting his carbine, lowered it with a bow, on receiving the contents of a well-filled purse.

Such events, however, seldom occur in these days; but amid so much poverty and wretchedness as exist among the inhabitants of the localities I am speaking of, there are many, probably, who would rather be bandits if they dared, than — as almost all of them are — beggars. It is in the latter character that they prove most annoying to the traveller; for miles and miles his steps are literally dogged by them, till his patience and purse are both exhausted — the latter long before the former. The continued sing-song of entreaty which they keep up — men, women, and children, in precisely the same tone and the same words — is like the constant buzzing of a mosquito, and nearly as irritating. It fairly drives all the legitimate associations of the scene out of one's head. How can one, in the midst of such pests, think about Marius in the marshes of Minturnæ, unless to wish oneself in the marshes too, to escape from the greater horrors of the highway?

It is a pity that there is not some way of paying a round sum by way of composition for this roadside almsgiving. Such an impost in favour of mendicity, I am certain most travellers would gladly tolerate, if it would spare them the annoyance of personal solicitation. It would be as well, too, if the licensed corruption, as well as the licensed beggary, could be put upon a more satisfactory footing than it is, at present, in certain parts of the Papal and Neapolitan dominions. Everybody who has travelled therein, is aware that he may be spared the inspection of his luggage, by an adequate gratuity. The officials look to it as part of their legitimate perquisites — in fact, without it, they either could not or would not live on their salaries — and as there is a great deal of trouble saved by this convenient form of bribery, and there is no chance of the delinquents being reported to any House of Commons, the practice is in very general use [...]

On arriving at the Railway terminus at Naples, our trunks were again taken into the custody of the Custom House authorities. These dignitaries were stationed at the door of an apartment bare of furniture, and not larger than a sentry box, in which they stood watching, with the eagerness of caged beasts waiting for their accustomed food, every arrival that promised the chance of a fee. As we approached, one of them stepped back, whilst the other exclaimed — as we drew out our keys, 'No, no, Signor, piccolo moneta.'

'How much?' said I; 'what do you *charge?*'

'Oh, we make no charge; what you please.'

'Well, here is a two-carlini piece; will that do?'

'Not enough, Signor.'

'Another two-carlini piece; will that do?'

'One more if you please, Signor; ah — that will be sufficient; (*to the porter*) take away the trunks.'

During the time the above conversation was passing, crowds of people were hurrying in and out, and a herd of vagabonds denominated *facchini* worrying us, and quarrelling among themselves, as to the tender of their services to carry our luggage, and call us a carriage. Having previously instructed one of my sons to call a carriage, and already hired a porter to carry our trunks, I obstinately declined any aid from the bevy of harpies by whom we were now surrounded, all screaming at the top of their voice, glaring at us with importunate fierceness, and clutching, whether we would or no, at the various carryable articles which we had under our arms and in our hands. Having made way through them, and found the carriage my son had hired, we attempted to get ourselves and our luggage into it; but we soon discovered that a second carriage would be necessary. I beckoned to one in sight which came up, whereupon there was a rush of some dozen facchini towards it, and then back again to us, each vociferating that here was the coach *he* had called for us. Then there was an indiscriminate seizure and transportation of luggage from one carriage to another, amid a screaming, hallooing, quarrelling, and confusion, that defy description. It was in vain that I pointed to the one man whose services alone I had engaged, and whose services alone I desired — it was in vain that I used every physical and verbal remonstrance I was capable of, against any further interference with our persons or our things — both speedily became beyond our own control; nor were suffered for a moment to be within it, until we found ourselves deposited in the respective carriages to which luggage and individuals had been so indiscriminately and unceremoniously consigned. Now reader, you will think, perhaps, the scene was over, and that we were fairly off, on our way to the hotel — Corpo di Bacco! as these desperadoes say, the worst of it was yet to come. No sooner had we given directions to our drivers, than there arose a cry from the whole mob of facchini demanding *qualche cosa* for their insolent interference. On my asking one of them, what he had done, the whole responded with a shrill shout which was equally savage and unintelligible. Pointing to the only man I had employed, I exclaimed — 'I have paid him, and will pay no more.' Then there arose a positive yell of execration, in the midst of which I ordered our driver to move on, but on his attempting to do so, two or three laid hold of him, others jumped upon the step of the carriage, and another laid hold of the horse's head, causing him to back and nearly upset the carriage. At this my eldest son jumped down, and seizing one fellow by the collar was about to strike him, when I begged him to desist; a similar remonstrance became simultaneously necessary to my second son, who was pushing another rascal away from the second carriage; meanwhile I was calling aloud for the police, abusing the driver for not going on, shouting alternately bad Italian, and good, but not very temperate English; till at length, myself nearly exhausted with rage, and my wife well nigh in hysterics, and amid a chorus of vociferation such as an Italian mob can alone give out, we broke away from the desperadoes that clung about our wheels and horses, and set off at full gallop towards our hotel. We had proceeded at a tremendous rate, for about half a mile, when suddenly down went the horse of the carriage in which were two of my sons, and at the same time was seen, lying on the pavement, in a pool of what looked like blood, a form that I feared, at first, must be that of one of the occupiers of the carriage. We were soon relieved by finding that it belonged to a man who had been carrying a cask of red wine, and who had been run over and knocked down in crossing the road, causing the horse to fall upon him, and his wine cask to break into pieces. The poor man was not seriously hurt, but made a piteous moaning about the loss of his wine, for which however four carlini entirely consoled him. If he had been killed, however, I doubt whether the emotion of the driver who had run over him, would have equalled the lamentation of the former, for his *povera bestia*, to which alone he seemed to think it necessary to pay the slightest attention. The animal was soon upon his legs again, and without any further disasters we got to our hotel, where, notwithstanding all our previous discomforts, we sobered down into a sufficient state of composure to enjoy a very capital dinner.

We arrived at Naples on a Saturday, and left it the following Thursday. A residence there of four months, from October 1829 until February 1830, had made me pretty well acquainted with everything worth seeing in the city and neighbourhood, so that, as far as I was concerned, I did not regret the short stay I was now enabled to make. The English, I was told, are not very popular in Naples just at this time, though to the hotel-keepers and shop-keepers they are always welcome, if only for the sake of their money. In the city we contented ourselves with a visit to Virgil's tomb, the monastery of St Elmo, the Museum, and the theatre of San Carlo. Puzzeoli, Baiæ, and Pompeii were the extent of our excursions in the suburbs. Unfortunately, during our visit to the latter, it rained nearly the whole day, so violently at times that we could with difficulty find sufficient shelter among the ruins to prevent our getting soaked through. Years ago my first visit had been made under equally unpropitious circumstances, the day being wet and foggy throughout. Perhaps it was all the more in keeping with the scene that Nature *should* hang her pall over these skeleton memorials of a destroyed city; but desolation's self grows beautiful beneath the blue of an Italian sky; and, though Pompeii was no more, the charm of its sunshine would have been as sweet to me amid its ruins, as it was to those who once tenanted its houses and peopled its streets. I was doomed, however, to depart without this gratification, and obliged to abridge considerably my survey of its remains. Hardly one-third of the city is yet exhumed, and it is remarkable what slow progress is made by the government in the excavation, or rather it is not remarkable when it can only afford to devote a sum equal to 6000*l.* per annum to carrying on the works. In our own country, or in America, the entire city would have been laid bare in a few years from its first discovery. Some have objected to the displacement of the objects discovered among the ruins, whether works of art or otherwise, contending that some contrivance should have been effected by which they might have been left in the exact position in which they were found, or even, if possible, restored to that to which they had originally belonged. Had such a scheme been practicable it would have added certainly to the interest and verisimilitude of the scene; but a measure requiring resources equal to the erection of a Crystal Palace, though an object of Neapolitan ambition, could hardly be possible to the capacities of a Neapolitan revenue.

Out of Harness (1854)

1865

Catherine Helen Spence in England

Born in Scotland, Catherine Helen Spence (1825–1910) arrived in the colony of South Australia in 1839. Governess, journalist and campaigner for electoral reform, women's suffrage and child welfare, she was one of the first Australian women to claim and maintain a high profile in public life. She also wrote novels, the best known of which is Clara Morison *(1854). In 1865, Spence was sufficiently free of the domestic responsibilities that stood between women and travel to make the trip Home. She spent half of her year abroad in Scotland visiting relatives and the scenes of her childhood, the normal pattern for her generation. But her travels also revealed an earnest sociological interest 'in people and in things that make for human happiness or misery rather than in the Beauties of Nature, art or architecture'. Her travel accounts focus on the people she met, on welfare policies and institutions, on electoral procedures. High points of the trip included her meetings with Augustus Hare (inventor of the Hare-Clark electoral system), John Stuart Mill, George Eliot and feminist Frances Power Cobbe. Catherine Spence made a second trip overseas in 1893, the year before her campaign for women's suffrage came to fruition in South Australia. She attended a number of international conferences and lectured in the United States and Europe. Spence's writing on her 1865 trip to Britain presents an interesting comparative analysis of traditional British society at home and the new society that was evolving in the colonies, one which highlights common features in the colonial discourse on Britain: the class system, inequality, poverty, and the greater independence and resourcefulness of colonial women.*

It is always interesting and often very useful to English readers to hear the opinions of intelligent foreigners with regard to their country and their society; and perhaps the first impressions of an Australian colonist, after twenty-five years' absence from Britain, may be worth a little attention. Those who, like myself, have left a provincial part of the mother-country when very young, and have grown up at the antipodes, must have as few preconceived ideas about England as any foreigner. Our knowledge has been hitherto derived from books and newspapers, or from conversations with new-comers or friends who have been on a visit to England, and is necessarily very incomplete; but at the same time we are of the old stock, born in Britain, and with a love and reverence for it greater than any American can possibly have. No spirit of rivalry or antagonism has ever arisen in any of the Australian colonies to prevent us from taking the kindliest view of the mother-country. Although our political institutions are different, and our social distinctions less marked, we are still emphatically English; and it will take several generations before we can have a distinct national character of our own.

It may be asked what there can be to strike us as new or strange if we are so English in character? The character may be the same, but the circumstances are so different under which we have grown up, that we cannot help being surprised at much that we see and hear. In our case, we have an enormous territory sparsely peopled by an agricultural, pastoral, and mining population, with here and there a town or city built on the sea-coast for the sake of imports and exports, and here and there a township close to a gold field or a copper mine; and in the other case you have a small country dotted over with large and populous towns, connected together by a network of railways, and crowded with industrious workmen. With us we only produce the raw material, and all our efforts are directed towards producing it with the smallest amount of labour. With you all invention is on the stretch to make as much out of the raw material as possible, by labour and by machinery. In England all land is private property, and is in few hands. In Australia a great proportion of the land is unappropriated, and held by Government in trust for the people; and those portions of it which are sold are in many hands, and often transferred. In England you have enormous wealth side by side with great want. In Australia labour and the rewards of labour are more equally divided. With you the suffrage is limited, with us it is all but universal. Here you have a State church and many Dissenters; in Australia, or at least in that part of Australia in which I have grown up, there is no endowment whatever given by the State to any religious denomination. Our climate is hot and dry, with no winter snows and no summer rains; our vegetation is different, our landscape scenery is different. So that, I think, it must be acknowledged that however English in character and feeling a colonist may be, he is likely to see much that will strike him as new when he visits England virtually for the first time in his life.

And the first thing that strikes him forcibly is the magnitude of the towns and cities, especially the enormous extent and population of London — not the first day or the second, but after living in it for a week or two, and seeing the miles of streets closely built and crowded with people in every direction. He, accustomed to think a great deal about the carriage of goods and about road difficulties, can scarcely conceive how such masses of people can possibly obtain their daily supplies of food and fuel, even by the bewildering number of railways that radiate from the great metropolis. He see little signs of manufactures, and he wonders how these millions can get a living. Do they live off each other, or off the country in general? Do foreigners, colonists, and provincials all flock to London to be fleeced, that the city population may be supported? He feels as if England must be small indeed, to necessitate men to leave the healthful, breezy country, to crowd into the streets and courts and alleys of London, Manchester, Birmingham, and Glasgow. The contrast between the wealth and the poverty of England strikes him with a strange feeling of awe when he compares the hideous slums of London with the miles of streets in which no one can live on an income of less than a thousand, two thousand, five thousand pounds a year; or when, 'in the season,' he contrasts the splendid equipages, the beautiful horses, the liveried servants, the perfectly appointed equestrians, the idle gentlemen, and the handsome and elegantly-dressed ladies in Hyde Park, with the ragged beggars whom he meets at every street-corner [...]

The great beauty of the English landscape, its undulations, its softness, its wonderful variety of mountain, wood, and shore, impresses most favourably a visitor from our far south land. Its perpetual verdure contrasts with our pastures scorched up for many summer months. The exquisite changes in the tints of the foliage of your forest-trees — from those of spring, when the young leaves are 'some very red, and some a glad light green,' as your oldest descriptive poet expresses it, to the luxuriant greenery of summer, and then to the mellow and russet tints of autumn — are always full of interest to eyes long accustomed to evergreen trees, almost all of one genus, with long narrow pointed leaves. We have, nevertheless, many very handsome trees, and I think the first impression we have of your English trees is, that they are very small compared with ours; and if we land, as I did, in the end of winter, the leaflessness is painfully cheerless. They also strike us as different from ours in having been planted and cared for by the hand of man, for our forest-trees do not shoot up straight to the light, or throw out their branches symmetrically, as yours do; but as we watch the development of the first bud into the tender leaf and the full foliage and the autumn decay, these varieties seem to compensate for the months in which there is not a leaf on the trees. The variety of foliage, too, in the beech, the oak, the elm, the ash, the pine, the birch, the chestnut, the lime, and the various firs and pines, makes us desire that we could add as many varieties to our gum-trees and wattles, and our stringy-bark forests [...]

But, on the other hand, the careful cultivation of Britain, the utilization of every little bit of land (even the narrow ridges on the sides of the railways), the rarity of commons or waste land, gives us a painful impression. We feel cribbed and cabined and confined. Colonial children rarely like England; they do not like every place to be private property not to be trespassed over. There is no doubt that the concentration of all the landed property in the kingdom into few hands, appears a much greater evil to those who have grown up in such a country as Australia than to those who have all their lives seen nothing else. Although I am not so much of a Radical as to suggest a division of property, I must say that I think every facility should be given to the transfer of land, and that some step should be taken to prevent the inheritance of colossal fortunes. In no country should there be any limit placed to what a man may acquire by industry and abstinence, but as to what he may inherit, I think a line may be drawn. Is it really for the benefit of a country, or for the good of the individual, that a fortune of two or three millions should be left to one man, or even to two or three?

In your England an agricultural labourer, working from the earliest days, when he is worth sixpence a week to frighten the crows, till he is worn out at sixty, earns in all his life about 800*l.*, or at the utmost, 1000*l.* This is the money-worth of his life's work. There are proprietors and millionnaires who have as much as that for every day of their lives without doing anything in the world for it, or, at least, without needing to do anything. No doubt, under such a system, England has grown up a very great country; science and art and invention and literature have all been encouraged, but the question arises, would it not have been a greater country and a happier country if there had not been such an enormous disparity of conditions? [...]

Perhaps nothing on the surface of society strikes a colonist more than the number of old people whom he meets. In travelling about in various ways, in public gatherings for any purpose, and in general visiting society, the number of grey heads is remarkable. It is not because England, as compared with Australia, is more conducive to longevity (though I believe that will be found to be the case, in a great measure, when our colonies are old enough to draw the comparison fairly), but because our colonies as a rule were settled and reinforced by young people, and thirty years is too short a period for our old people to appear numerous.

And the next thing that strikes a stranger like myself, who goes a good deal about, and visits both his own friends and relatives and colonial friends' friends, is the extraordinary varieties of society he meets with in England. I think on the whole that this is the most remarkable feature in England [...]

You enter one circle, and you are in the heart of that large world known as the religious world. You see it in the books on the table, you hear it in the conversation; and the visitors and the engagements of the family are all of one class.

You enter another, and you are in the scientific world. Papa's spare hours are devoted to the prosecution of some branch of science, or some invention which is dearer to him than his daily work. Some part, often a very large part, of his family sympathizes with him and works with him; and he surrounds himself with those books and men who are congenial to his researches.

You go to another, and find a number of people living for society — in town going out four or five nights a week, besides doing a good deal in the way of luncheon-parties and flower-show fêtes, and, as a general rule, going everywhere to see and to be seen; and in the country, unable to exist without the aid of picnics, water parties, croquêt parties, and volunteer reviews.

You may next, through a letter of introduction, drop into the very heart of all sorts of philanthropic movements, and there you meet with a variety of people each with his or her panacea for the existing evils of society. One says, Educate the people; another, Wash them and give them decent homes; another says, Give votes to the people, and raise them so that they will educate and provide for themselves. One works for children, another labours in prisons, a third visits workhouses [...]

Your next visit may be to quiet people, who are a world to themselves. You see there simple domestic life, and hear nothing about gay parties, or science, or politics, or progress, or woman's rights, or religious movements in whatever direction. You would scarcely think that any public events took place at all; for though Paterfamilias reads the newspaper, he never talks of it. Mamma looks after her servants, who give her a good deal of trouble; the girls do fancy-work, have each a friend — the sweetest girl in the world — and are very glad to play a game of croquêt with any one; and the young men are far more tiresome than the girls, inasmuch as a lack of ideas in them is more intolerable in the sex which has had the greater advantages.

Again, you may meet with a circle of people who are devoted to art, who are great admirers of some kinds of poetry, and who have travelled a great deal. In such a circle an Australian feels his deficiencies very much. He has no picture-galleries at home; he does not know what to admire or how to express his admiration, and often makes distressing blunders in the opinion he gives. Though he may have taken long bush rides, and made narrow escapes from death by thirst or starvation, he has not travelled in their sense of the word, for he has not seen any antiquities, or stood on any world-renowned height to view a classical land [...]

I used to fancy that we, in Australia, thought too much about money, and made it too much our object of existence, but I believe conversation runs more on money in England than with us. The manner in which young people speak of *unearned* money — of what may be left by relations, or what may be gained by an advantageous marriage, and not of what can be earned by industry, or saved by economy, strikes me painfully. There is a sadly worldly tone in the manner in which the sacred subjects of death and marriage are discussed. In a new country, like ours, girls very rarely have any money, and young men are generally the architects of their own fortunes; marriage takes place at an earlier age, and need not be so very carefully weighed beforehand as it must be in England. We have here and there an old maid, but the mass of our women are wives and mothers, and too full of domestic duties, either to have the high cultivation or the desire for a wider field, which we see so general among middle-class educated Englishwomen [...]

One consequence of our high wages is, that we do not see anywhere the exquisite finish and completeness in our domestic arrangements that you have in England. We have some very handsome and well-furnished houses in Australia, but it is the little details, the little conveniences, the many arrangements made that the family should be saved any avoidable trouble or annoyance that must strongly impress a colonist. I think it is very likely that we in Australia will have a taste for sumptuous furniture and appointments and equipages, but I do not think we can ever come up to the old country in the little details which give completeness. From our wealthy class not being a permanent class, we are never likely to have the old-established magnificence, the collections of pictures handed down from father to son, and added to by each generation, the ancestral woods, the beautifully-kept pleasure-grounds; so that, to see these things, our young Australians must visit Europe, and, in the visit, let us hope that they will learn somewhat beyond pleasing the eye.

I, gathering my ideas of England hitherto almost exclusively from books, have had to rectify and modify many of them on closer knowledge. I do not see, for instance, that England is filled by tuft-hunters and match-makers, by worldly parents and calculating children. There is a good deal more regard paid to appearances and to position, and, as I think, a more concentrated love of money here than in the colonies; but I believe these things are rather on the wane than on the increase. The real goodness of England is not to be seen in a superficial glance through what is called society, but in the homes of the people. I am satisfied that English society is sound at the core, and that it is neither heartless nor altogether conventional.

'An Australian's Impressions of England', *Cornhill Magazine* (1866)

1876

John Smith in Paris and Interlaken

Born at Peterculter, Aberdeenshire, Scotland, the son of a blacksmith, and educated at the University of Aberdeen, John Smith (1821–85) first came to Australia for health reasons in 1847. He returned in 1852 to become foundation professor of Chemistry at the new University of Sydney, a position he held until his death, and which permitted him several trips to Europe. Smith was an influential adviser to colonial governments, on education, water supply and public health, major issues of the day, and was appointed to the New South Wales Legislative Council in 1874. His interests included photography, theosophy and occultism. En route to Britain in 1882, Smith called in at Bombay and joined the Indian section of the Theosophical Society. Smith wrote up his travels in articles for the Sydney Morning Herald, *which were collected and republished in two series of* Wayfaring Notes. *These extracts are taken from the second, dealing with his 'holiday tour around the world' in 1876, when he joined one of the already ubiquitous touring parties of Thomas Cook, in the aftermath of the Franco-Prussian War and the Paris Commune. He is fascinated by signs of progress in the rapidly developing tourism industry but follows convention in scorning what is already a stereotype, the American tourist. Smith died in Sydney.*

PARIS, *January 23.* — We left London last night with a party of Cook's excursionists on the way to Italy, and arrived here this afternoon by way of Dieppe and Rouen. It has rained all the way, and the passage across the Channel was very rough. In coming along the valley of the Seine it was hard to realize that the country had so lately been in the possession of a hostile army. Not till we got near Paris did we encounter any visible signs of the great struggle, in the shape of ruined houses and bridges, and in military earthworks. Immediately after getting located in a hotel we had a long walk through the city to visit the wrecks caused by the Communists. Being in the neighbourhood of the Madeleine we began with that magnificent temple, and were surprised to find that it bore marks of cannon shot on the principal front. We had missed, while travelling, the detailed accounts of the Communist episode, and did not know that any part of the suicidal argument had been carried on here. In the Rue Royale, in front of the Madeleine a block of houses had been burned and was being rebuilt. From this we passed into the Place de la Concorde. Its numerous ornaments have not suffered much, although its great fountains are quiet. I was surprised to see in the neighbouring Champs Elysees and Tuileries Gardens that so many trees were still standing. Many no doubt have been recently planted, but a large proportion of old trees survive. Along the Rue Rivoli we found wide gaps left by ruined houses. The Palace of the Tuileries was a grievous sight, and it was with a feeling of some relief that I found the Louvre apparently unharmed. Eastward from the Louvre were more burned houses. Taking the line of the quay we walked on to the Hotel de Ville, now a mere skeleton of tottering walls. On the opposite side of the river we could see the gutted buildings of the Palais de Justice, Cour de Cassation, &c. Returning by the Rue St Honore, we passed the ruined front of the Palais Royal. The back part, with its glittering shops and cafés and agreeable promenade, is unharmed, and as lively as ever. With the last of the daylight we could just see the pedestal in the Place Vendome, on which once stood Napoleon's triumphant column. This walk made me feel very sad, remembering as I did, these buildings in their glory, and considering that down below the surface of this gay Parisian life there still brood the fierce passions and wild theories that wrought all this havoc. Before starting from London I thought we should probably arrive just in time to witness another revolution, which almost certainly would have occurred had Thiers not speedily withdrawn his resignation. But along with this gloomy side of the picture, I must notice that Paris seems to go on just as before; the streets as noisy and bustling; new buildings going up rapidly; fresh trees planted along the Boulevards; and in a few years, if peace should be preserved, this will be a finer city than ever.

[...]

February 15. — Early this morning our fellow-travellers in Cook's party started for Milan in accordance with their programme; while myself and nephew remained behind in order to see more of Italy. Thus far our experience of Cook's Excursion has been of a mixed character, but on the whole decidedly favourable. To join one of the 'personally conducted' tours saves a good deal of trouble, and perhaps some expense. All arrangements connected with railways, hotels, and guides, are made for the traveller; and, in the case of those whose time is limited, and knowledge of Continental languages deficient, this means a great deal. But then they are bound to a fixed programme; and to visit interesting places with a crowd of people, many of them unsympathetic, must often be inconvenient and even disagreeable. We have been fortunate in being members of an unusually small party, and we have got on very well, especially as we have had an agreeable young German for our guide through the whole round, and Mr Cook himself as far as Rome.

The system of 'hotel coupons', introduced by Cook, on the whole promotes economy, and it obviates the necessity of carrying much money about, and frequently changing its denomination. Mr Cook has selected about 150 good hotels on the Continent, where his coupons are taken. These coupons are made up in little books, each containing so many for breakfast, so many for dinner, and so many for lodgment; and such as are not used are taken back at Cook's office in London at a small discount. Supplementary coupons of one and one-and-a-half franc value are also issued to cover extras. The coupons are now in such demand that fully 150,000 were issued last year, their value about £20,000.

[…]

Walking out after dinner, we met a couple of fellow-travellers, who during the day had attracted a good deal of notice. They were unmistakably Americans, and the husband was a rough sort of man, who probably had 'struck ile' in his own country, and was now enjoying the proceeds. He smoked a big pipe the whole day long, except during lunch, and first drew attention to himself on board the steamer from Lucerne by his inconvenient mode of expectorating. His wife was a handsome little lady, pale and fragile, but got up in an exquisite tourist costume, so complete in all its appointments, that no amount of travel seemed commensurate with its capabilities. Her small feet were encased in neat but strong boots thickly studded with nails. She supported herself with an alpenstock, already branded with a few names; while, hung from her leather belt, there were a natty umbrella, and a tiny silver bugle to recall, I suppose, her husband or attendants, should they happen to get separated in their too adventurous labours, besides a small flask and other little odds and ends, such as scissors, screw-driver, and such like, believed to be useful in arduous Alpine climbing. Her hair (not nearly all her own, I fear) was dressed Swiss fashion, hanging in two plaits, as thick as one's wrist, far below her waist. Altogether she was an agreeable and amusing picture — amusing because of the manifest incongruity between her accoutrements and her delicate frame. Well, this couple must have had a tiff before starting in the morning, for on board the steamer they sat far apart, and never spoke to each other. We could not, indeed, have supposed that there was anything in common between them, had it not been for an active little boy — a four-year-old — who kept running from one to the other, and addressed them as papa and mamma. At lunch in the wayside inn, the lady made a feeble effort to eat, but soon got up and left the room in tears. A kindly German looked appealingly to the husband, and suggested that madame was ill, but only got a scowl and a half-articulated grunt for his pains. By-and-by, however, he went and got one of the maids to attend to his wife. The same German expressed admiration of the little boy, and asked why he took so little dinner. The father explained that he seldom ate butcher meat — 'Guessed he had raised him on bread and potatoes'. In the *diligence* the lady kept in the interior, while the husband sat on the box and smoked. This sort of thing went on all day, and no one could help feeling sympathy with the delicate lady, and indignation towards the boorish husband, whose case we prejudged, and made sure he was in the wrong. When we met them after dinner, however, it was gratifying to observe that the quarrel had been made up; for the lady was hanging on her husband's arm, and looking up lovingly into his face; and the little boy, holding his father's hand, gave us a roguish smile in passing, as if conscious of the little drama that had been enacted.

The principal street of Interlaken is lined on one side with grand hotels, rich in floral and aquatic decorations. On the other side are magnificent walnut trees overshadowing the road. The number, size, and elegance of the hotels were surprising to me when I remembered how the place looked when I passed through it on foot, with knapsack on my back, one-and-twenty years before. Things have greatly changed since then, and the comforts of travelling in these parts much improved. We have found the hotels generally very comfortable, their meals excellent, and the charges not extravagant. At breakfast, the bread and butter and honey are so delicious, that it is difficult to use them in moderation, and anything else seems superfluous. The attendance is also generally good. The hotels are now frequently supplied with electric bells, such as are commonly used in America, and now also in the newer hotels of England. In these countries, however, the usual arrangement is that the bell rings only so long as the small button, that completes the electric circuit, is pressed; but in some of the hotels we have frequented on this tour, for example at Cologne and Lucerne, the bell begins to ring as soon as the button is touched, and goes on ringing till some one answers the summons and stops the noise. It is tolerably effectual in procuring prompt attendance, but, on the whole, not pleasant to visitors, as, in a large and busy establishment, there is rarely any cessation of the irritating clatter from early morning till late night.

We spent a pleasant evening at Interlaken, rambling about till dusk under the great walnut trees, and in the public garden, and watching the last rays of the sun creeping up the snows of the Yungfrau, and tinging the mountain and the cloud masses resting on it with delicate rosy hues. At night there was a *soirée dansante* in our hotel, with good music and spacious rooms, but, although a number of young people assembled, evidently eager for the fray, everybody seemed afraid to begin, and at length we lost patience with them and went to bed.

Wayfaring Notes (Second Series) (1876)

1876

Alfred Blannin in Dover and Paris

Sport has provided the means to travel for many Australians, whether participating in international competitions like the Olympic Games or engaging in cricket tours around the Empire. One of the first groups of Australian sportspeople to tour overseas was a five-man Victorian rifle team. Led by Captain Alfred Blannin (1842–89), the riflemen left in 1876 and spent six months abroad travelling to Britain and Europe and then through North America. The trip had its origins in an invitation from the National Rifle Association of America. Captain Blannin's account of the trip records the competitions in which the team participated and the prizes that were won as well as giving his impressions of foreign places and people. As this extract suggests, abroad was a place for high jinks as well as for culture, and the team's activities no doubt provided their hosts with an early example of the 'Bazza' McKenzie image of the Australian abroad. Nevertheless, even the larrikin could have his moral susceptibilities outraged by the doings of degenerate foreigners.

When we arrived at Dover we felt greatly inclined to stay there, but neither of us liked to say so. I forget how it came to pass, but we agreed that a good night's rest was necessary before commencing our journey; so it was agreed upon [...]

Next morning woke up and found King asleep with his mouth open, so I amused myself trying to throw small pellets of paper into it; but he was too far off, so I woke him up and said, 'Good morning, King.' But, instead of answering my salutation, said, with a yawn, 'I could drink a soda and milk.' 'So could I,' I replied. 'Then ring the bell,' said he. 'Ring it yourself,' I answered; 'it's nearer you than me.' So we lay and looked at the bell rope, which hung temptingly between us. Suddenly a brilliant idea struck me. I took my stick, which was leaning against my bed, and, reaching out, struck the end of the bell rope over towards King, and told him to catch it. After two or three attempts, which gave us ten times more trouble than getting out of bed would have done, he secured it and gave a tug; but, as he had to pull sideways, he was forced to pull heavily. Suddenly I saw the fastening at the ceiling giving way. 'Stop,' I roared, but it was too late; he gave a final tug, and down it came, bringing about two feet of plaster with it. As the next fastening was in the corner over my head, the whole lot swung over to me, and dashed over me up against the wall, nearly blinding me with dust. Then I laid hold of the wire (the rope was lying uselessly on my bed) and began to pull; but, as the next fastening was giving way, I dropped it. We then held a council of war, and decided on making that bell ring, at any cost; so King went out in the passage to where all the wires met, and, not being able to distinguish our wire from the eleven others, took hold of the lot and gave a vigorous pull. The result far exceeded our most sanguine expectations — such a peal of hotel bells was surely never heard before. About four waiters, three chamber-maids, and two small boys all rushed up together and dashed about from room to room in a perfect frenzy of excitement. When the hubbub had subsided, I called a waiter. Said he, 'Did you ring, gentlemen?' 'I rather guess we did,' said I. 'Yes, sir,' he said, 'I thought I heard a bell ring, but wasn't sure; and — ' 'Two sodas-and-milk,' said I, cutting him short: he was getting too funny by half. We had our drinks, dressed, and went down to breakfast, when King went in a perisher at a large round of beef. Wrote our names in the visitors' book, as all *distinguished* people do, and went off to the steamer quickly, for fear we should find bills from plasterers, paper-hangers, and bell-hangers in our account. Kept a sharp look-out for Sleep, but he did not turn up; so we left by ourselves, and, after a short trip, found ourselves once more in France. Took tickets for Paris, and settled ourselves comfortably in the train for a seven hours' journey, which always takes eight to do.

I think the soda-and-milk must have got into our heads, for we slept nearly all the way to Paris. Arrived there at 6.45. Profiting by my former visit, I at once went into the street and hailed a passing cab. We entered, and proceeded to the Hotel de Maurice, made ourselves look smart, and that was no easy work, for the journey had made us awfully dirty — by reason, as much as anything else, of the confounded clouds of smoke and soot which continually pour in at the windows; and the only choice is between getting sooty almost to blackness, or being smothered. We had our dinner, and a most *recherché* dinner it was in every respect. I always think of that meal with the most lively satisfaction. We then strolled out in search of adventures, and made our way to a large garden, brilliantly lighted up, in which was a first-class orchestra playing operatic music. There was a tremendous crowd, and a roaring trade was progressing in cigars, wine, ices, &c.

We strolled round, and, as we had other places to call at, made our visit a short one. As we were leaving, I asked the man if we could return without checks, and he was proceeding to give me the information when King turned round to hear what was going on. The man saw his unlighted pipe in his hand. He roared at King, in French, that he was not to smoke pipes — only cigars — and darted his finger at him as if he would transfix him. King could see well enough what the man meant, but being unable to reply, he could not put his indignation into words. He leaned over the table, glared at the man, and shook his pipe in his face, and at last burst out with, 'Frenchy, you're an ass!' It was very comical to look on, and see King almost foaming in his desire to talk French, so that he could slang-wang the foreigner. It took King half an hour to cool down.

As we wished to see the Mabille we strolled off to find it, but decided to go in a cab. Seeing a cab-stand, we approached, and, as no one was about, took a seat in a cab and waited for the driver. We were having a pleasant smoke and chat, when a burly cabby came up and wished to know what we wanted. I told him, and he said he would take us. So we went off, and in about as long as it takes me to write it we were there. '3 frs,' said he. It was no use arguing with the beast, so we paid it, and entered the Mabille. There is nothing very striking about it: a large garden, prettily laid out, with fountains, cigar shops, drinking bars, a large dancing rotunda, and a skating rink — the whole affair something like our Cremorne was many years ago; but what we saw really staggered us. I had heard of the games carried on here, but was not prepared for the lengths to which they went; as it was only curiosity (and perhaps thirst) we wanted to satisfy, an hour was sufficient. As we were proceeding to leave the place we met Mr Taylor, a *Hindostan* passenger, who joined us in our ramble.

Our next move was to the Bal Boullier, and we were told that, if possible, it was worse than the Mabille. We chartered a cab, and took the precaution to agree, before we started, as to the fare. It was a long drive, and I touched cabby on the shoulder with my stick and asked him to drive quickly. He replied, 'All right! Plenty of time!' In a few minutes King touched him, with the same request in English. Cabby turned round and told King he mustn't hit him, in French; and they indulged in a little lively conversation, neither understanding what the other said — he inciting the man to increased speed, the man threatening to turn us out if King hit him again.

After a long drive through any amount of Boulevards, Rues and Squares we arrived at the Bal Boullier; and what we were told of it was not in the least exaggerated. It is a very large building, with about 100 feet square to dance on, surrounded by tiers of boxes for those who do not dance. It was crowded — men and women dancing in a most excited state, throwing themselves about wildly, and working themselves up to a state of frenzy, putting themselves into attitudes which would not be tolerated in any assembly having the most minute appreciation of decency — the men going almost head over heels, and the women nearly disrobing themselves in their terrible abandonment. The music was beautiful, and it seemed almost sacrilegious that that grand art should be used to pander to the tastes of people who were indulging in the most disgusting exercises it is possible to conceive. It must have been very bad, for King and I were quite satisfied with about ten minutes of it. 'Let a man go alone to such a place of amusement, and the sight for him is perfectly terrible. The horrid, frantic gaiety of the place puts him in mind more of the merriment of demons than of men. If a man falls, woe be to him! — ten thousand screaming fiends go trampling over his carcass. They have neither power nor will to stop.' But as we had come to see these things, so that we could pass our opinion thereon, we could scarcely be called participators; and, besides, we are now enabled to warn other young men possessed of sensibility not to be seen at these places.

Coming out, King remarked to me — 'Well, if that doesn't beat everything I ever dreamed of, chop me in two.' 'It's awful,' I added. 'Oh! that's nothing,' said a voice close to our elbow, and, turning round, we saw an Englishman, who was addressing us. Said he, 'You come over to that café, and you will see Paris in quite another light.' We both said we were sick of it, and declined.

*Hasty Notes of a Flying Trip with the Victorian Rifle Team
in England and America in 1876* (1877)

1879

James Hingston in Asia

Born in London, James Hingston (1830–1902) arrived in Victoria in 1852 to try his hand on the diggings. He gravitated towards journalism, writing for the Argus, *the* Age *and the* Victorian Review. *There is no question that his major achievement was the two-volume travel epic,* The Australian Abroad: Branches from the Main Routes Around the World, *first published in London in 1879 and reissued in Melbourne in a single volume in 1885, replete with two pages of laudatory press notes. This extract sums up his travels through Asia from Japan to Beirut as a Western consumer's guide to the smorgasbord of the Orient. Though confident of the superiority of British imperialism, Hingston offers a more complex appreciation of Asian civilisation than many of his compatriots would have been comfortable with. Hingston achieved instant celebrity as a travel writer and humorist and was compared with Mark Twain, often to the American's disadvantage. At the height of his fame, he wrote a lively commissioned travel guide to the West Coast of New Zealand for the NZ Union Steam Ship Company. Hingston was a remarkably accomplished and justly celebrated travel writer whose work was utterly neglected for more than a century, despite the recent enthusiasm for revivals, reprints and the regular rediscovery of lost genius.*

The fancy for such travel and such notes of it came upon me in Japan, with its novelties of a newly-opened country added to those of an Eastern one. China next displayed its immensity of territory and humanity to my wondering vision. Cochin China and Malasia then followed. The Thousand Islands led me up to their Queen in that united Sunda and Java which, but for Dutch defilement, were as Paradise regained. Resumption of the journey took me to and through Ceylon on to India from Madras to Calcutta, and thence through the heart of Hindoostan, for three thousand miles, to Bombay.

Passing thence down the Red Sea by Aden to Suez, Lower Egypt was entered upon and traversed to Cairo, its capital; and headway then made up the Nile to Assioot, the chief town of Upper Egypt. Down the Nile to Alexandria, and thence by sea to Joppa, brought me to the shores of Palestine. Tent-life then commenced in a journey up country to Jerusalem, and thence down to the Dead Sea and the valley of the Jordan. The route of travel took me onwards to Caipha, Carmel, and Damascus, and thence over Lebanon down to this sea-side Beyrout. Having given the ideas of the East suggested by such journey, a recount may be made of some of its characteristics most observable to outer vision.

Long shut-up Japan made a pleasant impression as a key-note to the music of these Eastern lands. All that was seen there was so novel and of such interest to one who travelled only to observe and remark. Its likeness to the British Islands in size, as also in population, was prepossessing, and its people might be thought to represent what the British would be, had Britain shut out the Romans, Saxons, Normans, and Danes, who have so mongrelized the native blood. The happy Japanee and his pleasant country, his French politeness and his frugal ways, were worth a visit, as showing what our mother land might have been like in the days when it was called 'merrie England,' and when it was as destitute of banks and poor-houses as is Japan, 'where every rood of land maintains its man.'

China and the Chinese show one a different picture. A nation is here found that would shut itself up, as did Japan, if it could, and that believes its knowledge complete, and that it can learn little or nothing from the rest of the world; which bought up the railway laid down in one of its ports by the British that it might destroy it altogether, and so have no innovations from other lands with which to disturb the minds of its people: a vastly extensive country, with rivers in their immensity like those of America, and a population equal to nearly a third of the whole world: a population that now we have broken into their house are swarming out of it, as ants do when we disturb an ant-hill, and who will likely overrun the modern world as the Goths and Huns did the older one.

Not to be forgotten either is the visit that has been made to Cochin China, and the sight of Saigon there and Cambodia further inland. Saigon has shown us one of the follies of the late French Emperor, that was similar to his bamboozling effort to distract the attention of his people from their own affairs to those of Mexico. The French settlement here, made on the line and on the low-lying marshy ground, is bad enough for climate, but to be surrounded by the odious Malays makes things worse. A place, this Saigon, that if made a penal settlement would leave nothing to be desired by those who wish to see justice dealt out to those of their fellow-men who may happen to be found out in their misdeeds.

Singapore presents the pleasant sight to a Victorian of a flourishing town supported by its position only. It stands to the land of which it is an outlying point much as Victoria does with regard to the rest of Australia — nearest to the busy world and its high roads. As a corner allotment this port of Singapore has a daily-increasing trade with those who use it solely as a house of call, for which purpose it seems to be the most favoured of places. A vessel there could probably have been found from most ports of the world, and several from some of them.

Any one will have a lasting pleasant remembrance who has seen the fair and fertile Java — Queen of the Eastern Archipelago and of all the islands of the East — a paradise of a place, in which is seen one of the saddest phases of Eastern life, and that in all its odiousness. Why the Spanish should be permitted by the world to enslave Cuba, and the Dutch to do the like with the eighteen millions of Java, are ugly questions [...]

Forgetting the odious semi-enslavement of its native races, the traveller through Sunda and Java will recall all the perfumes of 'the Spice Islands,' the grandeur of the verdure-clad mountains, and the sweetness of the flowering valleys, the groves of tree-ferns, and gardens laden with fruits found nowhere else, chiefly to be remembered amongst which will be the delightful mangosteen and the strangely-smelling dorian. The beauty of Nature's work in Java is seen to have greatly stimulated an artistic race who in past ages, before Dutchmen disfigured the place, dwelt there, and have left away up in the interior, for our wonder and delight, some of the finest temples the world can show, and notable above all the wondrous 'Temple of Boer Buddha.'

Ceylon showed a fine reverse to the hateful side of the picture presented by Java. The Dutch had sought to make it a similar wealth-producing source to the exchequer of Holland; but England, having obtained possession of it, allows man there to labour for his work and its produce. The true greatness and fair dealing of England in relation to its conquered possessions was not fully appreciated until one came upon Ceylon, and going through it from Galle to Colombo, and on to Kandy, Rambodda, and Newera Eliya, learnt the ways of its tea, coffee, and quinine-growing population, and how nothing in the island was made, as in Java, a Government monopoly for the enrichment of a distant land.

The same story was taught by great India itself in visits paid to Madras, Calcutta, Benares, Lucknow, Cawnpore, Agra, Delhi, Allahabad, Jubbulpore, and Bombay — a run rapidly made, but sufficient to show the system of government, which is without doubt the best that Hindoostan has ever enjoyed. Always the possession of some foreign power, and always probably so to be, India has never had that done for it, and for its advancement among the nations, that Great Britain has there accomplished. Such is shown in its railways, schools, newspapers, local courts, and those other aids to enjoyment of life and protection of property that none of its former owners gave to it. The great names they have left in the story were achieved by the splendid wonders with which they encumbered the land. At these decorative but useless works the toiling millions worked as slaves for the whims of some idiotic or half-drunken despot. Such was India's sad fate, until England became its owner. If not always to be so, that which her Government leaves behind will be memorials whereof any nation may be proud — the story told by them being one that men may always read as they run on every side of their course throughout the country.

Any one may be glad that he has seen India. It is a sight to satisfy the dream of a lifetime, and, to understand fully by outward vision what Shakespeare saw so well in the mind's eye of the world's glory in its outer and visible way.

The cloud-capp'd towers, the gorgeous palaces,
The solemn temples,

are here all to be seen at their best, and such as no other land can equal. They are also mostly visible in that state of dissolution that tells of days of splendour of which the 'revels now are ended,' and 'the insubstantial pageant faded' like to the 'baseless fabric of the vision' that called them into existence.

The visit to Egypt showed another phase of existing Eastern despotism — the land groaning under the oppression of the Turk as Java does under that of the Dutchman. The despotism of the old Roman Emperors we are too apt to think of as a thing of the past, and much as we think of the days of Louis XIV, and of his belief that the State was himself — *'C'est moi!'* Egypt is now in much the same sad condition as was France when its first revolution asserted the rights of its people to a share in the benefits of government.

It is scarcely possible to credit, without personally visiting Egypt, that one man can be allowed to recklessly dissipate the earnings of millions, and go on building Versailles-like palaces out of the hardly wrung and grossly burdensome taxation of millions of starving slaves. If any one imagines slavery as a thing the world has done with, a visit to Egypt will dissipate that delusion in the shortest of time. The humanity that is there not bought and sold, but obliged to cultivate the land for a living, and then robbed of all earnings, and left, half beaten to death, to a wretched starvation, is cursed with the most hideous form of slavery. Of such, disgraceful alike to Egypt and the world, enough was seen and heard in the visits made to Suez, Cairo, and the towns and villages on the right bank of the Nile from Boulac to Assioot, and from thence down to Alexandria.

Gladdest, or perhaps saddest, of all, as a Briton and Christian, will be he who has seen something of Palestine and Syria. Its crusading and other historical associations are pleasant to his memory, and all its Holy Land ones touch his soul. Beyond those, however, there are financial and political ones which touch his pocket, in the millions of British taxes paid to keep Turkey in possession here and elsewhere [...]

What the curse really is that overlies the Holy Land has been made plain by such visit. Every land misgoverned as Palestine and Syria are would appear similarly blasted. Egypt might equally be called accursed, subject to such tyranny as now afflicts it. These lands that were earliest in the van of civilization, and were, with neighbouring Persia, once foremost in fame, are now all the more, for such reasons, mournful and sickening to the traveller's eyes [...]

It will be strange indeed, after ten months of tawny, yellow, and other shaded skins, to see white ones again, and to look upon beings 'cloaked from head to foot.' The human form divine in its unadorned state has been so familiar to one's eyes that it may be a question if the change to its all-clothed state will be a pleasanter one. The compensation for any loss in missing the living Apollos Belvidere and Venuses de

Medici whose forms have been so often seen, will be that in the white and Western world we shall see the all-uncovered faces of womankind.

In leaving the East we leave, too, its old forms of locomotion, the palki of Hindoostan, the jinrikishaw of the Japanese, and its centaur drawers; the palanquin chairs of the Chinese, as also their humbler wheelbarrow street-vehicles. From those to the Egyptian donkeys and the Syrian mules has been a move in a more humanitarian direction. It must be pleasanter to one of right feelings to be dragged about by quadrupeds than by two-footed beings, to which latter form of conveyance an unconquerable repugnance may be honourably indulged. The camel can be dispensed with as a mode of conveyance by those disliking aching bones; but the Eastern donkey is an institution that might be acclimatised in the West to better results than have been there seen of it.

Of the outdoor sights which may be called amusements of the East we shall miss many: — the Japanese drama as enacted *al fresco*, and their wondrous ground and lofty tumbling and posturing; the Chinese tea-house life by land and water, and their street and stall gambling-stands; the Hindoo conjurors also, who were as enjoyable to see as their doings were mysterious, doings that helped to confirm the faith of our youth in the powers of darkness, and in the reality of the moving spirit of Milton's *Paradise* and Goethe's *Faust*. Neither will the Oriental story-teller at the market stands and street corners be forgotten as a pleasant change from the all-musical devotion of the Western world. The good old practice of lively narration which we in our youth recognized when asking our elders to 'tell us a story' has been with the Western world altogether replaced by the too-much-twanged piano, and that singing which as often as not scares away those listeners who are musical enough to understand it.

Gone with those sights will be the magicians who can see into the past and future unaided by packs of cards, who consult drops of ink as better indications for such purpose than the coffee-grounds of our breakfast-cup, and who sell me, as in China, my horoscope for a shilling, in which I see my future as unintelligible as it really is. Departed also will be the street water-carriers, and the sight of those picture-book Eastern wells that are now as they ever were. We shall not perhaps miss the beggars even in the Western world, but we shall not see the lepers, which will be at least one relief. Painted faces are common enough all over the world, so far as both Eastern and Western ladies are concerned, but not out of the East will be visible those facial 'caste marks' on men that tell us what they are, and of their attention that morning to their religious formulas [...]

Some of the sights to be lost on leaving Eastern shores may not be grievous. No more opium-smoking will be seen, nor anything of the wretched-looking faces of its votaries; nor any betel-nut and chunamb lime chewing, nor the reddened saliva with which, as with blood, it fills the mouth; nor any inches-long finger nails on men, nor reddened ones on women. No more shall we see the nasty fashion of carrying infants as packs upon the back or excrescences upon the hip; nor any *al fresco* washing and head-combings; nor any cowdung-disfigured exteriors to cottages; nor men too holy to wash themselves and their clothing. Sanctity so expressed and otherwise shown in shaved heads and yellow garments will be now looked for in other forms. Cathedrals, churches, and chapels, will henceforth replace the temples of the Eastern faiths — the Brahminical, the Buddhist, the Sintoo, the Jain, the Parsee, and the Mohammedan, that with other sects, as the Druses and Maronites, make up the faiths of three-fourths of the people of this world — a people impenetrable to all missionary power, and in their several faiths strong as martyrs.

And so here at this Syrian seaport we men of Australia and America leave that Eastern world that knew nothing of ours — that great East that once held all the world, and is now as the Sleeping Beauty of the fable. On the state of its possessions, their dilapidated condition, and the supine and somnolent state of its folk, our eyes have looked as did those of the Wandering Prince upon her castle and its drowsy surroundings. A great world nevertheless this Eastern one, in that it still holds three-fourths in number, if not in value, of the human race — has made two-thirds of all history, and cradled all the existing faiths worthy of the name.

The Australian Abroad (1879)

1883

A. F. Morrison in Moscow

Alexander Morrison (?1856–1904) was the eldest son of parents who arrived in Victoria in 1856. He was educated at Scotch College. It seems that he studied law at the University of Melbourne before reading for the Bar in London in the early 1880s. He returned to Melbourne in the mid-1880s, but was in Europe again by the end of the decade. He died in England. Morrison's urge to get off the beaten track, beyond the reach of Thomas Cook, took him to Russia in the winter of 1883. His account of his experiences and impressions was first published in the Argus *and then reissued in book form, to provide information about 'one of the most interesting countries in the world, a country which is comparatively little known and hence imperfectly understood'. He found much that delighted him in Russia and his criticism was reserved for the extravagance and indolence of the aristocracy and bureaucracy. The account of his travels in Russia included not only the sights but also information and opinions on food and drink, the police 'and their ways', foundling hospitals, bazaars, the church, manners and morals.*

One of the greatest delights for the stranger in Russia is to find himself beyond that zone of Europe blighted by circular tours and Mr Cook's tickets. He is not in a tourist stricken country. This has several practical advantages. He is an object of some curiosity and interest to the inhabitants, and it is pleasing to find that he is not at once pounced on as a victim for extortion. When I was in Moscow in the depth of winter — to say nothing of tourists (that term which somehow no rambler considers complimentary) — there were very few travellers of any sort there. A pleasing result of this dearth of strangers was the absence of the usual Continental guide-fiend. In Moscow, if you want a guide in winter you must search for him. You need not follow Ruskin's well-known advice, 'Always pay a guide — pay him well — to go away and leave you.' Even if you find a guide, he is not usually that most malignantly tiresome member of the species — I mean the one who gives you a foretaste of the linguistic torture in store for you by the sickening assurance, 'I spik English quite.'

[...]

When the traveller gets tired of the numberless churches and the snow-covered streets of Moscow, there is one short excursion to take out of the town which is worth coming all the way to Russia to do. It is to the Sparrow Hills, about four miles to the west of the city. You go there to get a view of Moscow just as you go to the Pincian to get a sight of Rome, or to the Seraski Tower for the marvellous panorama of Constantinople. The view of Moscow from the Sparrow Hills is frequently compared with these views, but there is no doubt that on the whole is surpasses them, and is perhaps the most brilliant prospect in Europe. Waiting for a fine afternoon, we go out to choose a sledge; in a moment all the isvostchiks are pointing to the desirable points of their respective turn-outs. One wishes you to feel the thickness of his sledge-rug; another, lifting the coat off his horse, ostentatiously indicates its good points; another shows an improvised foot-warmer in his vehicle, and so on. At last, half deafened by their shouting arguments, we choose a charioteer, and the porter brings out the encumbering paraphernalia always needed in Russia — rugs, wraps, greatcoats, with sketch-books, etc., which altogether take up more room than the passenger himself. As we drive off, the servant bends down and looks at the horse's feet. This is a Russian ceremony which wishes you good luck setting out on a drive or journey; it is a specially good omen if the person who bends sees all the four shoes of the horse, and the idea is that if your charger shows only one of its leather shoes as it dashes off you are sure to be upset or run away with. Our road at first skirts the western side of the Kremlin; its white crenelated walls, red towers, and gold domes are painted in brighter tints than usual by the sunshine. Crossing the Moskwa by the stone bridge, we see several immense loads of timber being dragged along the frozen surface of the stream in sledges consisting of a simple floor of wood without sides. The great beams are tied together by chains, pulled to the side of the river course, and anchored by the chain to the bank. Then, when the river melts in May, they are there ready to be floated down the stream. Several million roubles worth of wood is annually floated down the Moskwa in this way. Crossing the bridge, on the right hand stands on an eminence the magnificent Temple of the Saviour, just finished after being more than half a century building. It is now almost the largest church in Russia. Its mountainous central gilt dome looks like some great gold balloon which has fallen and rested on the roof. Soon we are skimming over a long straight road, with various sorts of buildings on each side; now a low wooden house separated from the road by a white wall; now a church, with its five silvery domes tin plated, their roofing in shape and colour resembling the scales of a fish; then on the other side a cloister church with indigo blue domes studded with silver stars. In the outskirts of the city the churches do not seem able to 'run to gold' (as an American would say) for their roofs. Indeed, readers must not suppose that all Russian church domes, in Moscow or anywhere else, are gilded. Most of them are green; whether this arises from rust on the brass, or is the original colour they were painted, it is hard to say. The church-owners like you to believe the former. Now and again we pass a garden about half an acre large. Some of its trees thrust their branches, white with ice and rough with hoar-frost, out over the high wall, and cast a skeleton-like shadow on the snow-covered footpath. On and on we glide over the glassy surface of the road, and it seems as if the houses and the city would never be left behind.

At last, however, the wooden buildings, which have been getting poorer in appearance, rougher in build, and dingier in their painted coats as we near the border of the city, stop all at once. We turn to the right, and are out in the open, with Moscow behind us. The country undulates in gentle swells, with miniature ravines between them. A large factory chimney appears on the south; its smoke is blown towards us by the gentle afternoon breeze; the woolly column and its feathery shadow flitting over the ground form the only stains on the blue cloudless sky and the white expanse of pure snow. Soon we have the road all to ourselves, and the isvostchik has to go slowly and cautiously in choosing his way, otherwise we might fall into a snow-drift six or eight feet deep. The depth of the snow is shown by looking at the fence which encloses the forest of birches and beeches on our right hand; only the tops of its posts are visible.

This wood, in which is situated a very pretty villa presented to the late Empress by Prince Orloff, runs with its interwoven network of branches right on to the Sparrow Hills. It is hard to imagine anything more lovely than a walk through such a Russian wood in the depth of a Russian winter. The thick stems of the trees are coated in a mantle of greyish white. The frost frames an icy fretwork in the branches, forming devices and strange zig-zag figures never dreamt of in Euclid or the higher mathematics. Sometimes the rain or the melting ice has commenced to drip, but is arrested by a frost reminding it that the time of thaws is not yet. Where this has happened you see hanging icicles, six inches or a foot long. They glisten in the sun like stalactites of transparent crystal, and beside them you see a bunch of infinitesimal ice needles, which the slightest breath will break. On a fine, still day nothing is more beautiful than to look up from the white ground through this inter-twining web roof of frozen white branches to the irregular patches of blue sky formed by their rigid lines. The silence of these Russian woods is very striking. The only sound is the crunching of the crisp snow under your feet, the small twigs cracking with the frost, or the soft thud of a slender bough falling on the ground. It seems hard to believe that these very woods which we drive past now will in a month or so be filled with the deafening twittering of the birds from whom these hills take their name. But in Russia the spring comes literally all at once; the trees and the earth make up for lost time, and do in two weeks what would take them twice as long in other climates [...]

All this may be very true when it comes, but just now the cold is so great that the very sweat is freezing on our sturdy, thick-set horse's back. We soon reach the tea refreshment traktir, from which the best view of Moscow is to be had. Visitors are scarce at this season, and we have to wait impatiently while the 'Traktirchik' and his man shovel a way into the house for us out of the deep snow. As we jump out our isvostchik mutters some words, the import of which we easily gather to be that he has no prejudice against partaking of liquid sustenance. 'Very well, Sidor, you can have some tea.' 'If it pleases my high-born lords,' answers the driver, grinning all over, and with a twinkle of his small grey eyes, 'may I have schnapps instead, to warm the corner of my soul.' This phraseology is, of course, irresistible.

We walk on to the verandah, part of which is roofed in with glass, from which you get an uninterrupted view to the east. The Moskwa runs below us, and takes a graceful curve to get round a projecting shoulder of the wooded hills. In the woods a mist is already rising off the snow; it is of that indescribable delicate mauve shade you often see in Russian thickets, and nowhere else. To the left, on the flat plain in front, lies the great fortress-like enclosure of the Novo Devitchi Convent [...]

But, further back, beyond all this, is the sight on which all travellers have exhausted the dictionary in terms of admiration. The undulations of the snowy plains seem to have gathered themselves together into one long wave-line, which has been arrested just as it hung ready to break over the plain. Facing you, three miles away, all along the length of this low hill, you have the overpowering view of all the churches, palaces, and buildings of Moscow in one glowing mass. Top-most of all is the cross of the great belfry, and round it, like the jewels of a crown, are clustered the golden domes, minarets, and towers of the Kremlin. As you stand and look out on this sight towards sunset, it is impossible to imagine anything more grandly picturesque. Those who have watched a sunset on the marble mosques or carved palaces of Agra or Delhi, or the flat roofs of Cairo, can form some idea of it. As the sun gets lower, the spectacle changes every moment; the wide surface of white walls of Moscow reflects its light, changing from a pale yellow to a deep orange, and again into a faint pink red. Every now and then some dome which has been in the shade is suddenly found out, and, struck by the sun's beams, is wakened up into a bright dazzling globe of polished gold, as if a half-transparent drab cover had suddenly been lifted off it. Viewing these hundreds of crosses, domes, and coloured roofs, it is easy to understand the effect this sight of Moscow has on the impressionable feelings of the Russian peasant. To this day, when he views it from these heights, it is to him as the first view of the towers of Jerusalem was to the Crusaders. He kneels the moment the city flashes on his eyes, and crying out 'Matouchka Moskwa Svataya!' (Holy Mother Moscow), touches the ground three times with his forehead, like the Turk in his mosque. It is easy, too, to picture the scene which took place here one bright afternoon in September, 1812. Napoleon stood here at the head of his army, inveigled on to their destruction by the artful retreat of the Russian forces. The soldiers, broken in spirit and half dead with the horrors of suffering endured in their long march, as soon as the glittering city — inviting to conquest — met their eyes, shouted out as with one voice, 'Moscow! Moscow!' 'All this will be yours' said Napoleon to his men. How this arrogant promise was never fulfilled; how the Muscovites, by a preconcerted plan and by a piece of noble self-denial, sacrificed their beautiful city to the flames; and how the retreat from Moscow entailed on the great army the horrors of torture worse than could be devised by the most blood-thirsty mediæval tyrant, everyone knows.

We wait — as everyone does — till the sun has set on this wonderful scene. The city and its lofty towers are seen standing coldly out against the sunset's reflection in the eastern sky; the horizon background is of that strange greenish hue only seen in the northern heavens. Soon the evening mists rise, forming a steamy atmosphere of a grey violet hue. In it the domes and towers seem to quiver and float in the air, and to recede farther into the distance, and as darkness comes on they gradually fade out of sight, almost like the enchanted castles of some old fairy tale. We are soon brought back to practical questions by being called to pay the usual 'Rubl adin' (one rouble) for our sip of tea. We know we are being cheated, but the view is worth far more than that; indeed, one cannot help being sorry when this afternoon's visit is over, and can only remind oneself of Heine's consolatory words to the sentimental young lady who sadly gazed on the sun dipping under the western wave — 'Don't grieve, mademoiselle; it goes down to-night, but it will come up again to-morrow morning.' Our five miles' drive home is very cold, and when we get into the streets they are ill-lighted by the few lamps; the houses carefully husband their light within their walls, and do not let even a spare ray gleam through a chink in the curtained windows and fast-closed shutters to redden the snow. As we drive past the Kremlin the burnished roofs which flashed so brightly an hour and a half ago are lost, sunk in the darkness; but when the moon rises they will shine out again over the pale snow, so as to almost rival the view you get of them from the Sparrow Hills, which is no doubt, in its way, the most magnificent of the kind in Europe, if not in the world.

Sketches in Russia (1886)

1887

James Hogan in New York

Born in Tipperary, Ireland, James Hogan (1855–1924) was one year old when his family emigrated to Victoria. He worked as a teacher and journalist, and in both occupations expressed the common fear that young nativeborn Australians were an inferior breed to their migrant parents. He was active in Irish-Catholic movements until 1887 when he went to Britain in search of wider exposure for his writing. In Britain he published a number of

books about Australia including The Irish in Australia *(1887),* Robert
Lowe, Viscount Sherbrooke *(1893) and* The Sister Dominions *(1896)
and became recognised as an authority on Australian affairs. In 1893 Hogan
was elected unopposed to the House of Commons as an Irish Nationalist
member for Tipperary and held his seat until 1900. He settled permanently
in Britain, making brief visits to Australia in 1895 and 1901. Hogan
recounted his 1887 travels to Britain via New Zealand and the United
States in* The Australian in London and America (1889), *a series of forthright and perceptive essays on the American way of life and on the joys and
drawbacks of life at the centre of the Empire. Like many others, he thought
the United States a model for the Australian colonies, and presciently saw the
role that parades of old soldiers could play in engendering patriotism in a
new nation on the 'one day of the year'.*

Monday morning ushered in the real Decoration Day with a wealth of
welcome sunshine. At an early hour Broadway and Fifth Avenue commenced to fill, and, long before 10 o'clock, the people were standing
twenty deep along the portions of those thoroughfares through which
the National Guard and the Grand Army of the Republic were about to
march, and be reviewed by the Governor of New York. Doors, windows, balconies, roofs — wherever a foothold was obtainable — all
were occupied by enthusiastic admirers of New York's great annual military spectacle. Women of every class wore the national colours conspic-
uously pinned on their breasts, and even the little children were
provided with the stars and stripes in miniature. First to move from the
starting-point were the veteran officers of the war, who came along
slowly in full uniform and riding in open carriages. They were greeted
with general cheers as they were recognized along the line of spectators.
Next in succession came the various sections of the National Guard —
a fine soldierly body of men — each division being preceded by a band
playing some one of those stirring tunes to which the war gave birth. I
was pleased to notice one division entirely composed of negroes, who
marched past with as military and dignified a bearing as any of their
white comrades in arms. It was very gratifying to witness the pro-
nouncedly cordial reception extended by the crowd to this contingent
of coloured men and its coloured band, for the universal cheering of the
masses in this connection testified to a practical recognition of equal
rights, and was tantamount to a popular declaration that the black citizens of the United States were fully entitled to become co-defenders of
their country side by side with the once so-called superior white race.
    Lastly came the Grand Army of the Republic — a phrase that has a
sort of majestic ring about it, and which seems to imply a military

organization of more than ordinarily brilliant calibre. But this interpretation is not the correct one. The Grand Army of the Republic is nothing more or less than a voluntary association of the soldiers who fought in defence of the Union against the Southern secessionists. They have banded themselves together in posts all over the country for the laudable objects of helping each other when necessary, and of perpetuating the memory of a glorious past. They are, in short, a reserve corps of veteran citizen soldiers — men who have borne the brunt of battle, and who would be ready to forsake their avocations and go to the front again if duty called. On this one day of the year — Decoration Day — they put themselves in evidence, as they have every right to do, and proudly march past to receive the plaudits of their grateful fellow-citizens — plaudits which they doubtless translate as meaning, in Biblical phraseology, 'Well done, thou good and faithful servant.' Of course, it goes without saying that their ranks must, in the ordinary course of nature, become thinner every year, and an experienced actuary of a life insurance company would doubtless be able to name with approximate accuracy the year in which the present Grand Army of the Republic will be represented by a solitary grey-haired survivor. Still, the year is yet a long way off, and the twentieth century will be out of its baby-clothes before it comes round.

About a thousand of the veterans turned out on this occasion, and, though not a few were observed to walk with difficulty, owing to advancing age and infirmity, the great majority, it must be said, presented a fine soldierly mien, kept the step with admirable precision, and seemed to the unprofessional eye in every way qualified to go through another arduous campaign with credit, if their country was in peril. They all displayed the letters G.A.R. (the initials of their organization) in gold upon their caps, and each of their divisions was preceded by some of those tattered silently-eloquent witnesses to deeds of heroism — which I had seen in the church of St Paul on the previous evening, and the sight of which now excited the immense concourse of spectators to such a pitch that they gave vent to their feelings as one man in a prolonged outburst of enthusiasm. One other notable incident of the procession was a beautifully-constructed model of a full-rigged vessel, named 'The Union', which was borne on high on the shoulders of a group of sturdy veterans, and displayed on either side the beseeching motto, 'Don't give up the ship,' the dying words of Captain Lawrence, of the *Chesapeake*. The resounding cheers that welcomed the appearance of this picturesque tableau all along the line of march, were a spontaneous response from the populace to the epigrammatic appeal to their patriotism.

Altogether, Decoration Day is a sight worth travelling some distance to see. Our processions in the colonies are pretty shows and nothing more. There is nothing in them to stir the blood or add a lustre to the eye. The elements of the heroic and the historic are absent. Who can estimate the value of such a procession as that of Decoration Day in New York, in enkindling an ardent love of country, in strengthening the popular fibre, in perpetuating the memory of a gallant struggle for the preservation of the unity of the States, and in placing a high ideal of national duty before the eyes of a later generation?

The Australian in London and America (1889)

2

1890–1913

Nationalists

The cultural vitality of the 1890s and the early Federation years has long been recognised. Nationalist rhetoric flourished, coloured by a growing and often uneasy awareness of the proximity of crowded Asia. In 1895 the ageing federationist Sir Henry Parkes drew attention to Australia's vulnerability in a homely travel metaphor: 'Our land was only situated the length of "a short holiday trip" from the vast over-populated countries of the old world'.[1] 'Empty' Australia occupied an uneasy place in a world that appeared to be growing smaller and becoming increasingly belligerent. The new nationalism was also underpinned by the increasing dominance of the native-born Australians in public life. They produced art and writing which looked inwards to the cultivation of an Australian spirit, and outwards to the future and a changing world order.

Best-known is the popular, self-consciously Australian school of writing associated with the influential Sydney *Bulletin*. It was a hybrid journal, though its dominant values were politically radical, masculinist and confidently nationalist, where nationalism assumed the need to keep Australia for the 'white man'. The work of Henry Lawson, 'Banjo' Paterson and others has often been seen as the most Australian of Australian literature, particularly when much of their work dwelt on the Australian bush as the source of distinctively Australian values. Their 'Bush' provided an imaginative escape for writers who thought of the city as stultifying, mean-spirited and materialistic, a response intensified by the 1890s Depression and by a willingness to see domestic relationships as restrictive. However the Bush legend tends to ignore the fact that just as often the escape could be elsewhere — for some men like Becke or McLaren to that other frontier in the Pacific, for many men and women to Europe. Lawson himself advised young Australian writers 'to go steerage, stow away, swim, and seek London, Yankeeland, or Timbuctoo — rather than stay in Australia till his genius turn to gall, or beer',[2] though his own trip to England, like his trip to the Bush, proved unsatisfactory. When the *Bulletin* writers turned to the rest of the world, they produced a new strand of travel writing that contained the same nationalism, democratic values and masculinist outlook. They readily found the natural wonders and social conditions of Europe inferior to those they had left at home, and they had no compunction about saying so.

However there were other styles of travel writing which assumed that Australians could comment on the wider world without being obtrusively Australian. This period also saw the development of an Australian imperialism, as Australian political and business leaders looked to the immediate north, east and south for opportunities for Australia to expand its influence and join the imperialist scramble. It began with

Queensland's abortive attempt to annex New Guinea in 1883, under-pinned Australian companies' domination of the Fijian economy and resulted in Mawson's scientific expeditions to the Antarctic from 1911. Mass tourism also came into its own in this period. The development of modern technologies such as the cinema, the mass-produced postcard, the travel poster, and the pocket camera, along with mass education, produced a greater knowledge of the outside world, and also the desire to see it. However the expense and time required still put an overseas trip out of reach of the vast majority of Australians.

1891

Alfred Deakin in India

Lawyer, journalist, politician and prime minister of Australia, Alfred Deakin (1856–1919) was born in Collingwood, Melbourne, and educated at Melbourne Church of England Grammar School and the University of Melbourne. His first trip overseas was in 1884 when he led a small party to California to investigate irrigation and conservation. Three years later he journeyed to London as Victoria's principal representative at the Colonial Conference of 1887. In 1890–91 Deakin was commissioned by the Age *to report on British-Indian irrigation. His brief also included the promotion of relations between India and the Australian colonies and an investigation of Hindu temples and architectural remains. Deakin's impressions were first published as a series of articles in the* Age *and then in two books,* Irrigated India: An Australian View of India and Ceylon, Their Irrigation and Agriculture *(1893) and* Temple and Tomb in India *(1893). Deakin's interest in spiritualism and theosophy predisposed him to the informed, appreciative and sympathetic study of Indian architecture, culture and religion that characterises his writing on India. However his preference for an idealised Buddhist past over a disconcerting Hindu present was a common response among educated Westerners to the mysteries of India. Here he makes a tourist's pilgrimage to the famous Buddhist temple at Karli, hewn out of rock, high in the Deccan.*

The tourist who leaves by an evening and returns by an afternoon train may have the advantage of beholding the Ghats by moonlight and by sunlight, and so of multiplying the effects, which succeed each other with dazzling rapidity as the train rushes from steep to steep, or winds along the edges of precipitous gulfs. The night journey, which possesses charms of it own, suppresses the bright greens of tropical foliage, and thus renders many of the aspects strikingly Australian. To have gone to

Mount Victoria by the Dubbo express, wound about Mount Lofty, or taken the direct route between Bacchus Marsh and Ballan by moonlight, is to have had glimpses which might be mistaken for some of those presented in the turns of the Indian hills. There is one marked difference in character, since the Ghats constitute the rough fringe of a great table land which comes to an abrupt conclusion at Lanauli, and falls almost sheer 1400 feet towards the coast plain [...] Below the winter sunbeams pour themselves through the mist upon a heaving ocean of verdurous hills with a faint purple setting that reminds one of the rich Australian haze.

It was Christmas eve as I made the ascent, and the one or two bungalows on the way occupied by English people were bright with flags and lights. It is Christmas morning as I wake to find the silver moonlight streaming in at the open woodwork of the lattice, which supplies the place of glass in this country, and so the plunge in the cool bath has to be taken by lamplight. By the time an early half breakfast, or chotah hazrah, of tea and toast is disposed of the whole eastern sky burns with a flush of intense rose and orange. The west is still filled with a mild radiance, but of diminished brightness, as (in Shelley's fine phrase) 'the pale white moon lies withering there.' Having resisted an attempt at blackmail, supported on the plea that the tongas in the village are all engaged, nothing has remained but to accept the alternative, offered as a challenge, and agree to ride. One's humanity protests against such a proceeding, because as a rule the so-called horse is generally a decrepit pony of disreputable expression and caparison, who is apparently in the last stages of starvation, and in the next place because the owner and guide usually accompanies one on foot, and though perhaps on the whole there is less effort required of him than of the rider, it seems an unchristian thing to keep a human being running afoot beside a horseman. Experience dissipates many of these sentiments. There comes familiarity with the practice among whites and natives, while the further and more satisfying knowledge is gained gradually that the pace of the Indian hired horse is never likely to seriously outrun an average pedestrian.

This morning there are two tongas already under way laden with gaily dressed Parsis, who make it rather too evident that they cherish high expectations concerning my progress. If they anticipate any intention

> To turn and wind a fiery Pegasus,
> And witch the world with noble horsemanship,

they are doomed to early and utter disappointment. My particular Pegasus, though he is a little bigger and somewhat better fed than most of his tribe, has no more ambition than his rider. The utmost extent of his abilities is soon learned. It is an irregular canter, with a stiff prop in the middle. Beyond this no persuasion can move him, and indeed it is not easy to rouse him to this point until the secret of his progress is discovered. After reasonable evidence of a determination on the part of his rider not to be contented with a walk which every passer-by outstrips, he is prepared, so long as his owner is in front of him, to distribute his legs in a kind of broken trot; but no sooner does he come up to his master than he stops as if shot, and prefers to jib altogether rather than accelerate his speed, if his achievement at any time could be dignified by such a word. The secret discovered, and the noble proprietor in his dingy sheet kept well ahead, we make better headway.

The morning is chill, and every native carries his cloak across his mouth to prevent the sharp air from entering his lungs. Some are rousing themselves in their little drays, in which they have slept, while other teams are on the road. The bullocks, the drays, and the drivers are all diminutive and rude. Then come strings of placidly chattering women, their robes of many colours tightly wound about them, bearing loads upon their heads. Men shake themselves and rise from under the banyans, where they have taken their rest. The roadside village is astir, naked children yawning in the roadway, a mother sweeping her doorstep with a handful of reeds, the father opening a shop as big as a trunk, and displaying with the greatest care a stock-in-trade of grains that might be bought retail for half-a-crown — unless dust were charged for, in which case it would realize a fabulous price.

After a further level stretch of well-made valley road we turn a shoulder of the hills and cross cultivation, passing the perhaps temporary mia-mias of the peasants, hardly sufficient in some cases to shield them from the dew, and certainly not from rain. The worst of them are not more than three feet high, while the majority, smaller than a two-roomed cottage, are built of mud and thatched with straw. The clothing of the inmates is of the coarsest and barest. This is the theatre of their life and labour; a level valley in which every available inch between the rocks is cultivated and irrigated. The marvellous capacity of the climate is proved by the fact that in one plot ploughing is proceeding, in another the young crop is springing, close by the stubble is scarcely dry, and near the huts threshing is going on. A rude, low dam in the tiny stream, one or two tanks, and a diversion higher up point to the means by which a hundred or two of human beings gain their bread. To judge from appearances they gain very little more.

The foot of the hill reached, my Arab steed is left, and a climb of about a quarter of a mile reminds one of the last pinch up the Camel's Hump at Macedon, or the slope of Mount Wellington just before reaching the Ploughed Field. Thanks to the projected visit of the Czarewitch the path has been smoothed, and the fact that his Imperial Highness has changed his mind and altered his route has conduced to keep it in good order. Rather more than half-way up a clump of trees in a sloping cleft marks the Chaitya plateau, from which a bell chimes slowly now and then, whose sound floats softly overhead until we attain the spot. Ages ago it sounded as now, while the gentle brotherhood looked forth upon a prospect perhaps even more beautiful than it is to-day. The opposite hills were steeped in full sunlight; the valley beneath was irrigated as now, by the same class of people and with the same implements and methods; but the richer plain upon which it opens, now sparsely tenanted and tilled, then stretched away populous and prosperous to its other verge, where swept the same range of hills, completing the same charmed circle of vision.

Turn now to the face of the mountain. An ugly little Hindu building dedicated to Siva must be removed in imagination. On the left are three long low clefts hewn in the basalt, only the upper one of which has two or three pillars as supports. These apparently natural rifts contain the cells of the ancient monks, which are as plain as the side cuts in a quartz mine. To the right of this Vihara [monastery] is the front of the Chaitya [shrine inside temple], hewn in the hill as Elephanta is, but without its splendid basaltic breadth, and by comparison almost Gothic, high arched, narrow and cathedral like. On one side a superb sixteen-sided pillar, upon the capital of which are four sculptured lions, still stands, while its fellow has disappeared. Beyond is a wide shallow porch, having on either side of it a square doorway so small and plain as to be scarcely noticeable; these open into the great excavation, but are not its chief entrances. This is in the centre, a splendid portal, disclosing a fine plain interior exactly like that of a church without pews, with a row of fifteen splendid columns on each side, leaving between them and the walls two dark and narrow aisles. The nave leads the eye directly to a large conical mass called a Dagoba, which fills its further end and rises bell-shaped to a wooden pinnacle and parachute, two-thirds towards the cupola-shaped ceiling. Although the whole Chaitya is hewn out of rock, there remain against the solid roof about eighty curved wooden rafters, probably of teak, looking like the ribs of a ship. These are all that have survived of what were once in all likelihood elaborate carved finishings within and upon the facade. Over the great door is a fine horse-shoe shaped window, rising to the roof, and casting its stream of light full upon the Dagoba. It is said by the authorities that worshippers were only permitted to look through the door, and not to pass it; so that while the wood work lasted, and before the front screen was broken, they would see its graceful shape solemnly surrounded by and revealed upon a background of darkness. The same effect, however, could have been obtained within, and by a far larger congregation, for whose entrance and exit doubtless the side aisles and doors were provided. This appears to have been the intention of the builders, since the seven pillars out of sight behind the Dagoba are perfectly plain, while those on view in the church are all richly carved.

The whole effect of this artificial cave is strikingly ecclesiastical. It is 124 feet in length, 46 feet high to the apex, its nave 25 feet, and the whole, with its aisles, 45 feet wide, admirably proportioned, and of an excellent simplicity — a place of worship, not a place to be worshipped, and perfectly in harmony with the creed to which it was devoted. Yet it is by no means unadorned. Its entrance is extremely tasteful and noble. Its octagonal rows of columns are symmetrically bold, while both in the porch and upon the crown of each capital are sculptures which unite freedom of conception to firmness of execution. They all breathe one spirit and disclose one motive; the panels to the right and left of the vestibule at its ends give in bas-relief the heads and trunks of elephants, most powerfully and faithfully rendered; the figures of their riders are male and female; those on the capitals of the columns within are similar in some cases, but more frequently portray two women, always upon elephants, and always embracing each other. The attitude and expression in each group is elevated, affectionate, and pure. Buddha appears above the outer panels of the porch in the place of honour, but not as an idol or object of adoration, he is revered rather than deified. Even such a tribute would have been distasteful to the sweet reasonableness of the gentle ascetic, and is in itself an evidence that the date of the Chaitya is considerably later than his. The character of its architecture and sculpture is refined, its feeling pious, and its sentiment humanitarian. It is an eloquent exposition of a lofty faith when in the full flower of its youth, in perfect concord with the aspect of the scene in which its site was selected, and of which it seems a part.

It is a far cry from Karli to Kandy, where stands one of the most famous modern shrines of the same faith, and hard to believe that both are dedicated to the same belief. It is still more difficult to realize that this flourishes in Ceylon while it has faded from India. Yet such is the truth: Buddhism as a separate religion has no abiding place, no followers here. As the soft chime again falls upon the ear, and dies gently in the recesses of the aisles, it might be deemed the passing bell of this once potent revelation of a high ideal. And why? The landscape is as fair to-day as when eager and earnest pilgrims climbed this mountain side to seek a momentary respite from their cares, a higher impulse for their daily living, a brighter prospect for eyes wearied with the selfishness and cruelty of their time. Is the need less keen now, or less heavy the burden than that of those who came to find a haven from its storms, an abiding place in which, forerunning their future, they could bid its discords cease in a life of charity and prayer? The bells' cadence still gives greeting to those that climb, but while long ago it called them from a grosser, cruder and more idolatrous teaching, blinded in a wilderness of mythology, harsh in social rigours, and coarse in tedious and meaningless ritual, to-day the Chaitya itself is silent and empty, and — deepest degradation of all — the summoning peal swells from the small, tawdry, plaster shrine of the terrible and hideous Siva, lord of the linga and the blood-filled skull.

Other faiths have faded, and more will fade, as the restless intelligence of man profanes or outgrows the highest he has previously attained. But the Dagobas of Buddha can never be entirely deserted. There will always be some to whom the grace and peace of this lofty inspiration of the past will appeal more deeply than the idols fashioned in the fevered present, half in doubt and half in dread. This sacred ideal, which has been the comfort and stay of millions, bringing them light, relief, and peace, has a claim upon the reverence even of those outside its pale. The bell note echoes and dies plaintively, as if thrilled and filled with an eternal regret. Is that regret for those who have wandered so far from its timid call, or for its own departed glory? Its own peoples have deserted it. And we strangers? —

> Men are we, and must grieve when even the shade
> Of that which once was great has passed away.

Temple and Tomb in India (1893)

1892

A. G. Stephens in the United States

Born in Toowoomba, journalist, editor and publisher Alfred George Stephens (1865–1933) did much to promote the development and recognition of Australian literature. He is best known as the editor of the Bulletin's 'Red Page' *(1896-1906), and as the publisher and editor of the literary journal* The Bookfellow *(1907–1925). Much earlier in his career, in 1892, Stephens made his eighteen-month tour of North America and Britain with a quick side trip to Paris. His impressions were first published as newspaper articles and then in book form as* A Queenslander's Travel-Notes *(1894). The identification of the author's place of origin in the title was not an uncommon practice in nineteenth-century travel writing. Stephens travelled across the Pacific via Auckland, Samoa and Honolulu to San Francisco where he encountered China town. As is to be expected from a* Bulletin *man of the 1890s, his views on the Chinese were decidedly racist. From San Francisco Stephens travelled on to Chicago where, like Catherine Spence, he attended the World's Fair. He found it 'splendid beyond description'. Stephens was appalled by the filth, vice and crime of the city whose main street contained 'wretched wooden shanties, which would be promptly condemned in any decent Australian town as unfit for human habitation'. After Chicago he went on to New York and Canada and then to Britain. On his travels, Stephens was above all interested in politics, social organisation and customs, and his strongly expressed views on everything from the American Girl to procedures in the House of Commons make lively reading. As a self-conscious Australian nationalist, he found much to criticise as well as admire in both the modernity of the United States and the traditionalism of Europe.*

Of course you cannot average the American girl. In the south she is not what she is in the north; in the east and in the west she is the same — but oh how different! Proteus never took so many shapes — or so charming. For the American girl is frequently charming. Indeed she tries to be — it is her duty to try to be — and if at first she doesn't succeed she tries, tries, tries again. Weak males generally succumb at the second try; tough ones can rarely resist more than three assaults. It is much pleasanter to succumb than to resist.

Yet, generalising as far as one may, one may say that the American girl is aggressive, audacious. Take an example — with a San Francisco maiden as exemplar. I should say that she was nineteen — this young person — bright, restless, piquante, with slim figure, dainty dress, and the tiniest of hands and feet. We were three days' acquaintances, walking along Market-street, and the conversation flagged. My companion looked up curiously at me, and was silent, thoughtful. Then, suddenly: 'Oh, Mr Stephens, why don't you wax your moustache?' 'I — I don't know — I never thought about it.' 'Oh, you should, really. You know what Rudyard Kipling says?' 'No, indeed.' 'Well, he makes a lady say that a kiss from a man who doesn't wax his moustache is like eating an egg without salt. And I think so too.' But later on there was found opportunity to convince this particular American girl that every rule has its exceptions. And we parted on the very best of terms.

The American girl fears God as little as man. I have mentioned one who thought He was 'a little *passé.*' This was farther east, when we were talking one evening on things sacred and profane, in a mixed company, with both sexes fairly represented. The lady this time was bony and angular, with short hair, short gown, spectacles and thick shoes. Distinctly blue, age about twenty-three, graduate of a university, doting on

Spencer. She listened half amused, wholly supercilious, to the mixed thoughts of the mixed company about humanity's alleged need for a God and a religion. Then she turned to me and let off her bomb-shell. I was shocked, or pretended to be, and ventured to remark that such was not generally the opinion of 'your fair sex' — this with elaborate sarcasm. 'Come, now, you must admit that the ladies are the best supporters of the conventional deity — and the unconventional priest.' 'Ah,' she said, 'it may be so in England; but — we manage these things better in America.' Yet my lady erred, for in every American congregation the males are in a dismal minority.

The American girl is generally a bundle of nerves, with bright eyes, an excitable temperament, and no complexion worth mentioning. Her sallow face is her sore point, and she often paints the lily. Heliotrope veils were in fashion when I was in Chicago; and, seen through these, the countenances of the north-end beauties wore a sunset glow delightful to contemplate. I praised their bloom enthusiastically to a drug-store assistant. 'Yes,' he said, 'they *have* a fine colour, a very fine colour — and cheap too, only twenty-five cents a box. Try a box?' I shuddered. Another fond illusion gone. But the drug-store man was right. American girls have nothing to compare with the healthy pink-and-white of the bouncing British maiden, nourished on rural bacon and taters, and kept moist and luscious by an all but continuous rainfall.

Just at present the American girl doesn't 'wear any frill.' Not round her neck, at all events. It has gone to decorate the bottom of her skirt. She wears her dress only to the base of the neck, and it has no ruching, no edging whatever. When the neck is plump and pretty one likes to see it rising a shapely column unadorned by drapery; but many American necks are scraggy; and then ——! In New York, the ladies were exposing not only all the neck, but a considerable section of shoulders as well. This was not an evening, but any ordinary walking costume, and seemed peculiar. Perhaps it *is* peculiar, but American girls rather like to be peculiar. I was introduced to one peculiar person who had done her best to rival the hero of Jarley's waxworks — 'Jasper Packlemerton, of atrocious memory, who courted and married fourteen wives, and destroyed them all by tickling the soles of their feet when they were sleeping in the consciousness of innocence and virtue.' My heroine had been courted and married by five husbands, had divorced them all, and was looking out for a sixth. She was a sylph-like thing with a baby face and big dreamy blue eyes. In short frock and sash she would have passed for a school-girl of sixteen just loosed from backboard and parsing. I gave her a warm invitation to come to Australia for Number Six — told her I knew a Gympie man who would just suit her. She said she would think about it.

America is the land of divorces, and American girls seem to like being divorced. A resident in San Francisco for twenty-two years told me, quite seriously, that fifty per cent. of Frisco wives were unfaithful to their husbands. I asked him how the figures worked out the other way. He couldn't say, but guessed the husbands were worse. 'I have always been true to Mrs. B.,' he alleged, 'and I'm looked on as quite a curiosity.' The number of divorces per 1000 marriages in California is something monstrous — 303 per 1000, I think — nearly a third at all events. In England divorces average 3 or 4 per 1000 marriages. Every fourth married man you meet in the western States has been, is being, or is about to be divorced. The process is ridiculously easy. You have only to swear that your husband doesn't cut his toe-nails (veritable fact), or that your wife gads about and won't mind the babies (actual case), and a complaisant judge cuts the knot at once. When a man and woman weary of one another — and they weary very soon in America — they simply shuffle the cards and have a fresh deal.

I was told of a lady who was divorced for chewing gum, but this lacked confirmation. So many ladies chew gum, in public and in private, at bed and board, at home and in the street, that the male American must be habituated to the sight and the practice. After all, it is only a *tu quoque. He* does it: why shouldn't *she*? But the unsophisticated stranger is apt to gasp and stare at the ceaseless wagging of so many daintily moulded chins. I stood at a Rochester street corner one fine afternoon, and counted the women passing by, distinguishing them as 'plainly dressed' and 'elaborately dressed.' There were twenty-two elaborately dressed and twelve plainly dressed in fifteen minutes. Nine elaborately dressed were chewing, and five plainly dressed. Only seven of the thirty-four wore gloves. In England or Australia, a lady's dress is not complete unless she wears gloves out-of-doors. But in America the fashion is growing of dispensing with the hand-shoes in the summer-time. 'Tis a sensible fashion, in truth; though it outrages sticklers for the female proprieties.

It doesn't follow that immorality is prevalent because the divorce average is high. On the contrary, the facilities for divorce make the idea of marriage more endurable. When the responsibilities of wedlock are so readily got rid of, there is less reason to shirk them. I am told, though I have not verified the statement, that a high divorce percentage means a low illegitimacy percentage, and *vice versa* — *i.e.*, the vice is all the other way. Even in pseudo-moral England there are fickle lovers, and the only reason why they never get divorced is because they never get married. I am wandering from the American girl in this letter, but I have not wandered from her in the spirit. She is an oasis in the desert of memory, and there is a great deal more to say about her. Yet most of it is better left unsaid. Like everything good, she must be seen to be appreciated. I met her with wonder, I knew her with delight, I parted from her with the greatest possible regret. But maybe these are thoughts which ought not

To be continued.

A Queenslander's Travel Notes (1894)

1894

G. E. Morrison in China

Journalist, traveller and adviser to the Chinese government, 'Chinese Morrison' (1862–1920) was the son of a headmaster of Geelong College. He was brought up on heroic tales of exploration, and compiled a history of Australian explorers when he was 16. Frustrated that he could not be another Henry Stanley, he began his life of travel by walking from Melbourne around the coast to Adelaide. His next journey, as a journalist for the Age, *was through North Queensland to Thursday Island and Port Moresby. He returned from the Gulf of Carpentaria to Melbourne on foot. A further visit to New Guinea resulted in severe spear wounds. After graduating in medicine from the University of Melbourne in 1887, Morrison travelled in North America and the West Indies, going on to Spain where he worked for eighteen months as a medical officer at a British-owned mine. He turned up again in Australia in 1890 but returned to his nomadic life after two years working at Ballarat Hospital. Morrison travelled through the Philippines and along the coast of China. After visiting Japan, he voyaged up the Yangtze from Shanghai to Chunking (Chongqing) and then travelled on foot another 2500 kilometres along the 'great overland highway into Burma' — though often, as in this extract, he was carried. He 'put his pride in his pocket and a pigtail down his back', and dressed and lived as a Chinese, though always maintaining a superior manner and trusting to a Christian convert to smooth his passage. In Britain in 1895 he wrote* An Australian in China *to show 'how easily and pleasantly' the journey could now be done. During the next two years, Morrison travelled through Asia as a secret special correspondent for the* Times. *In 1897 he became the first permanent correspondent of the* Times *in Peking, which was to be his base for the next twenty years. He reported on the Boxer Rebellion, the Russo-Japanese War and the overthrow of Manchu rule. In 1912 Morrison was asked by the president of the new Chinese republic to become a government adviser. He worked to bring China into the First World War and helped to prepare her submissions to the Paris Peace Conference. Morrison died in England, spared the knowledge that these submissions failed to secure their objectives.*

On the morning of March 14th I set out from Chungking to cross 1600 miles over Western China to Burma. Men did not speak hopefully of my chance of getting through. There were the rains of June and July to be feared apart from other obstacles.

Père Lorain, the Procureur of the French Mission, who spoke from an experience of twenty-five years of China, assured me that, speaking no Chinese, unarmed, unaccompanied, except by two poor coolies of the humblest class, and on foot, I would have *les plus grandes difficultés*, and Monsieur Haas, the Consul *en commission*, was equally pessimistic. The evening before starting, the Consul and my friend Carruthers (one of the *Inverness Courier* Carruthers) gave me a lesson in Chinese. 'French before breakfast' was nothing to this kind of cramming. I learnt a dozen useful words and phrases, and rehearsed them in the morning to a member of the Inland Mission, who cheered me by saying that it would be a clever Chinaman indeed who could understand Chinese like mine [...]

I was dressed as a Chinese teacher in thickly-wadded Chinese gown, with pants, stockings, and sandals, with Chinese hat and pigtail. In my dress I looked a person of weight. I must acknowledge that my outfit was very poor; but this was not altogether a disadvantage, for my men would have the less temptation to levy upon it. Still it would have been awkward if my men had taken it into their heads to walk off with my things, because I could not have explained my loss. My chief efforts, I knew, throughout my journey would be applied in the direction of inducing the Chinese to treat me with the respect that was undoubtedly due to one who, in their own words, had done them the 'exalted honour' of visiting 'their mean and contemptible country.' For I could not afford a private sedan chair, though I knew that Baber had written that 'no traveller in Western China who possesses any sense of self-respect should journey without a sedan chair, not necessarily as a conveyance, but for the honour and glory of the thing'.

[...]

We were high above the river in the mountain gorges. The comfort of the traveller in a chair along this road depends entirely upon the sureness of foot of his two bearers — a false step, and chair and traveller would tumble down the cliff into the foaming river below. Deep and narrow was the mountain river, and it roared like a cataract, yet down the passage a long narrow junk, swarming with passengers, was racing, its oars and bow-sweep worked by a score of sailors singing in chorus. The boat appeared, passed down the reach, and was out of sight in a moment; a single error, the slightest confusion, and it would have been smashed in fragments on the rocks and the river strewn with corpses.

We did a good stage before breakfast. Every few li [about 580 metres] where the steepness of the valley side permits it, there are straw-thatched, bamboo and plaster inns. Here rice is kept in wooden bins all ready steaming hot for the use of travellers; good tea is brewed in a few minutes; the tables and chopsticks are sufficiently clean.

Leaving the river, we crossed over the mountains by a short cut to the river again, and at a wayside inn, much frequented by Chinese, the chair stage finished. I wished to do some writing, and sat down at one of the tables. A crowd gathered round me, and were much interested. One elderly Chinese with huge glasses, a wag in his own way, seeing that I did not speak Chinese, thought to make me understand and divert the crowd by the loudness of his speech, and, insisting that I was deaf, yelled into my ears in tones that shook the tympanum. I told the foolish fellow, in English, that the less he talked the better I could understand him; but he persisted, and poked his face almost into mine, but withdrew it and hobbled off in umbrage when I drew the attention of the bystanders to the absurd capacity of his mouth, which was larger than any mule's.

I must admit that my knowledge of Chinese was very scanty, so scanty indeed as to be almost non-existent. What few words I knew were rarely intelligible; but, as Mrs General Baynes, when staying at Boulogne, found Hindostanee to be of great help in speaking French, so did I discover that English was of great assistance to me in conversing in Chinese. Remonstrance was thus made much more effective. Whenever I was in a difficulty, or the crowd too obtrusive, I had only to say a few grave sentences in English, and I was master of the situation [...]

The inn, where the sedan left me, was built over the pathway, which was here a narrow track, two feet six inches wide. Mountain coolies on the road were passing in single file through the inn, their backs bending under their huge burdens. Pigs and fowls and dogs, and a stray cat, were foraging for crumbs under the table. Through the open doorways you saw the paddy-fields under water and the terraced hills, with every arable yard under cultivation. The air was hot and enervating. 'The country of the clouds,' as the Chinese term the province of Szechuen, does not belie its name. An elderly woman was in charge of the oven, and toddled about on her deformed feet as if she were walking on her heels. Her husband, the innkeeper, brought us hot water every few minutes to keep our tea basins full. 'Na kaishui lai' (bring hot water), you heard on all sides. A heap of bedding was in one corner of the room, in another were a number of rolls of straw mattresses; a hollow joint of bamboo was filled with chopsticks for the common use; into another bamboo the innkeeper slipped his takings of copper cash. Hanging from the rafters were strings of straw sandals for the poor, and hemp sandals for moneyed wayfarers like the writer. The people who stood round, and those seated at the tables, were friendly and respectful, and plied my men with questions concerning their master. And I did hope that the convert was not tempted to backslide and swerve from the truth in his answers.

My men were now anxious to push on. Over a mountainous country of surpassing beauty, I continued my journey on foot to Fan-yien-tsen, and rested there for the night, having done two days' journey in one.

On March 24th we were all day toiling over the mountains, climbing and descending wooded steeps, through groves of pine, with an ever-changing landscape before us, beautiful with running water, with cascades and waterfalls tumbling down into the river, with magnificent glens and gorges, and picturesque temples on the mountain tops. At night we were at the village of Tanto, on the river, having crossed, a few li before, over the boundary which separates the province of Szechuen from the province of Yunnan [...]

The mountain slope does not permit a greater width of building space than on each side of the one main street. And on market days this street is almost impassable, being thronged with traffickers, and blocked with stalls and wares. Coal is for sale, both pure and mixed with clay in briquettes, and salt in blocks almost as black as coal, and three times as heavy, and piles of drugs — a medley of bones, horns, roots, leaves, and minerals — and raw cotton and cotton yarn from Wuchang and Bombay, and finished goods from Manchester. At one of the villages there was a chair for hire, and, knowing how difficult was the country, I was willing to pay the amount asked — namely, 7 d. for nearly seven miles; but my friend the convert, who arranged these things, considered that between the 5 d. he offered and the 7 d. they asked the discrepancy was too great, and after some acrimonious bargaining it was decided that I should continue on foot, my man indicating to me by gestures, in a most sarcastic way, that the 'chiaodza' men had failed to overreach him.

At Sengki-ping it rained all through the night, and I had to sleep under my umbrella because of a solution in the continuity of the roof immediately above my pillow. And it rained all the day following; but my men, eager to earn their reward of one shilling, pushed on through the slush. It was hard work following the slippery path above the river. Few rivers in the world flow between more majestic banks than these, towering as they do a thousand feet above the water. Clad with thick mountain scrub, that has firm foothold, the mountains offer but a poor harvest to the peasant; yet even here, high up on the precipitous sides of the cliffs, ledges that seem inaccessible are sown with wheat or peas, and, if the soil be deep enough, with the baneful poppy [...]

A chair with three bearers was waiting for me in the morning, so that I left the town of Laowatan in a manner befitting my rank. The town had risen to see me leave, and I went down the street amid serried ranks of spectators. We crossed the river by a wonderful suspension bridge, 250 feet long and 12 feet broad, formed of linked bars of wrought iron. It shows stability, strength, and delicacy of design, and is a remarkable work to have been done by the untutored barbarians of this land of night. We ascended the steep incline opposite, and passed the likin barrier [toll-gate], but at a turn in the road, higher still in the mountain, a woman emerged from her cottage and blocked our path. Nor could the chair pass till my foremost bearer had reluctantly given her a string of cash 'With money you can move the gods,' say the Chinese; 'without it you can't move a man.'

For miles we mounted upwards. We were now in Yunnan, 'south of the clouds' — in Szechuen we were always under the clouds — the sun was warm, the air dry and crisp. Ponies passed us in long droves; often there were eighty ponies in a single drove. All were heavily laden with copper and lead, were nozzled to keep them off the grass, and picked their way down the rocky path of steps with the agility and sureness of foot of mountain goats. Time was beaten for them on musical gongs, and the echoes rang among the mountains. Many were decorated with red flags and tufts, and with plumes of the Amherst pheasant. These were official pack animals, which were franked through the likin barriers without examination.

The path, rising to the height of the watershed, where at a great elevation we gain a distant view of water, descends by the counterslope once more to the river Laowatan. A wonderful ravine, a mountain riven perpendicularly in twain, here gives passage to the river, and in full view of this we rested at the little town of Taoshakwan, with the roar of the river hundreds of feet below us. Midway up the face of the precipice opposite there is a sight worth seeing; a mass of coffin boards, caught in a fault in the precipice have been lying there for untold generations, having been originally carried there by the 'ancient flyingmen who are now extinct.'

A poor little town is Taoshakwan, with a poor little yamen [mandarin's official residence] with pretentious tigers painted on its outflanking wall, with a poor little temple, and gods in sad disrepair; but with an admirable inn, with a charming verandah facing a scene of alpine magnificence.

We were entering a district of great poverty. At Tchih-li-pu, where we arrived at midday the next day, the houses are poor, the people poverty-stricken and ill-clad, the hotel dirty, and my room the worst I had yet slept in. The road is a well-worn path flagged in places, uneven, and irregular, following at varying heights the upward course of the tortuous river. The country is bald; it is grand but lonely; vegetation is scanty and houses are few; we have left the prosperity of Szechuen, and are in the midst of the poverty of Yunnan. Farmhouses there are at rare intervals, amid occasional patches of cultivation; there are square white-washed watch towers in groves of sacred trees; there are a few tombstones, and an occasional rudely carved god to guard the way. There are poor mud and bamboo inns with grass roofs, and dirty tables set out with half a dozen bowls of tea, and with ovens for the use of travellers. Food we had now to bring with us, and only at the larger towns where the stages terminate could we expect to find food for sale. The tea is inferior, and we had to be content with maize meal, bean curds, rice roasted in sugar, and sweet gelatinous cakes made from the waste of maize meal. Rice can only be bought in the large towns. It is not kept in roadside inns ready steaming hot for use, as it is in Szechuen […]

We were still ascending the valley, which became more difficult of passage every day. Hamlets are built where there is scarce foothold in the detritus, below perpendicular escarpments of rock, cut clean like the façades of a Gothic temple. A tributary of the river is crossed by an admirable stone bridge of two arches, with a central pier and cut-water of magnificent boldness and strength, and with two images of lions guarding its abutment. Just below the branch the main stream can be crossed by a traveller, if he be brave enough to venture, in a bamboo loop-cradle, and be drawn across the stream on a powerful bamboo cable slung from bank to bank

We rested by the bridge and refreshed ourselves, for above us was an ascent whose steepness my stuttering coolie indicated to me by fixing my walking stick in the ground, almost perpendicularly, and running his finger up the side. He did not exaggerate. A zigzag path set with stone steps has been cut in the vertical ascent, and up this we toiled for hours. At the base of the escalade my men sublet their loads to spare coolies who were waiting there in numbers for the purpose, and climbed up with me empty-handed. At every few turns there were rest-houses where one could get tea and shelter from the hot sun. The village of Tak-wan-leo is at the summit; it is a village of some little importance and commands a noble view of mountain, valley, and river. Its largest hong is the coffin-maker's, which is always filled with shells of the thickest timber that money can buy.

Stress is laid in China upon the necessity of a secure resting-place after death. The filial affection of a son can do no more thoughtful act than present a coffin to his father, to prove to him how composedly he will lie after he is dead. And nothing will a father in China show the stranger with more pride than the coffin-boards presented to him by his dutiful son.

Tak-wan-leo is the highest point on the road between Suifu and Chaotong. For centuries it has been known to the Chinese as the highest point; how, then, with their defective appliances did they arrive at so accurate a determination? Twenty li beyond the village the stage ends at the town of Tawantzu, where I had good quarters in the pavilion of an old temple. The shrine was thick with the dust of years; the three gods were dishevelled and mutilated; no sheaves of joss sticks were smouldering on the altar. The steps led down into manure heaps and a piggery, into a garden rank and waste, which yet commands an outlook over mountain and river worthy of the greatest of temples.

On March 30th I reached Tak-wan-hsien, the day's stage having been seventy li (twenty-three and one-third miles). I was carried all the way by three chair-coolies in a heavy chair in steady rain that made the unpaved track as slippery as ice — and this over the dizzy heights of a mountain path-way of extraordinary irregularity. Never slipping, never making a mistake, the three coolies bore the chair with my thirteen stone, easily and without straining. From time to time they rested a minute or two to take a whiff of tobacco; they were always in good humour, and finished the day as strong and fresh as when they began it. Within an hour of their arrival all these three men were lying on their sides in the room opposite to mine, with their opium-pipes and little wooden vials of opium before them, all three engaged in rolling and heating in their opium-lamps treacly pellets of opium. Then they had their daily smoke of opium. 'They were ruining themselves body and soul.' Two of the men were past middle age; the third was a strapping young fellow of twenty-five. They may have only recently acquired the habit, I had no means of asking them; but those who know Western China will tell you that it is almost certain that the two elder men had used the opium-pipe as a stimulant since they were as young as their companion. All three men were physically well-developed, with large frames, showing unusual muscular strength and endurance, and differed, indeed, from those resurrected corpses whose fleshless figures, drawn by imaginative Chinese artists, we have known for years to be typical of our poor lost brothers — the opium-smoking millions of China. For their work to-day, work that few men out of China would be capable of attempting, the three coolies were paid sevenpence each, out of which they found themselves, and had to pay as well one penny each for the hire of the chair.

An Australian in China (1895)

1890s

Louis Becke in the South Seas

Born in Port Macquarie, George Lewis Becke (1855–1913) began his life of adventure early. At the age of 14 he took passage with his brother to San Francisco. The young Becke's return to Australia nineteen months later was short-lived, and he stowed away on a ship bound for Samoa. His ensuing adventures included gunrunning, pearling, trading, fishing and some time as supercargo to the notorious blackbirder, 'Bully' Hayes. He was arrested — and eventually acquitted — for piracy. After engaging in a variety of more mundane occupations in Australia, Becke was again trading in the South Sea Islands from 1880 to 1885 and from 1890 to 1892. Unable to find employment in Australia, he turned to writing, took the name Louis Becke and, with the encouragement of J. F. Archibald, published a number of short yarns in the Bulletin. *His books,* By Reef and Palm *(1894),* The Ebbing of the Tide *(1896),* Wild Life in the Southern Seas *(1897) and* Pacific Tales *(1897) gained him the reputation of 'a born story teller', a facility he also deployed to write Australian history. But writing did not bring an adequate living, and in 1894 Becke was bankrupt. Two years later, he left Australia for London where he was received as a celebrity. In 1908 he returned to the South Pacific to record the local folklore. He died five years later in Sydney. In his writing Becke tended to rework the same themes, mixing fact, memoir and fiction, and more often than not playing with the themes of interracial romance and violence. At a time when many Australian writers were looking to the Bush, some looked to another frontier, the South Pacific. Becke was the most successful practitioner of what was to become something of a genre, the South Seas romance. Many of its elements — pagan innocence, subdued eroticism, the celebration of the senses and the white man's life of ease — are evident in this account of surfboard riding (complete with board-shorts) twenty years before the sport was introduced to Australia.*

Just as my wild-eyed, touzle-headed Gilbert Island cook brought me my early coffee and hard ship biscuit, Toria and Vailele — brown-skinned brother and sister — peeped in through the window, and in their curious bastard Samoan said 'twas a glorious morn to *fahaheke*.

Now I had learned to *fahaheke* (use a surf-board), having been instructed therein by the youths and maidens of the village individually and collectively. And when you have once learned surf-swimming the game takes possession of your innermost soul like unto cycling and golf. So I said I would come, and instantly my young friends handed me in a surfing costume, a highly indecorous looking girdle of thin strappings of the leaf of the pandanus palm. This I blushingly declined, preferring a garment of my own design — a pair of dungaree pants razeèd from the knees down. Then, bidding me hurry up and meet the swimming party on the beach, Toria and his sister ran back to the village to attend early morning service, to which the wooden cylinder that did duty for a church bell was already summoning the people.

Now, in some of the Pacific Islands surf-swimming is one of the forbidden things, for many of the native teachers hold the sport to savour of the *po uli* — *i.e.*, the heathen days — and the young folks can only indulge in the innocent diversion away from the watchful eye of the local Chadband and his alert myrmidons, the village police, among whom all fines are divided. But in this particular little island we had for our resident missionary a young stalwart Samoan, who did not forbid his flock to dance or sing, nor prohibit the young girls from wearing flowers in their dark locks. And he himself was a mighty fisherman and a great diver and swimmer, and smoked his pipe and laughed and sang with the people out of the fulness of his heart when they were merry, and prayed for and consoled them in their sorrow. So we all loved Ioane, the teacher, and Eliné, his pretty young wife, and his two jolly little muddy brown infants; for there was no other native missionary like him in all the wide Pacific.

The simple service was soon over, and then there was a great scurrying to and fro among the thatched houses, and presently in twos and threes the young people appeared, hurrying down to the beach and shouting loudly to the white man to follow. A strong breeze had sprung up during the night, and the long rolling billows, which had sped waveringly along for, perhaps, a thousand miles from beyond the western sea-rim, were sweeping now in quick succession over the wide flat stretch of reef that stood out from the northern end of the island like a huge table. Two hundred yards in width from the steep-to face it presented to the sea, it ceased, almost as abruptly as it began, in a bed of pure white sand, six feet below the surface of the water; and this sandy bottom continued all the way from the inner edge of the reef to the line of coco-palms fringing the island beach. At low tide, when the ever-restless rollers dashed vainly against the sea-face of the reef, whose surface was then bared and shining in the sun, this long strip of sheltered water would lay quiet and undisturbed, as clear as crystal and as smooth as a sheet of glass; but as the tide rose the waves came sweeping over the coral barrier and poured noisily over its inner ledge till the lagoon again became as surf-swept and agitated as the sea beyond. This was the favoured spot with the people for surf-swimming, for when the tide was full the surf broke heavily on the reef, and there was a clear run of half-a-mile from the starting-point on the inner face of the coral table to the soft, white beach. Besides that, there was not a single rock or mound of coral between the reef and the shore upon which a swimmer might strike — with fatal effect if the danger were not perceived in time.

The north point was quite a mile from the village, and, the tide being very high, we had to follow a path through the coconut groves instead of walking along the beach, for the swirling waves, although well spent when they reached the shore, were washing the butts of the coco-palms, whose matted roots protruded from the sand at high-water mark. In front of us raced some scores of young children ranging from six years of age to ten, pushing and jostling each other in their eagerness to be first on the scene. Although the sun was hot already, the breeze was cool and blew strongly in our faces when we emerged from the narrow leafy track out upon the open strand. Then with much shouting and laughing, and playful thumping of brown backs and shoulders, Timi, the master of ceremonies for the occasion, marshalled us all in line and then gave the word to go, and with a merry shout, mingled with quavering feminine squeaks, away we sprang into the sea, each one pushing his or her surf-board in front, or shooting it out ahead, and trying to reach the reef before any one else.

And now the slight regard for the conventionalities that had been maintained during the walk from the village vanished, and the fun began — ducking and other aquatic horseplay, hair-pulling, seizing of surf-boards and throwing them back shorewards, and wrestling matches between the foremost swimmers. The *papalagi* (white man), swimming between the boy Toria and a short, square-built native named Temana, had succeeded in keeping well in the van, when he was suddenly seized by the feet by two little imps, just as a sweeping roller lifted him high up. And down the white man went, and away went his surf-board shoreward amid the shrieking laughs of the girls.

'Never mind,' shouted Temana, shaking his black curly head like a water-spaniel; and seizing a board from a girl near him, and pushing her under at the same time, he shot it over towards me; and then Toria, with a wrathful exclamation, caught one of the imps who had caused my disaster and, twining his left hand in her long, floating hair, pitched her board away behind him. This little incident, however, lost us our places, and amid the merry gibes of some naked infants who were in the ruck, we swam on in face of the slapping seas, and at last gained the edge of the reef, which was now alive with nude, brown-skinned figures, trying to keep their position in the boiling surf for the first grand 'shoot' shoreward.

Between the lulls of the frequent seas the water was only about four feet deep, and presently some sort of order was formed, and we awaited the next big roller. Over the outer reef it reared its greeny crest, curled and broke with thundering clamour, and roared its mile-line length towards us. Struggling hard to keep our feet on the slippery coral against the swift back-wash, we waited till the white wall of hissing foam was five feet away, and then flung ourselves forward flat upon our boards. Oh, how can one describe the ecstatic feeling that follows as your feet go up and your head and shoulders down, and you seem to fly through the water with the spume and froth of the mighty roller playing about your hair and hissing and singing in your ears ? Half a mile away lies the beach, but you cannot see it, only the plumed crowns of the palms swaying to and fro in the breeze; for your head is low down, and there is nothing visible but a wavering line of shaking green. Perhaps, if you are adept enough to turn your head to right or left, you will see silhouetted against the snowy wall of foam scores and scores of black heads, and then before you can draw your breath from excitement the beach is before you, and you slip off your board as the wave that has carried you so gloriously in sweeps far up on the shore, amid the vines and creepers which enwrap the sea-laved roots of the coco-palms.

Then back again, up and down over the seas, diving beneath any that are too high and swift to withstand, till you reach the ledge of the reef again and wait another chance. Not all together do we go this time, for now the swimmers are widely separated, and as we swim out we meet others coming back, flying before the rollers under which we have to dive. Here and there are those who from long practice and skill disdain to use a board; for springing in front of a curling sea, by a curious trick of hollowing in the back and depressing the head and neck, they fly in before the rolling surge at an amazing speed, beating the water with one hand as they go, and uttering wild cries of triumph as they pass us, struggling seaward. Others there are who with both hands held together before them, keep themselves well in position amid the boiling rush of waters by a movement of the legs and feet alone. But, that day, to my mind the girls looked prettiest of all when, instead of lying prone, they sat upon their boards, and held themselves in position by grasping the sides. Twice, as we swam out, did we see some twenty or thirty of them mounted slopingly on the face of a curling sea, and with their long, dark locks trailing behind them, rush shoreward enveloped in mist and spray like goddesses of the waves. Their shrill cries of encouragement to each other, the loud thunder of the surf as it broke upon its coral barrier, the seething hum and hiss of the roller as it impelled them to the beach, and the merry shrieks of laughter that ensued when some luckless girl over-balanced or misguided herself in the midst of the foam, lent a zest of enjoyment to the scene that made one feel himself a child again.

For two hours we swam out again and again to fly shoreward; and at last we met together on the beach, to rest under the shade of the palms, the girls to smoke their banana-leaf *sului* of strong negro-head tobacco, and the men their pipes, while the younger boys were sent to gather us young drinking-coconuts. And then we heard a sudden cry of mingled laughter and astonishment; for, tottering along the path, surf-board under arm, came an old man of seventy, nude to his loins.

'*Hu! hu!*' he cried, and his wrinkled face twisted, and his toothless mouth quivered, 'is old Pakia so blind and weak that he cannot *faha-heke*? Ah, let but some of ye guide me out and set me before the surf — then will ye see.'

Poor old fellow! Like an old troop-horse who dozes in a field, and whose blood tingles to some distant bugle call, the ancient, from his lit-tle hut near by, had heard our cries, and his brave old heart had awak-ened to the call of lusty youth. And so, earnestly begging the loan of a board from one of the swimmers, he had come to join us. And then two merry-hearted girls, taking him to the water's edge, swam out with him to the reef amid our wild cheers and laughter. They soon reached the starting-point, and then a roar of delight went up from us as we saw them place the ancient on his board, his knees to his chin, and his hands grasping the sides. Then, as a bursting roller thundered along and swept down upon them, they gave him a shove and sprang before it themselves — one on each side. And, old and half blind as he was, he came in like an arrow from the bow of a mighty archer, his scanty white locks trailing behind his poor old head like the frayed-out end of a manilla hawser, his face set, and his feeble old throat crowing a quavering, shaking note of triumph as he shot up to the very margin of the beach, amid a roar of applause from the naked and admiring spectators.

Poor old Pakia! Well indeed art thou entitled to this stick of tobacco from the white man to console thy cheery and venerable old pagan soul in the watches of the night.

Wild Life in the Southern Seas (1897)

<hr>

1895

George Wirth in Montevideo

Many children have dreamed of running away and taking to the road with a circus. Joining the circus took George Wirth (1867–1941) around the world. His father, an itinerant musician from Bavaria, arrived in Victoria in 1855 and formed Wirth's Band with his brothers and sons. From time to time they played with touring circuses, including Ashton's in 1870 and 1881. In the following year, Wirth's Band branched out on its own to become Wirth's Circus. The overseas touring of the circus began in 1888 in New Caledonia.

Five years later with the onset of the 1890s Depression, the circus took off for more distant places, and between 1893 and 1900 performed in South Africa, South America, Britain, India and Java. George Wirth retired from the circus in 1930 and became involved in Australia's film industry. He died a wealthy man in Sydney in 1941. His accounts of moving a circus around the world and the attendant tribulations and triumphs make for entertaining reading about a not so common form of Australian travel.

We arrived in Monte Video on Sunday morning, September 1, and opened at the 'Nuevo Politeama' there on Saturday, September 14. A long distance telephone from our theatre to the Theatre San Martin in Buenos Aires conveyed to the manager of that theatre an idea how our show was taking on. They spoke to me through the 'phone, and told me they could hear the applause of the audience after each act, and I right there arranged with them to open in their theatre when we played Buenos Aires. This was the first time I had ever heard of a long-distance telephone, as it was not in Australia in those days.

The manager of the Theatre San Martin told me over the phone that night that he had heard that we had a troupe of black people who were walking about Monte Video nearly naked. I told him that they were in their native dress as they were semi-wild Zulus. He said he had heard that the citizens there were taking objection to them walking about like that, and when I explained that it was their native costume, and that I thought it a good advertisement for the show for wild Zulus to be seen in the streets of beautiful Monte Video, he advised me to clothe them properly or we would get into trouble with the authorities. True enough, we were ordered to clothe them properly in European clothes, and as most of them had never had on a pair of trousers or a pair of boots in their lives, they objected to wearing them, so we had trouble both ways. But the Zulus themselves solved the question by clearing out from us. We never heard where they went, but we had an idea that they were taken away by someone on a ranch and made work.

We found Monte Video a beautiful clean city with wonderful hotels. We had to wait a fortnight before we could open as the 'Politeama' was occupied by an Italian Grand Opera Company. We played in the theatre the night after they closed. The place had been built expressly for theatre and circus, so there was no trouble at all. The circus ring was right in the middle of the auditorium. The floor had to be taken up, and underneath was the ring. Then the stage came away in the middle, about 10 feet, for our artists and horses to come through on to the ring, while the stage itself was turned into a dress circle with upholstered chairs.

We found the populace, who were Spanish, very emotional and enthusiastic. If they liked a person they would make him or her their hero for the time being.

A few nights before we opened in the 'Politeama,' and just after we had retired for the night at the St Martin Hotel, we heard a great commotion up the town. We could distinctly hear firearms, as well as shouting, and bands playing. On looking out of our bedroom windows we saw a great crowd turning from the main street into the street we lived in. They were chairing some person shoulder high, and cheering him madly. We were positive it was a newly-elected President of Uruguay, and expected to see the Government troops open fire on them. We were all excitement and got more excited when we saw the crowd turn into the front door of our hotel. We now expected that we would be right in the middle of it, so we all got up fearfully and dressed, and, looking down the well of the hotel to the vestibule, saw the crowd still making a fuss over the same man. He was being hugged and kissed by both sexes in the crowd. One of our company — Gil Eldred — had been in Manila and could speak a little Spanish, so when we saw a 'mozo' (waiter) he asked him if they had elected a new President, and was that he they were making such a fuss over. The waiter replied that the hero was the celebrated tenor of the Italian Opera Company, who had been making his farewell appearance, and who was such a favourite that the public could not make enough fuss of him during this his send off.

During the fortnight we were idle in Monte Video, both my brother and myself were learning Spanish. It is not the real Spanish, but we did not know that. We only wanted to learn their language, as I had to clown, and Philip had to answer me as ring-master. He also had to drill a school of horses in Spanish. Our efforts in that direction on the first night brought down the house, as we were saying things all backwards, and this made a bigger hit than if we had spoken the words perfectly.

We became great favourites in Monte Video, and when my sisters had finished their acts they were encored and call upon to 'Baile' (dance), whereupon my sister Marizles broke into a Highland Fling. She had to respond again, and this time she did a Sailor's Hornpipe. The audience threw their hats into the ring, and now she had to return these to their owners personally. I thought they were crazy, but this was part of the performance that went on night after night. Madeline, who didn't dance, was kept very busy returning hats. We had engaged some Spanish clowns, but after the first night the audience would not have them, and would call out, 'Fuera' (get out). I asked them why they left the ring, and they said if they had stayed, they would have had chairs

thrown at them. The audience would call out for the 'Clown Aus-
traliano' or 'Clown Englishe,' so I had to clown two and three times a
night, as well as ride, do the horizontal bars, an acrobatic act with Philip
and Eldred, and a carrying act with my sister Madeline, or Olympians,
with either my niece Edith, or Eldred.

We played four weeks in Monte Video to good business and
arranged to open in Buenos Aires on October 12. We had packed up
everything ready to go on the steamer on October 7, but the theatre
with all our wardrobe, harness and paraphernalia was burnt to the
ground during the early morning. The horses had been removed to a
stable after the performance, or otherwise they would have gone with
the rest of the things. We were searching among the ruins the following
day to see if we could find the steel frame of a pad, but everything was
burnt to a cinder.

Round the World With a Circus (1925)

<u>1897</u>

Henry Lawson in Wellington

*Henry Lawson (1867–1922) was born on the goldfields at Grenfell. By the
time he made his first trip to New Zealand in 1894, both his reputation as a
poet and writer of short stories and the pattern of his life with alcohol were
being established. After six months working as a telegraph linesman, he
returned to Sydney. Two years later, Lawson married Bertha Bredt, and in
March 1897 they moved to the South Island of New Zealand where Lawson
worked as a teacher with Maoris in the remote settlement of Mangamaunu.
In organising the transfer to New Zealand, Bertha intended to separate Lawson from alcohol and his escapades with his drinking mates of the Dawn and
Dusk Club. The move was not successful and after eight months Lawson and
the pregnant Bertha were back in Sydney. In 1900 the family left Australia
again, this time to go to London where, like so many Australian writers,
Lawson hoped to achieve literary success and a commensurate income. In
London he wrote the four Joe Wilson stories, generally regarded as his finest
writing, but the metropolis did not meet his hopes and the family came home
in 1902, and Lawson's terrible period of decline began. His description of
Wellington, three years after New Zealand introduced votes for women, suggests the view from the bar-room window with its yarn-spinning and nostalgia. New Zealand was the only 'civilised' country Australian travellers felt
they could patronise.*

About the first thing that strikes an Australian on coming to Wellington is the quantity of alluvial soil packed up all round. It would seem as if the Lord had a lot of waste dirt left over when he finished the North Island and stacked it on this end.

Wellington looks like a good place for a workman to be in. Auckland has about it an atmosphere of conservatism not here apparent to the intelligent southern workmen's nose, which has become sharpened to such things in these hungry times.

About the first thing an Australian does in Wellington is to have a beer, then he goes to look for lodgings, falls into the hands of an unprincipled hash-house tout, and gets run into the worst 'diggings' in the city; then he has another beer. New Zealand beer is far superior to the stuff we get in Australia. Wellington pubs have generally two or three openings on to the bar; if you go in the front door you pay 3d. or 4d., if you go in through the side entrance it costs you 6d. for the same drink, and if you go into the private bar you pay 6d., and it costs you about 15s. in the end. If you stay out you get thirsty. Some of these things puzzle Australians.

It is said that there is less drunkenness over here than in Australia, but we think that there's just as much drinking going on, in comparison, and more gambling connected with it. You seldom see the dice box in Sydney bars. The Sydneyite drinks to get boozed and happy, not to gamble.

Wellington has a good harbour, bold scenery, splendid climate and perhaps the most Liberal Government and the biggest wooden building in the world. The Government will make the biggest blunder, by-and-by, and the building would make the biggest fire.

Wellington is also the seat of the National Joke of New Zealand, for New Zealand has a national joke [...]

The National Joke of New Zealand, which has not been immortalised yet, is that you can always tell a Wellingtonian by the way in which he grabs his hat when going round a corner.

Sometimes you hear it on the boat coming over; the boarding house runners will tell it to you as soon as you step ashore; men to whom you have letters of introduction will fire it at you as soon as they decently can; chance drinking acquaintances will tell you; perfect strangers will take you aside and try the damned old joke on you; and, if you meet an old friend over here, you will find him bursting to introduce you to the National Joke of New Zealand.

Another thing that strikes a new-chum is the way the footpaths are half-paved. There are flags from the kerb to a line running along the centre of the path, and the rest is gravel. The stranger is told that the

Council agreed to pave one half, if the ratepayers did the other. The city fathers fulfilled their part of the contract, but the respected citizens didn't come up to time: they declined to shell out. They walked on the paved half and chuckled.

The harbour and city are in a basin which looks like the bed of an old crater — and it's to be hoped it don't blow up. The hills have the advantage of not reminding an 'Othersider', vaguely, yet painfully, of some other hills that he has seen somewhere before. There ought to be more rock cropping out in those hills. There'll be a landslip some day in the vicinity of Wellington — and Auckland too, for that matter — and a good many respected townsmen and their families will be buried before they're ready.

Boys in knickerbockers, and tall strapping girls of fourteen, and intelligent women, and earthquakes are peculiar to Wellington. There have been four earthquakes since a friend of mine has been here, and he says the fun of it is that he didn't feel any one of 'em. But then, he's a solid citizen in every sense of the word, and it would take a good old-fashioned earthquake to shake him up to any considerable extent.

There are no earthquakes now-a-days, like there were when our grandmother was a girl. At least she says not. We only feel the weak dying kicks of the volcanic age, with a last convulsive kick now and again — like the one up at the terraces lately.

But there is always a chance of the earth yawning and swallowing Wellington, together with the biggest wooden building in the world, the women's franchise, the most Liberal Government, the National Bank and the National Joke of New Zealand — and E. M. Smith with his jam tins full of sand and cement. What a chance it would be for that gentleman to study mineralogy — if he survived.

There is always a likelihood of New Zealand cities being taken into the bowels of the 'yearth'; and, therefore, we would suggest more churches, more people going to them oftener, and more Sunday schools, and less cricket and cigarettes for the boys in knickerbockers, and more prayers said generally and less dice boxes in pubs.

Up on the top of the hills behind the city there is good scenery, a good view, and a pretty little town called Wadestown. A Sydney man tramped up there on a hot day, and struggled through the heat and dust until a thirsty voice from the bottom of his soul cried out aloud for a long shandy. Then he reached Wadestown, and made for the Post and Telegraph Office under the impression that it was a pub. But his companion told him that the town was called 'Prohibition town', and explained that the name was a joke which was kept on hand to relieve the National Joke when the National Joke got tired and wanted a spell

— a sort of relief-duty joke in fact. He further explained that the National Joke would die if it didn't have a rest now and again.

But the name of the town wasn't a joke, and the Sydney man was so disgusted that he packed up his traps and took the next boat back to Sydney. He should have gone out to Kaiwarra first.

The Botanical Gardens, Wellington, are a relief after the painfully artificial gardens of Sydney. There's an Australian emu up there somewhere, but we couldn't find him. We would like to have had a yarn with him — for the sake of Auld Lang Syne. But perhaps he's dead.

They say that an Australian wrote recently to one of your local papers complaining about the way in which the emu was lodged and fed. He said that he objected to a native of his country being treated like that. A blackfellow, a kangaroo, or an emu can always find a big place in the heart of the Australian abroad.

But there is a fountain in Wellington with a little trough on each side for the dogs to drink at, and a town that's good to dogs can't be such a bad, hard-hearted place, after all. Over in Sydney the dogs have to take their chance for a drink, and are sometimes driven by thirst to sneak in behind bars and lap up the droppings from beer engines. This demolarises 'em.

We might as well state, for the benefit of outsiders, that Wellington is mostly built of wood, because of the earthquakes — or rather the fear of them. But a good many brick buildings are going up round now (the *Times* Office for instance), and things are getting nicely ready for a big sensation when the next volcanic kick comes. We wouldn't advise New Zealand papers to build their offices of brick — because they are the most unprincipled pirates on the face of the earth.

This reminds us that the last big earthquake here happened when Wellington was born. It raised the settlement four feet and the hair of the population as high as it would go. They got on board the only ship in the harbour, intending to go away, but there came a big tidal wave which washed the ship up on the beach and wrecked her. So the people had to stop. They 'batched' together in the wreck for a while, or until someone said they might as well go home. So it might appear that Wellington owed its origin to a tidal wave.

The Wellington Museum is interesting and the Maori carvings less startling to the modest stranger than those in Auckland. But there are a lot of things outside the Wellington Museum that ought to be in; and — and, well we don't believe in the big fossil egg. We've studied the bones of the extinct New Zealand fowl, guessed her size, and compared it with the size of the egg, but we couldn't swallow it. There is a cast of a foreign egg in the same museum, and it makes us wild to think that anyone (except an Australian) had the cheek to lay such a big lie in New Zealand.

In conclusion, Oh, men of Wellington! Your literary men are good sorts and just about as sinful as their brothers in any part of the world; your artists are promising, ambitious young fellows, and I'm sorry to hear that their ideas and style are paralysed, or stolen to such an extent by men like Hopkins and Phil May; your scenery is a relief, after Australia; your climate good; your leading men are liberal, broad minded men, and your action with regard to your women has immortalised the land and will, perhaps, revolutionise the world — only you don't seem to know it. And now, if you only put the Upper House and a few other things into the National Museum, and cease to blow about the big wooden humpy, and abolish the National Joke — and provided you don't get taken into the bowels of the earth by a 'quake — you stand a grand chance to lead the nations.

Leonard Cronin (ed.), *A Camp-Fire Yarn* (1984)

1901

Randolph Bedford in England and Italy

Journalist, novelist, poet, farmhand, actor, theatrical manager, mining entrepreneur and politician, Australian-born Randolph Bedford (1868–1941) identified himself with that 1890s triumvirate, the Bulletin, *Bohemia and the Bush. Bedford took his family to England in 1901; a journey undertaken because it was hoped a long sea voyage would benefit his sickly young son, and to continue his search for financial backing for his mining ventures and publishers for his novels. He arrived in Dover not with the usual deference and awe but as a patriotic and self-conscious Australian, with, as he himself wrote, the 'curiosity of a puppy ... who must find what is behind everything'. As an Australian nationalist, assertive and defensive by turns, Bedford was highly critical of the British establishment, the class structure, free trade, the tolerance of appalling poverty, the unjustified race pride and sense of ethnic superiority. It was his desire to escape England, and an interest in Italian mines, that first took Bedford to Italy. But once encountered, Italy 'tugged at my heart strings', and much of his time overseas between 1901 and 1904 was spent there. His family was established for a time in a villa at Bellosguardo on the outskirts of Florence, which was used as an Italian base by some of his* Bulletin *mates such as Lionel Lindsay. While in Europe, Bedford wrote a series of travel sketches for the* Bulletin *and these were republished in 1914 as* Explorations in Civilization. *In a brief preface he explained that 'these travel notes' were written in the 'first flush of experience' and were therefore*

more 'truly observed' than when experience had made their content familiar.
He was even more enthusiastic about promoting travel within Australia, an
enthusiasm that is present in his autobiography, Naught to Thirty-Three
(1944). Bedford continued his colourful career as a Labor member of the
Queensland parliament from 1917 until his death.

All the books and all the Englishmen that I had met had exaggerated
the 'Albion' part of the description — the cliffs are not white, but a
dirty grey. Up to the feet of the cliffs the saddle-colored channel staggered, and there was neither color nor sunlight in the scene.

Stay! There was some color. A score of red-faced porters in neat blue
guernseys and trousers. There was still some hope — here was the genuine
John Bull, ruddy, kindly, cheery and strong. I selected a porter, bound my
burdens on him, and we moved shorewards along the pier; past a train
whose passengers were attacked by small pirates, whose faces were also the
color of smacked infants, and who called incessantly, 'Tea Bawskits.'

We found a hotel, and a good-looking German waiter, gazing with
the yearning gaze of a dying saint, at a two-penny tip on the horizon;
and there was also a very plain lady clerk, grey and acerbitous.

There was no joy here, so I went out to find a barber. I found him in
a small low-ceilinged evil-smelling shop. I knocked at the door and he
suddenly opened it; and I fell down five steps into the cellar he called
his 'saloon.' He produced a small towel that looked and smelled as if it
had been a cemetery for cockroaches, and I begged him to get another
one that dated no further back than George 4th. He went away, muttering, and returned with a new towel he had evidently been saving up.
It was a cheap honey-comb towel; the kind that is called honey-comb
because it is never sweet.

He put the towel round my neck, and I talked.

'Seem to be a lot of Germans here.'

'Yus sir, a big lot. Them Germins are all over this place.'

'Are you the only barber here?' I asked this because he had spoken so
bitterly of Germans that I knew there must be direct German opposition.

'No, I ain't. There's a Germin barber 'ere. Gets all the tryde. Don't
know why, eether.'

His razor was unspeakable — simply a sharp curry-comb. I had
been weeping unobtrusively while he spoke and my agony moved me
to say —

'I suppose he gets the trade because he has good razors.'

Then the brute abraded me for the fifteenth time, lathered me again
with cockroach soap, and said:

"We'll never get rid of 'em, I 'spect.'

'Protection and alien exclusion,' said I, 'why not try that?'

'Purtection,' he repeated scornfully — at least as scornfully as his rudimentary nostrils would allow him. 'Wy! ain't this a free counterey? Ain't it? No. Free tryde we wus born, and free tryde we'll die.'

I was hoping that he would die soon and I didn't care what he died as — this leper who was proud of his spots.

'Well, then, if you're a free trader don't howl about German competition.'

'That's a different thing that is,' he said very quickly. 'That's comin' at a man, that is — but it ain't nashern'l.'

'Then in business you're an Exclusionist,' I said, 'and Nationally, you're a Tory.'

'A' course I am — them there Liberals 'ud take away a man's livin'. I'm a Tory, I am.'

He finished me with a triumphant parade of the razor all over the sore places, and I paid him and fled from the shambles.

Rails came in from all points of the compass, and crossed over, and dived under our line, and went away in all directions, and came back again. The train ran through half-a-dozen miles of terraces and squalid streets, and thousands of chimney pots; crossed a muddy stream showing the flat black beaches of ooze that belong to low tide — there were barges and warehouses sitting down in the mud, and riverside factories up to their knees in slime; a yellow fog that smelled like bad coffee covered us; the train stopped, and the porters cried 'London Bridge.'

So the miracles that brought me over 12,000 miles of sea had really happened, and this was London. It seemed such a weight of endeavour for such a light result.

Out of London Bridge again, and trembling — haltingly — to Cannon Street, the train feeling its way through the yellow mephitic fog. Once or twice the dense chokiness lifted, and then I saw in the wilderness of houses we passed that in London the usual style of measurement suffers a revolution. Elsewhere three feet is a yard; here a yard is a foot square, and the majority of the houses have no yards at all.

The train started out of Cannon Street again, and backed and filled through the murk for half an hour; then it stopped suddenly, and the fog-choked voices croaked 'Charing Cross.'

My ignorance had brought me back to the Strand, although I wanted to land in the City, but this mistake being explained, I took a hansom, and voyaged eastward. The outlook was all very gloomy — a fog of Egyptian darkness in places; in others a miasma only as thick as starlight. The Cross in the station yard is dirty white from the impurity of pigeon droppings. The tower of St Martin-in-the-Fields whitened also with guano — all the ugly lines of fog-blackened architecture gradually disappearing under white manure. There was a street as wide as the narrowest parts of George Street, Sydney; a thousand 'busses tied and tangled in the fog, their drivers becoming blastiferous, and not thankful, when the liftings of the fog came; and hundreds of pigeons swooping down on the horse droppings, standing in the centre of the traffic, dodging horse hoofs and wheels with side-way flutterings; but never really taking flight. They had the perfect hunger which casteth out fear. For the 150,000 dockers or so are not the only living things to whom fog or strikes brings starvation.

Along the Strand, this dirty street, reverberant to the hoof beats of thousands of horses, the footways were lined at intervals with hawkers of various things for a penny, and their hands and faces were of the same flayed appearance and the same tint of chilblain red [...]

We had lunch at the 'Ship and Turtle' — an ordinary place of extraordinary charges, and run by the original forty thieves and the brother of the impenitent malefactor. Turtle soup 5/- a plate — salmon 3/- a portion — and not much to talk about when you had them. Henceforth I shall keep my appetite for rare dishes for the places where the rare dishes grow. Townsville has the atmosphere for the eating of turtle steaks and beche de mer.

'How many breads, sir?' said the waiter, preparing to write the items with a very short pencil on a very long slip of paper.

'Breads?'

'Yessir, breads sir, an' butters, sir?'

'Do you mean to tell me you want to know how many bits of bread I ate, and how many of these little pennyweight bits of butter?'

'Yessir — breadssir and butterssir — 'ow many, sir?'

'I don't know; you'd better average.'

He averaged; with 10 per cent on for the risk.

'I had two salts,' I said gravely.

'Two salts, sir?'

'Yes, and two peppers, and two mustards.'

'Peppers sir, an' mustards, we don't charge for.'

I took the docket and moved towards the cash desk.

He coughed, 'Beg pardon, sir, forgotten somethin', sir,'

I gave him fourpence.

'Thanky, sir,' and he was gone to another customer.

The tip system is a curse in England — a curse which has become law, partly by reason of the studied carelessness of a leisured class with regard to the money it has never been asked to earn; and partly because the employer, recognising the existence of tips, engages waiters at no wages at all, leaving them to make a living by this organised blackmail of customers.

Certain police-court evidence given in London during my visit showed that in many, and presumably in all of the principal hotels and restaurants, the proprietors *charged* the waiters anything over £1 a week for the privilege of working; and in some cases insisted on a division of the tips in addition. The injustice of this struck me at first, and I fought it. Now, having things to do so much more important, I fall in with the rest, and tip for everything. A waiter opens the door — he expects a tip; he tells you the time, and waits for a tip; and if you are busy, and therefore absent-minded, you pay the penny and go away a spineless worm, and not a man. There is nothing more lowering of self-respect than this continuous and shameless hunger for unearned pence.

[...]

At Paris, there was a clean, clear city to rest the eye on after the soreness of the London fog. I dined at the Cafe of the Black Cat, and inquired vainly for garlic. Was told by the waiter, who appeared shocked at the inquiry, that they did not keep garlic. The world is growing weaker — at least, its breath is.

December 23. — Reached Modane — on the Italian side of Mt Cenis — at 10 this morning. Snow everywhere — covering the railway track and the great mountain behind it; which is as steep as the little hill of Byjerkerno. Mt Cenis is very fine — the sort of unnecessary hill which calls for an unnecessary tourist to climb it for no especial reason.

Around Modane there are a few farms, each with a fine barn and a tumbledown shed for a dwelling-house. The cockatoo farmer is the same in the Alps as on the Hawkesbury River.

In Genoa I found the beginning for me of Italian art; and the worst refreshment room on earth, not even excepting in Westralia. But the newness of it all stopped any criticism of the dinner. Even that vile refreshment room was frescoed and painted till it became a little hall of wonder, and opposite me there was a bright-eyed, blue-haired Italian woman, whose teeth flashed with the whiteness of milk — one of Shakespeare's Italians she was.

From Genoa to south of Spezzia the rail runs in and out of the cliffs by the Mediterranean. It is curiously like Tasmania. There is a bay like Penguin and another like Emu Bay. The air has been very mild since we left the snow, and I found myself half believing that I was on the road from Ulverstone to Emu Bay, looking out for the red lantern on Table Cape.

At Pisa my bedroom was coved and domed and frescoed: and the use of marble, to eyes accustomed to the cemented brick of England, was prodigal, on the threshold and on the window lintels — the windows that opened on to Juliet's balcony with a big white moon shining on it, and below in the garden the red gold of ripe oranges against leaves of magnolia green. I sat on that balcony and smoked for an hour, and looked at the oranges and the oleanders, thanking my luck that had sent me from the fog of the antipodes of Australia into an imitation of my own land.

[...]

How like is Australia to Italy in atmosphere. There is in my garden in Grey-street, East Melbourne, a cypress as beautiful as any here, and as calm — it looks east to the Dandenongs, which are lovelier than the Apennines.

We want in Australia to kill the imported abuses of the old world — to imitate in our art our trees and our climate — beautiful, generous, and strong, as these Italians did. The magnificent simplicity of the Pitti and Strozzi palaces were suggested by some great rock in the Apennines, and they are as far above the over-ornamented houses of new Paris or new London as the best of Michel Angelo's figures are above Cellini's flashy Perseus — which is mere goldsmith's work. Of course, we are too young in Australia to consider art or beauty before breakfast; but we have spent a lot of money on building for little result, and surely it is at least as cheap, if not cheaper, to build with brains and taste as without them.

Explorations in Civilization (1914)

1904

Nathan Spielvogel in Germany

Born into Ballarat's Jewish community, Nathan Spielvogel (1874–1956) spent most of his life in the Wimmera district of Victoria as a teacher, writer and historian. In 1904, with his savings of 120 pounds, this 'backblock State Schoolteacher with an ambition to see the lands of the past' took off for Europe, visiting Britain, Holland, Germany, Switzerland and Italy. Although both of his parents were born in Germany, his own grasp of the language was tenuous, as this extract shows. While delighting in German food and music halls, and his first escalator, Spielvogel was disturbed by other features of German life, particularly the all pervasive militarism. Everywhere he travelled Spielvogel was very conscious of being Australian, and having seen the ancient lands he came home 'feeling proud that I have come back to a country where freedom is more than a name'. Spielvogel's tales of his adventures abroad were first published in the Dimboola Banner. *Reissued in book form in 1905,* A Gumsucker on the Tramp *proved immensely popular, reaching its fifth edition in 1913 with some 20 000 copies being sold. Equally successful were his sketches of Australian life such as* The Cocky Farmer *(1907) and* Old Eko's Note Book *(1930). The popularity of his*

books owed much to his gently iconoclastic style, and to his intention of amus-
ing as well as instructing his readers. Spielvogel retired as head teacher at
Dana Street School, Ballarat in 1938.

Neue Konigstrasse, Berlin.
My last glimpse of London was of London Bridge, with all its lights
gleaming and mirrored in the great silent highway of the Thames. The
night is dark, so I turn to my travelling companions. One is a commercial traveller off to Moscow, the other is an Austrian returning from the
great fur sales in London. Both spoke English well, and we chatted away
merrily, till we came to Port Victoria at the mouth of the Thames at
10.15 p.m. (70 miles in 85 minutes). We embarked on the little packet
steam boat belonging to the Zeeland Co., a Dutch firm, and so away. I
looked over the rails till the lights of Queensbro' sank from sight — and
so good-bye to dear old England! The accommodation on board was
wretched — a big room with 18 beds ranged around it anyhow, beds
20ft long, with pillows and blankets at intervals along them. I woke up
to find the man sleeping next me further along, cursing me for putting
my foot in his mouth. What he objected particularly about was that I
had my boots on. Anyway, he shouldn't sleep with his mouth open. We
had to pay extra for our beds, in fact extra for everything we had. I have
a receipt for a penny for the use of a clean towel. There were eighteen
men sleeping in the one room — all strangers, so I slept in all my
clothes — boots and all. The passage was extremely smooth, but at 4.30
a.m. I had had enough of the air laden with the exhausted breath of
eighteen gentlemen of assorted nationalities, so I made my way on deck
and got a whiff of clean salt air. At five the long low coast of Holland
came in view, and soon we disembarked from the wretched little tub at
Flushing. Tips to the stewards! Not much. Passing through the Customs
House we boarded the 'wagon-lit' for Berlin. And what a train! What
comfortable carriages. Corridor cars, the entrances to which were at the
ends. No doors in the cars, but instead, splendid large windows, $3\frac{1}{2}$ ft
by 3ft, which gave an unbroken view of the scenery. The window
spreads the whole width of the compartment [...]
    Six came and I prepared to meet my unknown cousins. I had sent
them my photograph and a German (?) letter from London, telling
them to meet me at the Friedrichstrasse station to-night. I must own
my heart beat a little quicker at the thought of meeting my mother's
folk, whom I had never seen. 6.58! Here we are! I picked them out!
Kissing and shaking of hands. They yabbering in German, I yabbering
in English. Grusse und Kusse! 'Welcome and glad to see you!' 'Sprichst
du nicht Deutsch?' (Don't you speak German) 'Sehr schlecht! Und ihr

English?' (Very bad, and you English?) 'Nicht ein Wort, aber Fraulein H—— kann ein wenig. Gertie sprich English zu ihm?' (Not a word, but Miss H—— knows a little. Talk to him English). And the pretty little maiden said to me unblushingly all the English she knew. (I'm wondering if she understood it): — 'O! You leedle darling! I lofe you! Oh! you leedle daisy! Dell me drue.' Not a bad welcome! I'm sleeping to-night in Berlin so, 'Leben sie wohl.'

Berlin is the finest city I have yet visited. London is great, Berlin is grand. London is impressive, but Berlin is majestic. Unter der Linden reminded me of Sturt Street, Ballarat, though the lovely Linden trees, all bursting out in their dainty light green shades were prettier than the formal flower pots of our Victorian show street. Berlin has the advantage over London of being practically a new city. Its public buildings and monuments stand in squares or facing wide streets, and so are seen far better than in London.

I got a shock the first day out. The typical German I had imagined was short, fat, and badly built, cap on head, scrubby moustache, pipe in mouth, and a generally easy-going manner — Hans Breitmann. But in every particular I was wrong. The typical Berliner is above the general height, with a bold military manner (if he is not a soldier he makes you think he is), moustache turned upwards (in many cases the moustache had been trained so much upwards that I wondered if the wearer intended to climb up to heaven on it) — and pipe in mouth? Never had an illusion of mine been so broken. I have hardly seen a dozen pipes in Berlin! Cigars! Cigars! The cabdriver smokes cigars at his work, likewise the man that sweeps the roads. Everybody smokes them! Ten cigars can be bought for a penny, and I have been paying a penny each for cigars worth fully 6d. in Melbourne. I've been smoking twenty daily.

Berlin seems to date from the Franco-Prussian war of '70. Its monuments — and they are many and magnificent — commemorate the victories of that war. The great National Denkmal, the most imposing monument I have yet seen; the great Brandenburger Thor, surmounted by bronze statuary; the Emperor's palaces; the majestic Reichstag (Parliament House), standing in a block by itself and surrounded by noble streets; the palace of William I, and the window where he stood every day to witness his subjects — (every man I passed this way pointed out this window to me, with the words — in German, of course — 'That's where our King William stood every day.' It got a bit monotonous after the seventy-third time I had replied 'Did he?') The Sieges Alleè, in the Thiergarten, is a magnificent avenue of fine trees, and stretching along on either side for a long distance is a collection of marble monuments to defunct German heroes of all times, while at the extremity of it is a great column of metal with an angel on top — the whole composed of the melted down guns captured from the French in 1870.

And right here I say that I wouldn't live in Berlin. No! not at any price. Berlin has a god we know not in Australia or England — Militarism! The soldier is everywhere! He is marching in squads in the streets, he is drinking in the bier hall; the police, postmen, railway officials, are all soldiers out of their time; he pervades the whole city. Even my cousin's coachman wears gorgeous military uniform. The officers, dressed in their dainty lavender top coats, and little undress caps, stalk along the street, turning an eye of contempt on anyone not in uniform. I stepped into a car the other day. Four civilians were sitting on one side, an officer alone on the other. The car started with a jerk. I dropped down rather suddenly, almost on top of the officer. He jumped as though something or other (I don't know what) had happened. I apologised in English. He looked too fierce for me to remember any German. Then, giving me a look of intense contempt, he said several things at me in German. (I wished I'd learnt more German). I don't think they were respectable. He flung himself in the far corner and left me alone [...]

The Berliners live well. Every evening my cousins have taken me to one of the great cafés — the Bauer, Victoria, Kaiser, National, etc. We have nothing like these in Australia. A large hall, with little tables scattered all round it. The walls and ceilings are most beautifully decorated. A grand band plays the best of music, while around sit ladies and gentlemen drinking beer or iced coffee (delicious), eating ice creams, etc. Friends come up and chat for a while and pass along. The gentlemen leave the ladies, and stroll off for a game of billiards or cards upstairs — I rushed the file of English newspapers — and so the evening passes. The account is made up — about 2s. was our usual bill for the three of us — and then home. Tips everywhere. If one buys a beer, the waiter expects a tip for bringing it — a half-penny is considered enough.

I also visited a students' beer party. It was exhilarating. A great glass with two handles, very similar to a soup tureen, was filled with the non-alcoholic weiss (white) beer. The first man, taking it by its two handles, stood up and let the beer roll down his throat, roaring out a drinking song, 'Ach Prosit.' When he had done his best, the next one took a turn, and so on round the table, until it was emptied.

Berlin has some beautiful streets, wide and straight with fine buildings on either side, but neither here nor in London have I seen our common shop-verandah [...]

To-morrow I leave Berlin to visit my mother's sister and relations in Kolmar, away in the north-east of Germany. I am looking forward to it with pleasure, and with just a trifle of unrest, as the Germans do not hide their feelings, and I hate being kissed by men.

I was in one of the great Warenhauser (shops like Foy's in Melbourne), where one can purchase anything, and found it tremendous. Going upstairs is an easy affair. There is a moving platform, on which one steps, and is carried up to the next floor. And cheap goods? I bought articles of clothing for 6s. 6d. that I regularly pay 17s. 6d. for in Melbourne! Pictorial postcards, 10 a penny! I'd like to earn my salary in Dimboola and buy my things in Berlin.

Though teetotalism is (as far as I can judge) almost unknown in Berlin, so is drunkenness. I ascribe this to the more rational method of drinking.

I hope, Mr Editor, that your fair readers will not think I am intending this as flattery. The Australian girl is easily first (so far as I have seen) in beauty and charm, but particularly that she always seems to be well dressed, no matter how cheap the materials may be of which her dress is composed. Now, the dresses worn by —— but stop! I must not get into a description of ladies' dresses, so to avoid that disaster I will close for the time [...]

My cousin has a furniture factory, and employs a large number of hands. The average wage is about 18s. a week, and the highest is 30s. — but see what he can buy with his money? I spent many hours in the factory watching these workmen take a lump of unpolished, unshaped wood, and with a few deft turns of a few simple tools turn it into a thing of beauty. Their world is small, and their prejudices and ideas are bounded by their tiny village, yet I felt respect for them for they were makers. There now! (My German improves fast).

My uncle has a restaurant, and when evening comes the folk of the village gather in the Gasthaus to see me. Had I dropped from the moon I could not have been looked on with greater wonder by these village wise heads. Of course I am not supposed to understand any German, and they criticise me openly. Says one, 'I suppose all Australians smoke pipes and have funny noses?' And another, 'They don't grow much hair in Australia. I suppose it's too hot?' 'Yes! And they all write without ink (I had a fountain pen), and what bad writing.' I sit till I can stand it no longer, and then bolt to another room.

Eat! I have scarcely stopped since I've been here! First breakfast, second breakfast, lunch, dinner, coffee drinking (like our afternoon tea — tea is almost unknown in these parts), even meal and supper, and each one of these is a solid meal. Besides these, aunt gives me a snack in between so I shall not get hungry. They live well! What do you think of roast larks on toast for breakfast?

My pockets are mysteriously filled with cigars, and I ask no questions but smoke them, about 20 a day.

I visited the neighbouring village at Kolmar, where my mother was born, and spent her early days. The cobble stones are worse here. I now understand why she left Germany. My cousin was with me, and after visiting about a dozen cousins to the third and fourth generation, we went down a street, past the priest's garden where mother had, uninvited, helped herself to fruit fifty years ago, past the street wooden pump where she had run for water many a time, and, finally, to the little stone house on the corner which she called 'Home.' With the permission of the inhabitants I went up into the attic where she spent her girlhood. People seem to live here till they die of old age. I visited my mother's aunt — she's a young person of 96!

The shops open on Sundays after church hours, and as the band plays in the market place, things are gay between 12 and 2 in the afternoon.

I notice that Socialism is becoming an important subject in Germany, and the party (Sozial-Demokrats) are gaining more power yearly. Still, 'the man in the street' in Germany does not take the same interest in politics as the Australian does.

Now that I am leaving all my kind relatives, who have treated me like a Prodigal Son, I'm the lamb that's being killed (with over-feeding) for the safe return. Off to Berlin.

A Gumsucker on the Tramp (1906 edition; first published 1905)

1907

Alf Vincent in Canton

Born in Launceston, Tasmania, Alf Vincent (1874–1915) moved to Melbourne and took over the main cartoon page of the Melbourne Punch *at the age of just 22. He was soon offered a staff position on the Sydney* Bulletin *as a cartoonist and remained there until his death. He drew heavily upon urban themes — Phil May was a significant, perhaps overwhelming influence — and was a prominent illustrator of the* Bulletin's *near-hysterical prejudices against non-Europeans, believing that anything Asian was in turn either dangerous or hilarious. Travel in Asia did not seem to temper his prejudice, though it is possible that too much of his reputation rested on an unambiguous defence of the White Australia policy. This piece first appeared in the* Lone Hand, *which J. F. Archibald, former editor of the* Bulletin, *established in May 1907. Vincent swung between melancholia and elation. He suffered a final nervous collapse in December 1915 and committed suicide at Manly.*

In Canton I met one who is probably the world's boss executioner. His record for helping his fellow-man to the Hereafter runs well into four figures. Barring generals, milk adulterators, and other people in a wholesale way of business, he is the best friend Death has. And yet about him there is no undue pride. He is, I should judge, some 60 years of age, with a manner at once friendly and reassuring. His smile smacks ever so little of the Notre Dame gargoyle. But its lurking devilishness is mitigated by a suavity that is altogether charming, and high purpose speaks clamantly from this official's bald, tall, bland brow.

If I haven't before, I may mention now that my guide, Wun Brick, did all the tipping in the course of our travels together. This saved me trouble, and pleased Brick infinitely. I noted, as an interesting psychological circumstance, that whereas Brick only donated a mere nickel at such places of minor interest as temples, silk shops, and the like, when we came to the execution-ground he squandered on the man behind the sword a piece of silver! Also he did the deed with a marked graciousness as though to say, 'Well, old man, we may meet some day in another capacity; and if so — well, remember that I was never a niggard, and let the job be done in quick and gentlemanly fashion.' I didn't stay to witness an execution, though with a professional vanity that appealed to me as inexpressibly naïf, my new friend was all for sending round to the gaol for a subject, and giving me a demonstration of his art straight away. The fact was I'd had quite enough of horrors for the time being. In the gaol which I had just left were scores of malefactors, their heads framed in heavy 'cangues,' and their faces miserable and woebegone to a degree. And if the 'cangue' subject didn't fill the bill in the way of horror, there were offenders to be seen having their hands withered in salt, and yellow miseries enduring other ingeniously agonising experiences. No, the man who wants more 'thrill' after seeing the inside of a Canton gaol is cut out for a waxworks impresario.

Anyhow, if one is after blood, one can see enough in the streets of Canton by simply looking at one's feet. It is everywhere. It forms the basis of all Cantonese color schemes. The execution ground, by the way, is a pottery yard, where they still make pottery, only halting for a brief space while the blood-letting business is in progress.

China is a place where the doctrine of 'one man one policeman' obtains largely. Each Chow is the Law unto himself, as it were. A, we will suppose, has a grievance concerning some commercial transaction he has had with B. What is A's method of procedure? Does he writ B? Does he slink to B's bank and garnishee the latter's account, or prate of judgment summonses and bailiffs? He does not. Simply he walks up to B, takes him gently by the wrist, and runs him in (all unresisting) before a J.P. And, big or small, B goes like a little child, and is probably 'cangued' for three months for his pains. A curious system this, but it seems to work well, and saves a lot of expense.

Babies, and again babies! They teem everywhere. The East fairly creeps with them. They are China's main product; and are all of them the dearest, smilingest, chubbiest little beggars in the world. If you take a sampan, the captain of the boat, who is always a lady, will be carrying one on her back. There are probably half-a-dozen more under the hatchway; and it is ten chances to one that you are unconsciously sitting on another. The only really safe thing to do to avoid this brand of mischance is to shin up the mast. But that has its drawbacks. It is a very unpleasant sensation for a sensitive person to find himself sitting on a new baby; and this Eastern habit, of leaving them littered casually about, develops in the visitor a cautious expression of countenance before sitting down. For my part, I haven't outgrown that yet. I find myself suddenly starting up from my seat in a tram, dreaming that I have been sitting on a mislaid infant. Imagine the humiliation of returning it to its parent, with excuses — the flattened remains of her offspring! One could hardly say, 'Pardon me, madam! I'm afraid I've spoilt your baby — but I will get you another!' And yet some sort of apology would be deemed essential.

Only on one occasion did I see a baby crying in China, and that was a Japanese infant. It was having its head shaved by a barber; and I didn't blame it for its tears either. For I was once (only once) shaved by a Jap barber — my chin, not my head — and if that kid suffered half as much torture as I did, and lived, I can only say that the Japanese baby of commerce is a sturdy bit of goods.

Nature-worship in the East is a remarkable institution. These kiddies, who represent the common or dirty urchin type of the community, are going round singing carols of thanksgiving to Mother Nature. The blossoming trees serve as inspiration to the youngsters, and, indeed, at this time of year the said blossoms make of Nature a thing that is absolutely boshter — or words to that effect. This Nature-worshipping is a pretty custom, and comes as natural to the immature Chow as does pitch-and-toss to our Australian youth.

'Vagabonding in Asia', *Lone Hand* (1907)

<u>1910</u>

Mary Gaunt on the African Gold Coast

Australian-born novelist and travel writer Mary Gaunt (1861–1942) was a 40-year-old widow when she moved to London in 1901 to establish her literary reputation and make her living from writing. She later recalled that she had felt the desire to travel in exotic places since her childhood in the Ballarat district, but the rules of female decorum had not allowed her to go 'a-roving' in the world. Protected by middle-age and widowhood, she journeyed to West Africa in 1910, exploring the west coast forts accompanied only by a retinue of native bearers. Indicative of imperial attitudes to the role of indigenous people, Gaunt gave the account of her travels the title of Alone in West Africa. *In this extract, she is travelling the old slave route from Kumasi, the Ashanti capital burned by the British in 1874, to Sunyani, in modern-day Ghana, nine years after its annexation by Britain. Africa was followed by two 'solo' journeys through China and Manchuria, described in her books* A Woman in China *(1914) and* A Broken Journey: Wanderings from Hoan-Ho to the Island of Saghalien and the Upper Reaches of the Amur River *(1919). Jamaica was the subject of her last book of travels,* Reflection — in Jamaica *(1932). The sister of admirals and generals, Mary Gaunt had no doubts as to the benefits of the British Empire, while at the same time always identifying herself as a strong independent daughter of Australia in contrast to the effete and useless women produced at the centre of the Empire. Mary Gaunt did not return to Australia after her departure in 1901 and lived the later years of her life in Bordighera on the Italian Riviera. Forced to flee Italy in 1940, she died in Cannes. As well as her travel books, her literary estate included some twenty novels.*

Here we know not the meaning of the word forest. England's forests are delightful woods where the deer dwell in peace, where the rabbits scutter through the fern and undergrowth, and where the children may go for a summer's holiday; in Australia are trees close-growing and tall; but in West Africa the forest has a life and being of its own. It is not a thing of yesterday or of ten years back or of fifty years. Those mighty trees that dwarf all other trees in the world have taken hundreds of years to their growth. When a slight young girl came to the throne of England, capturing a nation's chivalry by her youth and innocence, the mahogany and kaku and odoum trees were old and staid monarchs of the forest. When the first of the Georges came over from Hanover, unwelcome, but the nation's last hope, they were young and slim but already tall trees stretching up their crowns to the brilliant sunlight that is above the gloom, and now at last, when the fifth of that name reigns over them, at last is their sanctuary invaded and the seclusion that is theirs shall be theirs no longer. For already the axe is laid to their roots, and through the awe-inspiring forest runs a narrow roadway kept clear by what must be almost superhuman labour, and along that roadway, the beginning of the end, the sign that marks the peaceful conquest of the savage, that marks also the downfall of the forest though it is not even whispered among the trees that scorn them yet, flows a perpetual stream of traffic, men, women, and children. Backwards and forwards from the north to Kumasi and the sea they come, and they bear on their heads, going north, corrugated iron and cotton goods, kerosene, and flour, and chairs, all the trifles that the advance of civilisation makes absolute necessaries; and coming down they bring all in their season, hides, and heavy cakes of rubber, and sticks of dried snails, and all the other articles of native produce that a certain peace has made marketable along the way or in the markets of Kumasi.

The spell was upon me the moment I left the town. That road is like nothing else in the world. The hammock and the carriers were dwarfed by the great roots and buttresses of the trees to tiny, crawling ants, and overhead was a narrow strip of blue sky where the sunlight might be seen, but only at noon did that sunlight reach the roadway below. We travelled in a shadow pleasant in that heat; and on either side, close on either side, were the great trees. Looking down the road I could see them straight as a die, tall pillars, white and brown; ahead of me and close at hand the mighty buttresses that supported those pillars rose up to the height of perhaps ten men before the tree was fairly started, a tall trunk with branches that began to spread, it seemed to me, hundreds of feet above the ground. And between those tree-trunks was all manner of undergrowth, and all were bound and matted together with thickly growing creepers and vines. It was impossible to step an inch from that cleared path […]

When there was a village there was, of course, a clearing, and on the first day I passed several villages until at last I came to Ofinsu, where I had arranged to spend the night. Ofinsu is on the banks of a river, and the road comes out of the forest and passes broadly between two rows of mud-walled houses with steeply pitched, high-thatched roofs, and my carriers raced along and stopped opposite a small wooden door in a mud wall and rapped hard.

For the first time on my travels I had really excellent carriers. They were Krepis from beyond the German border, slight, dark men with slim wrists and ankles, and crosses cut as tribal marks on each cheek, and they were cheerful, smiling, willing. When I remembered my before-time tribulations I could hardly believe these were actually carriers who were going along so steadily and well, who were always up before me in the morning, and in as soon as I was at night, who never lingered, never grumbled, never complained, but were simply ideal servants such as I had never had before in my life save perhaps for a day, as when I went to Palime from Ho, and such as I shall count myself extremely lucky if I ever have again.

'We *have* got good carriers,' the transport officer had said, 'though you don't seem to believe it'; and he proved his words, for never have I travelled more comfortably than I did on that one hundred and sixty miles to Sunyani and back.

The knocking at the little door brought a black lady with a shaven head and a blue cloth wrapped round her middle. She was a woman past all beauty, and very little was left to the imagination, but she threw open the door and indicated that we were to enter, and she looked at me very curiously. Never before had a white woman come to Ofinsu.

I entered, and this was my first introduction to an Ashanti house, a house that seems to me singularly suited to the climate and people. It is passing away, they tell me, and I for one am sorry.

We went into a courtyard open to the sky, and round it, raised at least two feet from the ground, were the rooms, I suppose I must call them, but though there was a roof overhead and walls on three sides, walls without windows, the fourth side was open to the central courtyard. When I entered the place was crowded; Hausas or Wangaras — I never could tell one from the other — were settled down on the platforms, and their loads — long bundles made up for carrying on the head — were all over the place. I said nothing. I am generally for the superiority of the white man and exact all the deference that is my due, but clearly these people were here first, and it seemed to me they had it by right, only how I was to bathe and sleep in a house where everything was so public among such a crowd I did not know.

But my hostess had other views. No sooner had I entered than she began clearing out the former guests, and in less than a quarter of an hour the place that had seemed so crowded was empty, swept and garnished for my accommodation. My bed was put up on one platform, my table and chair on another. 'Get table quick and chair, so can play cards,' Grant instructed my headman, and behind, through a little door that may be seen in the picture, was a place that answered for a kitchen, and a cup of tea was quickly produced for my comfort. It was weird going to sleep there in the open, but it was very, very delightful. I rigged up in the corner of one of the rooms — I have no other names for them — with ground sheet and rugs, a little shelter where I could have my bath in comfort, but I undressed without a qualm and went to bed and slept the sleep of the woman who has been in the open air the livelong day and who, happily for herself, can indulge her taste and sleep in the open air all night.

I took a picture of my open-air bedroom with my valuable headman and two small children who belonged to the household I had invaded in the foreground. But that was before I went to bed at night. At earliest dawn, before the dawn in fact, my headman was at my bedside wanting to pack up and start.

That night's lodging cost me one shilling and threepence. The headman told me one shilling was enough, so I bestowed the extra threepence as a dash on the shaven old woman who had done all for me that my servants could not do, and she seemed so delighted that I was left wondering what the Wangaras who had given place to me had paid.

Just as the sun was rising we crossed the Ofin River, and I found there assembled the entire population of the village to look at the strange sight — a perfectly courteous, polite people who never crushed or crowded though they looked their fill. I can only hope I was a success as a show, for certainly I attracted a great deal of attention, but of course I had no means of knowing whether I came up to expectations. It took some time to get my goods and followers across the river in the crank canoe which is only used in the rainy season, for usually the Ofin River can be waded, and while I waited on the farther shore I looked with interest at the other people who were waiting for their loads to be ferried across.

The men were Hausas or Wangaras, some wearing turbans, some with shaven heads, and clad in long, straight, shirt-like garments, while the women excited my deepest compassion. They may have been the men's wives, I know not; but by whatever name they were called they were slaves if ever I saw slaves. They had very little on besides a dirty, earthen-coloured cloth hitched round their loins, their dark faces were brutalised and depressed with that speechless depression that hardly realises its own woes, and their dusty hair that looked as if it had not been washed for years was generally twisted into short, thick, dusty looking plaits that were pressed downwards by the weight of the load they one and all carried. They carried children, too, on their backs, tiny babies that must have been born on the journey, or lusty youngsters that were a load in themselves. But a Hausa will carry an enormous load himself — sometimes up to 240 lbs — so it is not likely he will have much consideration for his women. It may be, of course, that their looks belied them, but it seemed to me that they cared little whether Fate drowned them there in the swirling brown waters of the river or brought them safely through to the other side to tramp on, footsore, tired, weary, heartsick — if these creatures who looked like dumb beasts had life enough in them to be heartsick — to their destination three months away in the north.

They waited there as I passed, and they looked at me dully and without interest; presently their loads would be brought across and they would be on the march again, and I went on pitying to Potsikrom.

The forest was getting denser and denser. There were fewer towns and clearings on this day — nothing but the great trees and the narrow ribbon of road with the strip of blue sky far, far away. It was very awe-inspiring, the forest. I should have been unspeakably terrified to pass through it alone, but my chattering men took away all sense of loneliness. There was not much to see, but yet the eternal trees had a most wonderful charm. It was like being in some lofty cathedral where the very air was pulsating with the thought of great and unseen things beyond the comprehension of the puny mortals who dared rashly to venture within the precincts. No wonder the Ashanti gave human sacrifices. Sacrifice, we all know, is the basis of all faith, and what lesser thing than a man could be offered in so great a sanctuary?

And that afternoon we came to Potsikrom, a little village deep in the forest.

The rest-house was a mud building with a thatch roof somewhat dilapidated, and built not after the comfortable, suitable Ashanti fashion, but after the European fashion, possibly in deference to some foolish European who probably regarded all the country as 'poisonous.' That is to say, it was divided into two rooms with holes in the clay, very small holes for windows, and, saving grace, a door at each side of one of the rooms. In the corner of one of these impossible rooms I saw, to my surprise, a camp-bed put up, and for the moment thought it was mine. Then I saw a suit of striped pyjamas which certainly were not mine, and realised it must belong to the medical officer whom I had left at Kumasi the day before. His boys had stolen a march ahead, and, thinking to do better than the white woman, had put up his bed in what they considered the most desirable place, thinking doubtless that possession was nine points of the law.

I certainly didn't desire that corner, but I felt my authority must be maintained, and so I asked:

'Who that bed belong to?'

'Massa,' said a grinning boy.

'Take it down,' said I.

Up came the Chief's clerk. All these Ashanti chiefs now have a clerk who can write a little English and so communicate for them with Government, and the clerk, interested as he was to see a white woman, was very certain in his own mind that the white man was the more important person. He probably regarded me as his wife come on ahead, and said that the Chief had another house for me.

I didn't like that rest-house, but pride has suffered pain since the beginning of the world, so I distinctly declared my intention of staying there and ordered them to clear out the medical officer's bed forthwith. My boys were very anxious to assert my superiority and out went that bed in the twinkling of an eye, and my men proceeded to put up mine between the two doors, and, having had a table set out for tea, I awaited the arrival of the medical officer with a quiet mind.

Presently he arrived and we laughed together over the struggle for supremacy between our men, and pledged our future good fellowship in tea. The Chief sent me in eggs and chickens and yams as dash, the people came and looked at me, and presently the evening fell and I had my evening meal and went to bed.

And when I went to bed I repented me of having stood on my dignity. What on earth had I wanted the rest-house for? It was the last house in the village, a little apart from the rest, the great solemn forest was all around me, and I was all alone, for Grant and the men had retired with the darkness to somewhere in the village. My bed stood under a roof certainly, but I should not have dared put up the door of the rest-house for fear of making it too close, and so it meant, of course, that I was sleeping with nothing between me and that awe-inspiring forest. I do not know what I was afraid of any more than I know what I feared at Anum, but I was afraid of something intangible, born of the weird stillness and the gloom. I put a hurricane lantern at the door to scare away any wandering pigs and goats — I did not really in my heart think there would be any wild beasts — and then I proceeded to put in a most unpleasant night. First there was too much light, it fell all over my bed, and though I did not like it, I still felt a comfortable sense of safety in the light. Then I began to itch. I twisted and turned and rolled over, and the more I moved about the more uncomfortable I became. I thought to myself, 'There, it serves you right! You are always nursing the fat little black babies and now you have got some horrible disease.' The thought was by no means consoling, but I was being driven so frantic that I began to think that no disease could really advance with such rapidity. Besides, all sorts of great insects were banging themselves against my mosquito curtains, so I came to the conclusion that probably the tiny sandflies were also attracted by the light and were getting through the meshes. There was nothing for it but to screw up my courage, get out of bed, and take that lantern away. I did it, crept back to bed again, listened for a little to the weird noises of the night, was relieved to find the appalling irritation showed no signs of increasing, and finally, in spite of my fears, dropped off into so sound a sleep that I was only awakened by Grant endeavouring to drive away by fair words my energetic headman, who was evidently debating whether it was not his bounden duty to clear me away, bed and all.

I told the doctor my experiences in the morning, and he confirmed my supposition that it was only sandflies and not horrible disease that had troubled my slumbers.

Very much relieved was I, for the little black babies are dear little round souls, and I should have been loath not to take them when their mothers trusted them to me. I should hesitate much before I took a baby of the peasant class in this country, but there, in the heart of Africa, it is always safe to cuddle the little, round, naked thing that has for all clothing a few beads or a charm or two tied to its hair. They are always clean and soft and round and chubby, and they do not invariably yell with terror at the white woman, though I am bound to say they often do.

We were in the heart of the forest now. There were but one or two villages and only one or two places that could be dignified by the name of clearings. At one, as big, perhaps, as a tiny London square, three or four huts had been erected, and an old woman was making pots. They were all set out in the sun to dry, and the good lady was very nervous when I wanted to take her photograph. She consented at last, and sat there shivering, in her hand a great snail shell which she used to ornament the pots. They were such a lonely little company, so cut off from all their kind, and we must have been such wondrous figures breaking in on their life and then passing on again. I gave them the last bright new pennies I had, and left them wondering.

And so we went on again through the forest, past Insuta, until, as the evening was falling, we created immense astonishment by arriving at Bechem.

Here again the rest-house was built uncomfortably, European fashion, and again my only alternative was to have my bed put up between the two doors so that I might get plenty of air. But at Bechem the town was full. It was a big town set in the midst of a great clearing, and to-day it was swarming with people, for the next day was Coronation Day, and the Chief had sent out word that all his sub-chiefs were to come in and celebrate. And here was another excitement — a white woman! How many chiefs came to see me that day I really would be afraid to say, and the Chief sent me in by way of dash a sheep, a couple of chickens, piles of plantains, yams, eggs, and all manner of native edibles. It was very amusing to stand there in the midst of the swarming people, receiving these offerings. Of course they all have to be returned with presents of value, and I was thankful they did not think me important enough to receive a cow; as it was it cost me a pound to get out of Bechem, but my carriers were delighted for I presented them with the sheep. He was an elderly ram with long horns, and I think he was the only person who did not thoroughly enjoy the entertainment.

The Chief sent in word through his interpreter to say that the people had never seen a white woman before; there were many people here because of the Coronation, might they come and 'look'? Never have I been so frankly regarded as a show. There was nothing for it but to go outside and let them look, and once more I can only hope they were satisfied. I had never seen such crowds of natives before, crowds that had not seen much of the white man and as yet were not arrayed in his cast-off clothes. All round us long Dane guns were popping off in honour of the great occasion, and tom-toms were beating half the night. When I waked next morning — I slept in the passage to get plenty of air, but I was not afraid because the rest-house was near the centre of the village — I found that at the earliest glimpse of dawn long lines of people had assembled outside my house and were patiently waiting for me to come out. I had my breakfast in the little courtyard behind the house, the people peeping through the fence of palm-poles, and when we set out on our way the Chief, in all the glory of silken robes and great umbrella, came a little way to do us honour.

Never, not even when I was married, have I been such an important person. The tom-toms beat, the umbrellas twirled, long Danes went off, horns blew, and as far as the eye could see were the villagers trailing away behind us.

The Chief escorted us for about a mile, we walking in the cool, misty morning, and then he turned, slipped his cloth from his left shoulder as a mark of respect, shook hands, wished us a prosperous journey, and bid us good-bye like the courteous gentleman he was, and we went on into the mighty forest again.

It is always cool in the early morning, and very pleasant here among the trees, so the medical officer and I walked on chatting about Bechem, when we came upon another little party of travellers, who stopped us and asked help. It was a Hausa with a couple of women, his wives in all probability, and a couple of other men, presumably his slaves. He was a tall, strong man in the prime of life, upon whose shaven head were deep lines graven by the loads he had carried. Our headman, who could speak Hausa, interpreted.

Men were following him from Nkwanta, he said, to kill him. A child had died in the town, and they said he 'had put bad medicine upon it,' that is, had bewitched it, and the penalty was death.

It was rather startling in this twentieth century to be brought face to face with the actors in such a tragedy, especially when we were powerless to help. We were unarmed and had with us only carriers and servants; it was the prestige of the white man that was carrying us through. The Hausa was going away from Nkwanta as fast as he possibly could, and apparently he did not want to trust himself within its bounds, even under the protection of a white man. He declined to come back with us, and what could we do? The medical officer, I think, did all that he could when he promised to report things to the Commissioner at Sunyani, and recommended the Hausa, since he would not avail himself of our protection, to get the Chief's clerk at Bechem to write his account of the affair to Sunyani and Kumasi.

And so in the early morning we went our way, and he went his, and he disappeared into the gloom of the forest, a much troubled man. I wondered how he would ever get back to his home in the north, for there is but this one road, and that road leads through Nkwanta. He would only dare it, I think, with a large body of his own people, for who is to report to Government if a travelling Hausa should disappear?

Alone in West Africa (1912)

1910

Ethel Turner in Holland

Born in England, Ethel Turner (1870–1958) arrived in Sydney in 1881 and was educated at Sydney Girls' High School. A prolific writer, best known for her Australian children's classic Seven Little Australians *(1894), Turner made her trip to Europe with her husband, lawyer and future judge, Herbert Curlewis, and their two children in 1910. Written as a travel book,* Ports and Happy Havens *(1912) recounts, in a light-hearted but observant manner, Turner's experiences and impressions on a long-desired pilgrimage to the famous sites of history and culture. Travelling via the Suez Canal, Turner described Colombo and Cairo before giving a detailed account of the family's progress through the Italian peninsula to Switzerland. More self-consciously literary in her writing than the average Australian traveller, Turner's descriptions of her time in Italy are framed and informed by English literature. But if Italy's past entranced Turner, she was at one with most of her compatriots in experiencing some relief in passing from the past into the present when she crossed the border into Switzerland, where she was among a people to whom she felt 'nearer akin' than the 'olive-skinned, dark-eyed race, whose hand we have just been shaking on the other side of the Alps'. The Swiss looked at the tourist 'mostly with straightforward blue eyes'. Holland was another clean, straightforward place. Turner did not pretend to be anything other than a conventional tourist, but put into her travels as much energy as Mary Gaunt, and found many of the same problems: the struggles to describe the peculiarities of the locals, to maintain one's dignity and to get a good night's sleep.*

From Holland the family went on to Belgium and then crossed the Channel to England. Turner does not include an account of her time in Britain. She did not count it as 'travel'. Her book concludes with the trip through France to catch the boat home from Marseilles.

In Italy it had seemed to me there were no homes — merely houses and ruins.

In Switzerland all the houses were homes — homes leaning lovingly together in the crowded parts, or standing apart on the hills, with wide spreading roofs brooding warmly over the hospitable walls.

Germany had homes too, as well as houses.

And here was Holland hastening to spread out her dwelling-places on either side of our train windows — Holland with her far-stretching, flat plains dotted everywhere with dwelling places.

Houses or homes in Holland? Homes every one of them, from the palaces that shelter Queen Wilhelmina to the tiniest roof-tree of the struggling tulip grower. Not a brick in any one of the edifices but has been solidly laid with the mortar so cheap in itself yet so priceless to a nation, the mortar of the goddess Home.

It is my private belief that there is a committee of lynx-eyed Dutch vrows who spend their lives travelling up and down to report at head-quarters 'How Holland Looks from the Train.' It is my belief that when these ladies see anything in the landscape to offend their searchlight vision — anything like a dustbin or an untidy backyard or a broken fence — they immediately haul away the householder, and administer such a punishment that the offence is never repeated.

All the distressing detail of poverty's squalor or household slovenli-ness that so often mars a lovely landscape is kept out of sight in Hol-land. It seems the Dutch ideal to be able to invite the train to look at the entire four sides of a home and garden, and to be able to defy it to find a bit of vagrant paper or an empty tin or an unswept path.

The very poorest houses we saw — very poor sometimes, pitifully poor — had their clean little curtains and their brilliantly polished brass pots in the windows and a glimpse of red geranium or the spring's tulips.

It is my belief that highly-paid artists go along with this 'Commis-sion to inquire into Holland's Appearance from the Train,' and when-ever they find that the expanse of flat fields grows monotonous, they carefully erect a windmill or plant pollard willows along a canal.

Yes, no one has deceived you; there are windmills in Holland's fields everywhere, everywhere. No one has deceived you, everywhere, every-where there are canals. Here is a great barge with clumsy square sails, and it seems to be solemnly sailing across a wide green meadow — you cannot see the narrow sunken canal at all from your window.

Here is a windmill; the artists made it of grey or warm brown or black timbers, according as was the necessity for contrast or harmony in the landscape's scheme.

Here are peasants in the fields; the artists have been round to see that they dress mainly in blues or browns, and always wear wooden shoes.

We reached Amsterdam so train-worn we promptly went to bed, a thing one seldom can do when just arrived in a new city. No matter how late at night it is, something compels one to go and peer about at the mysterious stranger.

But here we only peered for ten minutes or so — saw the immense concourse of people in the streets (in no other city that we visited did we find the entire population so unanimously turned out of doors each night, parading the streets and quays or drinking coffee, as in Amsterdam), were run into half a dozen times by boys and girls on roller skates — caught whiffs and visions of hyacinths and tulips at the frequent florists, and then went to bed, if not to sleep.

As in Switzerland, and as in some of the towns in Germany, the sole bed-covering we find here is the feather bed. It is made ornamental with rich red damask, and is swollen to incredible proportions — feet deep in very truth. One creeps under it cautiously, and in a few minutes is asleep as sweetly as if in an oven. And then in a few minutes one is awake as indignantly as if in an ice-box. The swelling feather quilt has slipped silently off on to the floor, and is lying there blandly, as if compassionately protecting the boards from the nip of zero.

Even if one is very provident, and pins or ties or weights the thing into security, cold currents of air steal in on all sides, much resented by nations immutably wedded to tucked-in blankets. Next time we travel in countries addicted to slippery mountains of feathers, we shall provide ourselves with tubes of seccotine for the edges.

The Kinder, however (nay, we are in a new country again — the Kinder have become 'Kinderen' or 'jonge volkje'), are entirely charmed with their beds. They have a huge four-post double bed, each with a red canopy and rich red damask curtains that run along the entire four sides.

To go to bed in Holland is to withdraw into the red solitude and fastnesses of an enchanted country [...]

We walk about the streets and quays and look at the forests of masts, and the tall narrow houses and the storks' nests, and the canals and the barges coming down them, laden from stern to prow with huge baskets of flowers.

We look at the people, and are amazed to find them so like ourselves — much more so than either the Swiss or Germans; more than once we are sure that a passer-by is English, and make some inquiry, only to be met by such a reply as, 'Ga recht vit, en dan de eerste straat links, rechts,' instead of, 'Go straight on and then by the first street to the right, to the left.'

In one respect we do not find them like ourselves. Once we stop on a bridge, and the perspective of trees and old houses down the canal is so tempting that we get our cameras ready.

Mine is shaped like a watch, the good old 'turnip' watch of our ancestors, and is encased in polished nickel; plainly it is not an everyday object in Amsterdam. I move away from the rest of my party and am engrossed for a few minutes with my 'finder,' a tiresome affair on so small a camera. When I look up I find I am in the centre of a crowd that increases every second — street boys and girls, labouring men, working girls; they cluster round me, fifty or sixty of them at least, and thrust their faces over my shoulder, and gaze with extreme eagerness and anticipation at the inoffensive little weapon in my hand; had it been a revolver and had I been about to shoot their city with it instead of attempting to take a microscopic — and most probably ineffectual — time exposure of it, they could not have buzzed and pushed and jostled and exclaimed more.

The exposure has yet to be made [...]

We spend a day in the Rijks Museum. An entire article devoted to it would just about touch the fringe of its interest.

Here we find Rembrandt, whom we never dreamed to be quite so fine as this. The finest photographs, copies, descriptions do not even begin to show the power of this painter, who for so many years made Amsterdam his home.

These are not portraits on the walls, they are flesh and blood men and women stepped out of the past centuries and come to speak to you. They are so full of vigour, so full of the red blood of rude health and reality, that there comes an uncanny minute when you feel half persuaded that it is they who are alive and the men and women who are moving about the galleries in sober suits and hobble skirts are the pale, ineffectual pictures.

To see a picture like 'The Night Watch' makes one pant to be a millionaire; one burns to be able to fling down a couple of hundred thousand pounds or so and carry off the canvas and hang it up in one's far country and call the students to come and look, and shout to them, 'This the way and this that portraits should be painted!'

[...]

I once met a man who declared to me that the Zuyder Zee was blue — an inconceivable thing. I once met a girl who seemed to have perfectly clear vision and yet maintained that the Zuyder Zee could smile.

But I declare that it was a yellow, turbulent monster, and that it showed its teeth and snapped and snarled without cease when we adventured on it.

It was an abominable day. A cutting, bitterly cold wind, laden with all the dust in the Netherlands — no negligible quantity after all, despite the careful vrows — swept over the city. It was the day for all sane persons to meet with a roaring fire and an armchair and the newest book. But sanity cannot always be the partner of the hurried tourist. We were due in Belgium in another day or two, and this special excursion to the Islands was not a daily affair. We must either give it up or adventure with set teeth.

The devoted tourist never gives anything up, so we set forth, some twenty or thirty equally insane persons in the same boat with us. The fares were expensive, and guides and interpreters were supplied. We confidently counted on just such glassed-in decks and comforts as we had been met with on the Rhine. But all provided was a narrow, open-decked launch, with a tiny, stuffy cabin.

The wind from the angry dam of the Amstel tore after us, and more than once blew people bodily out of their deck chairs. Other steamers scudded hurriedly on the way; fishermen's boats went to shelter against the kindly land.

Several very sick persons were profoundly glad when we made our first port, the Island of Marken.

And now we felt we were indeed in truth in Holland.

Amsterdam is a great city, and in all great cities people dress with a monotonous sameness, one nation as like as possible to another. But here were 'Miss Hook of Holland' people stepped off the boards and engaged in the plain duties of life. Here were men in huge baggy trousers, mostly blue or black, but sometimes red and green, men with gaily embroidered waistcoats and tight little red or blue coats decorated with many solid silver buttons, men with earrings in their ears, with round caps and fat cigars, heavy knitted stockings and huge wooden sabots.

Here were women in many petticoats — many, many petticoats. The hobble skirt will never catch on in Holland, for the wife of the Dutch farmer and peasant expresses her wealth and status mainly by her petticoats [...]

It is the cap that lends three parts of the charm to the Dutch woman's appearance — it is the cap that brings the artists from all parts of the continent and England eager to make pictures of it, and incidentally the face beneath it. If the face beneath it, the typical Dutch female face, fresh-coloured, fair-skinned, high cheek-boned, were surmounted by the Hat as we know it — the lower-class hat, trimmed with draggled feathers or tawdry flowers, or faded ribbons — the artist would not want to turn his head.

But take the same face and surround it by a close-fitting cap of snow-white lace or muslin, with stiffly starched wings standing out behind the ears, and at once it has character, dignity, modesty [...]

All the sabots that we met were of white, natural wood, or varnished brown or painted black, but different villages, we were told, incline to different colours; in one the wooden shoes are painted red; in another, green; in another, blue. A single pair will often last for years, a coat of paint from time to time making all as good as new. As some we bought, quite superior ones, carved and pointed at the toes, cost only a gulden (one and eightpence), the family boot bill in Holland cannot be the tragedy it frequently is in poverty-stricken English families. The stockings are always heavy knitted ones, and in these islands everyone's odd minutes are frugally cast upon four knitting needles and turned to account. Grave-eyed little maidens clatter up and down the roads knitting swiftly at stockings as long as themselves; fishermen knit as they lean at the wharves; vrows 'step over' to see one another and turn a heel and work a foot what time they are drawing a breath of leisure between the violent cleansings of their houses. Every window in a Dutch house is cleaned inside and out daily; the outside walls and the outside painted work are scrubbed and washed weekly, just as much as a matter of course, as are inside floors and painted work in countries less startlingly clean. I suspect the very gravel on the neat paths of being scrubbed, pebble by pebble, daily. One cannot, therefore, credit Dutch vrows with drawing over-many breaths of leisure [...]

The only method, by the way, of telling a boy from girl up to the age of six in Marken is to look at the top of the cap; if there is a button there, the child in question is a boy; if there is no button, you may safely call it Marie.

After that age the boy goes into wide trousers and cigars, in strict imitation of his father, but frequently the top half of him remains in girl's dress for two or three more years. When Goldsmith let his fancy fly,

> Embosomed in the deep where Holland lies,

he did not fail to note the persevering work of her 'patient sons,' attributing it in a great degree to the incessant care and vigilance that, as a nation, they are forced to exercise to keep out the encroaching ocean from their hard-won lands —

> Thus, while around the wave-subjected soil
> Impels the native to repeated toil,
> Industrious habits in each bosom reign,
> And Industry begets a love of gain.

This 'love of gain' is nowhere more plainly to be seen than in these islands and villages.

No sooner has one landed than one is beset by these children, who carry baskets filled with miniature sabots, cheap ornaments, knitted mittens, and so on. The instant they see cameras they surround one like eager bees, and strenuously insist upon being taken. So used are they to the coming of the camera-carrying stranger and the artist, that they fall into poses and studied groups and set smiles, the while one is considering if the light is good enough to take a picture. And then, at the well-known sound of the shutter's click, they rush forward with eager hands outstretched.

'English sixpence,' they shout, 'English sixpence.'

Ports and Happy Havens (1912)

1912

Ada Holman in England

Ballarat-born Ada Holman (1869–1949) was a journalist, feminist and reformer, and the wife of Labor politician W. A. Holman. She made her nine-month trip overseas in August 1912, spending most of her time in the United Kingdom. The trip was partly undertaken for the education of her daughter in Europe. Holman's travel impressions, which focus on Britain and France with some observations on the Eastern ports, were first published as articles in the Sydney Daily Telegraph. *The articles, collected in* My Wander Year, *are of interest because of the range of her observations and the combination of prim respectability with outraged social conscience. Holman was intent on evoking London, 'not so much a city as a world', but was also pursuing a political agenda, casting her reformer's eye over the slums of the East End and the working conditions of women in the cotton mills of Manchester. When Holman crossed the Channel to visit France, she wrote not only about the layout and monuments of Paris, a city that is more 'compact and manageable' than London, but also about her visits to the theatre, both the Comédie-Française and the Moulin Rouge, and about housekeeping and fashion. It was not so difficult to describe the chic Parisienne in 1912 since 'at first sight every woman seems the replica of the other': black was de rigueur. In the year after Ada Holman's return her husband became premier of New South Wales, from 1913 to 1916 as a Labor leader and then, after campaigning for the introduction of conscription, as leader of a National Party government from 1916 to*

1920. In a later work, Memoirs of a Premier's Wife *(1947), she again reflected on the famous places and people in her life.*

London is not so much a city as a world, wherein every phase and aspect of life finds expression. The seller of philosophy and the seller of cats' meat alike find a mart. There is no fad too eccentric, no article too bizarre to lack adherents or buyers in sufficient numbers. The most amazing feature is the number of sectional papers. To know London in the true sense one should read them all. Every cause has its voice, from the Suffragettes' and Socialists' to the Anti-vaccination League and the 'no-hat' brigade. Merely to read the posters dislocates the mind, and it is necessary to keep fairly alert for the task of finding the way in and out of tubes, and for springing off motor-'buses going at full speed down crowded thoroughfares. It is unfortunately impossible to get lost nowadays and have picturesque adventures. One must pay some price for a well-ordered life! Comprehensive directions allowing for the minimum of intelligence salute one at every point, and if amid the fascinating announcements of strange journals and new plays the directing sign is overlooked, one has but to jump into a taxi. Given the merest outline of an address, the driver unerringly discovers one's destination. The taxi men, like the policemen, must spend all their off time learning London's bewildering topography by heart. No one else knows anything. Each Londoner lives in a water-tight compartment. The world of Peckham Rye has no knowledge of the whereabouts of Park-lane. It is useless to ask a resident of Kensington to direct one to Brixton. Most of the notices are very politely worded, though 'Don't spit here' is a little too pervasive, and 'Beware of pickpockets,' displayed prominently in every lift, is not calculated to increase the amity of nations. In Westminster Abbey one can easily picture a Mrs Humphrey Ward Bishop delicately penning the mild list of prohibitions ending with, 'The dean and chapter would be exceedingly pained by any infringement of these regulations,' and I particularly like the suave warning in the halls glittering with glass cases at the British Museum: 'Ladies with hammers not admitted.' The trail of the suffragette is over all!

[…]

A visitor anxious to investigate the social conditions of London naturally asks to be shown the East End, having almost unconsciously pictured the great metropolis as marked off into distinct areas of light and darkness, misery and magnificence. One, perhaps, has received this impression of clear-cut demarcation from Douglas Jerrold's 'St James' and St Giles',' Gissing's 'Nether World,' or the stories of Whiting and Morrison. There is, most assuredly, an East End where one may go through miles of streets and their ramifications without encountering one beautiful object, one hint of the culture and charm centred in the capital, but one has not to go to Whitechapel or Shoreditch to find these conditions. The East End, in the sense of pauperism, though unseen if unlooked for, is pervasively present throughout London. One has only, as it were, to peep behind the scenes to find its ugly presence in wait. Within a stone's throw of hotels in which life is regulated by the champagne standard, there are courts and purlieus filled by poverty of the most abject description, where existence is sustained on the merest margin. The dwellers in these areas live and move and have their being within restrictions the most peculiar. By some unwritten law, all their life goes on in their own street or alley. In the fashionable squares a child occasionally begs a penny, while quite a number eke out a livelihood by hanging about in wait to open a taxi door or drop a white-gloved lady's letter into a pillar box; but the adult beggar is seldom seen in wealthy districts. Even the pavement artists and the blind singers attach themselves only to semi-fashionable or merely 'respectable' quarters. It seems almost understood that the smart set must not be distressed by the sight of affliction and want. But for those who wish to see how the poor live, it is another story. Get away from the broad streets, from the squares and locked gardens, go behind the luxurious mansions, the millionaires' hotels, and follow the twists and turns of ever narrowing streets, from which lanes off-shoot, with in turn their off-shoots of alleys or somebody's 'rents,' and a quite sufficiently appalling 'East' will be found to satisfy the most sensational lover of contrasts. And just as whole areas are given up to struggling poverty, so other areas are given up to the criminal population, who perhaps may be classed by the sociologist as revolted poverty. Of these latter districts in the East it is extremely difficult for the outsider to obtain any real knowledge. Hither one can only come safely with an officer of police, or, preferably, of the Salvation Army. Coming thus ticketed as an enquirer, one gets little but sullen looks. There is no admittance into the home life of Bill Sykes or into the confidence of Moriarty spinning his webs of intrigue against the community and Sherlock Holmes. It seems very obliging of the main criminal mass of London thus to settle themselves in a recognised quarter. It must, and does, simplify the work of the police immensely. When a burglary or act of violence takes place, they know just where to look for the perpetrators, who spend their days between their chosen haunts and gaol. But analysed, the thieves' place of residence is presumably — like everybody else's — dictated by circumstances rather than by choice. Only a complacent class of landlord, one imagines, selects his tenants from the depraved section. The submerged is another matter. As Bernard Shaw shows in

'Widowers' Houses,' slum property is good-paying property, and many investors ask for nothing better. Rents are very high in proportion to accommodation, and whoever goes unpaid, the landlord does not. For the poor find in the London of to-day a tremendous difficulty in being housed, and will stick to the vilest kind of insanitary den, for which an inadequately high rent is paid, because of the impossibility of finding any other shelter within their means. I saw some clear examples of this when visiting a very poor quarter with Mrs H. B. Irving, who has now practically given up her career on the stage to devote herself to social organisation. She is a poor-law guardian for the North-eastern District of London, a most active member of several other bodies, such as the St Pancras School for Mothers, the Tuberculin Depot, and other institutions, which aim not so much at giving relief in doles as at altering conditions and raising the standard of hygienic education. Many of the most capable women in London are closely devoting themselves to such work. Although the organisations are in no sense political, they largely include women of political intelligence, who understand that conditions can only be altered by the people themselves, and who are trying to work side by side with legislation.

We visited one poor woman to whom a third child had just been born, in a basement to which no sun and scarcely any light penetrated in the December weather. She was in a comfortless bed, the covering of which was made up of an odd assortment of pieces — not one good blanket in the lot. There was a fairly good fire in the room, and on the hob stood the kettle and a saucepan, which, with the frying-pan, made up the entire culinary service of the family. A small cupboard, a shaky table, two or three chairs, and a few boxes (which supposedly contained the family's wardrobe) pretty well made up the room's catalogue, and even so, left it rather crowded for the adults. There was, however, a sort of folding bed in a corner, piled with more indeterminate covering, on which lay a sleeping child, hectic flushed. To an enquiry as to whether that was also hers, we were told 'No, that was a child of a neighbour who had gone out charing.' Thus the poor get over the servant problem [...]

Pervading all, was a most sickening smell. I was ill in five minutes, though my guide said one quickly got used to it, and the inmates would have been quite surprised to hear of its existence. One can imagine people becoming accustomed to evil sights and sounds, but fetid odours — never! It would have been a miracle had the atmosphere been pure, for apart from the position of the den below the street level, the sanitary arrangements of the yard were indescribably vile, and this, I would emphasise, within a quarter of a mile of a hotel whose guests cannot get the barest elements of food, shelter and ablutions under £10 a week. When one knows how magnificently science is at the service of every Londoner in the good quarters, it does seem a marvel that arrangements which would disgrace Port Said or a wayback town in New South Wales, are existent in the crowded alleys of the great city.

[...]

By the courtesy of the Right Hon. Samuel Royse, Manchester's Lord Mayor, I was enabled to go over the biggest cotton mill in Lancashire. Trade rivalry is so great that visitors are not encouraged for fear of espionage into secret processes, but I was able to give an entirely honest assurance not to understand a thing I saw. Machinery to me is just an inscrutable demon. There I beheld bare-footed, dirtily-clad girls, rushing to and fro on slippery floors, mixed up inextricably, as it seemed, with swift monsters darting tearing knife blades towards them with sinister import — monsters which have their almost weekly toll of human hands or fingers — with whirring spikes that revolved 200 times a minute, able to snatch a nail from a finger while one might say 'knife,' with machine belting seeking an unwary moment of its jaded devotees to compass their destruction. Later on I saw a young woman whose scalp had actually been torn from her head at one such unguarded moment. Over and above all was a deafening, maddening noise, which refuses to be hushed for one moment of the insatiable twelve hours. Conceiving this as the life of young girls, some of them pretty, all of them with a human right to happiness, and knowing it was preferred to the sheltered life of the house in its guise of 'service,' I saw that inevitably the feudal system of our homes is doomed — short or long as its final over-throw may be. The hatred extends even to the appearance of the accursed thing. It was sad to see the hair of young girls, most of it the pretty, soft brown tint so characteristically English, repulsively flecked and matted with cotton fluff. No ordinary washing can cleanse or brighten it after such daily punishment. Every woman loves her hair, but these mill hands would go bald before they would wear caps and 'look like housemaids.'

It is pathetic to see vanity finding its own to the extent of tight curling pins in the dust-laden heads. Such trusting faith in the redeeming effect of a curl is worthy of better results. The curls are for the evening, when the long, tense hours are over, and the glee club, the choral society, the church choirs, claim the imprisoned souls of music that lurk within these grimy, imperfectly nourished bodies. One young man, with the thickest possible variety of Lancashire burr, told me he was studying Wagnerian roles, not with any intention of a stage career, but simply for his own joy and comfort. It is a tradition of the mill hands to be singers or instrumentalists. They scarcely read at all. Their hours of leisure, it will be understood, are scanty, and the muse is very exacting. By laws of recent date the female operative's day must not exceed ten working hours (the men's are longer). She commences her work at 6 a.m., winter or summer, and leaves at 5.30 p.m., within these hours taking time for breakfast and dinner. In the fairly comfortable rest room that the proprietary had established for the girls, I saw, I think, copies of three periodicals only, and no books. Newspapers, with the tendency of some of them to preach revolutionary doctrines, are not permitted, for reasons obvious from the owners' point of view. The girls' comfort is not disregarded outside the deadly machinery rooms. The mill has its own restaurant, where an employee may for twopence obtain a satisfying hot meal, or, if she elects to bring her own food, it is cooked for her free of charge. Every mill hand has a number, like a convict. At unindividualised work, where humanity is dealt with in the mass, identity is apt to be lost. There are three thousand 'hands' in the mill I visited, of whom nearly one-half are women, from the age of 14 to any age one likes to imagine—married and single.

For their labors, the remuneration does not strike an Australian as high. In the weaving rooms, the most thunderously and whirlingly noisy of them all, an expert worker may have six looms in her charge, for each of which she receives 1s. per day. Most of those I saw were able to undertake four only, and as Saturday is a half-day, I do not think the pay can run to many extravagances. One woman in the spinning room was pointed out as very expert, 'able to make her 30s. per week.' I happened to go upon pay day and saw each 'number' allotted her dole, which was usually a sum of from 10s. to 16s. Low as the individual wage is, the yearly paysheet of this mill is £120,000, but that is not excessive when the production of these workers is contemplated. In this mill (covering 13 acres of ground), 150,000 spindles and 3,000 looms are at work. The various interesting processes of manufacture annually transform 25,000 bales of raw cotton, equal to 12,500,000 pounds of yarn, into 116,000,000 miles of thread and 30,000,000 yards of calico and flannelette. The engines total 4,700 horsepower, and 18,000 tons of coal are consumed every year. One deals with figures on the grand scale in a Lancashire cotton town.

My Wander Year (1913)

1912

Douglas Mawson in Antarctica

Travel includes not only pilgrimages and holidays but also exploration. Douglas Mawson (1882–1958), one of Australia's most famous explorers, arrived in Australia from England at the age of 2. He studied mining engineering at the University of Sydney and soon after graduation undertook a geological survey of the New Hebrides (now Vanuatu). More and more fascinated by geology, he returned to further study, taking out a science degree in 1905. Two years later, Mawson's scientific interests led him to join Shackleton's expedition to Antarctica. In 1910 he launched an appeal for support for what was to be the Australasian Antarctic Expedition which sailed at the end of the following year. It was during this expedition that the seriously debilitated Mawson, after the deaths of his two companions, made his thirty-day journey alone through the ice to reach the base camp. While recuperating, Mawson began writing his account of the expedition, The Home of the Blizzard *(1915), which was to become a classic of polar literature. He was knighted in 1914 and seven years later was appointed professor of Geology and Mineralogy at the University of Adelaide, a position he held until the age of ninety. Mawson led two further expeditions to the Antarctic, in 1929–30 and 1930–31.*

'Then on the shore of the wide world I stand alone.' — KEATS

Outside the bowl of chaos was brimming with drift-snow and as I lay in the sleeping-bag beside my dead companion I wondered how, in such conditions, I would manage to break and pitch camp single-handed. There appeared to be little hope of reaching the Hut, still one hundred miles away. It was easy to sleep in the bag, and the weather was cruel outside. But inaction is hard to bear and I braced myself together determined to put up a good fight.

Failing to reach the Hut it would be something done if I managed to get to some prominent point likely to catch the eye of a search-party, where a cairn might be erected and our diaries cached. So I commenced to modify the sledge and camping gear to meet fresh requirements.

The sky remained clouded, but the wind fell off to a calm which lasted several hours. I took the opportunity to set to work on the sledge, sawing it in halves with a pocket tool and discarding the rear section. A mast was made out of one of the rails no longer required, and a spar was cut from the other. Finally, the load was cut down to a minimum by the elimination of all but the barest necessities, the abandoned articles including, sad to relate, all that remained of the exposed photographic films.

Late that evening, the 8th, I took the body of Mertz, still toggled up in his bag, outside the tent, piled snow blocks around it and raised a rough cross made of the two discarded halves of the sledge runners.

On January 9 the weather was overcast and fairly thick drift was flying in a gale of wind, reaching about fifty miles an hour. As certain matters still required attention and my chances of re-erecting the tent were rather doubtful, if I decided to move on, the start was delayed.

Part of the time that day was occupied with cutting up a waterproof clothes-bag and Mertz's burberry jacket and sewing them together to form a sail. Before retiring to rest in the evening I read through the burial service and put the finishing touches on the grave.

January 10 arrived in a turmoil of wind and thick drift. The start was still further delayed. I spent part of the time in reckoning up the food remaining and in cooking the rest of the dog meat, this latter operation serving the good object of lightening the load, in that the kerosene for the purpose was consumed there and then and had not to be dragged forward for subsequent use. Late in the afternoon the wind fell and the sun peered amongst the clouds just as I was in the middle of a long job riveting and lashing the broken shovel.

The next day, January 11, a beautiful, calm day of sunshine, I set out over a good surface with a slight down grade.

From the start my feet felt curiously lumpy and sore. They had become so painful after a mile of walking that I decided to examine them on the spot, sitting in the lee of the sledge in brilliant sunshine. I had not had my socks off for some days for, while lying in camp, it had not seemed necessary. On taking off the third and inner pair of socks the sight of my feet gave me quite a shock, for the thickened skin of the soles had separated in each case as a complete layer, and abundant watery fluid had escaped saturating the sock. The new skin beneath was very much abraded and raw. Several of my toes had commenced to blacken and fester near the tips and the nails were puffed and loose.

I began to wonder if there was ever to be a day without some special disappointment. However, there was nothing to be done but make the best of it. I smeared the new skin and the raw surfaces with lanoline, of which there was fortunately a good store, and then with the aid of bandages bound the old skin casts back in place, for these were comfortable and soft in contact with the abraded surface. Over the bandages were slipped six pairs of thick woollen socks, then fur boots and finally crampon over-shoes. The latter, having large stiff soles, spread the weight nicely and saved my feet from the jagged ice encountered shortly afterwards.

So glorious was it to feel the sun on one's skin after being without it for so long that I next removed most of my clothing and bathed my body in the rays until my flesh fairly tingled — a wonderful sensation which spread throughout my whole person, and made me feel stronger and happier.

Then on I went, treading rather like a cat on wet ground endeavouring to save my feet from pain. By 5.30 p.m. I was quite worn out — nerve-worn — though having covered but six and a quarter miles. Had it not been a delightful evening I should not have found strength to erect the tent.

The day following passed in a howling blizzard and I could do nothing but attend to my feet and other raw patches, festering finger-nails and inflamed frost-bitten nose. Fortunately there was a good supply of bandages and antiseptic. The tent, spread about with dressings and the meagre surgical appliances at hand, was suggestive of a casualty hospital.

Towards noon the following day, January 13, the wind subsided and the snow cleared off. It turned out a beautifully fine afternoon. Soon after I had got moving the slope increased, unfolding a fine view of the Mertz Glacier ahead. My heart leapt with joy, for all was like a map before me and I knew that over the hazy blue ice ridge in the far distance lay the Hut. I was heading to traverse the depression of the glacier ahead at a point many miles above our crossing of the outward journey and some few miles below gigantic ice cascades. My first impulse was to turn away to the west and avoid crossing the fifteen miles of hideously broken ice that choked the valley before me, but on second thought, in view of the very limited quantity of food left, the right thing seemed to be to make an air-line for the Hut and chance what lay between. Accordingly, having taken an observation of the sun for position and selected what appeared to be the clearest route across the valley, I started downhill. The névé gave way to rough blue ice and even wide crevasses made their appearance. The rough ice jarred my feet terribly and altogether it was a most painful march.

So unendurable did it become that, finding a bridged crevasse extending my way, I decided to march along the snow bridge and risk an accident. It was from fifteen to twenty feet wide and well packed with winter snow. The march continued along it down slopes for over a mile with great satisfaction as far as my feet were concerned. Eventually it became irregular and broke up, but others took its place and served as well; in this way the march was made possible. At 8 p.m. after covering a distance of nearly six miles a final halt for the day was made.

About 11 p.m. as the sun skimmed behind the ice slopes to the south I was startled by loud reports like heavy gun shots. They commenced up the valley to the south and trailed away down the southern side of the glacier towards the sea. The fusillade of shots rang out without interruption for about half an hour, then all was silent. It was hard to believe it was not caused by some human agency, but I learnt that it was due to the cracking of the glacier ice.

A high wind which blew on the morning of the 14th diminished in strength by noon and allowed me to get away. The sun came out so warm that the rough ice surface underfoot was covered with a film of water and in some places small trickles ran away to disappear into crevasses.

Though the course was downhill, the sledge required a good deal of pulling owing to the wet runners. At 9 p.m., after travelling five miles, I pitched camp in the bed of the glacier. From about 9.30 p.m. until 11 p.m. 'cannonading' continued like that heard the previous evening.

January 15 — the date on which all the sledging parties were due at the Hut! It was overcast and snowing early in the day, but in a few hours the sun broke out and shone warmly. The travelling was so heavy over a soft snowy surface, partly melting, that I gave up, after one mile, and camped.

At 7 p.m. the surface had not improved, the sky was thickly obscured and snow fell. At 10 p.m. a heavy snow-storm was in progress, and, since there were many crevasses in the vicinity, I resolved to wait.

On the 16th at 2 a.m. the snow was falling as thick as ever, but at 5 a.m. the atmosphere lightened and the sun appeared. Camp was broken without delay. A favourable breeze sprang up, and with sail set I managed to proceed in short stages through the deep newly-fallen blanket of snow. It clung in lumps to the runners, which had to be scraped frequently. Riven ice ridges as much as eighty feet in height passed on either hand. Occasionally I got a start as a foot or a leg sank through into space, but, on the whole, all went unexpectedly well for several miles. Then the sun disappeared and the disabilities of a snow-blind light had to be faced.

After laboriously toiling up one long slope, I had just taken a few paces over the crest, with the sledge running freely behind, when it dawned on me that the surface fell away unusually steeply. A glance ahead, even in that uncertain light, flashed the truth upon me — I was on a snow cornice, rimming the brink of a great blue chasm like a quarry, the yawning mouth of an immense and partly filled crevasse. Already the sledge was gaining speed as it slid past me towards the gaping hole below. Mechanically, I bedded my feet firmly in the snow and, exerting every effort, was just able to take the weight and hold up the sledge as it reached the very brink of the abyss. There must have been an interval of quite a minute during which I held my ground without being able to make it budge. It seemed an interminable time; I found myself reckoning the odds as to who would win, the sledge or I. Then it slowly came my way, and the imminent danger was passed.

The day's march was an extremely heavy five miles; so before turning in I treated myself to an extra supper of jelly soup made from dog sinews. I thought at the time that the acute enjoyment of eating compensated in some measure for the sufferings of starvation.

January 17 was another day of overcast sky and steady falling snow. Everything from below one's feet to the sky above was one uniform ghostly glare. The irregularities in the surfaces not obliterated by the deep soft snow blended harmoniously in colour and in the absence of shadows faded into invisibility. These were most unsuitable conditions for the crossing of such a dangerous crevassed valley, but delay meant a reduction of the ration and that was out of the question, so nothing remained but to go on.

A start was made at 8 a.m. and the pulling proved more easy than on the previous day. Some two miles had been negotiated in safety when an event occurred which, but for a miracle, would have terminated the story then and there. Never have I come so near to an end; never has anyone more miraculously escaped.

I was hauling the sledge through deep snow up a fairly steep slope when my feet broke through into a crevasse. Fortunately as I fell I caught my weight with my arms on the edge and did not plunge in further than the thighs. The outline of the crevasse did not show through the blanket of snow on the surface, but an idea of the trend was obtained with a stick. I decided to try a crossing about fifty yards further along, hoping that there it would be better bridged. Alas! it took an unexpected turn catching me unawares. This time I shot through the centre of the bridge in a flash, but the latter part of the fall was decelerated by the friction of the harness ropes which, as the sledge ran up, sawed back into the thick compact snow forming the margin of the lid. Having seen my comrades perish in diverse ways and having lost hope of ever reaching the Hut, I had already many times speculated on what the end would be like. So it happened that as I fell through into the crevasse the thought 'so this is the end' blazed up in my mind, for it was to be expected that the next moment the sledge would follow through, crash on my head and all go to the unseen bottom. But the unexpected happened and the sledge held, the deep snow acting as a brake.

In the moment that elapsed before the rope ceased to descend, delaying the issue, a great regret swept through my mind, namely, that after having stinted myself so assiduously in order to save food, I should pass on now to eternity without the satisfaction of what remained — to such an extent does food take possession of one under such circumstances. Realizing that the sledge was holding I began to look around. The crevasse was somewhat over six feet wide and sheer walled, descending into blue depths below. My clothes, which, with a view to ventilation, had been but loosely secured, were now stuffed with snow broken from the roof, and very chilly it was. Above at the other end of the fourteen-foot rope, was the daylight seen through the hole in the lid.

In my weak condition, the prospect of climbing out seemed very poor indeed, but in a few moments the struggle was begun. A great effort brought a knot in the rope within my grasp, and, after a moment's rest, I was able to draw myself up and reach another, and, at length, hauled my body on to the overhanging snow-lid. Then, when all appeared to be well and before I could get to quite solid ground, a further section of the lid gave way, precipitating me once more to the full length of the rope.

There, exhausted, weak and chilled, hanging freely in space and slowly turning round as the rope twisted one way and the other, I felt that I had done my utmost and failed, that I had no more strength to try again and that all was over except the passing. It was to be a miserable and slow end and I reflected with disappointment that there was in my pocket no antidote to speed matters; but there always remained the alternative of slipping from the harness. There on the brink of the great Beyond I well remember how I looked forward to the peace of the great release — how almost excited I was at the prospect of the unknown to be unveiled. From those flights of mind I came back to earth, and remembering how Providence had miraculously brought me so far, felt that nothing was impossible and determined to act up to Service's lines:

Just have one more try — it's dead easy to die,
It's the keeping-on-living that's hard.

My strength was fast ebbing; in a few minutes it would be too late. It was the occasion for a supreme attempt. Fired by the passion that burns the blood in the act of strife, new power seemed to come as I applied myself to one last tremendous effort. The struggle occupied some time, but I slowly worked upward to the surface. This time emerging feet first, still clinging to the rope, I pushed myself out extended at full length on the lid and then shuffled safely on to the solid ground at the side. Then came the reaction from the great nerve strain and lying there alongside the sledge my mind faded into a blank.

When consciousness returned it was a full hour or two later, for I was partly covered with newly fallen snow and numb with the cold. I took at least three hours to erect the tent, get things snugly inside and clear the snow from my clothes. Between each movement, almost, I had to rest. Then reclining in luxury in the sleeping-bag I ate a little food and thought matters over. It was a time when the mood of the Persian philosopher appealed to me:

Unborn To-morrow and dead Yesterday,
Why fret about them if To-day be sweet?

Home of the Blizzard (1934 edition; first published 1915)

3

1914–39

Travel and culture

The outbreak of the First World War made European travel a possibility for many Australian men who otherwise would never have expected to leave Australia. It would be more than half a century before Australians would again travel overseas in such numbers. About half the eligible men joined up, for a variety of motives including patriotism, Empire loyalty, money, status and security — but also for the one chance in a lifetime to see the world. One result of the devastating death-toll was to make that world look a dangerous and degenerate place. Australian war memoirs inevitably included much that is in fact travel writing, their authors usually though not always concluding, like many tourists, that Australia was a haven of peace and commonsense in a hostile and confusing world.[1]

The two decades following the Great War were the romantic heyday of safe, and indeed luxurious, ocean travel. Following the democratising effect of the war the cultural élite reasserted their dominance over travel to Europe, and it became a more self-consciously cultural affair, as their family ties with England frayed. They wished to distinguish themselves from the culture of the masses, increasingly identified with America. While would-be film stars set off for Hollywood, Rhodes scholarships and art scholarships sent the bright young things off to Europe. Travel to Europe was less about family reunions and natural wonders, more about art, history and intellectual life. Travel also became a more self-consciously political experience — to have an opinion on Italian trains or English cooking or Russian folksongs was to take sides in the great geopolitical and intellectual questions of the day. The ordinary Australian's view of the world, which Bedford and Spielvogel celebrated, now became an embarrassment; the travels of those who were not 'cultured' were only of interest if they were romantic adventurers or vagabonds.

From the 1920s, Asia became a more common destination for tourists. Shipping lines like Burns, Philp and Company, and the Orient Line increased their advertising for Asian stopovers on their routes to Europe and trips to Asian destinations in their own right. 'The trip to Java and back occupies fifty days', one brochure pointed out, 'and is one of the most attractive on the list — especially for Australians in winter'.[2] The Royal Packet Navigation Company placed alluring advertisements in quality journals for travel 'Over Sunlit Seas to Java–Bali–Sumatra', while the Orient Line assured readers that it maintained the highest standards of imperial service in bringing the Orient to the traveller. The Orient had become a destination with status, all the more so for being exotic and drawing on fashionable taste for chinoiserie and Japanese flower-arrangements.

1914

Hilda Rix Nicholas in Tangier

Born in Ballarat, Hilda Rix (1884–1961) studied painting at the National Gallery School in Melbourne between 1902 and 1905. In 1907 she left Australia for Europe, accompanied by her widowed mother and sister, both of whom were also artists. On arrival in England, Rix enrolled at the New Art School in Kensington. In September 1907 the family moved to Paris, where Rix studied with a number of artists and where she remained until the outbreak of war. From 1910 she passed the summers in Étaples, Brittany, where a large community of artists lived and worked. Rix spent two months in Morocco early in the spring of 1912, and returned there for another period of painting in 1914. In her letters and other writing on her experiences in Morocco, Rix reveals something not only about the artist as observer but also about the ways in which Europeans have understood and constructed 'the Orient'. The Tangier of Hilda Rix was 'like a beautiful dream', 'fairyland', 'an Arabian night's story', 'a Bible story', a place of exotic, colourful street theatre. It was a place too where, because of their identification with the colonial powers and their clear sense of racial superiority, women could enjoy a little more authority and independence than at home. With the outbreak of war Rix had to abandon her Étaples studio and its contents. The paintings were discovered by an Australian soldier, Major G. N. Nicholas, whose admiration for her work led to marriage. Six weeks after the wedding he was killed in action. After some success in England and France in the 1920s, Hilda Rix Nicholas returned to Australia, remarried, and settled at Tombong, New South Wales, where she remained for the rest of her life.

I've come right up on to the roof of the hotel to write to you. It seems like a strange dream to be in Morocco again. I am high up near the sky and looking down and around at all this crowded town and peaceful country, now bathed in the orange glow of the setting sun.

To-morrow is big market-day and the 'Soko' down there below is a seething mass of people. The country people have come in with their loads, carried for long miles on their backs, or the backs of their weary little donkeys. And to-night there will be huddled groups camped around the faint lights of their lanterns, to be ready to start market early to-morrow morning.

There! The big glowing half-orange of the sun has just dipped behind the mountain's edge to my left, leaving the sky a pinky gold — and the dips between the mountains are hung in rosy veils. The sky on the horizon's edge melts upwards into a lemon blue — then on to warmer blue in the hollow of the 'inverted bowl,' and down again in a powder-blue mist to the sea. Above the sea in the sky opposite the sunset is a great hand of pink clouds stretching forth and reflecting the happy glow.

Below me, beyond the big garden of this hotel, with its huge palms, bamboos, roses and mimosa all abloom, there is a ceaseless passing up and down of my beloved fairy-tale people. To-day there has been a European fête, and a mad rollicking car full of carnival revellers has hurried up the hill below me, laughing and scattering before it to all sides donkeys, Arab men and women.

A party of Arab women have just mounted the hill bearing enormous loads of faggots on their backs; they look like huge snails bent forward to their toil, but nearly all are cheerful and many pretty, beneath dirt and charcoal-dust. Their tired donkeys, also heavily laden, trail slowly behind them. Beyond and below in the twilight of the Moorish cemetery quiet forms are hovering over the graves, tending them noiselessly.

Oh! such a buzz of strange tongues is coming up on the breeze from the crowded Soko, and people of the hotel are entering the big gates in ones, twos, and threes, for the day is done. I must follow the sun's example and go below, for I am keen to make an early start at my work to-morrow.

Enthusiasm is a fine thing, but I wonder if the general public realise what miseries an artist has often to undergo. To-day I congratulated myself on occupying a fine strategic position — it was on an elevation that raised me above the throng and there was a row of little shops behind that prevented me being ringed in by a curious crowd. But no sooner had I become deeply engrossed in my subject than a man came and dumped down beside me a revolting heap of animal offal. It would have been unheroic to give up my position because my subject was enthralling, but oh, the horror of it! My sister very kindly rushed back to the hotel for eau-de-Cologne and smelling-salts to help me to endure the situation.

One has to risk horrible diseases quite often in the East, for in the closely pressing crowds there are often visions of smallpox and leprosy — people who have lost noses and eyes from some frightful malady. Then there is always the risk of sun-stroke, or getting a chill through staying in the shade. It takes a lot of moral and physical courage and a vivid enthusiasm to carry one through, but, thank Heaven, the beauty overpowers the discomfort or nothing would be produced.

At last the blazing sun beating on the offal made the odour insufferable, so, turning to the butcher who had placed it there, I implored him with signs to take away the offending mass, at the same time making great play with my bottles of smelling-salts and eau-de-Cologne. He shrugged his shoulders to show that such a thing meant nothing to him; but a kind inspiration dawned on him and he not only removed the offensive heap but sent post-haste for an incense burner, who, swinging his censer, filled the tormented air with a delicious perfume.

Having heard so much of the difficulties of working amongst the Arabs because of their religious principles, I am delighted to find that they do not look upon me as an enemy, and I am happily overcoming their prejudices and continually finding them doing little graceful acts.

Naturally the idle crowds on the market-place surround me, but so engrossing is the task of catching the ever-moving people that one becomes unconscious of the crowds behind, for they never get between one and one's subject. Of course many subterfuges have to be employed to keep the victim unsuspecting, but unhappily some one in my audience invariably recognises my prey and calls to Mohammed or Absolam that he is being captured on paper. Sometimes the said Absolam only looks sheepish, wriggling, alas! out of position, or sometimes completely disappearing. If one feels that there is a resentful spirit growing one gracefully melts away.

Often in the heat of work I am not conscious of the ring of people until with a snap a pencil breaks, and I hear a chorus of gentle groans of sympathy — and when I dropped a pencil the other day, an Arab picking it up and seeing the point was broken whipped out his large knife and sharpened it and presented it to me with a beaming smile. Would that all were as complacent! The other day, coming up from the Soko, I saw two camels stalking superciliously down the hill into the market with huge cases and baskets of dates and oranges. I was delighted to see them because since the war they have not been able to enter Tangiers as the Spaniards hold the roads. So with my bag of ammunition and my big drawing board I followed them. They descended the hill to the foot of the Soko where their master made them kneel to be unloaded. I began my work, and immediately a merry crowd formed around me; but the owner of the camel, a man from the interior, unused to my naughty ways, at once became agitated — fearing harm to his camel through my 'evil eye.' So he planted himself in front of the beast, and a friend, looking equally fierce, joined him; the two of them holding out their wide jelabas succeeded in blocking out my entire view.

Well, I looked pathetic for an instant, saying 'La, la!' (No, no!). But finding them adamant, I went away amid much heated comment and laughter. Instead of going quite away, however, I made a little detour and returned to that corner of the Soko, but on the other side of the camel, and stood on a two-foot-high wall from where I got a splendid view of my game. I proceeded to draw feverishly. Presently the crowd spotted me, and caught on, laughing; this caused the two angry men to look up, and seeing me at it again unbaffled, one of them again placed himself in front of the camel's head. In spite of this and the excitement around me, I managed to get the whole squatting body of the beast. But the owner's rage was at fever heat when my merry audience called to him that I had potted his camel. He jumped up, joisted the loads on to its hump, untied its folded knees, and prodded it to get up and run.

They ran — but so did I, drawing all the way while running, with a torrent of laughing, cheering Arabs beside and behind me. Oh such fun! I chased them right up the hill, my pencil flying at work, head bobbing up and down — dodging squatting people, and laughing with the joy of the sport as I ran, until my game vanished round the corner up the hill. But I had won my point and got my camel's head, midst cheers and roars of laughter from the crowd of onlookers who had been intently watching my exploits.

The owner's friend who had been so furious before, came behind me and said — 'Mizziaan! mizziaan!' which means 'splendid.'

Oh it is an unending feast of form, colour and light. If only one had months here and a big studio to attack big canvases, and gradually entice models to pose for one, as well as doing the moving people on the market-place! I have already succeeded in persuading several splendid types to give short sittings.

I had the opportunity the other day to draw an escaped slave in the tribunal of the French Embassy. If only one could succeed in banishing their fears — what an unending field of work there is amongst these beautiful, dignified people!

'Sketching in Morocco', *Studio* (1914)

1915

David Doull in Egypt

Until the 1960s, the highest annual figures for overseas travel from Australia were recorded by soldiers, not tourists. For the majority of soldiers who have served in wars overseas, it was the only occasion on which they left Australia. The large collection of war diaries, particularly of the 'six bob a day tourists' of the 1st AIF, often slid into the genre of travel writing. David Doull was a lieutenant with the 17th Battalion of the 1st AIF and served at Gallipoli. He returned to Australia in November 1916 and, as 'one of the Gallipoli heroes', published a short account of his war in A Story of Gallipoli: With the 5th Brigade, *a conventional memoir expressing pride in his men, as 'cheerful as schoolboys', a horror of war and sentimental nationalism. At the same time, he published a far more substantial and more reflective work,* With the Anzacs in Egypt: Life and Scenes in the Land of the Pharaohs, as Seen Though Australian Spectacles. *What is striking is that, though taking the form of a war memoir, it finishes before the Australians have seen any action, and consists entirely of travel description. Doull is a thoughtful if blinkered social commentator on Egypt and its people, though he admitted 'the laughter and the inexpressible delight with which Australians have greeted each novel scene in this strange land cannot adequately be expressed'. While impressed with a society he imagined 'unchanged throughout the long ages of the past', he looked forward to the 'leavening of the culture and civilisation which everywhere follows British rule and influence'.*

Every Australian soldier within a week after arrival in Egypt visits the great Pyramid of Cheops at Ghizeh, under the shadow of which the Australian contingents had their camps.

The journey from Cairo to the three Pyramids of Ghizeh is now made by electric tramway in forty-eight minutes, the starting point being where the magnificent Kasr el Nil bridge crosses the Nile from the Island of Gezirah [...] For miles a canal runs parallel with the tramway, and one of the most picturesque scenes of Egyptian life is the crowd of native children, lazy buffaloes, and flocks of ducks and geese sporting in the cool water.

On Saturdays and Sundays, when the Australians have general leave, a constant stream of trams, motors, carriages, camels and donkeys pass and repass on this beautiful avenue, which ends at a small cluster of buildings — Mena House Hotel, refreshment rooms, photographers, etc. Here the overseas warrior falls into the hands of camel drivers, donkey boys, guides, and a whole tribe of 'backsheesh' begging Arabs, who never leave or cease to importune him till he shakes the desert's dust off his feet in the solitude of his room or tent. The great pyramid looms up, a vast ruinous, hoary mass of stone, only a few hundred yards away, but the road is an inclined sandy path which the sweltering heat renders still less inviting. You decide to take a camel. Had you been wiser you would have selected a donkey for, despite his strong objections to moving, he is a far more comfortable mount. Having selected the ship of the desert, the camel driver utters a peculiar guttural sound, the animal falls on his knees, lurches up with you on his back and away you go swinging and bouncing past the mighty tomb of Cheops to where, some three hundred yards away, the mysterious Sphinx has been watching the sunrise for the past six thousand years.

The level sand fronting the temple of the Sphinx is the rendezvous for the remainder of the Arab tribe that lay in wait for you. It consists of guides innumerable, native photographers, vendors of lemonade, sakkars (water carriers), sellers of worthless curios and scarabs. The latter are carved representations of the sacred beetle, and are found in the tombs, many bearing the genuine seals of the Pharaohs. The heterogenous collection of picturesque humanity is augmented by scores of fellah children from the adjoining village of El Kafr. From this spot the three great pyramids, Cheops, Khephren, and Mykerinos are seen in a diagonal line to the south. The remains of fortification walls, numerous tombs, the granite temple and the tracks of ancient roadways leading to the plateau complete the collection of imposing ruins [...]

Having been photographed with these ancient monuments for a background as everybody does who visits Egypt, you turn your camel's head towards the entrance to the great pyramid, the driver again utters his peculiar guttural sound and the animal falls upon its knees and you are promptly surrounded by the third and final band of brigands at the great heap of huge stones that represents all that is left of the mighty steps.

'Will the captains climb the pyramid first, or will they visit the royal tomb?' asks your guide.

Looking up in dismay at the immense pile which contains enough stone to build a wall around France, 'the Captains' unwisely decide upon inspecting the interior [...] Ten piastres, equal to 2/2 in English money, is the usual charge made for a visit to the interior of the tomb. Soldiers, however, are admitted free. If this charge were still levied, though, it would be the least of the sums the Australian finds himself called upon to pay, for, although the guides and attendants inform you there is no charge for visiting the interior of the pile, they do not omit to point out that the amount of backsheesh you give them is entirely optional. You are thereupon conducted to the granite entrance to the pyramid, and prepare for a space to say farewell to the day.

Filled as the dark weird passages were with perspiring soldiers and Arabs on the day on which the writer made the inspection, the experience was such as few would care to repeat, and was well expressed by a stalwart soldier, who, upon emerging into the light again, dashed the sweat from his face, and exclaimed 'You go through hell and see nothing.' Undeterred, however, by this opinion, you surrender yourself to three or four Arabs who have assumed temporary ownership of you, stoop down and begin to descend a narrow passage 4 feet high, $3\frac{1}{2}$ feet wide, which penetrates into the rock to a depth of 320 feet. The passage is of granite worn smooth and slippery by the feet of thousands of long dead Egyptians. Farthest from the entrance the air, like that found in mines and deep wells, becomes unpleasant and you perspire as freely as if you were in a Turkish bath. During all this time two greasy, sweltering niggers are holding on to your hands, another is hanging on to your coat behind, while a fourth is preceding you with a spluttering candle that scarcely penetrates the intense darkness. Whichever way you look there are flickering candles, crouching forms, and a long line of chattering Arabs. Your friends may be immediately behind you, but in the awful din of Arabic tongues you do not hear them. You simply growl and slip and sweat until you reach the closed entrance to a gallery where the Arabs, under the Khalif all Namum, in their search for hidden treasures, cut round the original block, and reached as far as the chamber of the sarcophagus. Following the same course we ascended another narrow granite passage, which eventually brought us into the king's chamber, in the exact centre of the pyramid. This is a tomb 17 feet high, 17½ feet wide, and 34 feet long. The granite blocks of which it is built show the same excellence of construction which is noticeable in the great gallery, a perfect evenness of the tiers, and the extreme exactness of the almost imperceptible joining. The ceiling, formed of nine enormous slabs of granite, is absolutely intact. It was in this chamber that the mummy of the king was laid. The sarcophagus of granite, without ornament or inscription, which enclosed the mummy is still in position, but the lid and the mummy have long since disappeared.

An Arab lights a short piece of magnesium wire, which gives a transient glimpse of the plain bare room, and splutters and dies out.

'Five piastres for the light, captain?'

'Is this all there is to see?'

'Yes, but there is the queen's chamber, but it is not so good as this.'

'Well, I'm hanged!'

As you stand and wring the perspiration from your clothes, as much inclined to laugh as to grumble at 'going through hell to see nothing,' the guides tell you they have 'worked very hard' and ask for backsheesh. Helpless amongst so many, for by this time the number has been reinforced by a few more spare cadgers, you waive the point, and express a longing to see the blue sky and the desert, which all at once has become lovely. Thereupon the whole gesticulating crowd catches hold of you, others hold your feet as they slip into the footholds in the smooth stone, and away you go on your rapid transition from the places of the 5,000 year old dead to the living world of to-day. With each step the guides become more solicitous and tender until they finally land you, a washed-out human relic, once more at the entrance, where you settle their claims and laugh at the experience.

The ascent of the pyramid, which is made on the eastern face, despite the recent accident to some intrepid Australian soldiers, is perfectly safe, and is less strenuous and exhausting than the visit into the interior. The height of the steps despite the assistance of the Bedouins who practically haul you up with little regard for your feelings, makes the ascent difficult. Inside a quarter of an hour, however, they succeed in hauling you to the 30 feet square top, where the Arabs provide you with tea, and your exertions are rewarded with a wonderful view of the surrounding country [...]

There is something subtly fascinating in the mysterious face covering of the women of Egypt. It touches the occult, and like all hidden things, plays powerfully upon the fitful imagination of man. It is something which Englishmen cannot understand; an Eastern fetish deep-rooted in antiquity; for, in the tombs of the ancients we find sculptures and paintings attesting the existence of this custom thousands of years ago.

The borko, or veil, is worn in Egypt by Turkish and Egyptian ladies, the former, when in the streets, being scarcely distinguishable from the natives of the country. The beautiful semi-transparent covering worn by the ladies of the upper classes is of the most delicate silk, covering up the face to within an inch of the eyes, the appearance of which, darkened at the brows and lashes with kohl, an aromatic resin, are attractive in the extreme. With few exceptions the eyes are large, black, almost almond shaped, fringed with long beautiful lashes, and have an exquisitely soft bewitching expression. Distinguished by a style of beauty possessing great sweetness of expression, many of the Egyptian women are considered to represent the perfection of female loveliness. These attractions, sufficiently alluring in themselves, are rendered more bewitching by the semi-transparency of their gauzy veils. The general effect of the veil is to render all the upper-class women attractive, as the veiling of the features gives additional prominence to the luminous eyes directed at the observer from behind them. Few of the Egyptian women permit themselves to be seen unveiled, except by very close relations, or when the exhibition of their features may appear to have been accidental. The fair Cairene, however, is not so modest but that she will turn an interested and sparkling pair of eyes upon any attractive member of the opposite sex who chances to pass her carriage. The adoption of the transparent covering in place of the suffocating black borko represents a widespread tendency towards its abolition, which Egyptian ladies favor and their lords and masters disfavor; which the progressives strive for, and the conservatives oppose.

Like many other social customs in Egypt, tradition holds the mass of the people so firmly that the few progressives find it impossible to break away, and the veil, instead of shielding the charms of the wearer from the gaze of the men, serves only to attract. Until a few years ago Egyptian women wore the veil from the face to the feet, but following in the steps of their Turkish sisters, they now only wear it as low as the bosom, the remainder being concealed by a long black silk costume, combining the head and outer dress.

The women of the lower classes, including the fellah, are easily distinguished by means of their black borkos, a heavy cumbersome veil, which is kept from pressing too closely upon the face by means of an ornamented piece of bamboo. During our marches in the environs of Cairo we frequently came across women tending goats who wore this kind of borko covered with heavy brass rings and other rude ornaments. What miseries these unfortunate people suffer during the heat of summer can easily be realised by those who have experienced its ordeals. As an illustration of the well-known fact that the covering of the face is due, not to any sense of modesty but to custom, it may be mentioned that Cairene women will upon the approach of strangers hastily cover up the face though the bosom or legs may remain exposed. It is quite amusing also to notice a young girl coquettishly covering up her face, though her feet are bare and her clothes in tatters. Many of the poor, lacking the wherewithal to purchase a borko, cover their faces with their head coverings, concealing the features so completely that only one eye remains visible. This practice is religiously observed even by the poor wretches one sees grubbing among the rubbish heaps outside of the city.

With the passing of the veil, should the progressives succeed in imposing their wishes upon the community, much of the false mysticism surrounding Oriental women will disappear, and with it will doubtless come their emancipation from their present condition of semi-slavery.

With the Anzacs in Egypt (1916)

1915

Martin Boyd shipboard and in England

Great-grandson of Sir William à Beckett, author of the first extract in this anthology, writer Martin Boyd (1893–1972) was born in Switzerland to an old and distinguished Australian family whose European ties had been maintained. All his life Boyd moved between and lived in two worlds as do the characters in his major novels, notably the Langton tetralogy. His early years were spent in Victoria but he returned to Europe in 1915 to join an English regiment and served in France, an experience that left him a fervent pacifist. On board a ship between the two worlds he could explore the ambiguities of his national and sexual identities. Italy, which he discovered in 1922 with 'an extraordinary sense of illumination', offered a way out. His arrival in Pisa gave him 'a sense of a homecoming of the spirit' and in Florence 'I was like stout Cortez on the peak in Darien'. Boyd was in Australia after the war but settled in Britain in 1921 where he remained until 1948. In that year, he moved to Australia to restore his grandfather's house, but he left for England again in 1951. Highly critical of Britain's ruling class, Boyd fled to Rome in 1958 where he remained until his death. Martin Boyd's life was also a quest for spirituality and his book on Italy, Much Else in Italy *(1958), takes the form of a series of religious and aesthetic meditations. He was received into the Catholic Church in the last week of his life. The story of his wandering life is told in two versions of his autobiography,* A Single Flame *(1939), from which this extract is taken, and* Days of My Delight: An Anglo-Australian Memoir *(1965).*

I left on the *Miltiades*, an Aberdeen liner that went round by the Cape. I had a great many presents of articles which were supposed to be of use at the Front. An aunt gave me a money belt, stuffed with golden sovereigns. I took with me a bag of golf clubs and someone said that was no way to go off to a war. My parents gave me everything they could and opened an account for me at a bank in London.

A great many people came to see me off at the ship. Among these was a girl with whom I was in love, though it was undeclared. I had a vague idea that it was dishonourable to make any advances to a girl 'of one's own class' unless one was in a position to marry her. Just before the ship sailed occurred one of the most shameful incidents of my life. I lured this girl round to a secluded part of the deck with the intention of kissing her, but when we were alone I found myself too inhibited to do so.

I shared a good deck cabin with a commercial traveller on his way to Perth. The weather was stormy, and after the excitement of departure I was very unhappy at leaving my parents and my small sister. At intervals to me in this sick and miserable condition appeared the commercial traveller, smoking a strong cigar, and saying: 'What you want to do is to get up and eat a hearty meal.' This went on for a week, while the ship plunged like a submarine through the Great Australian Bight.

At Perth the commercial traveller was replaced by a Rhodes scholar. After a day ashore I suddenly became well again and took an interest in my fellow passengers. I became more friendly with a young man named Lord whom I had known as a child, but who had since been to one of the famous English public schools. He enjoyed telling me about England, and in which areas of London it was possible to live, and where to have one's clothes made. For all his knowledge of the correct thing he was a sentimental and engaging young man, and when the ship drew away from Fremantle, he said: 'I wonder when we shall see Australia again.'

I gave an indifferent reply and he was shocked. I had cut my umbilical cord on the day I left Melbourne. Yarra Glen and Kew Hill were holy places to me, but I had no feeling for the soil of Fremantle merely because it was Australian. Lord had some reason for his sentimentality, as before he returned he had been badly wounded in the stomach and had undergone seven operations.

Most of the young men on the ship spent their time reading *Infantry Training*. I read Max Beerbohm's *Zuleika Dobson* which had been given me by Susan, and pored over Mrs Carruthers' Baedeker. Mrs Carruthers and her son, a youth of about twenty, who was also on his way to the war, were aristocratic in appearance and very consciously gentlepeople. Mrs Carruthers as well as Lord told me about London, and talked a lot about nice people and nice neighbourhoods: 'The part about Knightsbridge' she most preferred. But she could be friendly and amusing, and in a certain dress she said: 'I feel like Rosie Rapture, the pride of the beauty chorus.' There was a very attractive Danish couple on the ship, who were avoided as German spies.

Older but more innocent than either of them, I listened to Lord and Carruthers talking about women. Carruthers was chaste in fact and intention, not from moral scruples, but because, as he said: 'I couldn't bear to have a paid woman messing me about.'

Lord startled me by talking not only of women but of boys with equally interested appraisement. I expressed surprise and he told me of the prevalence of homo-sexuality among public-school boys, sailors, and Egyptians. I thought this rather more funny than shocking and said: 'Then really it's quite virtuous just to go with a woman.'

We called at Durban and Capetown, where some South Africans joined us, young men who had been in the campaign in German South-West. The ship had at one time been cut in half and lengthened, and a dummy funnel had been added for the sake of appearance. Its spacious gloom, reached from the boat-deck, made a rendezvous for lovers. Carruthers said that one heard sensual chuckles coming from it at night. 'Sensual chuckles in the dummy funnel' became a stock phrase with us.

The ship rolled lazily northwards through a sweltering ocean. I felt as if I were suspended between two incarnations. Part of me had died in Port Phillip Bay. The past and the future were dreams, and the only reality was this ship, where from Mrs Carruthers and Lord I gleaned brief glimpses of the life to come. The life on the ship had a curious unreality, with the lazy games under the awnings; the pseudo-smart people from the tropics who talked of *sahibs* and *tiffin*; the bogus spy and his lovely wife; the slight excitement of flying-fish; the pock-marked and bejewelled woman at my table who complained about the perfectly good food; and at night the queer phenomenon of sensual chuckles in the dummy funnel. It was unlike anything I had known hitherto.

At concerts the third officer, who had a broken nose and a tenor voice, used to sing very sweet songs, which stirred my still adolescent longings. He sang about a girl who was brown and bright and made for love, and about another whose two grey eyes and two white arms were waiting for him. In the evening, when before dinner I lay in my bath of warm sea-water, with the sub-tropical sun streaming through the sky-light, I thought sensuously of the impersonal acquiescent girl waiting for me somewhere.

We called at Teneriffe, my first contact since infancy with an old civilization. The water was bluer in the shadows of the boats that came out to meet the ship, and more opalescent than I had ever seen it in Australia. The golden brown Spaniards dived from the bridge for coins. One could see them deep down, like fishes in the clear water. I went ashore with the Carruthers. We visited the bullring, the cathedral, where there was a flag captured from Nelson, and then drove up the hill to luncheon in a hotel garden. The cobbled streets and the crumbling walls, all this sun-drenched antiquity, filled me with delight.

Lord had gone off with the Rhodes scholar to the brothel. In the evening in my cabin they were describing, for the benefit of Carruthers, their afternoon's experience. Lord said:

'I didn't do anything. She was too much like a cow.'

He had, however, bought some obscene post cards. I looked at them and they affronted my imagination. I had not thought that it would be like that. Those leering men and black-stockinged women bore no relationship to my dreams of the nymphs in the olive groves.

Lord and Carruthers and the Rhodes scholar went on talking about the brothel, and took no notice when I told them to shut up. So I soaked a bath towel in water, crept along the deck, and flung it through the port-hole, where it caught fairly their three heads, bent over the post cards. I fled and dodged them all over the ship, through places forbidden to passengers, and finally lay in a lifeboat, and heard them a few feet from me, wondering where in the devil I had gone. I had the feeling of elation which the foxhunter, excusing his sport, says the fox enjoys. But I doubt if I would have enjoyed it so much if I had known that if I were caught, I would not merely be ragged, but broken up, and pieces of my body hung on a wall.

On the last four days of the voyage there was the chance of our being torpedoed, and some people did not dress for dinner, though I could see no particular argument against being drowned in a dinner-suit. I was very anxious not to be torpedoed, as one of the consolations for coming to the war was that I would see England before I died.

I landed at Plymouth and spent two or three days walking about Devon and Somerset to get myself into good condition after the seven weeks on the ship. I saw the cathedrals of Exeter and Wells and the ruins of Glastonbury. I became gothic drunk. For fifteen years my imagination had been historically stimulated, and when for the first time I visited the scenes of the ancient dramas, their beauty and significance struck me more forcibly than they could ever have done if I had grown up amongst them. A young man is more likely to fall in love with a girl whose face is strange to him, than with one who has always lived next door. In every cathedral and church and inn the remembered pages of John Richard Green leapt to brilliant life. I had this reward for my long exile.

[...]

One morning after parade on Hampstead Heath, we were told that members of the Inns of Court O.T.C. had been seen in the company of undesirable women, and that commissions would be refused to men who spoke to women 'to whom they had not been introduced socially.'

I was twenty-two and saw no prospect within a tolerable period of marriage, so in spite of this injunction I decided to speak to a woman to whom I had not been introduced socially.

I went alone to a musical comedy in a theatre decorated with plaster nymphs. Afterwards I walked, timid and feverish, about Piccadilly and the Strand. I must have looked inhibited as none of the many prostitutes I passed gave me a word or a glance, and I was much too shy to take the initiative. I did ask one, a handsome, Jewish-type young woman with a black velvet hat and imitation diamonds, if she could tell me the time, which she did, amiably enough, but made no attempt to follow up the conversation. At that time I looked much younger than my age, and a year later when I was a subaltern, Canon Victor Horsley, who was dining at a house where I was staying, made a gesture towards my uniform and said: 'What's all this? Are you in your school O.T.C.?'

At last in a dark street by Charing Cross Station, a woman said 'Hullo' to me. I turned, my heart beating violently, and said 'Hullo.' She asked if I would come home with her and I said 'Yes.' I could not see her face in the dark. I walked beside her up towards the brighter lights of the Strand. She smelt of whisky and I sensed that she was old. When we came out into the light I saw that her face was leering, furrowed, and bibulous. She asked me if I would wait while she went into the lavatory of Charing Cross Station. This completed my disgust. She said 'Promise?' I said 'Yes.'

When she had gone I was torn between the impossibility of going with her and the dishonour of breaking my promise. I waited for a desperate minute and then fled.

But my intention not to go to bed alone that night survived. I walked on, tired but determined. In the Tottenham Court Road, a rather bony woman of nearly thirty spoke to me pleasantly, and hailed a taxi. What I was really seeking was the release in an act of sensual worship of all the beauty I had seen and imagined, I believed that with the fusion of bodies would come the fusion of souls. I did not know that it was grotesque to expect this from a casual encounter.

In the taxi the woman began to haggle about money. I was so stupid as to have forgotten this part of the business. I told her that I only had a pound and a few odd shillings. She did not believe me, and said that she wanted two pounds. I said that I was sorry but I simply had not got it, and if she insisted I would have to leave her. She then believed me, but as soon as we were in her room, which had a print of Queen Victoria over the mantelpiece, and some pious motto over the bed, she demanded the pound. I gave it to her, one of the last of the golden sovereigns that I ever used as currency, and she rolled it in her stocking. I was still unwilling to believe that this incident would not give some revelation of beauty, and I attempted a gesture of tenderness with her, but she was terse, matter-of-fact, and mechanical. As I had only given her a pound she soon got rid of me, and having directed me towards Seymour Street she went to look for further clients. I walked home, depressed at having spent a pound on anything so unsatisfactory. I have since learnt that this disillusionment with prostitutes is one of the commonest experiences of young men who have been brought up to respect girls of their own class. My conscience bothered me, as I had broken my promise to the hag at Charing Cross Station, though I could see no alternative.

A Single Flame (1939)

1916

Hector Dinning in France

*The son of a clergyman from Maryborough, Queensland, Hector Dinning
(1887–1941) was educated at Brisbane Grammar, graduated in Arts from
the new University of Queensland in 1914, and became a schoolteacher. He
enlisted in the 1st AIF and, never having been out of Australia before, served
at Gallipoli and in France and Palestine, rising to the rank of captain in the
Australian Army Service Corps. He published two accounts of his war years,*
By-Ways on Service *(1918) and* Nile to Aleppo *(1920), as well as descriptive works on Australia, the best known of which is* Australian Scene
*(1939). The war opened other opportunities: he spent a year in England
after the war, pursuing a postgraduate course at the London School of Eco-
nomics and marrying an English woman, Margaret James. Returning to
Australia in 1919, he took up an orchard in the ill-fated soldier settlement
scheme, lectured in English literature for the Workers' Educational Association, and worked on the* Toowoomba Chronicle *and the Brisbane* Telegraph. *After war broke out in 1939, he became State publicity censor in
Queensland. This extract from his war memoir is one of many examples of
how war literature can spill over into lyrical travel writing. The yearning for
another more peaceful and arcadian world becomes all the more powerful
and poignant because of the contrast with life at the front.*

It is a joy to walk down the Authie on a spring morning. The Citadelle
towers above you on the left. You are conscious of its graceful immensity long after you have passed it. The little French cottages straggle
down-stream from the Citadelle base. They are white and grey, red and
white — French in construction from their tiny dormer windows to
the neat little gardens with their bricked-up margins flushed by the
stream. Long tree-lined boulevardes start away from the road which
skirts the river; you can see for many kilometres along their length. The
wine-barrels are piled beneath the plane-trees. The children play about
them. You will come upon a château standing stately in its low ground
fronting the river. And beyond the château, which marks the border of
the town, you are in the richness of the river fields and the river slopes.
Here are the elm-groves, and the clumps of soaring poplar, and the
long lines of stubby willow clipped yearly by the hand of industry; they
sprout long and delicate from the head.

Groseille and hop tangle about the bank. Far off on the ridges the
white road traverses under its elms, picking a way among the hedged
terraces. You see no denizens here other than the old men and the girls
who are at work in the fields. From them you will have a cheery

'*Bonjour*' and some shrewd remarks on the weather: '*Ah, oui! — toujours le travail, m'sieur — toujours! Mais ça ne fait rien: nous sommes contents — oui.*' And so they are.

Then you come to Gezaincourt. That fine old château in its *parc*. The *parc* is of many acres, and there are deer in the woods of it, and a lake where the wild-fowl are.

To return we left the river and struck up into the ridge. We came to Bretel, midway between Gezaincourt and the Citadelle. We entered a private *maison* standing back in its garden; it was, none the less, marked *café*. Madame received us unprofessionally, inviting into the kitchen to drink. There she was preparing the dinner. *Je ne sais pas pourquoi* — but the French are deliciously friendly with the Australians. They take us into their homes with a readiness that is elating. They will not do it with the English. But, after all, they are frank, and we approach them frankly. We are given to domesticity, and they are intensely domestic. Indeed, the Australian temperament is far nearer to the French than is the English. The Australian tendency to the spirit of democracy finds sympathy in the provinces of this splendid Republic. The national spirit of democracy has its counterpart (may even have its roots) in the local trend towards communism which, in France, makes you welcome to enter the *maison*, chatting easily about its domestic affairs, and, in Australia, makes you welcome in the house of the country stranger, where you drink and eat without embarrassment at the hospitable table for the first and last time. The Australian is guiltless of the habitual industry of the French — of their intense interest in the detail of their lives and work; but he has their unconventionality and their lightness of heart and their hospitality. He understands their communistic way of life in the provinces. And when a French girl on a country road looks him directly in the eye for the first time, and with the smile of friendly frankness gives him a '*Bonjour, m'sieur,*' he is no more embarrassed than she. He meets and returns the greeting with an understanding of which an Englishman knows nothing. The French and the Australians are allies by nature. There is nothing amazing in their immediate understanding of each other. How, on the other hand, the English and the French continue to do anything in conjunction is a source of continual wonder. Between their temperaments there is a great gulf fixed.

By-ways on Service (1918)

<u>c. 1921</u>

Jack McLaren in Fiji

Born in Melbourne, the son of a puritanical Presbyterian clergyman, Jack McLaren (1884–1954) was educated at Scotch College before running away from home at 16. After a year's wandering in the bush, he became a cabin boy on a sailing ship on the South Africa run. He later recounted these early adventures in Blood on the Deck *(1933). Much of McLaren's life over the first two decades of this century was spent in a variety of occupations in the Pacific, New Guinea, Java and northern Australia. During these years, McLaren established himself as a freelance writer first in Sydney and Melbourne, and then from 1924 in London where he settled permanently. McLaren's adventures provided the material for more than forty books, travel writing, autobiographies, novels and collections of short stories.* My Odyssey *(1923) describes his experiences during the period 1900–11 in Papua New Guinea and the Pacific Islands, which included working as a gold prospector and trader and 'recruiting' and overseeing indigenous labour. From 1911 to 1919, McLaren ran a coconut plantation on Cape York, described in* My Crowded Solitude *(1926). When he visited Fiji, he went as an established writer, rather than a South-Seas trader, and thoroughly enjoyed his new status.*

And after many days and wanderings I came to the Civilized Wild, which is Fiji. I was no longer seeking adventure or a job. For some peculiar reason of their own editors no longer regretfully declined my stories, but bought them with commendable avidity; and I had been encouraged to the manufacturing of numbers of longer manuscripts for which certain publishers paid me real money and made into books. My odyssey was over. I went to Fiji as a tourist, a man of leisure, intent on comparing the Civilized Wild with the Palæolithic Wild of my roamings [...]

But despite their superiority, dignity and civilized ways, the Fijians retained many of their old beliefs and superstitions. In a Suva back street there was a large banyan tree which no native would willingly go near after dark. It was said that the spirit-bodies of still-born children hung from the branches by their feet, like bats, and that at night they became phosphorescently visible, which was certainly a sight to be avoided. One native explained to me that there were only a certain number of lives in the world and that a child born without life was a case of a body too many, wherefore the pre-natal spirit hid in the banyan tree, not knowing what to do with itself. There was, it appeared, a sharp distinction between pre- and post-natal life.

At Uluvata, a salt-water village, the people were forbidden to whistle in the vicinity of the houses, as whistling was said to attract mosquitoes.

On the shore reef near by was a large block of fossilized coral which was alleged to be the shrine of the Mosquito God, and plantains and sweet-potatoes and other propitiatory offerings were regularly laid there.

They had many such superstitions, and further, they were possessed to the full of that sensitiveness to shame I had seen so often in Papua and other places. The last outstanding feature of my visit to Fiji was a personal experience of it.

Accompanied by a planter friend who knew the local language, I was journeying about the upper reaches of the Rewa River, some two days' journey from the coast, and everywhere the people exhibited the kindness and courtesy of their race. But at a village called Siria the people, responding to the planter's extremely exaggerated account of my importance, set out to make themselves extra-pleasant. In the house of the biggest chief they held a kind of reception. Kava roots were ground and the liquor made and consumed in large quantities. Girls inadequately attired specially for the occasion came to me to have their breasts rubbed with oil; and afterwards they danced and sang and placed about my head and shoulders garlands made from the beaten inner bark of the hibiscus plant. In accordance with age-old custom, men and women squatted before me on the mats of the floor and made highly complimentary comments on my appearance and attire, the chief out-doing the others in these remarks.

For a time all went well; then one man stated that he liked my trousers. He was enamoured of my trousers. They were the best trousers he had ever seen, he said; and he asked the planter if he thought the great Turaga (Master) beside him would give away the garment if he were asked.

There was a sudden hush at this, for it was a recognized custom among these natives that when a thing was asked for, or even extravagantly admired, it should be handed over. Seeing that the people had been so kind, I would willingly have given the man the garment; but I was travelling light and my only other trousers were sopping wet from a long day's journey in the rain.

I had this explained to the chief. He undertook to relieve me of the necessity of either wearing wet clothes or being considered mean. He was an elderly man who prided himself on his knowledge of white men and their countries. He rose and spoke, and the planter translated his speech for me. It was something in this fashion:

'Listen, my brothers. A great shame has come upon Siria this day, and my stomach aches at what the people of other lands will say and the mockery they will cast when they hear. This Turaga is a great white man. Oh, a very great white man! He writes things in books. In many books. Also in the papers with pictures in them. Even now have your eyes seen the machine with which he makes the pictures. He writes things that are wise and true, and many people read those things and rejoice. They rejoice exceedingly. Everyone speaks of how great a man is he. He has sailed all the seas in the big steamer-ships, and has written down the things he has seen. In America the people speak his name continually, so great a man is he; and he sleeps in the house of he who is king. Many presents come to him. When he goes in the steamer-ship to Beretami, King George Number Five sends to him the women of his house laden with yams and bananas and kava roots the thickness of a man's leg. The best house is made ready for him. Oh, I tell you he is a great man!

'And now he comes to Siria. He comes to make the people of Siria proud of his presence amongst them. And what do the people of Siria do when this great Turaga is with them?

'One man — a man named Musilami — seeks to beg his trousers!

'*To beg his trousers!*

'It is a great shame that has come to Siria indeed. For the Turaga will put it down in his books, which all people read, that a man in the village of Siria tried to beg his trousers!

'And in the papers which have pictures will be the village where this thing happened. Truly has this man Musilami brought shame to his village. For many people will read, my brothers, and they will see the pictures. And they will laugh and speak in scorn of Siria. In Suva and Levuka will they laugh and talk and mock. On the beaches of Samoa will the news be passed from mouth to mouth. And many will ask: "Who is this foolish man called Musilami who sought to beg the trousers of the great Turaga?" And others will ask: "What kind of place is this Siria that its people do things like this? Truly must they be ignorant people." And they will hear in Tahiti and in Lifu and in Tonga; and the singers will make new songs about the people of Siria. And the king of America will carry with him the book and the papers with the pictures that he may look often and laugh. And King George Number Five will ask that the Turaga tell with his lips the story of Musilami that he may hear with his own ears how a foolish man brought mockery on his village. Even now, before the news has gone forth, is my heart bowed and sore with the shame ——'

He was interrupted by Musilami approaching on his knees and begging that the Turaga be asked to forgive him. He had not really meant to ask for the trousers, he said; it was only that he had been over-anxious to show his deep respect for the great white man who honoured the village with his presence. He had admired the trousers and spoken so only that the Turaga might be pleased. Would the chief ask that the Turaga write not in the books of this foolishness of Musilami, who was so deeply sorry that his blood was as turned to water?

In keeping with my mythical importance I signified regally that the man was forgiven and the incident closed. Then Musilami smiled, the girls resumed their dancing, and the kava-cup started on its rounds once more.

And I, watching, concluded that in the matters of superstition, tradition and, above all, keen sensibility to scorn the man of the Palæolithic Wild and the man of the Civilized Wild were brothers all the while.

My Odyssey (1923)

1926

J. B. Murray in the United States

This extract takes us into another area of travel, that of the hobo and the tramp. Born in Melbourne, J. B. Murray (1907–), whose identification may well be a pseudonym, set off as a 19-year-old to join his married sister in California. Between 1926 and 1937, he worked at a variety of casual jobs from fruit picker to farmhand to salesman. He also met and married Iris, an English girl, and they returned to Australia. In American Trails *(1944) Murray recalled his travels and struggles to survive in the era of the Great Depression and the New Deal, of Hoover and Roosevelt. The book concludes with his reflections on America and the world during the Second World War, by which time Murray was in the AIF. He later retired to Queensland.*

Swinging along the highway on a bright sunny morning, I felt an almost gay sense of freedom, glad indeed to leave the city and head into the wide open spaces. The miles that lay ahead did not worry me those first few hours, and, anyway, a ride would be sure to come along sooner or later. That night found me sleeping in a shed close to a small town about twenty-eight miles from the city. I say sleeping. Actually, I lay on a pile of sacks shivering with the cold and battling with the rats, one brute chewing a piece of hair from behind my ear. By dawn I was stiff, cramped and dog tired, and set out for the town to get some breakfast. After buying a pair of heavy shoes in San Francisco and a few other essentials, I had about four dollars, which I intended to hang on to as long as possible. At a service station I washed, and had a shave in cold water, and feeling refreshed, proceeded on to a restaurant and enjoyed coffee and hot cakes.

By ten o'clock I began to look for rides. The cars swept by. The highway was never free of their roaring motors, but at mid-day I was still walking. The sun shone hot, and the dust mingled with the little rivulets of sweat that streamed down my body, until my clothing rasped like sandpaper. The new shoes were a deadly mistake, and by evening my feet were swollen and sore with blisters on the heels. That night I slept in a field, protected to some extent by armfuls of wild oats, which I made into a kind of covering. Early next morning a truck picked me up, and the driver, stopping at a town for breakfast, invited me to a most welcome meal of steaming hot coffee, a couple of eggs and hot cakes. I rode for about ninety miles, asleep most of the time, and when finally our roads divided, felt much revived. A week of this tramping found me with only a dollar left, and only one hundred and ninety miles from San Francisco. I must have presented a spectacle like the prize-winning scarecrow, and was even in the early stages of developing a beard, just that period of growth when a beard looks more like a dirty smear. At garages and service stations where I tried to get a wash, they waved me on. In the towns 'cops' eyed me with suspicion, and women detoured in a wide arc giving me the right of way undisputed (very unusual), while along the roads the cars honked and hooted, and farmers were hostile. In the past I'd heard stories of the free life on the open road. Some fools had even written songs about 'swinging along the broad highway.'

I met a number of tramps travelling north, and spoke with a few, who warned me that there was nothing in the way of work down south. The afternoon I spent my last nickel I met two guys going my way, and we joined forces. They laughed when I told them I was walking to Los Angeles, especially as one foot was so sore that I was limping badly. 'Look here, Bud,' said one of them, 'I guess you're plenty green, but we'll show you the ropes. To-night we can pick up a goods train for Bakersfield, just a little further from here, and from there on it's easy.' We soon came to a stream and found a good spot to rest under a bridge. Stripping off, we bathed in the cool water and washed our underwear and socks. Jim and Harry made coffee, and produced some canned beans. My foot was red raw across the heel, and Harry fished about and found some bacon fat, with which he bound it up with a strip torn from the tail of a shirt. The salt stung, but it felt better right away.

A couple of hours later, under cover of darkness, we took up a position alongside the railway track and waited for the freight. There was a grade here which would slow her up to about ten miles per hour. I was told to follow them when the time came, and swing myself up behind on to whatever car they considered we should 'grab', preferably a box car, if the door was not fastened. After a long wait we heard her coming, and presently the white beam of the headlight stabbed the darkness. We lay hidden from the glare, until the engine hissed and gasped its way past. I waited tense and ready to spring. 'Now!' cried Jim. Both of them swung themselves to the passing box car, but I stumbled and the next minute it had passed me. Determined not to be left, I made a frantic grab for the iron of a coal truck and the next moment was whisked off the ground, scrambling like a maniac to climb up the side and over. I made it, conscious that both arms felt as though they had been nearly pulled from their sockets. That train had been travelling faster than it appeared to be.

I soon discovered that a bed of coal is not so comfortable, and once the goods topped the rise and gathered speed the wind whistled by and cut like a knife. All that night I rode on top of the coal, absolutely numb with cold. Just before daylight I must have dozed off in spite of the discomfort, for suddenly I heard a tough voice demanding that I 'get the hell out of there.' Looking up, I beheld a railroad bull glaring at me. 'Come on there! Up you get, and jump pronto before I come and lift you off on the toe of my boot.' The train was doing about twenty or twenty-five as near as I could guess, and we were passing through some cultivated fields. 'I'll be killed,' I yelled back at him. We were entering a stretch of up-grade and began to slow a little. If only I could delay a few minutes, I thought, almost terror-stricken. 'Go on, you Goddam bum, or I'll let you have it!' Thoroughly alarmed by the menace in his voice, and not sure whether I could see a gun in his hand or not, I gritted my teeth and jumped. A sudden swift sensation of space, a sharp pain with a roaring in my ears, and then — blackness. The next I knew was that voices were murmuring somewhere, and then I felt water on my face. Opening my eyes, I was aware of lying on the ground, and there were Jim and Harry. No damage had been done fortunately. I had been lucky enough to miss a fence, and had landed in the midst of an alfalfa field. The crop was tall and the ground comparatively soft, so, apart from bruises, and having the wind knocked out of my sails, and from being as black as the ace of spades, as cold as an Eskimo, aching from head to foot, with a blinding headache, feeling giddy and miserable, apart from these things I was all right, and even able to grin a bit in appreciation of not having any broken bones.

Half a dozen others had been ejected further along the line. Two of them coming up to us, we all held a conference, from which it was disclosed that Bakersfield was within easy reach, and that a good 'jungles' was not far distant. One of our new friends fortunately had a water bottle, Jim having used all of ours in reviving me. A long drink and I felt well enough to accompany them to the jungles, so with Jim steadying me by holding my arm, off we went over the fields and on to the highway. We had traversed about half a mile when Harry, who had been carefully studying the fences as we went along, announced that we were in the vicinity of the jungles and must look out for a foot trail on the right side of the road. We found it a few hundred yards further, bearing away from the road toward a belt of timber a short distance ahead. He had been guided by signs not apparent to the casual observer, yet clear enough for the hobo to read easily.

The hobos, often known as the 'knights of the road', are travelling workers, roaming wherever fancy dictates, working their way in towns and cities, on farms and coastal ships, or riding the railroads. Among the ranks may be found all manner of men, from ordinary tramps to tradesmen, and even professional men. The business of living along the roads is often hazardous, calling for courage, resource and endurance. Camps are established all over the country, adjacent to towns and railroad junctions, under bridges, beside streams, or in any other sheltered place that may be suitable. These camps are known as 'jungles'.

The professional hobo sets a standard of achievement, ever pitting his wits against obstacles for the glory of overcoming them. Let it be noised about that some particular railroad is too dangerous to ride, and some hobo will ride it, in defiance of the hazards and the strong arm of the law, which has often been enforced by the companies to a ruthless extent. Hobos have been shot dead by the railroad 'bulls' or armed guards. The man who masters such a road, or runs the gauntlet of some hostile town, or crosses some great sandy waste land on foot, is one to be respected and emulated. His name becomes known far and wide, and everywhere hobos are anxious to meet him. These hobos have a *nom-de-plume* known as a 'moniker', such as 'Slim Jim', 'The Frisco Kid', or 'Society Slim'. This last is the moniker of a well-known writer and newspaper man, and may be seen cut into the woodwork of railroad sidings, on sign posts, water tanks, and in jungles throughout the United States; his moniker is derived from the fact that he was able to get professional jobs on newspapers and associate with 'the big shots' in the higher social circles.

Wherever the hobo goes he leaves behind him information in the form of signs, known to the initiated, who read them as unerringly as the Australian black tracker traces his quarry. Such information refers to the possibilities of some town, or railroad, or of some hazard to watch for, and other items of interest to the wanderer. He will cut his moniker into the wood as a signature, and state where he is heading from that spot; thus one may read, 'Slick Joe, Going north', together with the date.

The hobo is the aristocrat of tramps, and directly responsible in many instances for the development of far-back rural districts and towns, being a source of ever-available labour for the harvesting of crops and the building of towns. He is generally regarded with easy tolerance, and even a degree of affection, along the highways.

The term 'bum' is applied to the type of tramp who more or less lives on charity. He seldom gets very far away from the towns, usually being lazy and shiftless, although harmless enough, often being the victim of circumstance, and not entirely at fault.

The ordinary tramp is more on the order of the Australian 'swagman', and is known as a 'bindle-stiff': this on account of his carrying a bundle (bindle) or roll.

The 'yegg' is a term applied to the cheap crooks, who roam the countryside and indulge in robbery and other crimes. They keep to themselves, and have their own signs and methods of getting about, and are responsible for many of the charges and injustices brought against the hobos and legitimate tramps. They are the cause of the railroads taking such severe methods to suppress the practice of 'riding the rails'.

Girl hobos and tramps were never numerous, until the years of the depression filled the roads with hosts of people reduced to the status of tramps and bums, including women and children.

The track we were looking for was just discernible from the road, and I entered it in thankful anticipation of the rest and food that my friends assured me was now only a matter of a few minutes, for I was feeling sick and dizzy, and could not have made the remaining few yards without assistance. Entering the timber the welcome odour of coffee tingled the nostrils, and we came suddenly into a clearing well screened by shrubbery. About a dozen men occupied the jungles and were engaged in various chores. Several small fireplaces made of stones, with frying pans and cooking utensils made from tins, were round about. At one of these a man was boiling some clothes in a kerosene tin, while a couple of late-risers were cooking breakfast at another. It was from this fire that the aroma of coffee emanated and hung in the crisp morning air. One or two were not yet up, sleeping in their clothes on pallets of grass under an overhanging branch across which was draped a piece of linoleum for a roof. Old boxes and sticks cut from trees had been used for rough furniture, and on such a table against a tree was a wash-basin made from half a kerosene tin, together with a piece of soap and a comb. Above, hung a broken piece of mirror, and a towel, stained but clean, hung alongside. An array of washing draped the branches of another tree. A stream of water close by made this retreat a perfect jungles, a hobos' club, where all comers had an equal right to the comforts and the hospitality of the camp, with only one condition that whatever was used was returned to its place and left clean. Fires must be carefully extinguished, and where possible some contribution be made to the camp in the form of clothing, or another comb or looking glass, tins, boxes, magazines, papers, or anything else that might be of use. In this jungles we found everything necessary for our comfort, and appropriated a position near a fireplace.

The others nodded or spoke a word of welcome, and a little concern was displayed over my foot and general condition. The two who were having breakfast contributed some coffee and sugar, together with oatmeal, and a couple of eggs that were fresh enough not to have come from too great a distance [...]

After a good hot sponge I stretched out on a mattress of grass and fell fast asleep, not waking until about six in the evening, feeling refreshed and hungry. The appearance of the camp had changed. Some of our acquaintances had 'hit the trail', and several strangers had taken their places. All fires were going, and I spied Jim and Harry busy setting out the evening meal. A couple of men were playing cards, while another was busy darning a pair of socks. One chap was engaged on a piece of fancy work done in coloured silk on a frame. It turned out to be a table centre of pleasing design. He sold these in the towns along the way. The boys had washed all the clothing that I was not wearing, and this was now dry and ready to don. That night after supper we all gathered round the fire. Tobacco was divided up, and stories of varied experiences were exchanged, covering the whole of America and many other countries besides. Every subject under the sun was discussed, and the world economic situation gone into fluently, if sometimes stupidly yet at times intelligently, one or two showing quite a little knowledge and apparent education.

Soon a banjo was produced, and before long we were all singing happily, without a care in the world. A couple of latecomers produced half a gallon of wine, which was freely passed round. During all this time I had noticed a man remaining by himself, lying under a bush some distance away and asked about him. It appeared that he was a regular 'bum' and a spirit-drinker recovering from a bout. No one bothered about him. When finally he would ask for coffee he would not be refused, but the 'bo's' were not particularly interested in his welfare. He would be tolerated, and could use the camp, as long as he behaved himself.

Such were the jungles before the depression caused many of them to grow into large camps accommodating up to a hundred persons of both sexes.

Close to the towns jungle camps were often raided by the police and everything burned. The 'yegg' and habitual 'bum' provided the excuse for such action, which often had its genesis in a desire to keep the down-and-outer on his uppers as an easily exploited source of cheap labour for the local community.

Next morning Jim, Harry and myself were on the road early. The sun came up red, and soon the road ahead shimmered in the heat. The cars raced by, choking us in clouds of dust. We walked more slowly and rests became more frequent. A truck picked us up at last, and that night we camped at another jungles sixty odd miles on our way, and close to a town. The following few days were much the same. We enquired all along the road for jobs on the ranches without success, and at last reached Los Angeles without a cent, dirty and dispirited. I wondered why the blazes I had ever left Australia, and why I didn't return. That thought grew, and once I went to the British consul and asked for advice about getting a job on a ship bound for Sydney. I was treated civilly enough, in a cold, impersonal way, which made me feel that Australians were not particularly worthy of notice, and informed that working one's passage was no longer permitted. No, they were very sorry, but could offer no advice about employment, and suggested that I contact the Benevolent Society. I departed, feeling more alone and wretched than ever, and wandered about the streets, wondering what to do and gazing in the windows of the food shops. While engaged thus I ran into Jim. He and Harry were 'travelling south', and he tried to persuade me to go with them, but I had enough of the 'roads', and only wanted a job. A steady job. One that one could take an interest in and work up from. Some day I would want to get married, and have a home of my own, and from what I had seen, travelling the highways would lead nowhere. Jim gave me a dollar, explaining that he had a little luck 'shooting dice'. First a cup of coffee and a slice of pie, next a cheap haircut and shave, and then away to Pasadena to see if Bill's oil was gushing.

American Trails (1944)

1927

Nina Murdoch in Nice

Born in Melbourne and brought up in New South Wales, Nina Murdoch (1890–1976) was a journalist, novelist, travel and children's writer, and founder of the ABC's Argonauts' Club. Although married, she was an independent career woman who preferred to travel alone. Her first overseas trip in 1927 led to an obsession with travel and with Europe and resulted in her first travel book, Seventh Heaven: A Joyous Discovery of Europe *(1930). She was titillated by Europe from her first morning in France, and had the romance writer's capacity to maintain that sense of titillation throughout her work, producing an unusually readable example of the 'gushing' style of Australian travel writing. The book proved very popular, reaching its fifth edition by 1934. Murdoch's next trip to Europe in 1934–35 produced* She Travelled Alone in Spain *(1935). She returned from this trip via South America where she travelled down the Amazon river. Back in Europe in*

1936, Murdoch described her experiences and impressions in Tyrolean June: A Summer Holiday in Austrian Tyrol. *Her time in Austria alerted Murdoch to the dangers of Nazism. Her last travel book,* Vagrant in Summer: Holiday Memories of Nine European Towns, *was published in 1937. Leaving an Australia which she represented as isolated, provincial and starved of art and history, Murdoch records the rapturous impressions of a traveller who could find enchantment anywhere in Europe. She was thrilled by flirtatious and vivacious Latins, by gipsy dancing in Spain, by the folklore of the Austrian Tyrol and by the orderliness of Switzerland. On the other hand, she responded negatively to the unromantic: other tourists, the English masses, pampered dogs and anything Belgian.*

When I am old, and life has lost its savour, I shall be able still to shudder with delight, remembering that golden summer Sunday, when for the first time I stepped into the heart of Venice, and stood trembling and abashed before the miracle of beauty that is St Mark's. Though I grow blind with age, I shall see still the green and blue of Genoa's Gulf spread out in sunshine like a peacock's tail. I shall still gloat upon the beauty of Lugano — a dream lake painted by a magician on enchanted silk. And though the thunder of the gathering years bring deafness on me, I shall hear yet the triumphant music of the carillon at Bruges — O jubilant memory! — listen again to the Arcadian ecstasy of peasants singing full-voiced to a great harvest moon, between empurpled vineyards on Italian hills; and once more give ear to the sound of water rushing from five thousand fountains through the cypress groves of the Villa d'Este. For one must be old, old, old indeed to forget the wild sweetness of surprise, the rapture and the wonder of the first exodus from a new world to the old.

For my part, I was scarcely sane, I think, the year that I found Europe! — I had slipped, it seemed, into a fourth dimension where, disembodied and exalted, I flowed from one enchantment to another — sublimated and adoring, humble and triumphant together; not knowing whether I wanted most to laugh or weep, so intense was the satisfaction of making contact with the beauty and graciousness of an old civilization. Sometimes in Italy joy rose to such a pitch in me that it was only by the grace of God and early discipline that I did not career — a Maenad drunk with delight — screaming with ecstasy across the face of the Continent!

[...]

'Il fait beau ce matin pour ma'moiselle!' says the waiter as he puts my petit déjeuner beside the bed.

Sweet insinuation that the morning should make itself fine on my account! And 'ma'moiselle!' With the scratches of nine years' service on my wedding-ring!

He is gone, the sly flatterer, and so, having taken coffee and rolls that are like a lovely benison, I lie exquisitely at ease with but one thought singing through my mind. 'I am in France! On the Riviera! At Nice! It is my first day! I am in Fr … !'

This goes on for half an hour and it must now be half-past nine at least. Yet there has been no furtive trying of my door handle to see if the stay-abed is moving. In a British country I should feel just a little guilty lying so, and the morning flying away. But not here! And how complaisant is the bed! I muse upon the genius of Providence who invented sleep and fresh water; and consider how Continental people, though they do not appreciate the gift of water to drink, have improved on God's idea of rest! — I never met a bed in Europe but it was soothing as a lullaby. And I am one of those to whom the wrong pillow can mean torture. Indeed in Holland the beds were so marvellously comfortable that I grew enthusiastic to the point of dissecting one! And I found that under the head of the mattress (which was neither too little nor too much stuffed) there was a cushion — not stupidly round like our bolsters, but wedge-shaped, with the thick part of the wedge toward the top of the bed, and the rest sloping gently away till it came to a wafer's thickness somewhere under the shoulder blades.

But to return to Nice! It is ten o'clock, and springing out of bed, I make for the cabinet de toilette attached to my room. How the Continent comprehends comfort! Here is no pretentiousness, but solicitude wedded with common sense. The large porcelain basin has round it a broad ledge, so that one's towel popped down stays there, neither falling to the floor nor slipping into the water. There is a glass shelf over the basin for one's toilet things; and above that a large mirror. And in exactly the right position over that, an electric bulb placed so that a man can see to shave without cutting his lip, and a woman can make up without looking as if she had cut hers. The walls are tiled, the floor of parquetry; the supply of hot and cold water abundant. In the bedroom itself is a roomy wardrobe supplied with polished wooden coat-hangers. A light hangs from the centre of the ceiling, and above one's pillow is another for reading in bed. An armchair, a writing-table and a straight-backed chair complete the furnishing of the room, since the cabinet de toilette obviates the necessity for washstand and dressing-table.

I can think of nothing more comfortable than a room in a Continental second-class hotel, where one pays en pension about thirteen shillings a day, which includes the regulation ten per cent for tips.

I have had my bath, and am clad in a single stocking when there rises from beneath the little white balcony of my room, the light music of a guitar.

Enchanting!

I creep to the persiennes and try to peer down into the garden through the slats, but can see only one sunny board of the balcony floor. The guitar plays softly on; and now above it rises the warmth of a baritone voice, in a rich little song of love, swelling with passion and dying at last on a note of optimistic despair. I am still at my jalousie, the second stocking in my hand when the guitar sounds again, this time in a Spanish air, with the beat of the castanets in it. The voice rises gaily provocative. He is not perhaps a great singer, my unseen seren-ader, but he has the essentials — full tone, sure ear, and the air of singing for such pure joy that I am constrained to drop my other stock-ing and execute a Spanish pas seul — not as practised or as graceful as his song, but, I assure you, no less filled with joy.

He drifts into the Toreador's Song; then to more lyrics, till in the midst of one slyly sweet, the metallic discord of a church bell clangs across the music of the guitar, and reminds us both that it is Sunday.

How much more good I think this Provençal minstrel has made me feel than the Salvation Army band at home! Why, I ask myself, do we permit our Sunday mornings to be ruined with bad music? Because forsooth, the performers mean well? How British! The French are not so kind, but I am not sure that theirs is not the greater wisdom which refuses to tolerate a bad performance even for Jesuitical reasons.

With the church bell clanging across his joie de vivre, the singer gives vent dolorously to Gounod's *Ave Maria*. And I, who have now man-aged more than my stockings, fling open the shutters and look down over the balcony to find him thinnish, brown, black-moustached and clad in a seedy grey suit and boots that turn up like gondolas. One should not expect too much! I ought to have stayed behind my jalousie. Yet, when I drop a franc over the white wrought-iron railing of the balcony, it is acknowledged with such a superb sweep of the hat, that fancy sees him clad at once in velvet and silk, scented and beplumed — a gallant catching the rose from his mistress' bodice. (And the franc worth less than twopence!)

But that, you see, is the magic of the Latin temperament to which nothing is so dull or insignificant, but a gesture, a trifling embellish-ment, can transform it to a thing of romance and beauty and art. Here, lest the workaday horse should take himself too sadly, he moves to the music of a hundred tinkling harness bells. And the hire-carriage horses that go klip-klopping along the Promenade des Anglais and the Boule-vard Victor Hugo, wear nodding on their brows, scarlet and blue hus-sar mounts, coquettish crocheted caps, or fillets of gaily-coloured ribbon.

In Alsace I saw horses wearing with joyous abandon, what looked like little red flannel trousers on their ears. That was a darling sight; but even more treasured is the memory of a mule's face under a Dolly Varden straw tied down with rosy ribbons!

I like to think that some day, when the ice of our Northern ancestry has thawed beneath the Australian sun, that we too, flinging away our Saxon self-consciousness and dread of emotion and vivacity shall insist on colour, colour, colour and joy and graciousness. That we shall in the end be Latin in appearance and temperament, I have no doubt. — Our skies demand it! [...] How many hundred years I wonder, before our voices lose the raucousness and our manner the abrupt harshness of our youth? How long, how long, before we realize that sturdiness without grace is a barren thing and that beauty must be served as well as strength?

So I sit dreaming in the hotel garden among oleanders and palms, loquat-trees and heavy-headed dahlias, soaking in the soft air of the Riviera on which comes delicately the faint, faint scent of magnolia like the bouquet, elusive and disturbing, of a paradisaic wine. An aureate breeze from the lapis-lazuli of the Baie des Anges stirs the fringes of the great tawny table-umbrella under which I sit, and dapples the still dewy lawns with bubbles of light. And, sitting a table or two away, a Frenchman in a strawboater (they are almost de rigueur here in summer) never takes his eyes from me in the hope that I may be feeling flirtatious on such a delicious morning. The patience of these Latins! He sits gravely staring, but ever ready to relax in case, as I look up from writing, I should show the slightest brightening of my coldly British eye. Only when noon, the Continental lunch-hour strikes, does he give up hope.

And now at luncheon the waiter — groomed like a Michael Arlen hero on the eve of romantic adventure — pours my humble glass of water as if it were an oblation. He serves the hors d'oeuvre with solicitude; the soup with gentle melancholy; the fish with a protective air; the entrée with an ecstatic sigh; and the roast chicken with a gesture of tenderness. He languishes over the meringue and serves cherries with suppressed passion. And as I rise, he bends as if above some delicately-scented flower to murmur with touching anxiety '*Est-ce que ma'moiselle a bien mangé?*' Thus no doubt, her beauty-stricken slaves served Helen! And oh, the sense of well-being such charming service gives — to him as well as to me! For, like all his compatriots, he is an artist who demands from life form and colour and a flowing graciousness. And so perfect is the gesture with which he serves, that (whether he knows it or not) he goes en prince clad in dignity.

In any case, how much more amusing life is for him, who, however humbly placed, cultivates a technique instead of labouring constrained and dull like an ox harnessed to the plough!

Seventh Heaven (1930)

c. 1928

Eric Muspratt in India

Born in London, the son of a clergyman who gave up the cloth, Eric Muspratt (1899–1949) left school at the age of 9 and soon entered upon his life as a global itinerant. There was hardly a casual labouring job that he did not try in hope or desperation in some part of the world. He was the classic adventurer, writer and professional stowaway, handy with his fists, reckless with money, always vowing to settle down with the girl of his dreams, but womanising in the meantime. He acquired firsthand knowledge of prisons throughout the world. In this extract from The Journey Home *(1933), he has just escaped from detention in an Indian government workhouse. Muspratt served with the AIF in both world wars, eventually marrying and choosing to settle down in Victoria with his parents. In most of his writing, travel and autobiography were closely linked, as in* Fire of Youth: The Story of Forty-Five Years' Wandering *(1948). Muspratt was fanatical about fitness and physical culture, welcoming opportunities for bodily display. A portrait of the author wearing almost nothing, fists clenched and muscles rippling, appears in* The Journey Home. *Promoted by his publisher as the 'world's champion hobo', Muspratt's mobile life raises the question whether for some people movement itself is home. Muspratt died from an overdose of sleeping draught in Concord Repatriation Hospital, Sydney, after suffering an attack of pleurisy. Whether his death should be interpreted as suicide or a characteristically heroic attempt at self-medication, prompted by the desire to look his best for a female visitor, remains unclear.*

The glorious fact of my freedom took hold of me and filled the little fact of life that was I and made a universal kingdom of it. How much better it was to starve or to die in the pure self-will of freedom than to have every sense for ever satisfied without it. I walked along strongly through the shadowy unrealities of other people. They were all being left behind by the swinging strength of my legs. The night air met my naked arms and legs as they swung. My eager muscles drove me forward. They lifted me along so lightly but so irresistibly. My lungs swallowed the air and sent it bubbling through my blood. My heart swelled with strength and happiness. I had come to life, seen it and conquered it. It all belonged to me by a sense of boundless strength and happiness. I was king of everything because I had suddenly become a free pauper. Whoopee! Saha! Bueno! Tik hai! Waha! Karasho! Kalos! Skoal!

Howra Bridge was one of the greatest spectacles I have ever seen. The road goes out across the dirty waste of moving water which is the Hooghly. An unbroken procession of people, drab Indian figures, move along at each other's heels so that they seem to flow as smoothly and ceaselessly as the waters beneath them. Calcutta must have a greater pedestrian traffic than any other place in the world. This flood of people spills out across Howra Bridge in two thin streams, one going one way and one the other. So there are three main movements in this spectacle. The third is the water. And the water and the people are so strangely alike. There is an endless hum of voices, like a cloud of sound that floats away into the vast silence of the sky [...]

It always takes some hours of steady walking to get clear of the suburbs and surrounding townships of a great city. But my excitement carried me along quickly. I wanted to put as many miles as possible between me and the workhouse before my absence was discovered. The police would be on the look-out for me, and I was a conspicuous enough figure. I decided that it would be advisable to leave the main road at Chandernagore and take quieter roads to a big railway junction called Burdwan. There I could jump a train on the main line going to Patna on the Ganges. Then I should have to jump trains for the thousand miles or so to Bombay. I had done many thousands of miles on goods trains and had jumped a number of passenger trains, so this part of the plan was quite possible.

But my escape depended chiefly on this first walk. Burdwan was about a hundred miles away. I must get there as quickly as possible and hide myself on a train. So I determined to do a record walk. Unfortunately I had walked about Calcutta quite a lot on the day of my departure. But I had once done fifty miles in eighteen hours over rough country in the Rocky Mountains, and that walk had started at the end of a hard day's work. Also I had won a walking-race of six miles in fifty-six minutes. And now I felt that enough of my old strength had returned [...]

With a couple of short spells for a smoke, I walked on all night. A wonderfully soft and misty sunrise saw me padding along a lonely road. It was marvellous to be away from everybody while the sun was rising over the tree-tops and sending its first rays down to the dewy road at my feet. I looked eagerly around at the tropic vegetation of this Indian countryside. It was a brand-new experience to be walking the roads of India. The dawn and the sight of the open country gave me a fresh burst of energy. I walked on strongly for several hours, here and there passing a cluster of *bustees*, the native huts built of sticks, grass and leaves. Half-naked black families stared curiously at me. They seemed much nicer and friendlier than the city people.

As the sun climbed up higher, I became hot and tired and sleepy. So I decided to stop in a bigger village and refresh myself. In the middle of this village there was a big pool of water with shady trees by its banks. I went down some wide, stone steps leading into the water, took off my shoes and singlet and bathed in my shorts. Then I sat on the steps and ate my little parcel of food. This was the last of the workhouse diet, but already I missed the morning drink of tea. I forgot *bungla* quickly and easily, almost automatically, but I craved tea for days.

It was a great relief to sit on those cool steps by the water and the trees, refreshed by bathing and eating, and to smoke a cigarette. While I smoked, an Indian girl came down the steps with an armful of clothes for washing. She went about her job as unself-consciously as if she were quite alone. I lay on the steps within two yards of her, but I did not talk at all, preferring to contemplate her and to think. There was something very beautiful and peaceful in the scene. Her movements in washing the clothes had the swift and sure rhythm of long practice. Her female ancestors must have done this work in exactly the same way for so many generations that the movements of it had been bred into her. The folds of her sari fell gracefully about her strong and supple figure. The dark brown arms were beautiful in their bareness as they stretched and swung from the covered body. She tucked back the sari when it slipped and uncovered a breast as carelessly as a white woman would pat her hair. She seemed to take my presence as much for granted as that of the water. This pleased me very much. It made for a wonderful ease in one's own mind.

I had lingered long enough, so I gathered up my things, put on my singlet, shoes and hat, and left. We each smiled and said the one word 'good-bye.' It had been a very happy little rest. I had drunk two mugfuls of the water from the pool, so I felt good for the road again. I put enough Condy's crystals in the mug to make the water a light purple. By this simple precaution I hoped to avoid any of the diseases that are brought about by impure water. I should not have much choice in the matter of drinking-water, because already this country looked very dry in the open stretches between the patches of jungle. I walked along for some miles, feeling rather sleepy in the hot sun. It was a relief to leave the main road at Chandernagore. The danger of being seen by police-men was much less now. Several motor-cars had passed me on the main road, and I had hidden from them as much as possible. A white man tramping along with only shorts, singlet, hat, tennis-shoes and a bundle was quite remarkable enough to have the news of it spread about [...]

Towards nightfall my feet became very sore. The soles of my tennis-shoes had worn through with over fifty miles of walking. I put soap on my blisters, but the sharp stones in the road stuck into my feet. The drinking- and washing-places were few and far between now. I had seen nothing since a little creek before noon. As it was getting dark I came to a couple of huts beside the roadside, and decided to ask for water and to camp for the night. But the people were very unfriendly. They made no attempt to call off their dogs that yapped and growled around me. And they became enraged at my requests for water. I spoiled whatever chance I had with them by cursing spitefully at the lot of them. They must have had some religious prejudice against strangers, particularly against sharing their water. I passed on in great disgust [...]

There was a small clearing on one side of the road where the jungle receded a little. A few big trees stood out in this clear patch of ground. I sat down by the foot of one of these trees, took off my shoes and started to eat the remains of my chapatti. Afterwards I felt quite soothed and comfortable in smoking a *biri*. My peace of mind returned. There were various small noises from the jungle near by, but this clear ground around me helped my confidence. After all, the animals in this neighbourhood would probably be small. They would be afraid to attack me. I hoped so, anyway, and tried to put the fear of them out of my head. This would probably have been impossible but for a great sleepiness which was overcoming all my thoughts. I lay down by the roots of a tree and fell asleep with the *biri* in my fingers.

I had been told that jackals hunted in packs, sometimes led by a hyena. The hyena was a hideous brute with a big head and jaws. And a native had told me, as I walked out of Calcutta, that in his village a hyena had bitten a man's face off as he lay asleep. This had been one of my unpleasant thoughts. Another native had pointed out a place where, he said, a panther had taken a sleeping man. Apparently these beasts even entered villages and descended on people as they worked in their gardens. All these things had worried me when I found myself alone at night in this jungle. I did not want to die like a miserable coolie. There were so many things I wanted to do before death overtook me.

My sleep must have been very sound while it lasted, but the awakening was the most horrible I have ever had. An animal's snout snuffled in my face. I opened my eyes on it and felt its presence all over me. The story of the hyena flashed into my brain. Like a jack-in-the-box I let myself go in a terrific spasm. I punched, kicked and yelled all at once. My body shot into a convulsive movement which landed me on my hands and knees. I snarled and trembled in panicky ferocity. There had been a scurrying in the dust and I was alone staring into the darkness. In the violence of my horror I felt that my hands could tear flesh and break bones. I crouched tensely and looked into the darkness. There were a number of dark shapes about twenty feet away. They must have been jackals. I put my head close to the ground and saw several distinct figures of about the size of a big dog. Then I lit a match and started a *biri* in order to frighten them. I had my back to the tree and faced them. The light of my match had dazzled me for a moment, so that I could not see what they were doing. I was still all strung up, so I caught up my blanket and rushed forward, stamping the ground, waving the blanket and cursing. They had disappeared. I picked up a stick and walked about a little. There were no shadows left in the clearing. I was alone among the few big tree-trunks.

Suddenly it occurred to me that I had made enough noise in this place to attract the attention of any big animals there might be in the neighbourhood. So I bundled up my things and quickly walked away. All the fatigue was startled out of me now. I was painfully active and alert. I stepped briskly along in the middle of the track and listened hard for sounds from the jungle. I cursed myself for not having a weapon of any kind. And I longed to see the light of a house or hut.

That was a painfully unpleasant walk, and with another bad shock in store. I had travelled well away from the scene of my first scare, but was still speculating as to whether anything had followed me. There were small noises and rustlings in the darkness on either side, but big jungle animals could move very quietly. So I was in a way prepared for the worst. But the shock I got was paralysing. A deep, chesty snarl came from a little way in the jungle on my right-hand side. It was slightly behind me. My legs stopped walking and my feet held the ground in horror. My whole body stiffened, so that I could not move or even think. I was paralysed by the sudden horror of it. This was something far bigger and more ferocious than a jackal or hyena. When my brain started to work, instead of being suspended in awful expectancy, I thought of panthers, pumas, leopards and such beasts, flashing claws and jaws. There was nothing that I could think of doing. It was useless trying to run away and I could not fight this thing with my hands. It seemed that the snarl had been a preliminary to attack, that it would spring as I stood there petrified.

Suddenly the thought of fire occurred to me. I sprang to the grass and bushes at the side of the road, scrambled my matches and box in a heap in the grass and set fire to them. It went quickly once it had started. But there were awful long moments when I crouched down expecting the animal to land on my back. I scratched and snatched at grass and sticks. Now the animal would have to spring straight at the fire to get me. Every second counted in my favour as the fire blazed up and grew bigger. I grovelled for more twigs and grass and leaves in the light of the fire. As it grew I saw more and more and gathered them in. The dead leaves flared up quickly and the little twigs crackled. I reached out for bigger fuel and found dead branches. Soon there was a mass of smoke and crackling fire. Luckily I had built many hundreds of fires, and everything was dry. So, even in my panic, I built up that fire with the maximum speed and efficiency. Now I was standing up, being scorched by the heat as I snatched in sticks and branches and broke them into the fire. It was wonderful the way those flames rose up to help me. The smoke poured round in the darkness and, I reckoned, got into the eyes of that jungle beast. My fighting spirit was rising with the flames. I pranced about in the growing circle of light and sprang at more and more fuel. I dragged in several big, dead branches and stood close to the fire breaking them up, tearing off the smaller sticks and smashing the bigger ones on my knees. There was now a circle of about fifteen yards of good light and no animal in it. I seized a stick which was burning at one end and rushed about my circle of light, brandishing my torch with one hand and dragging in fuel with the other. It was a wonderful place for firewood. My fire was spreading among the leaves and bushes on one side and I was throwing on fuel from another. I became wildly exhilarated as it grew into a great, blazing fire. I must have worked for about half an hour to get it as big as it was in the end. I stood beside it to rest, sweating and panting, when there were six-inch logs burning.

It was a glorious feeling standing there and feeling that I was saved and that the battle was won. I snarled and spat and cursed at the darkness. I had long sticks thrust into the fire so that one end would be red and blazing, and I could use them to ward off an attacking animal. I could charge with one of these sticks as with a lance. I practised with a couple of them, running to the edge of my firelight and waving them round at the darkness. I actually enjoyed myself now, feeling quite safe. My hands were burnt and scratched and the sweat ran all over me. But I was glowing with strength and a wonderful, happy ferocity. I felt inexpressibly proud of myself — me and my fire. We had beaten off the beasts of the jungle. I talked a lot to myself. And I had actually had the great presence of mind to kick my bundle out into the road. I laughed loudly over this, knowing that it was pure accident.

I stopped my fire from spreading, and pushed the bigger logs together. Then I sat down to smoke a *biri* and to contemplate the brave adventurousness of my situation. I felt absurdly pleased and proud. I wished that I had seen the beast, or taken a stab at it with one of my fiery lances. Best of all would have been to have slaughtered it. I snuggled down on the warm earth, wrapped in the warm air and light. What a wonderful and beautiful thing fire can be. It can be warmth, protection and guidance. As a companion in cold, darkness and danger it can be better than the best human being in its comfort, assurance and cheer. I reflected for a long time on fire that night, and felt rather like a god in having created it so efficiently.

The Journey Home (1933)

c. 1930

Ambrose Pratt in Malaya

Born into a wealthy and cultivated medical family in Forbes, New South Wales, Ambrose Pratt (1874–1944) studied law and was admitted as a solicitor in the Supreme Court of New South Wales in 1897. He was unimpressed by legal life and joined a trading vessel to the South Seas in search of adventure, sailing for England soon after to pursue a literary career. He returned to Australia and joined the Age *in 1906. Pratt wrote over thirty novels, mostly with red-blooded themes and historical settings. He accompanied Prime Minister Andrew Fisher to South Africa for the opening of the Union Parliament and published his account of the trip as* The Real South Africa *in 1913. Pratt was enthusiatic about 'the Orient' (he had a Chinese amah as a child) and critical of the White Australia policy. He joined the staff of the* Industrial Australian and Mining Standard *in 1917 and travelled extensively in Southeast Asia. He had mining interests in Malaya and Siam (now Thailand), some of which are alluded to in* Magical Malaya *(1931), an unusually glowing account of Asian cultures whose cuisines he clearly relished. Food has always been a great test for the traveller: the ultimate way to open oneself to another culture is to actually eat it. For many Australian travellers foreign food was a great ordeal. For Pratt, it was a joy. The Order of the White Elephant was conferred upon Ambrose Pratt for services to the Siamese government. He died in Sydney.*

Show me a man who is not interested in 'good eats' and I shall show you a dyspeptic misanthrope. It does not abash me to confess an abiding fondness for palatable food. One of the richest treasures Malaya has to offer the healthy epicurean traveller is a profuse choice of strange, delectable dishes and a wide variety of fruits unknown in the Occident. One can get French cooking in all the cities, but I pity equally the chefs who are condemned to practise their fine art on canned and frozen meats and the unfortunates who condemn themselves to consume the products of so tragical a mésalliance. Earnestly do I advise every visitor to Malaya not to await the destruction of his digestion and the ruin of his appetite by sticking to the foods to which he is accustomed, but to 'go native' at the earliest moment after he lands. Courage is needed, but the rewards of intrepidity are very satisfying.

Beef, mutton, pork and lamb are eschewed by the indigenous population, not merely because they are costly and forbidden by religious law. Flesh meats are unsuitable to the climate and should be eaten sparingly if at all. The Malays and Siamese are very wise people. They live chiefly on rice, but they garnish their staple diet with fish and fowl and an abundance of tropical fruits. Their cooking is partly Chinese, partly Hindoo; sometimes a mixture of both. It is said of the Chinese that they have ten thousand ways of cooking rice. The Hindoos know how to make at least as many different sorts of curry. The cuisine of Malaya, therefore, is undisfigured by one suspicion of monotony. Approached in the right spirit every meal is an exciting voyage of discovery, every menu card a sign-post to thrilling and unpredictable adventures.

The traveller of real bravery absents himself from his hotel at tiffin time and eats out, preferably at Chinese restaurants, for at such resorts every kind of Oriental cooking is dispensed. The supreme purpose of Eastern cuisine is to marshal all the senses into an amiable co-operation to ensure a maximum assimilation of food and a minimum of bodily inconvenience in the process. Every ingredient of every genuine Malayan dish has a special mission to fulfil. The reason why every Oriental dish has numerous ingredients is that there are numerous organs of digestion. No digestive organ is ever neglected by an Eastern cook. This vegetable is flung into the pot to stimulate the pancreas, that to diminish or increase the flow of gastric juices. Here is a fungus that goads the colon; here another that regulates peristaltic action. This grated nut explosively affects the liver cells, and so on. Talk about our household chemistry and culinary science! These fellows have forgotten more than we shall ever learn. And what wonder? They were great cooks thousands of years before our ancestral Picts and Scots knew how to boil an egg. And they use in their everyday cooking scores of roots, mushrooms, herbs, fungi and vegetables of which our botanists have yet to learn the names. The knowledge of innumerable centuries is theirs and nobly do they use it. My mouth moistens as sweet recollections surge.

Numberless varieties of fish are almost everywhere obtainable. Most of the sea fish that are liked by the natives appeal strongly to the Western palate. The Malayan seas swarm with edible fish, and Siam is busily developing a big export industry. Game birds are plentiful in Northern

Siam, but in the Malay States one has to be content with snipe and pheasants. Peacocks infest the northern jungles, but they are rarely used as food, although they are not a sacred bird. The natives love them for their beauty too much to destroy them willingly. Chinese coolies eat anything in the way of meat, including snakes and the flesh of tigers. Deer roam the forests and fresh venison is often served in back country rest houses, but I did not like it. I tasted sladang once (wild ox) in North Siam, but it was cooked by a Kling who did not know his business, so I am giving sladang the benefit of the doubt.

Some of the indigenous fruits are wonderful. The best are the rambutan, the mangosteen, the lichee and the pomelo. The two former are not unlike in flavour, but resemble nothing else on earth, and they are as salutary as they are delicious. The durian is acclaimed by those who have acquired the taste for it as the king of fruits, and it is said to be a powerful aphrodisiac. All animals love it and it is often used as a bait for tigers. But it effectually protected itself from me with a perfume I found impossible to combat. It smells so urgently of prehistoric man imperfectly preserved in petrol that I was always forced to fly before its terrible approach. Lichees, however, are heavenly and they deserve all that Elia said of them.

Good English spirits and malted liquors and the finest vintages of France are obtainable at all the leading hotels; and spirits and wines of a more indifferent quality at every rest-house, shop and restaurant. The vast majority of Siamese and Malays, however, do not drink intoxicating beverages. They prefer tea and coffee and sweet bottled drinks. The most popular and certainly the healthiest tipple dispensed in Malaya is a squash composed of crushed fresh limes. Faintly tinctured with quinine and well sugared and iced, it is extremely palatable and refreshing. The consumption of ice is enormous. There is an ice factory in every town and the ice carts ply daily to every mine and plantation, and almost every native village.

It is the universal custom at least once a week to eat curry spiced with chile. These dishes are tremendously pungent and they bring tears to eyes of stone, but they are necessary. The climate of Malaya plays havoc with the hepatic cells, and experience has taught that the chile alone can be relied on to inhibit the disorders that attend congested livers. The chile curry is usually built upon a bed of either prawns or chickens' wings; and is thickly sown with bamboo shoots, soya sprouts and rice meal noodles. Mangosteens are usually served afterwards to soothe the tortured tongue and cool the blistered lips.

On waking of a morning it is the proper thing for Europeans to drink a cup of iced pineapple juice; then eat a slice of lime-sprinkled papaia and top off with a cup of unsweetened Chinese tea. To ward off the possibility of evening faintness (dinner is never served before 8.30) makan kichy, consisting of oubis (crisp chipped potatoes) and all manner of dainty native savories, are available in every hotel and in every home. One seems to be always eating or drinking or both in Malaya. Of course they do other things there; but I was sometimes tempted to wonder why. They have contrived to make the main business of life so very pleasant.

It is only in sweet-meats that the cooks of Malaya display a hesitating genius. They make legions of different kinds of comfits and pastries, but of all the scores I sampled I discovered one alone that I can affirm to be superlatively good. It was the simplest of the lot. 'Gula Malacca' it is called. It consists of a small shape of jellied sago that is served in a shallow bowl of nipa-palm syrup and deluged according to taste with the milk taken from a fresh young coconut. To eat this dainty is to forget one's troubles and to slide into a voluptuous dream of gastronomic joy. Lest my readers should mistakenly suppose my culinary lucubrations are self-revelant I shall bring this chapter to a close.

Magical Malaya (1931)

1933

Katharine Susannah Prichard in the Soviet Union

Born in Fiji, Katharine Susannah Prichard (1883–1969) had lived in Tasmania, Melbourne, Gippsland and outback New South Wales before she made her first trip to Europe in 1908 at the age of 25. As she noted in her autobiography, Child of the Hurricane *(1963), it was still not acceptable at that time for a young woman to travel alone. Her purpose in travelling to Britain was a common one among Australian writers, to establish her reputation, to make her name. This she did when her first novel,* The Pioneers, *won the colonial section of the Hodder & Stoughton novel competition. Not so common was her decision to return to Australia. She left again in 1912 to go to North America. Feeling ill at ease in New York, Prichard moved on to Britain where she spent the war years working as a journalist. She returned home in 1916 and in 1919 married war hero Hugo Throssell VC, whom she had met in England, and they moved to Western Australia. In the following year, Prichard became a founding member of the Australian Communist Party, which led to her touring Russia in 1933 as an officially sponsored guest, a participant in the political pilgrimage undertaken by so many*

Western intellectuals of the day. Prichard's account of her travels abounds in enthusiasm and admiration for life and work in the Soviet Union, but Betty Roland, with whom she stayed in Russia, recalls a Prichard who was more disillusioned. If Prichard seems uncritical, we need to remember the background of the Depression in Australia and the fact that the only alternative at the time to uncritical admiration of the Soviet Union was an equally blinkered condemnation. While Prichard was abroad, Hugo Throssell committed suicide, a tragedy that must have had an impact on the way she chose to represent her time in Russia.

In my wanderings through Soviet Russia and Siberia, I travelled something like thirty thousand miles. From the villages about Moscow and Leningrad to the Ukraine, the Kuban, the North Caucasus, through the Mordva, Baskir, Chuvash and Tartar Republics to Western Siberia and the Altai Mountains.

I want to write about them in splashes of colour, gouts of phrases as Walt Whitman would have, or Mayakovski: paint them after the manner of the French symbolists, images seething and swarming over each other, as they lie in my mind.

'The shapes arise.'

Ancient buildings of dead beauty, slums of the middle ages, sullen rivers, dark pine forests, pink and white churches with gilded domes, wild waste places, ragged mountain ranges under perpetual snow, fretted scaffoldings stretching above them: new cities of glass and steel, dove-grey concrete, crowding in on them: a black mouldering village beside its striped fields: harvest fields flooded with sunshine, a kolkhoz (collective farm) village of new pine logs in a forest of golden birches.

Novosibirsk from the air, the great theatre in a diagram of widespread suburbs, the Obi river winding away into the Arctic; the aerodrome, its fleet of grey Soviet-made planes sunning themselves on a frosty morning, airmen in black leathern uniforms pointing the way to Australia over the mountains of Central Asia.

Peasant markets and lumber camps, big square old-fashioned wooden houses, laced with icicles, splendid horses, the grey Orlovka and sturdy Tartar ponies — Red Army soldiers in long blanket coats bestriding them and galloping away into the distance. Blast furnaces pouring their golden syrup of iron into huge cauldrons heaped with snow: the fiery slag, fuming and casting a rosy glow on peaks of the Altai.

A panorama of cabbages, blue sky, and Ukrainian women stooping over them in bright skirts and red kerchiefs. Fields of sunflowers, more cabbages, acres of beetroot and potatoes, bean fields, harvest fields, shorn harvest fields, fields green with springing wheat going right up to the blue-dark wedge of the steppe. Kazan and the Volga. Zvenigoret, where Techekov lived and wrote, and the barbarous monastery of Zagorsk.

Flower-decked factories and foundries, machines garlanded for opening of a new wing: sanatoria and school kitchens. Theatres packed to the doors with men and women from the factories and workshops, symphony orchestra concerts in the open air: Tchaikovsky's 'Eugene Onegin' at the Grand Opera House in Moscow, a group of udarnik peasants in the Royal Box.

A conference of children in Siberia, Komsomols demonstrating in the rain, hundreds of thousands of them — young men and women of the Young Communist League — streaming through the twilight streets, ten and twelve deep, their bands playing, scarlet banners flying. Celebrations of November 7, on the Red Square in Moscow, snow falling, diplomatic representatives of all the powers of Europe standing with their hats raised for nearly a quarter of an hour, while the guns of the Kremlin boomed and massed bands played the Internationale.

Yarns recur — yarns with trappers and hunters from 'the frozen North' — yarns about reindeer, wolves, polar bears and sable, yarns with Itin who wrote 'Commercial Routes of the Soviet Arctic,' and other poems: with a Shortsi mother whose log cabin was decorated with collective farm slogans and whose baby lay in a cradle swung from its father's hunting bow, while the grandmother sat at a spinning wheel, making thread from a heap of dingy wool and crooning a song as old as the hills. Yarns with a Tele-ut patriarch, once the only man in his village who could write, now proud of his twelve-year-old grand-daughter, in the sixth grade at school, who can tell him how the moon and the stars were made, and about all the strange peoples of the earth.

[...]

I did not want to be a tourist in Russia; to have it said that I had made a 'conducted tour,' 'saw only what the Soviet Government wanted me to see.'

The criticism is sometimes made that people who visit the Russian Socialist Federated Soviet Republics under the auspices of the Intourist Agency are not free to go about as they wish. But all the tourists I spoke to, said that this was not so. They made their own programmes, used the Intourist guides, interpreters and cars when they wished, and filled in the rest of their days as the spirit moved them.

In any foreign country, on account of differences of language and currency, strangers find it convenient to travel with Cooks, The Polytechnic, or some other organization; so visitors to the Soviet Union, in order to get about easily and make the most of their time, agree that it is decidedly an advantage to travel Intourist.

There is no difficulty, in ordinary circumstances, about making a visit to the Soviet Union. It is no longer considered a great adventure even. The ships I travelled to and from Leningrad on were filled with tourists from all parts of the world, and it is certainly less costly to travel Intourist. On the 'Co-operatzia,' I heard two frugal Yorkshiremen, whose political opinions were those of the time of Queen Anne, say that they 'had never spent so cheap a holiday as they had in the Soviet Union.'

As for me, taking my own wilful way, I roamed about by myself, during my first days in Moscow. Nobody suggested what I should do; where I should go. I just arrived, and proceeded, as I have done in London, Paris, New York, Melbourne or Sydney — but feeling rather a motherless foal, so dazzled and bewildered by the beauty and strangeness of everything.

Moscow, the old city, with the Kremlin, its red walls, white palaces, gilded domes, reflected in the river, the new city spreading out from them with its green parks, flower-bordered boulevards, austere blocks of workers' flats — looked like an aged courtesan beloved by a peasant lad, so the virility of youth, a vigorous vitality was permeating its mediaeval veins.

How stupid and dazed you can feel, though, in an unknown city whose script is a fantasia of obtruse symbols, and where nobody seems to understand the carefully prepared questions you hurl at them from a phrase book. I had studied Russian, however, and when my ear was tuned-in, managed with odds and ends of French and German, to find friends and a room with them in a working-class quarter.

It was just what I had been hoping for — an eyrie from which I could watch the every-day life of the people. And so I saw children going to school in the square below. Squads of them, sturdy, well-fed, neatly clad boys and girls gathering at 8 o'clock in the morning to do physical exercises, with a child as leader of each group, and then running off into the school, a lovely building with a facade of white nymphs on yellow ochre walls and a columned portico.

I saw many schools in Russia and Siberia. Some of them, the finest I have ever seen. But this one was particularly interesting because there, in a quarter where in Tzarist days the children would have been ill-fed, verminous and uneducated, they had this model of a Greek temple to learn in. Among the surrounding blocks of workers' flats were still the cobbled courtyards, mouldering arches and rotting wooden houses of that time; but the villa a prince had built to hide a favourite mistress in, had become a school. Renovated and preserved, elegant and pagan, it was serving the gods of new Russia as it had done the gods of old.

In the square, too, was a garden with benches and tables workers of the surrounding flats had made as their contribution to what is known as the 'greening' of Moscow. There in the afternoon, women sat with their sewing and knitting, toddlers played on a sand-patch. In the summer evenings, men spread their chess and draughts boards on the little tables, or played cards; little girls practised the peasant dances, and lads sang folk songs and songs of the revolution to the tunes they churned out of their big accordeons.

All the women in Russia do not work in factories and business offices, as is generally imagined. Many with young families stay at home to mind their children as women do in other parts of the world. The only difference is that women who have specialized in any particular work, and wish to go on with it, may do so, after marriage as before. Nurseries and kindergartens attached to the big factories, and situated at convenient points throughout the cities, make it possible for them to. I knew teachers, doctors, writers, as well as factory workers and women in charge of public departments who took their children to a nursery or kindergarten in the morning and brought them home again in the afternoon.

[…]

The happiest folk I met in Russia or Siberia were the collective farmers, men and women. They were rejoicing after a record harvest and busy with plans for the next season's sowing, more machinery, new houses, improvements to schools and clubs, winter courses of agricultural study for their udarniks (best workers) and brigadiers, the leaders of field brigades […]

It was late in the afternoon when we reached Ulitena, where four villages have united in a kolkhoz not of an advanced type, but boasting two banners won for development of its agricultural and industrial resources.

Large log-built houses with carved and painted window frames, on either side of the wide grassy street, hens, chickens, and a flock of geese strutting across it, this was Ulitena. Every house had a garden with bushes of lilac and syringa before it. Hollyhocks and sunflowers bloomed beside them: at the end of the street, a light graceful tree leaned out, spraying the pale blue sky with scarlet berries.

A crowd of peasants collected to know who we were: where we came from. The chairman of the kolkhoz and secretary of the Communist Party for the district were summoned. They greeted us cordially, and took us to the house of Marya Ivanovna Romanowa, near by.

Bare-legged, as she came from hay-making, a faded coloured apron caught up over her full grey skirt, a flowered handkerchief tied round her head, Marya set out her cups and saucers, and prepared a meal. A serious, dark-eyed woman, tough, sinewy and weather-tanned, we had a strange affection for each other the moment we met: became friends for life.

Soon the samovar was steaming, tea made: bread and butter, honey and eggs spread out. Marya asked me to stay with her while I was in the village: and I lived for three days in her big house lined with golden pine. A cow, calf and hens were stowed away in plenty of straw, in a barn attached to the rear; but Romanowa's house and the barn were so clean and scrupulously kept that they smelt only of new-mown hay, resinous pine wood, and big bunches of birch leaves she had hung from the rafters.

Luria exclaimed to see the ikons, small old oil paintings of the Madonna and saints set in tarnished gilt, still on a shelf in the sitting-room, white crocheted mats spread beneath them. Marya said they had belonged to her family for generations and she liked to keep them, just as she liked to have flowers in her window boxes. Geraniums and fuchsias made a gay border to the carved white frames of her windows and outside, a thicket of lilacs tempted imagination of what they must look like in the spring.

The Real Russia (1934)

1935

Jack Hides in Papua

Born in Port Moresby, Jack Hides (1906–38) joined the Papuan Public Service in 1925, becoming a patrol officer in 1928. In 1935 he led without radio or aerial support an expedition into the region between the Strickland and Purari rivers, the last significant portion of Papua to be explored by Europeans. His account in Papuan Wonderland *(1936) records the first white contact with the 'lost tribes' of the densely populated Tari basin, and his expectation that Australia would be the bearer of civilisation there. The expedition, which lasted six months and comprised a patrol officer, eight police and twenty-eight carriers, was involved in at least nine skirmishes, during which some thirty-two tribesmen were killed. One carrier and a police constable died of exposure and exhaustion. Hides was later to be widely criticised for the bloodshed, which took some of the gloss off his reputation as a handsome and dashing young explorer. He died in Sydney at the age of 32 of pneumonia contracted in Papua. The four books that Hides based on his New Guinea experiences,* Through Wildest Papua *(1935),* Papuan Wonderland, Savages in Serge *(1938) and* Beyond the Kubea *(1939) are a combination of adventure fiction, travel description and ethnographic studies.*

We cut a track up the remaining two thousand feet of Landslide Mountain, and reaching the summit, advanced along it for some distance westward; then, towards late afternoon, we came on to a spur leading gently down northwards and followed it. The final crossing of this mountain had taken ten hours, and by this time the carriers were spent men. The weeks of incessant toil and the short rations of poor food were now telling on them severely.

But we all went on eagerly down this spur, thinking of what lay ahead, when quite suddenly, at a spot where a large tree had recently fallen, we came to a break in the forest. And as we looked excitedly northwards, O'Malley and myself stood spellbound gazing at a scene of wild and lonely splendour.

Below us, on the opposite side of the Ryan, a large lake lay on a platform of the divide, while the Ryan itself was seen to emerge from a deep gorge about two miles to the northwards; and beyond the gorge, gold and green, reaching as far as the eye could see, lay the rolling timbered slopes and grasslands of a huge valley system. On every slope were cultivated squares, while little columns of smoke rising in the still air revealed to us the homes of the people of this land. I had never seen anything more beautiful. Beyond all stood the heights of some mighty mountain chain that sparkled in places with the colours of the setting sun. As I looked on those green cultivated squares of such mathematical exactness, I thought of wheatfields, or the industrious areas of a colony of Chinese. Here was a population such as I had sometimes dreamed of finding.

The carriers and police came along to gaze in amazement on this wonderland; it meant food and life to them all.

'My mother,' said Sergeant Orai. 'People like the sand. They have plantations. What people are they?'

'Maybe Chinaman?' said another of the police.

I only heard one of the carriers speak, and that was to ask in a querulous voice: 'What if they are bad-tempered?'

And Dekadua told him, with the greatest assurance: 'Well what? We are ten.'

We made our camp a little below the view, and O'Malley and I talked until late upon our discovery. I had taken observations, and I found that the border of the two territories still lay some distance to the northward. These people and this wonderland belonged to Papua. This fact gave me the greatest satisfaction.

We were away at daylight next morning, cutting on down that spur to the northwards, and some time about noon, with great relief, we emerged from the forest on to a large cultivated area of sweet potatoes.

We found ourselves in a pretty canyon three to four miles in diameter, and surrounded by steep mountain walls of sandstone. The whole floor of the little canyon was under cultivation, while the stream that watered it flowed into a lake on the lip of a precipice, and then tumbled in a 1500-foot drop to the main river in the eastward.

Set apart all over the flats below us, and generally one dwelling to every two or three of the cultivated areas, were the homes of these people. They were like little farmhouses, oblong in shape and built low to the ground, while surrounding them all were straight hedges of coloured croton and hibiscus. A pretty sight; indeed, an unforgettable sight.

Some of the inhabitants were in the fields below, and on calling to them, a number of short, stockily built men, all carrying bows and arrows, appeared not more than a hundred to a hundred and fifty yards away. They looked at us queerly, with their heads to one side, and appeared to be whispering excitedly amongst themselves; then they started to call in pretty, yodelling tones, and soon we saw women and children hurrying away across the fields towards the top of the canyon.

The men stayed, however, and for more than an hour we endeavoured to induce them to approach us; but they appeared afraid, turning every now and then to bolt like wild horses when we approached any closer, or when there was a movement in the party. O'Malley and myself showed them axes, and tried to make them understand that we were hungry and wanted food. They pulled up potato vines, smacked their abdomens, and indicated that we might take all we required; but still they would not approach us.

We made our camp at one end of the cultivation, for there was no other convenient place to stretch our rotten canvas. With the limestone behind us, we were now enjoying fine weather, and, luckily for us, I afterwards learned that we had entered this country in the dry season, because in the wet months conditions are particularly unpleasant. We took what food we wanted, and filled ourselves to contentment, with the men watching us from below all the while. The yield of the potatoes, and their excellent quality, was extraordinary; the soil was as loose as sand, and the inhabitants appeared to till the ground in a manner peculiarly their own. The whole of the cultivated area had been dug up by some primitive means, the vine roots of the potato being placed in square plots or terraces.

Towards evening three men approached to within a hundred yards, and waving their arms to us several times, indicated that we must go back whence we came. When I showed them a bright steel tomahawk, called in friendly tones, and indicated they come up to us, they shook their heads vigorously.

We watched them slowly disappear across the cultivated fields, and listened in wonder to their pretty yodelling as they went.

As the sun went down over the sandstone walls that evening, and the shadows started to creep across the canyon, O'Malley and I sat on the edge of a terrace outside our tent ravenously eating baked potatoes and juicy bundles of spinach and native asparagus. It was wonderful to taste green vegetables again, to feel that our appetite could be satisfied, and to know that for some time ahead there was easy country and the security of food.

I looked across the canyon, but there were none of the inhabitants about now, and the spirals of smoke rising from the little farmhouses told me their women were preparing the evening meal. I set to wondering about these new people, their extraordinary methods of cultivation, and this valley wonderland of yodelling natives who lived in farmhouses. Whence had they come? and for how long had they lived in this forgotten world of theirs? Perhaps they had been here before Hannibal crossed the Alps? or even before corn was discovered in Egypt? for we are told that the migratory whirls that populated the Pacific date back many thousands of years.

But what did the people in the little farmhouses think of us? I pictured the males gathering in certain of the houses below; I saw them eating and talking excitedly, and asking one another what was to be done with the strange devils above. Should they fight, or should they leave well alone? They would be superstitious; they would fear us, for we were something they could not understand; and to-morrow they would probably come and find out more. I went to my dirty blanket that night and slept comfortably for the first time in many days.

The next morning the carriers lay on the ground in the sun, too full of food to walk comfortably about. They all complained of headaches, and it was as well that we were not to move off that day. I wanted to establish friendly relations with these people, for in view of the population ahead on our path, it was necessary that there should be no trouble, no misunderstanding with the first of them.

Not long after sunrise, six men, all unarmed, slowly approached the camp. As they came, they stooped to pick up potato vines, and pointing to their abdomens, kept calling 'Tomo Tomo'; and when we did likewise, they indicated that we take as many potatoes as we wanted.

These six men were presently joined by others, and about thirty of them were induced to come right into camp. They stood warily off us, not daring to allow us to touch them with a friendly hand. I was astounded at their appearance. They were all of short stature, they were clean and light skinned, and they had girlish mops of brown hair adorned with flowers. Three or four had rosettes of bachelor buttons; others had bands of eidelweiss across their foreheads; some had parrot feathers; while all of them had bone daggers stuck in the cane girdles around their waists. A knitted sporan, tucked between the cane girdles, was all the covering they had. I was greatly interested in their Asiatic-like features; their cheek bones were high, and their noses and lips were all finely moulded.

For some time they looked queerly at us; then when I managed to get close enough to one of them, and patted him in an assuring manner, they all became graciously friendly, cutting us bunches of bananas with their bone daggers and indicating that we eat to our hearts' content.

[...]

For days upon days we marched across this valley system, northwards and eastwards over the great rolling slopes, always getting higher and higher as we climbed the eastern country. We travelled along wide roads, past farmhouses and cultivations, with guides ever ready to show us the way.

It was beautiful country, and appeared to be extremely fertile. Even the police talked about what wonderful taro and sugar-cane would grow here. As we would come to the end of each farm section, the guides would always leave us to be replaced by others from the new section. At the end of each section, too, the road passed under an arch made of long wooden slabs pointed at the end, as in a picket fence; while on both sides of the road, and marking off the farm areas, ran long contour drains eight to ten feet in depth. It made me wonder who had taught these people their excellent methods of husbandry, their system of splitting timber for building, and their burial practices. And as I stood in their great fields of potato, it made me realize just what corn would do for them. They grew potato, spinach, banana and sugar-cane, and a native asparagus; and unlike other Papuans, who plant their gardens haphazardly, these orderly folk set out their cultivated areas in neat terraces. They bred pigs in large numbers, and housed them in proper pens.

When the harvest had been taken from an area, the pigs were driven into it and allowed to grub about in the stubble for several days. Then they were transferred elsewhere, and a curious type of cane grass was planted. When this had grown to a desired height, it was cut down, burnt, and turned into the ground. After a short time another crop of potatoes was put into the soil. To us, who were conversant with the rather lackadaisical farming methods of the average Papuan, it was an amazing sight to see this primitive race of people employing a procedure of husbandry that is only of comparatively recent introduction in civilized countries. These people were not Papuans as we knew them. As I have already said, they had no villages; each family seemed to have its dwelling on the particular cultivation of the farm section to which it belonged. Burial was in the open, the bodies being placed in small coffins of wood and rested above enclosures formed like the picket fence of the sections. The coffins had painted characters in red, yellow and black, and most of them were in clusters at the corners of the farm sections.

When we came to rest in their parks of casuarina and poplar, these pretty light-skinned men would make us sit down. They would give us their leaf tobacco to smoke, cultivated and cured by themselves; they would give us sugar-cane to quench our thirst; and before we went on, our hosts would sometimes take out their Pan-pipes from the net bags that every man carried and play us tunes of a forgotten age.

As we camped on a high tableland one day, many miles to the eastward of the point where we entered the valley, a wide area of country lay spread out before us to south, west and north. The valley of the Tarifuroro was a wonderful sight, its broad slopes reaching far away from the river and extending on and on, west and north-west, with cultivations on every slope.

To the north-west, about twenty-five miles distant stood a high cone-shaped mountain, the highest I had seen in all Papua. It was a glorious monument, and its glistening summit seemed to beckon to us with pride. We named it Mt Jubilee, in commemoration of King George's Silver Jubilee. The two main sources of the Tarifuroro appeared to lie north-west and north-east of this majestic peak, and from the two broad valleys thus formed on both sides of it the Tarifuroro came down between valley slopes fifteen to twenty-five miles wide. It then carried on south, drawing to it the waters of numerous small streams of the cultivated lands, and then this mighty mountain river could be seen sweeping south-east to thunder through a deep limestone gorge of the barrier, and from there out on to the plains of the great plateau. I had no doubt now that it was the Kikori. Its connecting course south and east of the Leonard Murray Mountains, and the highest point reached by the Staniforth-Smith expedition, could only be imagined.

As I gazed on this fertile valley, this wonderland where practically any crop will grow, the question of the future of these people occurred strongly to me, and I wondered whether the introduction to civilization would make them any happier than they appeared to be when we first came in contact with them.

[...]

Thus we went on south-eastwards. We travelled along wide roads with hundreds of natives to watch our passing. Crowds of curious women and old men with sticks stood by the sides of the road, or followed at the rear. Our hats were of great interest to them, and as we walked along O'Malley and I continually raised them for the benefit of the sightseers. We frequently met new people, and always it was the same questioning gesture: 'Where are you going?' And always we waved our arms down the length of this densely populated valley. For five days we travelled through friendly people, but late in the afternoon of the fifth day we arrived among a new section of people. I did not like the shifty looks of some of the men, while an evil-looking chief particularly came under my notice. None of them would answer our appeals for food, and the forced friendliness of this scoundrelly old chief, who thought we concealed pearl shell in the tin box of medicines that we carried, could not be mistaken. With over two hundred men in the park as we made camp that evening, their intention to massacre the whole lot of us with their stone battle-axes, which every man at that time held in his hands, was most obvious.

[...]

Morning came with a cloudless sky, and the sun over the mountains in the east to make the heavy dew sparkle in the grass of the park. With hungry stomachs life seemed hard indeed. Three men, carrying unstrung bows and bundles of arrows, came in to lead us as we prepared to move off. I asked them again for food, but they explained that we would get it at some place farther on. I knew that they were up to something, but we had nothing else to do but follow them.

We crossed a grass basin covered with snow-white balsam and heliotrope stock — a pretty sight — and followed the guides to some small limestone pinnacles two to three miles distant from the park where we had rested for the night. Through a gap in these pinnacles, and extending south-eastwards, we could see another valley system, a tableland of hollows and mounds, all covered with grass and cultivations. The three natives pointed to it, and called the country the Wen.

A large crowd of men now began to appear at our rear. Some of them trailed their bows behind them. Whenever they saw us look back, they would drop their weapons and stand with arms akimbo. Others carried their arms covered with green pandanus leaves, or hidden in bundles of sugar-cane.

A terrific din of yodelling was going on all the time, in front as well as in the rear; but apart from watching the men carefully, we made no sign.

Climbing to the top of the gap, where one track led up both ways of the saddle, and the other down into the south-east, we found about twenty unarmed men ready to receive us. Their friendliness was overdone — obviously forced — but I did all I could to show that we neither feared them nor anything they could do. We followed closely their every move. I took photographs of them, and explained that our way was down the valley of the Wen; they in turn told me that they were of the Injigale people, and the place where we now stood was called Bangalbe. I knew what they were up to, and I wanted to ask them why they wanted to kill us, and to explain that our rifles were not things to be despised; but some of those smirking, self-possessed faces would have taken a lot of convincing.

While all this was going on, a man appeared on the saddle about twenty yards away above us, and with an impatient, plain gesture told the unarmed natives with us that they were to move the patrol on down the track. With that he disappeared down a side-track, and the men to whom we had been talking now nervously urged us to be on our way. The yodelling on the by-tracks had ceased, and we were told there would be no guides, that the people were going back. This was an obvious lie; how cheaply they took us! I turned to Sergeant Orai standing by me. His beard was black and fuzzy, his uniform torn and dirty with a hundred and fifty days of breaking across as many miles of mountains, and in the haggard and worn face of this great Papuan was a grim coolness. I did not speak to him, but he uttered my thoughts.

'It is here that we find it, Taubada,' he said.

I ordered all the police to load their carbines, and getting the carriers bunched closely together, we went down into the timber following the track south-eastwards. Of the four police in front, two watched the right-hand side of the track and two the left side.

We had not gone more than two hundred yards when a terrific din of yodelling arose on all sides of us, and the whole line was attacked. It all happened with remarkable suddenness, but every man was ready for them, and Borege was the only one to take an arrow. I fired in front of me and at the back of me, at men not fifteen feet away, rushing with short stabbing spears. The poor carriers got new strength; they yelled and screamed and threw their steel tomahawks at the attacking natives. To give some idea of how these people regarded us, and how closely they attacked, Constable Budua, rushed at close quarters by spearmen, started swinging his rifle instead of firing. He was pulled to the ground, a man with a battle-axe on top of him; and had I not heard Budua's call for help, and seen the incident, he would have been killed by two other natives assisting his assailant. I shot one of them as I rushed to Budua's assistance, and, pulling his assailant off him, after hitting him with the butt of my rifle, allowed him to run off. The struggle was over by then; it had only lasted about fifteen seconds. The thunder of the rifles had brought silence in the country around us, and we walked out of the timber into cultivations again.

Our attackers came to meet us with presents of food. They stood and offered the bunches of bananas and bundles of spinach; but the food was thrown back at them, and I explained that we did not take presents from people who tried to murder us; and further, that when we were ready for the food, we would take it. They stood like down-hearted schoolboys, and for all their treachery, my heart went out to them. So that when a little later about twenty venerable old men met us, and with great difficulty and care explained by gestures that this was not the section that had attacked us, I pretended to believe their story. At the same time I told them that we would now take the food we wanted.

Their answering gestures could have been read as: 'Go to it, old man.'

We killed two pigs in a pen nearby, dug what potatoes we wanted, and then handed the old men axes, which they all smilingly accepted. Then with large fires going, and food cooking, we gorged ourselves to contentment.

The attitude of these people was extraordinary. Within an hour or so of the attack, fully three hundred men, all of them genuinely friendly, were sitting around the party; and it would have been indelicate, I thought, to have even suggested to them that only a short time before we had been fighting with them. They seemed to treat a fight like a football match. They could be treacherous, but they could also be gentlemen.

That night we slept contentedly in one of their parks, with the natives sleeping in the farmhouses within a hundred yards of the camp, and the next morning at daylight we were on our way following a good road down the western side of the Wen plateau. I could see contour drains cutting across every acre of country. At first I believed that they were for irrigation, but now I could see that they were to prevent erosion of the soil, for in many places in this Wen country I could see sections of the drains supported with timber to keep the soil in place.

We now had plenty of guides, and as we proceeded on hundreds of men came to join our party from all points, all of them unarmed, and those not carrying presents of food were walking uprightly and with their arms folded. It was all so pleasant; women could be seen in the green potato fields, and little boys ran with the party. How we wished it would continue always. There was no hooting or yodelling now, no derisive laughter to follow stumbling police and carriers: the people were genuinely friendly, courteous and respectful. And our party were equally courteous and respectful, and considerate of the smallest detail. Not even a potato leaf was taken without the asking, no road was followed without invitation, and presents of steel were exchanged for food. As we rested at one point, I heard Sergeant Orai addressing his police and carriers.

'You must forget the fight,' he said. 'You must remember that this is not your mother's country, that it belongs to these people; and you must not forget to treat these people as you were treated yourselves when the Government first came to your village.'

It was the finest thing I had ever heard from a native, and it showed the great feeling of common brotherhood that has come into the minds of these Papuans.

Australians should learn more about this colony of theirs, for they can stand in front of the world to-day and show the results of their administration of a subject race.

Papuan Wonderland (1973 edition; first published 1936)

1936–37

H. M. Moran in Abyssinia and Germany

Herbert Michael Moran (1885–1945), who was born into an Irish work-ing-class family in Woolloomooloo, achieved distinction as a rugby player, surgeon and writer. Always a controversial figure, in 1935 Moran sold his medical practice and went to live in Italy. He had long actively promoted Italy and its language and culture in Australia. Enthusiastic about Mussolini and his fascist experiment, Moran worked in Rome to create a more sympath-etic hearing for fascist Italy in Australia and Britain, though his visit to Abyssinia (now Ethiopia), following the Italian invasion, tempered his enthusiasm. He was much less impressed by Nazism when he lived in Ger-many for most of 1937. By the time of Italy's annexation of Albania in 1939, Moran had also become disillusioned with Italian fascism and moved to Britain where his previous activities made him somewhat suspect to the For-eign Office. During the war he worked as a medical officer with the Royal Army Medical Corps. His scathing criticism of procedures and morale in the Corps, of the poor standard of recruits and of an overall moral degeneracy in Britain helps to explain the appeal of Italian fascism to Moran. He died of cancer in Britain in 1945 and his memoir of the last ten years of his life, In My Fashion, *which contains a very moving account of the progress of his ill-ness, was published posthumously. Moran wrote two other largely autobio-graphical works,* Viewless Winds *(1939) and* Beyond the Hills Lies China *(1945).*

In March 1936 I finally got permission to go to Abyssinia as a freelance doctor. I went out in an Italian transport crowded with Italian soldiers whose medical examination must have been of the most superficial character. During our trip to Massaua I spoke with many of them. Few indeed were those who had in them any fire of martial ardour. Almost without exception they were from small farms, sons of large families, men living on a pocket-handkerchief of land. Indeed their one dream was that from some conquest in East Africa they would get farms for all. I have no doubt that the land hunger of the Italian people was genuine. Mere figures mean nothing; the fertility of the soil and the people are everything. I have no doubt also that any scheme for the future peace of Europe is doomed to certain failure which does not take into account the needs for expansion of the highly compressed European races.

The immediate causes of Mussolini's adventure into East Africa were undoubtedly the economic difficulties of his country. These had no doubt been quickened by the extravagance of a Government for ever seeking publicity for spectacular works, but an important factor also was the denied outlet for Italian emigration. The entry of Italians into North America and Australia since the last war had been rigidly curtailed. We Australians must for ever have our own scruples of conscience when we remember that we refused admission not only to restless Southern European races, but even to our own in Great Britain, while we refused ourselves to populate a continent as large as Europe. The northern territory of Australia will never be close settled with any British race.

I was impressed far more with the laboriousness of individual Italians than with their capacity for organisation in Eritrea or Abyssinia. Massaua seemed the most horrible town I had ever visited, and even allowing for its situation and its climate, was not a possession to be proud of. The engineering feat by which on a little train we climbed up to Asmara cheered me as a remarkable example of what Italian skill and effort could do. Asmara itself possessed a somewhat pretentious building which then housed the Ministry of Propaganda. Its façade was showy, but its sanitation abominable. There was one lavatory to be sure, whose flush never worked, yet none of the Italian high officials working in the building seemed to care. I had to live with journalists from many countries in huts set up in the grounds of the only hotel (occupied largely by officials and the great industrialists who were making the roads or supplying goods). The lavatories in these huts were malodorous, yet the Italians when told about it just shrugged their shoulders. I went to Makalé at the heel of the army which had conquered it. There I stayed at a hospital under canvas. I had arrived late in the afternoon after a most unpleasant journey from Asmara round hairpin bends in a constant fog of yellow dust. My first question to the friendly Italian doctor who was my host was: 'Where are the latrines?'

He answered: 'Oh, there aren't any.' Politely I enquired why. He said latrines were a nuisance and they brought flies; everyone just goes up into the bush a couple of hundred yards away. This was depressing. The ground outside the tented hospital was dusty, but for the lesser conveniences the Italian officers did not go far. Yet in that hospital and in another one adjoining where a leading surgeon from Bologna used to operate, there were air-conditioned rooms and they were doing surgical work that was first class. The nursing itself was poor, but that was typical of the Latin attitude towards nursing, which has never reached the standard of British or German countries. I argued frankly enough with the medical staff of that hospital over a bottle of wine after dinner on that first evening, but I convinced no one.

Later I was to hear from some of the American correspondents how in advancing behind the troops over battlefields they had always to watch their steps because of the primitive habits of the Italians in matters of defecation. They also told of unpleasant incidents caused by the altitude at which they were living. Owing to the close proximity to the Equator the air was very rarefied and everybody on the plateau gasped for breath after any effort. As flies abounded there was always the danger of them trapping a fly in their open mouths. One of these Americans was mentally ill for weeks following one such unpleasant experience. It was only the mobility of the Italian Army, which was, after the first few weeks, always on the move, which saved them from dire medical disasters.

I was in Makalé seated among many foreign journalists, of whom only one was English, when one evening I heard the languid voice of a B.B.C. commentator announcing that there was no truth in the statement that the Italians had yet occupied Makalé. The derision of the foreign journalists, especially the French and German, was very great. Another memory I have is of a night in April 1936 at the camp of the Alpini during a battle called after the neighbouring lake of Asciangi. From the open door of the little tent in the valley of Chercos, which is beyond Amba Alagi, I looked up at what had been only a few weeks before a mule track circling the mountain, being converted into a motor road by manual labour. Before me was a great bastion of a mountain, a path round which led to the treacherous Pass of Aiba. This was being widened in feverish haste. I could hear at times the sound of explosives as the workers blasted a section of the rock surface or blew up some obstruction in their way. Rain was falling, for the small rains had begun. There was no moon, but over against the massive black shadow faint dots of light were moving; winding now to the right, now to the left, but always mounting upwards. The column of motor vehicles was passing through. Here was the warning symbol of mechanical wars to come.

I did not enjoy my two months' stay in Eritrea and Abyssinia. I thought Abyssinia a vile country and the Abyssinians the most unpleasant native race that ever I had the misfortune to meet. The Italian workers, sitting by the side of small heaps of stones, breaking them up for the new roads which were rapidly being thrown across the country, depressed me terribly. They worked in intolerable heat with no more than a branch cut from a tree to give them some pretence of shade. Trees indeed for the first 200 miles from Asmara were extremely rare. Stones and boulders everywhere abounded. The dust covered everything. Of vegetation only the giant *euphorbia candelabra* raised its ugly form at frequent intervals along the way. I was later to see its first flowering, red bulbs standing up like lights on a grey-green candlestick.

I visited Adua with its odorous lepers. In the cathedral grounds leprous natives were lying about in the dust. Native mendicants crowded round us all the time; they had sores on their faces upon which flies settled undisturbed. There were great ceremonial stone slabs still in the courtyard of the cathedral which showed still the gutters along which the blood of human victims had once flowed on ceremonial occasions. From the Coptic church was coming the sound of chanting voices. On approaching I saw a priest reading out of a great book, a crowd of bowing clergy around him. The odour of the lepers was heavy everywhere. A cruel country. I saw the instruments of torture which are called Mencor and Civgraf. On my way back to Italy I motored from Asmara to Massaua with an American journalist, subsequently to be killed in Spain. He was by profession a sporting writer, more at home among baseball players and boxers than among soldiers. He had become greatly depressed during a long stay in East Africa, and everything there had disgusted him. He had nearly been captured at one time by the Abyssinians. All the journalists, as well as the Italians, had an intense fear of the little scalping-knife with which the Abyssinians practise a radical ablation of man's sexual organs. I myself had visited a spot where some eighty Italian workers had been evirated and mutilated. This lovable American journalist became during one visit to the front separated from his fellows, and seeking to make his way back had stumbled on a group of the Abyssinian enemy. He had suffered considerable shock at the anticipation of himself having to submit to the Abyssinian methods of mutilation. In Massaua the heat and the dust, the general air of desolation, the absence of every amenity, now smote him hard, and, full of an infinite contempt for everything Abyssinian or Italian, before the surprised and inactive native policeman on duty in the main street he publicly urinated to express his feelings.

I carried away one ineffaceable memory, that of a white-robed Abyssinian poised on a slope of Amba Alagi, what time the snub-nosed motor lorries were grunting their way up towards Toselli's Pass. Glory and defeat for the Italians had been there nearly forty years before. Behind the Abyssinian stood his servile woman, docile and apart, the submissive bearer of his burdens. The Abyssinian man stood holding his stock with two hands behind his shoulder; his loosened white robe was flowing free in the wind like a signal of surrender, and he himself was gazing in silence upon the plains which stretched far away below and which at that moment it seemed unlikely his people would ever possess again.

[...]

At the end of 1936, a little disillusioned and much disappointed with all that had taken place in Rome, I went to live in Munich. There I remained a year plodding away at the German language which previously I had learnt only to read, and then solely in order to keep abreast with the German medical work in cancer.

I liked Munich and I liked the Bavarians. But the whole city was haunted, haunted with suspicion. Everyone had become distrustful of his neighbour. No one knew who next would become informer. I observed and I noted things, but only in my mind: I never dared to set them down. My letters were constantly being opened; I was conscious that I was under surveillance. What indeed could be more sinister than the presence of an elderly British subject of no apparent occupation in their midst? I used to spend one hour of each morning speaking German to an elderly fraulein to whom I had been recommended for a German teacher. Naturally, in the course of desultory conversations, paid for fifty at a time, I made casual enquiries about the life and customs of the people. One morning quite suddenly she turned on me with her face blazing, and shouted: 'Are you a British Intelligence agent?' That was the last lesson I ever had: I was content to forfeit all the others still due to me.

I lived then in an excellent *pension* frequented chiefly by Germans and Americans. I gathered the impression that not 40 per cent. of the Bavarians then sympathised with the National Socialism of Hitler. But in spite of my letters of introduction they remained shy and fearful: fearful lest through some indiscretion on my part persecution should be their lot. One disinterested German Catholic doctor, whose fate I can scarcely doubt, an excellent surgeon, asked me almost imploringly for his own sake not to call again. He knew that he himself was under

close observation by the Secret Police; a visit, therefore, from any foreigner must inevitably make his position still more difficult. There
were numerous such frightened people in Munich. I remember being
surprised one morning at breakfast in my bedroom to see the house-
maid, after first looking along the passage-way, close the door mysteriously for the purpose of asking me in a whisper did I believe there was
going to be a war. Such is the evil infectiousness of nationalism that I
suspect the percentage of supporters had doubled itself by 1940, after
the unbelievable collapse of France. I well recall that winter of 1936–37
in Munich. A heavy fall of snow had slowed down all communications
within the city. When I used to go out for promenades and heard the
muffled footsteps of other pedestrians, they seemed to me to symbolise
the hushed restricted lives of the inhabitants. In the smaller cafés men
would sit in groups of two or three reading the newspapers provided on
wooden holders. Of free discussion there was none. I used to listen
intently to them, but never once heard any of them refer to the Leaders
by name. It was dangerous, even if the remarks made were complimentary. The Catholic churches were always crowded, but I noticed that it
was with men and women past middle age or with very young children. The women were always in much greater numbers than the men.
The age group from fifteen to thirty-five years was conspicuous by its
absence. Everywhere even in the church there was an atmosphere of
repression and of persecution endured, of fear, of reticence even among
one's own family. At the Dom one Sunday morning I found it difficult
even to get standing room inside, because Cardinal Faulhaber had been
announced as giving the sermon. But I could make out no word of his
address. A Nazi loud-speaker arrived to blare away patriotic political
addresses and tunes in the square just outside the cathedral door. The
blare completely drowned the cardinal's sermon. In my country young
men would have pulled these Nazi propagandists out of their car and
done them violence, but in the Munich cathedral there were few or no
young men. The middle-aged men and women had no other option
but silently to endure the insult.

In this city, as in Rome, the most contemptible were always those
followers who did not believe in the new form of Socialism but who
went through all the business, making the required signs for their own
material benefit. Moral courage in both places was at its lowest ebb.
Even those who hated the Leader genuflected when necessary before
the new god. They dared only to have outwardly the courage of the
opinions of the mob. It was very interesting to watch at this time the
almost mechanical obedience of the German people to a sign. At any
road crossing the pedestrians would wait patiently for the given sign to

cross. But even after the correct colour had been switched on there was always an appreciable pause. They were waiting for someone to take the first step and to lead them on. In France half the undisciplined pedestrians would have been already across the road, in Australia they would have been sprawling at all angles across it all the while. But the Germans, obedient to the regulations, dreaded even to take the first step for fear of making a mistake.

In My Fashion (1946)

4

1940–69

The world expands

The Second World War did not offer such expansive travel opportunities to Australians as the First. More served overseas, but on the whole they served closer to home for shorter periods of time. However the long boom that followed the war put travel in reach of a whole new market. It was still expensive and time-consuming, still conceived as a 'once in a lifetime' experience. But with an expanding middle class, greater affluence, secure work and low unemployment, it became far more common for young people to travel before 'settling down', and for retired couples to join a *Women's Weekly* World Discovery Tour. Europe, with London as home-base, was still the primary destination.

Diplomatically, strategically and economically, however, Australia's place in the world was changing after 1945. The decline of Britain as a world power, the American alliance, increasing trade with Japan, and immigration from so many places other than Britain and Ireland meant that the route 'Home via Suez' was no longer the umbilical cord it had once been. Australia played host to the Queen, the Olympic Games, the Beatles and the Pope. Television brought the world into the suburban lounge room. The popular interest in a wider world saw the remarkable efflorescence of the professional Australian travel writer. The many books of Frank Clune, F. J. Thwaites, Shirley Deane, Peter Pinney, George Johnston, Charmian Clift, Cynthia Nolan, Colin Simpson and Nancy Phelan made travel writing possibly the most popular Australian literary genre of the time.

1940

Frank Clune in the Dutch East Indies

Born to Irish-Catholic parents in humble circumstances in Sydney, Frank Clune (1893–1971) was selling newspapers at 7 and left home at 15. He travelled the world for five years, joining and deserting the US Army in 1911, taking whatever jobs came his way. He joined the AIF, was wounded on Gallipoli and returned to a succession of colourful jobs — fireman, recruiting sergeant, steward, vaudevillian, opera singer, mousetrap salesman — and a marriage that failed. In 1923 he married Thelma Smith, later proprietor of an art gallery, and set up a successful accountancy business. The publication of his autobiography, Try Anything Once, *in 1933 was the beginning of his career as one of Australia's best-selling writers. Autobiography, biography, exploration, popular histories, historical novels and travel form the substance of his prolific output which ran the full gamut of popular*

literary taste, and was often ghosted by P. R. Stephensen while Clune contin-
ued his tax consultancy. This extract, a characteristic example of Clune's racy
if somewhat artificial vernacular, is taken from All Aboard for Singapore
(1941), based on a trip by Qantas flying-boat across what is now Indonesia
in November 1940. Clune was encouraging Australians to look north just as
Japan was looking south. His book attracted the attention of the censors for
observations made about defence arrangements in Darwin. In the 1930s the
novelty of air travel, as flying-boats opened up the new air-route to Europe,
seized the imagination of Australians, ever ready to enthuse about any new
technology. Altogether, Clune wrote around twenty books on overseas travel
between 1940 and 1970.

The engines of *Cleopatra* drone sweetly across the Timor Sea as I think
back to the caravel of Magellan, the yachts of the Dutch and the brigs of
the British in days of yore. Across this brazen sea, the proas of the Malays
came and went to the muddy shores of mysterious Australia, in quest of
sea-cucumbers to tickle the palates of mandarins; and across this sea also
toiled the shipwrecked mariners and escaping convicts, bent-backed in
open boats, skins blistered, tongues parched, sweating gallons ...

The scene changes to Parer and McIntosh, a nine hours' flight with
a single-engined plane.

Time drifts on, and here I am in a four-engined skymaster, scheduled to reach Timor in three and a half hours' flying time — with
breakfast and a multigraphed newspaper *en route* and no more danger
or discomfort than sitting in your armchair at home.

We fly across the Timor Sea on our set course, by automatic pilot;
and the engines purr as gently as a Dutch dovekin, for they have been
given a check overhaul during our overnight spello at Darwin. Nothing
is left to chance on the mechanical side of Qantas. In the workshops at
Sydney, the engines undergo rigid tests in complete overhauls on the
bench, where they are electrically and mechanically timed and
'motored-in' and all details carefully checked, including petrol consumption, pressures, temperatures, and revolutions. This routine is
repeated on the running overhauls at the end of each day's flight. There
are so many gadgets for taking an engine's pulse and diagnosing its diseases, that the risks of stoppage in flight are reduced almost to zero, and
the odds against a stoppage of the whole four engines in midair are so
astronomical that a bookie wouldn't bother to shout them.

We left Darwin at seven o'clock in the morning and at nine-thirty
the shores of Timor came into view. Then the steward pushed back the
hands of the clock in our cabin to eight o'clock.

The march of time — backwards.

We sight land at the native village of Kalbano, on the southern shore of Timor, sixty miles east of Koepang. This is a Qantas emergency alighting basin. But we don't need it, and on we go along the shore of mountainous and rugged Timor, its contours contrasting markedly with the muddy mangroves we left behind on North Australia, a few hours ago.

Jade-green seas lap long sandy beaches, palm-fringed. The jungle is cleared in patches, and there are many native villages on the hilltops. It is the end of the 'Dry', and soon the brown landscape will be green-clad with the coming of the monsoon. A long white motor-road links up the villages.

At eight-thirty we are flying above the U-shaped bay of Koepang, which is sheltered by an isle off-shore, a protected haven at the western end of 240-mile-long Timor Island. The pilot banks over the town, and we see below us the jungle-swathed ruins of Fort Concordia, where Billy Bryant batched in durance vile and Billy Bligh sat in state at the Governor's table. It's all gone now; stone forts are out of date, in these days of blitz-hate. A river runs over a white sandy bed through the jungle, with trees and thatched villages on its banks. We ignore the landing-ground, a star-shaped white 'drome with many runways, used by the Dutch land-planes of K.N.I.L.M., on their Batavia–Sydney journey.

Our destination is the harbour, at Tenau, six miles from Koepang quay. Engines hushed, we glide above islets, with tall palms, and a multitude of triangular-sailed craft, to touch down like a footballer scoring a try. Skimming the surface, we come to rest at 8.45 a.m. (Timor time), a fast crossing of 3 hours 15 minutes, aided by a following wind.

All roads lead to Timor. We're here! [...]

Sydney's old-time trade contact with Koepang, in the days of the brigantines and brigands, was neglected throughout the nineteenth century. But the coming of Ross Smith, in the Air Age, resurrected the route and re-established it for ever and for aye.

Fast to our buoy in the bay, we are approached by the refuelling launch, while globules of lubricating oil drip from our engines on the still waters, and float in a rainbow circle.

How clear the water is! the sandy bottom ornate with coral. Another launch approaches, with port officials, flaunting the tri-coloured flag of the Netherlands. The boat's crew are dusky, with inverted straw hats, like washing-up basins. We are in a foreign country, and our ship's papers must be examined with ceremony and formality. The white officials are in speckless tropic twill, topee'd and cool.

While *Cleo* is refuelling for half an hour, I yarn with Mynheer Van t'Pad, the Qantas agent, who has lived in Timor many years. His boat's crew are Koepangers, of a famed seafaring breed, often recruited by pearlers of North Australia for service in their luggers as seamen and divers.

Mr Van t'Pad is proud of Timor's lore, and yarns interestingly about the historic isle [...]

The forests abound with monkeys, birds and snakes, while crocodiles roam in the rivers. In olden days the rajahs of Timor claimed descent from the Crocodile Tribe. At their coronation, a ceremony of sacrifice was held. A virgin and a red-haired pig, salved with sweet-smelling oil, were thrown to the crocodiles in a sacred cavern by the seashore, as a propitiation for the nation's sins. The aborigines of Timor are pagans, with anthropological affiliations to the people of Polynesia. They used to worship the sun, moon and stars; nowadays many of them have been converted either to Allah or Jehovah. Their houses are like beehives in shape, thatched with long grass or the leaves of the lontar-tree, and are called *kopas* — hence the name Koepang [...]

Cleopatra droned again, then roared and smoothly climbed from Koepang Bay at 9.15 a.m. (Timor time) on her ever-westering hustle.

Beyond the blue horizons the beckoning horizons were bluer, as we started our flight above the isles of the Indies which stretch for 1800 miles between Koepang and Singapore, like the skeleton of a mighty dragon with its back broken. We are traversing the southern chain of the Indies, comprising the isles of Timor, Flores, Komodo, Sumbawa, Lombok, Bali, Java and Sumatra, with attendant isles and many straits betwixt and between.

One hundred and twenty miles' flying from Koepang, across the sail-studded Savu Sea, brings us within sight of Flores, a mountainous island, its peaks towering to Mount Ineri, 7363 feet high — an alert working volcano. The chief town of the two-hundred-mile-long island is Ende on the south coast, where there is also a volcano — a fierce one, not high, but a corker [...]

At eleven o'clock the teacups rattle, as we pass the western end of Flores, cross the strait and see below the isle of Komodo, a jewel in this immense necklace of the Indies; a unique isle famed as the home of *Veranus komodensis*, alias the Komodo Dragon. This prehistoric creature, like the Australian platypus, is a freakish survival into the modern motor age. He's a giant goanna, a lizard twenty feet long, of great strength and agility, who feeds on wild horses and wild men — when he can catch them [...]

We dodge the dragons of Komodo and, crossing above another narrow strait, see below the isle of Sumbawa, with high cliffs, and star-fished coastline sprawling in promontories and bays. A steamer, flying the tricolour of Holland, is passing through the strait, trailing a white wake on the dark-blue sea. Near the coast, the lowlands, covered with parched rice-fields densely cultivated, are backed by steep, wooded hills. We fly directly over the big native village of Sape, and begin to lose height for our descent to Bima, twenty miles westward.

At 11.30 a.m., we are flat out in Bima Bay, an all-point alighting, perfect. Bima is 350 air-miles from Koepang, and *Cleopatra* is thirsty for more petrol, so we pause here for half an hour, and most of the passengers go ashore for a stroll along the coral pier to the village.

Bima Bay is six miles long and about half a mile wide, a perfectly sheltered haven, an ideal all-weather alighting basin. The village is the residence of a rajah and his retainers; but we have time only for a leg-stretch ashore, so we do not make a ceremonial call on the potentate.

Almost all the houses of Bima are of thatch — cheap, cool, and dry — with a few European-style dwellings and shops, and a multitude of native and Chinese booths, selling everything from frying-pans and fish-hooks to carpets and *kains*, with fresh fruit, betel-nut, corncobs, rice, copra, knives, beads and all the fun of the market, chaffered by a motley mob of Malays, Sundanese, Chinese and bare-torsoed toilers — some wearing fezzes, some caps of Bali batik, some just fuzzy-topped with nature's thatch.

Here we are, only fifty-five hours after leaving Sydney, but in an amazingly different world — the world of coloured skins and teeming millions, on Asia's island fringe, where the White Man is a big fellow master — not just one of the mob, as he is in Sydney. Now we're in the 'East', which is really Australia's 'North'. We have to keep up the White Man's prestige, and try to look the part of bosses of the world, God's Chosen People, enlightening the poor benighted heathen with our culture and commerce.

In the village I noticed a licensed opium store, but time did not permit a puff of the stuff that dopes and raises hopes. A Macassar proa, two-masted, beats into the bay, a beautiful sight, with many sails set, glowing white in the sunshine. She has two rudders — one port and one starboard — with a steersman on each. These craft, traditional traders of the isles of Indonesia, originate in Celebes Isle. Its chief port is Macassar, only two hundred miles north of Bima. The mariners of the Macassar proas are considered to be the world's best yachtsmen, handling their sturdy sailing vessels with a skill born of centuries of experience...

We stroll back to the pontoon and, while awaiting the launch, watch a sailing race between two outrigger fishing-canoes, each with one Moslem turbaned occupant, returning from a haul.

One canoe has a white leg-o'-lamb-shaped sail. Its owner takes the lead from his rival, whose hobo craft is propelled by a yellow oblong mat-sail. Leg-o'-lamb wins the race to market. As he nears the shore, I note with a thrill of patriotic pleasure that his all-white sail is made of cut-up Australian flour-bags bearing the brand of a Melbourne miller.

Australia will be there! Too right.

All Aboard for Singapore (1941)

1940

Paul McGuire in Bali

Born in Peterborough, South Australia, and educated by the Christian Brothers and then at the University of Adelaide, Paul McGuire (1903–78) married Frances Cheadle in 1927, a biochemist and author in her own right who collaborated with McGuire on several projects. He was overseas correspondent on several papers before the Second World War in which he served in the RAN Volunteer Reserve. McGuire's Westward the Course! The New World of Oceania *(1942), from which this extract has been drawn, went into several editions and helped establish his reputation as a speculative and professional travel writer, one of the new Catholic intelligentsia, confident in his Australian identity but ready to admire older, more deeply religious societies. At the end of the war, McGuire became European correspondent for the* Argus. *In the early 1950s, he was closely involved with Robert Menzies in the anti-communist 'Call to the People of Australia'. He was appointed as Australian delegate to the General Assembly of the United Nations in 1953 and in the following year became Australia's first ambassador to Italy, a post he held until 1959. McGuire was also a poet and prolific author of popular crime novels.*

I suppose that most people are pretty bored by Bali. I was, until the first hour in which I saw it. How long it will remain as it is, how far it has already declined from what it was, you may variously guess. But it still has a rich creative life which raises query after query for our western values.

I have never quite discovered what our educators are doing unless to turn us all into clerks, stenographers, factory hands and readers of *Esquire*. But if it is a fair test that education should leave us with ideas and the capacity to express them, I do not know how we shall compare the Balinese peasant with the drab inhabitants of our suburban cots.

To the Balinese, life is packed with meanings. A primrose by the river's brim would never be a simple primrose and nothing more to him. With its spirit his own soul would dwell in whatever communications a man may have with a primrose. And so with the rice and earth, the mountains, fields and waters, even the familiar peg where the house-holder might hang his hat. He reveres and mingles with this life in all the round of the seasons. In the new leaf and old, at seedtime and at harvest, he shares and celebrates with fruits and flowers and feasts; and, that his thoughts and feelings may have more lasting representation, with his arts: the arts of music, of the dance, of architecture, of carving, of drawing, of metal-work.

He greets, on the whole, his gods joyously. His agriculture is itself an art and conducted according to the canons, for the spirits of the fields and plants have their own rights. The peasant co-operates with them: and so he tends his fields with the diligent care that makes all cultivated Bali and most of Java like a gentle garden. When his day in the fields is done, he turns, as the mediaeval European did, to give divinity a local habitation and a name. He works at his temples and shrines as the English villager worked at the parish church and roadside crucifix. Again like the mediaeval villager, he develops extraordinary dexterity, and as he carves creates, often with furious fancies whereof he is commander. Every Balinese is a carver, for he builds his little shrines in every corner of a field, by trees, on hillocks, above a running stream: and because the stone of Bali is soft he must be constantly renewing them, and endless practice perfects skill and provides for every play of idea and humour. He is quite capable of putting a god on a bicycle, and motor cars appear amongst saints. About the shrines, he plants gardens and builds altars, and makes festivals, for he can find as many holy-days as the fourteenth century did to sing and dance and play through.

As in the mystical stones and glass of the Gothic, all forms and colours have meanings. That conventional bird is Garuda, the steed of Vishnu; the tortoise bears the earth; the elephant god is good fortune; Nandi the Bull is Shiva's mount; the swan is Brahma's bird. Red belongs to Brahma, white to Shiva, black to Vishnu, yellow to Baruna, god of the ocean. All these signs are a familiar language of the Balinese, and in them they write their poems of wood and stone. You can have a deal of fun in trying to read them.

The arts grow in the worship of the gods, for religion represents what men have most deeply thought and felt. That is why an atheistic age so often seems arid and its arts without grace. Old cities raised great churches like our Lady of Salisbury, our Lady of Wells: but the modern city is dominated by its insurance houses, banks and cinemas, for these, I suppose, are the things we believe worth celebrating. But I doubt whether even the Temperance and General Assurance Company is likely to feed and flower in the drama, the dance and the music which grew round the Gothic churches and still flourish in the temples of Bali.

The drama both of shadow-plays and human actors is drawn from Hindu cycles and local legends. Some themes are ritual, some merely entertainment; and the theatre, like the dance, is vigorous and alive. A deal of ribald and topical stuff and local allusion finds its way into the play through the 'penasar,' who comment on the doings of the classic characters, like a Greek Chorus but much more freely in every sense. The classic plays are usually in the old literary and priestly tongue of Java which the people seldom understand but running comment and improvised dialogue provide the popular stuff and are apparently rich and dirty.

Both plays and dances need the gamelan, the fascinating orchestra which develops and immeasurably improves the principles and range of the xylophone with percussion instruments of wood and metal, and bronze vessels rather like soup tureens, gongs, drums, suspended tubes, flutes, and rebab, the one- or two-stringed viol. The gamelan of the play sets the characters to music, with recurrent motifs, and dramatic description. It has measures of yielding sweetness, and sharp, metallic effects that seem to etch a pattern on the air.

If you wander through the villages, you may hear the gamelan and see a play on most nights of the year. People make feasts and shows on the slightest provocation or none at all: for a marriage in the family, a birth, a meeting, a successful deal, a return from travel, the building of a house, the bringing in of rice, the birthdays of Queen Wilhelmina or Princess Juliana or Princess Juliana's children, the arrival of a friend. When a gamelan is not performing publicly, it is probably rehearsing in some one's house, and as you hear it at evening through the scented trees, you should pursue it, and climb in under the low door and sit in the dusk amongst the men and boys and try your hand. The European has become a passive spectator at his mass entertainments, but the Balinese still makes his own pleasures with exquisite patience, love, and art. He is so much more a man [...]

The Balinese, like the rest of us, have some nasty superstitions and dirty tricks. They also have qualities of life that we have lost. Allowing for the gulf between the Christian mind and theirs, you may recall the world reflected in the bright mediaeval artists, in the Miracles and Chaucer, with its feasts, holidays, pilgrimages and popular theatre, its light, cheerfulness, piety, broad humour, lustiness, earthiness, shrewdness and the air of well-being that belongs to those who find many things to do and learn to do them well. The man whose life is reduced to mechanical routines, crabbed offices and factories, who spends his days adding up other people's profits and losses, is the discontented, empty, angry man. Can you blame him?

The Javanese must once have been much like the Balinese. They lost half their arts when Islam broke the images. But Bali's peculiar misfortune was to be discovered not by fanatics and fierce adventurers but by dilettantes, art-dealers, and the tourist business.

Artists and some who pass as artists introduced the Balinese to pretty Western forms. The Balinese have such skill that they imitate with distressing fluency. Their imitations sell for a few cents to the dealers who trafficked in souvenirs from Bali. The litter of cheap imitative stuff was now spread from here to Minneapolis, and endlessly repeated birds and fish and carved heads of dancing girls poured out of Bali as if the place were a mass-production factory. You saw whole cases of identical heads being packed across the street for Sydney and New York. The Balinese had entered our money-economy, on the bottom rung. They had learnt what we will buy. And what we will buy is muck. So those who were goldsmiths, silversmiths, weavers, dancers, players, sculptors were now hands for hucksters.

Until the war, the place was becoming an international peepshow. The girls of Bali are delicate and their young breasts are bare. So they drew a Casino-de-Paris sort of audience. With normal smut came nastier stuff and some of it settled in comfortable bungalows. The Dutch a while back had done some bungalow-cleaning, but the perverted dilettantes who cuss at missionaries and despise the patient officers of Empire did immeasurable damage in a few years.

So a boy who could draw like an angel was carving suburban knickknacks, cheap, very cheap, sir; and he could take you where there were plenty girls, very hot, sir; for he had discovered what the customer wanted.

Many influences worked against European prestige in the East, but the most deadly was from moneyed and perverted idlers. They spread their corruption even where they were despised. Hearty, hard-living planters and soldiers and sailors are one thing and taken much as a matter of course in the East: languid degenerates are another, and an item of export we certainly cannot afford if we intend to recover Asia's respect. Let them stick to their own elegant metropolitan sties.

Westward the Course! (1942)

1945–46

Patrick White in Athens

For Australia's wealthy pastoral dynasties, regular trips to England were a mixture of business, pleasure and the intricate demands of social status. The parents of Patrick White (1912–1990) were in London when he was born, but returned to Belltrees, their property near Scone, when he was 6 months old. White began his education in Australia but was packed off to a 'four-year prison sentence' at Cheltenham College, England, when he was 13. He returned for two years jackerooing before continuing his English education at King's College, Cambridge, where he read modern languages. This time he stayed away for fourteen years, writing plays, poetry and novels, travelling extensively, mixing in artistic and homosexual circles, and spending the war in Greece and the Middle East in the Intelligence section of the Royal Air Force. It was then that he met Manoly Lascaris, a Greek officer, who returned with him in 1948 when White, rather than becoming 'the most sterile of beings, a London intellectual', decided to settle permanently in Australia. He completed The Aunt's Story *(1948), which takes up themes of travel and otherness, on the voyage home. In Sydney, living first on a small farm at Castle Hill, and then from 1964 at Centennial Park, White wrote the novels that established his reputation. Among numerous awards, he received the Nobel Prize for Literature in 1973. His 1958 essay 'The Prodigal Son' and his novel* The Twyborn Affair *(1979) are important statements regarding White's perception of the cultural relationship between Australia and European civilisation, a theme taken up again in his acerbic autobiography,* Flaws in the Glass *(1981), which provides this description of Athens at the end of the Second World War and Greece's civil war.*

Athens was a city of contrasts and conflicts in those winter months after liberation, in the final stages of civil war. The less fanatical, or middle-class supporters of the Left had begun trickling back into the city, to lose themselves in what they hoped in their hearts would be a return to life as they knew it before. There was a final skirmish in the outer suburb of Kephissia, where the actress Miranda, the Maud Gonne of ELAS, rode a white horse in support of freedom. The rebels were quickly dispersed.

The city's face remained pocked with bullet holes, the stucco of formerly great houses and bourgeois apartment blocks chipped and peeling. Inhabitants too poor to deal with the black market were still hungry; they did not fit their clothes, neither their old shabby ones, nor the incompatible garments sent by relatives abroad or dispensed by

UNRAA. Yet never since have I seen Athenians of all classes so demonstrably happy.

The weather was capricious: forays of snowflakes alternating with hopeful sunlight and jagged windows of blue. There was a procession through the streets when they brought the icon of the Tinos Panayia to the Metropolis, banners and gilded emblems pagan to western eyes slowly parading, accompanied by the great patriot-prelate Damaskinos, the armed services, and pallid civic personages, some of them reputed collaborators. At the Metropolis the icon was exposed for homage. I joined the queue. A peasant woman overcome by emotion at the prospect of kissing the Panayia fell to the ground in what looked like a fit. She was whisked away. The queue advanced towards the vision of glassed-in diamonds outshining a face as archetypal and unadorned as that of the peasant who had just fainted. Though the glass was wiped after each kiss with a wad of medicated cotton wool, I had been brought up to fear 'germs'. Perhaps I could not exclude the divine ones; anyway I bent and kissed the air this side of the contaminating glass, and shuffled on, full of regret for my hygienic Protestant upbringing. It did not even allow me to carry away a close-up of the miraculous face. My consolation was in recalling that Queen Sophia, after dedicating her pearls to the Tinos Panayia when praying for her husband's recovery, took them back after he was out of danger.

Athens always reacts through its gut. Food however crude was appearing again in the tavernas. The streets were full of heartfelt song, the dusk loaded with perfume of stocks, the comforting smells of roasting chestnuts and *kokkoretsi*. It was still a village; you could meet a peasant in University Street, a lamb slung across his shoulders like Apollo or Christ. The island of Aiyina was still visible across a blue Saronic Gulf. Rising above the city the Parthenon had not yet begun to look like an archaeological artefact; it suggested pure spirit for this last moment in time before human cattle from the four corners of the earth began shaking its foundations as they trample in herds over the Acropolis.

No doubt these will be interpreted as elitist sentiments in 1981, but on afternoons with winter verging on spring in the aftermath of a terrible war, when apart from a custodian I was the only visible character among the *dramatis personae* who haunt the Acropolis, I saw the Parthenon as the symbol of everything I or any other solitary artist aspired to before we were brought down into the sewage and plastic of the late Twentieth Century. Don't despair however, any of you who have continued reading; it is possible to recycle shit. Could this be my positive message to the Australian optimistic jingle-writers of today?

When I was discharged from hospital I began meeting Athenians during the hours when I was off duty. There was Manoly's youngest sister, Elly, one of the Lascaris family's three solid mandalas, the first being Elly the aunt who brought up the six abandoned children and who starved herself to death after the Germans invaded Greece. Elly the younger, when I first saw her, conjured up certain roses and certain apples. In the Athens markets apples had begun appearing out of Thessaly, a rosy vision to one who had spent several years in the Middle East. Elly's crisp, rosy beauty as a young woman and mother was closely related to all that is admirable, all that is real, in the only country to which she could belong. Her second son Notis (Epaminondas) was born on the kitchen table during the Occupation. (Elly's grandfather underwent a serious operation in Smyrna, also on the kitchen table, anaesthetised by hammer blows, while his wife stood holding his hand.) Elly was delivered by her husband Elias, of peasant stock from Agrinion, the tobacco country in the west of Greece. In the early days of his dedication to medicine, Elias used to ride a donkey to patients in remote mountain villages. He and Elly married against their families' disapproval. The Lascaris of Byzantium found it hard to take a peasant. The Polymeropouloi of Agrinion resented the Athenian intruder as an affront to local brides. The first child was born in a house where Elly used to coax the fire with a turkey-feather fan, her first maid a prostitute examined daily by Elias for the pox. In time Elias became the one on whom the Lascaris family most depended, director of a leading Athens hospital, a heart specialist while remaining a GP at heart: he will respond to a call in the middle of the night from any of his patients suffering from a bellyache as the result of overstuffing with *stifatho*. Costas, the Polymeropoulos firstborn, became Professor of Thermodynamic Engineering at Rutgers University, Notis the second, has spent recent years researching Chemical Physics at Göttingen.

In Athens I resumed my Greek lessons. My teacher was Julia Pesmazoglou, an elderly Smyrna spinster who spent her time between two sisters, one married, the other widowed, on opposite sides of the city. Julia gave me my lessons in the widow's house, possibly because there was a marriageable daughter. Mrs G. the widow had been a beauty, 'white — white as a statue, and cold' according to Despo, the Lascaris aunt with elegance and spiritual pretensions, who copied verses from Tagore into a leather-bound notebook.

You would not have guessed at the marble beauty of Mrs G., congested as a turkeycock, kneeling on one arthritic knee to wrest from the back of a lower shelf in her dresser a packet of sugar hoarded since before the war. Most of the Smyrna ladies were hoarders. Remembering the Turk, they never failed to prepare for a siege — unless the spiritual Aunt Despo, who fainted on catching sight of a worm in an apple, or on cutting into a tomato (that smell!) during the Occupation.

Not only sugar, Mrs G. had hoarded gossip, which endeared her to a novelist. Rising to her feet unsteadily, clutching the burst packet of sugar, she returned to the fray, '... their grandmother Cleopatra went to bed with half Smyrna — which explains why the family came out slightly Jewish.'

Mrs G.'s flat had been taken over by a band of *andartes* towards the end of the Civil War. She was given no choice. But, she implied, they were decent men. She, her sister, and her daughter, had enjoyed their company; their lives were enlivened by the presence of such unlikely lodgers.

There was a tune played on a concertina which haunted the streets of the Lykavittos my first Athenian spring, the first the inhabitants were able to enjoy since the liberation. It was an exhausted tune, sad but hopeful. I had taken a room in a house on the upper slopes to escape from the RAF officers' mess when off duty. It was another of those ochreous houses pockmarked by foreign occupation and civil war. There was no lavatory, but I was invited to visit that of an adjoining flat. Rather than inconvenience my neighbour and myself, I used to do it in a cigarette tin and throw the contents out of the window. Apart from this, the room was a great joy to one of a solitary disposition.

As I lay on the crude cotton bedspread on those solitary, watery, spring afternoons, the concertina's melancholy tune, breaking and mending, would meander down through the labyrinthine streets of the Lykavittos expressing everything I felt at the end of those tumultuous years, everything of the Greek fatality, which was also my own, and why I was drawn to Greece from a distance, and one Greek in particular. Advancing, the frail tune was quelled, like faint flurries of rain-laden wind, before taking up again at the phrase where it had left off. Like hope itself. Around the corners of the ochreous, pockmarked houses, and into the future.

It was some time before I caught sight of the musician, a small, insignificant man, who could have been a bit unhinged, like most of us who are creative. Walking slowly, deliberately. Pressing a squeeze-box as though it were part of his own chest. From which the vital tune was trickling. Winding through the streets. In and out my half-sleep as I lay goose-fleshed on the coarse-textured counterpane. Should I risk overfilling the the cigarette tin? Or could I hold out till the concertina-player had passed before emptying it out the window?

There were the parties celebrating liberation. To one of these, farther up the Lykavittos, Elly, Manoly, and I took turns pushing a child's pram with the ice Elly had made from Morello cherries. The party was given by a group of gilded young Greek pilots trained together in Rhodesia, whose age had spared them operational hazards. The women guests were mostly disappointed wives and hopeful spinsters. The cherry ice and some of the clangers dropped by Catina, the eldest Lascaris sister, were the high moments of the party.

Another good gossip and inspired clown, Catina continually shocked her husband Dimitri by interpreting life in physical terms and imagery. Surviving the shocks his devoted wife dealt him, and exile amounting to imprisonment for his political beliefs, Dimitri Photiades became in old age President of the Greek Writers. At the time when we met he was editor of an intellectual magazine too abstract in content to succeed, the author of a play, more historical than dramatic, in which Miranda of the white horse played the part of the Empress Theodora. Dimitri finally made his mark with his histories of modern Greece written in demotic Greek.

In the days after Hitler's War the Photiades, Dimitri and Catina, were living on the roof of the building where the Polymeropouloi, Elias, Elly, and their two children, occupied a ground-floor flat which also served the doctor as a surgery. Catina could hardly be described as a housewife. In the kitchen of her cramped hutch you were likely to find one of several cats stretched out beside the sink, along with the odd shoe, a clutter of unwashed dishes, and a few ageing *bourekakia*. Catina accumulated cats. They pissed on the corners of the furniture; one of them fell from the parapet into the street below. Dimitri finally put his foot down, and Catina would take the unreliable lift and feed her cat family in the street.

Dimitri was born into another great Asia Minor family. Perhaps due to his Anatolian background, the sitting position has always come naturally to him. 'Ssh!' his wife would warn. 'He is thinking.' Perhaps as an apology for the family estates, Dimitri became a communist. Twice he was exiled to rocks in the Aegean, where his wife was allowed to visit him, but rarely. There is a snap of Catina standing in front of the wire-netting of a fowl-shed where the Photiades mended the temporary break in what has never been less than a conjugal idyll, if rather a disordered one.

As a result of her trials by Greek history, Catina has become an organiser. She got herself a job at the Hungarian Embassy in Athens. She acquired two country properties, and a flat in the city superior to the cramped, converted wash-house on the roof, but could not help introducing a similar clutter into the flat. Catina is synonymous with clutter. When she retired from the embassy, the Hungarians gave her a dinner-set large enough for a state banquet in recognition of her services. The many pieces remain in their cartons all but blocking the entrance to the lavatory and kitchen. There they will probably continue standing as insurance against the future, while Catina's chatter makes her *kephtedes* blench and reduces the rice or spaghetti on her stove to the porridge one has come to expect.

Variations on Athens Transport: the child's pram with the water-ice in it; during the Occupation, the wheelbarrow in which a husband pushed his wife, already in labour, to the hospital where she was delivered of an enormous baby; the buses, the never quite destructible buses...

The Athens buses have always been falling apart; in thirty-five years they would seem to be the same buses. You could fracture your skull during a leap over a pothole, break a limb rounding a corner. These ramshackle, immortal contraptions are murderous if you succeed in emerging from a queue never less than eight abreast, to squeeze on board, pressed together with other human sardines, inhaling petrol fumes, cigarette smoke, body vapours, till acceleration churns the victims into a protesting mass, all livery skins, rasping hair, rancid laughter, invocation of saints and the Panayia.

On our excursions to Maroussi in the hectic months at the end of the war, when the scent of stocks from the surrounding fields still prevailed over petrol fumes, Catina was the great queue-jumper. I can hear her screeching at the top of her voice as she mounts the step, protecting her precious husband with an arm. A father protecting his child turns on her and shouts, 'Anyone can see you aren't a mother!' If only one could have explained that she was the mother of this great child, her husband-baby — and however many cats...

Elly and Elias gave a party when the war was over. There were those hopeful spinsters expectantly gathered in the small room. (The optimism of Athenian spinsters at this period could only have been brought on by memories of hunger during the Occupation. They were desperate for a meal ticket. Nothing else could account for some of the marriages they made.) The male guests included a few airmen, and pongo officer friends of Captain Aristo, eldest of the Lascaris brothers. More British than the British from spending a war in their army, the Captain could not leave off singing *A Troopship is leaving Bombay*... in close harmony with Miss A. who didn't know English. Jilted by the Captain as a girl after he had carried her off through a convent window, her hopes had been revived by rumours from Alexandria. The Captain was not yet divorced, but without a doubt he meant to be. Miss A., still a young woman with faultless legs and dramatic bust, was biding her time. Always knitting, garments for the family, toys for the children, as well as joining in songs on convivial occasions. She had the voice of a peacock from competing against the winds which harry her native island. The Captain obviously appreciated Miss A.'s charms as she lounged against him, an arm laid along his shoulders in her role of *vivandière*, but on getting his divorce he jilted her a second time; he married a girl of fifteen.

The future has not dawned, however. This evening the Captain and Miss A. are united in singing with appropriate abandon,

> A troopship is leaving Bombay
> Bound for old Blighty's shore,
> Heavily laden with time-expired men,
> As well as cunts signing on...

Aunt Despo had a somewhat exhausted voice even at less confusing moments. Now she professes, 'This Miss A. is so kind — attentive — I don't understand what she expects of me...' as the words of the song are belted out,

> ... you'll get no promotion
> This side of the ocean,
> So cheer up, my lads,
> Fuck 'em all...

The walls of the small room had begun contracting — joy, relief, expectation, melting, running, congealing. Through the glass doors the remains of the feast Elly had got together in what were still starvation times had dwindled to skeletons of fish and pools of oiled mayonnaise, still symbols at least, of peace and plenty.

> ... so cheer up, my lads,
> Fuck 'em all!

Aunt Despo stuck it out. In her old age she was an etiolated beauty of true distinction, who had admired the Duse as an actress, and possibly adopted something of her style. I see Aunt D. in her *saloni*, surrounded by leather-bound volumes in the several languages she spoke, photographs of the Smyrna sisters, the spindly, protesting furniture. When young she had literary aspirations. I was shown the fragment of a novel written in prim English, in which Despo as an aviator was forced down behind the lines during the Asia Minor War.

For all her intellectuality, her spiritual airs, and devotion to high ecclesiastics, Aunt D. had her practical side. During Hitler's War when her friend Iphigenia who lived at Porto Raphti brought her the present of a chicken, she took a room in a hotel so that she wouldn't have to share the chicken with her family.

Anyone who has experienced hunger will remember a destroyer of the spirit even greater than lust. Relatives have fought over a bowl of pap left at the bedside of the dying.

Flaws In the Glass (1981)

1948

Alan McCulloch in Italy

Painter, cartoonist, art critic and writer, Alan McCulloch (1907–92), who is best known as the author of the Encylopedia of Australian Art *(1968) and as the art critic of the Melbourne* Herald *for thirty years, spent his early adult life working in a bank. In 1947 he took off for America with the quixotic aim of walking from San Francisco to New York. Having taken ten days to reach Los Angeles, he gratefully accepted the invitation of a friend, Ellen Bromley, to drive across North America. McCulloch recounted their adventures in his travel book,* Highway Forty *(1951). He married Bromley in New York where he drew for the* Saturday Evening Post *before setting out for Europe. After exploring the painter's Paris, McCulloch and his wife travelled by tandem bicyle through France and Italy.* Trial by Tandem *(1950) is a light-hearted traveller's tale of encounters with places and people during the 2000-mile trip from Paris to Positano on the Amalfi coast, where the McCullochs briefly joined an artists' colony. While as alive as any tourist to the delights of art and life available so cheaply in postwar Italy, McCulloch was unusually sensitive to the poverty and hunger of the slums. In this extract he finds the ideal artists' Italy between the poverty of Naples and the sumptuous beauty of Capri.*

Naples!

The dirtiest, filthiest, foulest city in Italy — yet fascinating — as fascinating as a mouldy old junk yard.

A sprawling, slovenly collection of buildings and ships — disconnected particles, clustered around an old castle on the water-front.

Galleria Umberto, a tantalising arcade of vast dimensions with a murky past and an exciting present.

Sybaritical shops on via Roma, and the neat jewellers' shops of the Vomero.

The Finicula, and the Underground railway.

Expensive fish restaurants where society gathers on the waterfront; sinister dives where thieves meet around Piazza Garibaldi. *Trattorias* and *Pizzerias, Cafés* and *Ristorantes* of all kinds. Thousands of voracious beggars.

Tiny donkey carts transporting enormous priests; mules and horses, belled and trapped out as though competing in a medieval pageant. Thieves and racketeers of every description; *carozella*, car, and camera men in every *piazza*.

And all the rambling, ramshackle, haphazard, hysterical, egotistical, conversational population of scoundrelly characters known as Neapolitans.

In all this our tandem created a sensation, a policeman on point duty on Corso Umberto almost piled up the traffic in his anxiety to stop us.

We were not permitted to traverse Corso Umberto on a bicycle he said. We could wheel it if we wished, but we could not ride it.

Later we found out that this was a safety measure introduced by the *carabinieri*, who had grown tired of retrieving the corpses of erratic Neapolitan cyclists from the wheels of the greater traffic.

But we found pushing the tandem infinitely more dangerous than riding it, the greater traffic whistled past us with only millimetres to spare. And we had to walk at least a mile to Piazza Amadeo, where we engaged a room at a *pensione* formerly recommended to us by a friend in Rome.

[...]

One morning we boarded the luxurious little steamer that runs from Naples to Capri.

It was really little more than a ferry, but the officers, accoutremented with a prodigious amount of gold embroidery, behaved like the commanding officers of a battleship or a large ocean liner, saluting, studying charts after the manner of old sea dogs, and engaging in all kinds of impressive formalities.

The second class passengers, consisting principally of peasants laden with products purchased at the market of Naples, descended to the saloon on the lower deck, where they promptly sealed all the windows and sank into slumbrous repose.

But above, on the upper deck, all was gaiety.

The first class bar and coffee lounge was crowded with the foreign residents of Capri, looking very sophisticated in the eccentric head gear, silk scarves, bandanas and Capri shoes which distinguished them from the crowds of cheerfully vulgar tourists who paraded the decks with guide books and cameras.

In the general melee we recognised an old friend, an Australian girl, and her Neapolitan fiancé; we greeted one another with mutual pleasure and decided to join forces.

Gradually Naples receded behind a pall of grey smoke and the towering volcano of Vesuvius became a purple shadow. We discharged some of our second class passengers and their cargo at Sorrento, and one or two distinguished-looking characters alighted from the first class saloon.

The sea was as blue as a sapphire, and against it the caps of the wavelets looked startling white.

Around the point from Sorrento, the Island of Capri at once came into view, rising precipitously from the bed of the sea in a series of inverted cones [...]

The steamer turned and a few minutes later put in at the wharf.

We ascended to the centre of the village in a *funicula*, with the sweet smell of jasmine and honeysuckle in our nostrils and our eyes filled with the beauty of the terraced landscape.

Three sides of the tiny *piazza* were comprised of colorful little shops, and the fourth, as well as being a parking place for the omnipresent *carozella*, opened on to a magnificent view of the island.

Two *carozellas* took our little party to Anna Capri, where we visited the truly beautiful villa of Axel Munthe.

One remembers a glorious walled garden, and a magnificent panoramic seascape unrolling like a gigantic blue carpet from the foot of the cliff half a mile or so below to the outline of the island of Ischia faintly patterned on the horizon. Fragments of ancient stone carvings, elegant gates of wrought iron and an atmosphere of complete serenity complete the picture.

Back in Capri we found a nice clean *pensione* for the night. That evening we dined in a charming café; the sky was alight with stars and the air soft and balmy as a dream.

Beauty, almost inconceivable, we found everywhere on Capri — from the ruins of Barbarossa which crest the isle, to the Faraglioni rocks which decorate the eastern corner — and the native Capriotes seemed as charming as their surroundings.

Yet Capri was not for us.

We could never have worked there.

One would tend to become a kind of lotus eater.

There was an unhealthy undercurrent of viciousness in the foreign community which we found psychologically interesting, but hygienically disturbing.

We couldn't stand the sight of womanish young men, wearing gold bangles on their arms, and dancing attendance on the tattered remnants of foreign aristocracies with faces painted like polished enamels.

We couldn't stand the sickly sentimentality of the representatives of Hollywood, who were concocting a romantic film about the island.

Perhaps these things were transitory, but even temporary acquaintance was enough.

Capri was to us an over-dressed shop window. Seductive, pleasant for an occasional indulgence, but intolerable to live with.

Nor were we ever really happy in Naples.

For all the color and excitement how could one forget the dreadful bundles of rag that squatted in the gutters with begging outstretched claws?

Or the voices of thousands of hungry children — the only 'Neapolitan Serenade' that we heard.

One was filled with a sense of impotence, of utter futility.

What hope was there for Italy, or any country, where such conditions existed?

There are some things that make one ashamed to be alive — and the seamy side of Naples is one of them.

[...]

Next morning we crossed the razor back above Sorrento and descended the winding road — to the beginning of the most beautiful coastline in the world, and the last stage of our tandem ride from Paris to Positano.

Ellen, with all her dislike of great heights, found this road thrilling as well as terrifying.

It was cut into the face of the cliff, and overlooked a sheer drop of two hundred feet or more into the sea. The contours of the coastline were such that to travel a mile as the crow flies meant a road journey of approximately ten times that distance.

At the end of a rugged point we came to a little, plump man, sitting by the roadside. He was gazing into the ravine and weeping copiously.

'Ah, Signora,' he said in answer to Ellen's sympathetic inquiry. 'Four weeks ago, at this place, a very sad thing has happened. An *autobus*, it has gone through the wall, over the side of the cliff, and all have been killed the people. Two only saved, and a little *bambino* found in the branches of a tree. It was the mercy of God signora. Both the parents lost, and the *piccolo bambino* saved by the tree. An olive tree, like a white bird in the branches, and noticed only at the last second as the rescuers were departing. I did not know the people, it was a very sad thing Signora. Take care with the bicycle Signor. It is a dangerous beast of a road.'

He raised his hat to us, sat down, and resumed his weeping.

We hugged the cliff side.

Occasionally, above us, we could see peasants cutting wood with heavy hand-scythes, feeling for toeholds in the precipice and climbing like mountain goats, their voices echoing musically from the surrounding walls of rock.

Wild flowers grew profusely in the small crevices, barns were cut from the living rock, and irregular flights of stone steps disappeared skywards as though on some heavenly mission.

From the end of each point we caught tantalising glimpses of Positano, but a considerable time elapsed before we rounded the last corner and the whole village came into view [...]

Broad flights of steps leading from the little *piazza* outside the church took one down to a solid line of stone houses inhabited by the fishermen, whose fishing boats and nets were drying on the warm, darkish strip of sand that formed the small beach. A smiling, intimate place in which to spend the winter; and for us, who wished to digest the experience of our travels, to write, to draw and paint, it seemed ideal.

Slowly we descended the hill, and taking the last elbow in the road, arrived at the gleaming white *pensione* where we had booked accommodation in advance.

The *pensione* was charming, and the proprietor, who extended us a warm welcome, turned out to be a most unusual phenomenon — an Italian *pensione* proprietor who was honest, elegant and dependable.

The prices of the *pensione* were very reasonable, but they were still more than we could afford for an extended period.

So a few days later we indulged an impulse to go house hunting.

With the exception of an upper and a lower road, the thoroughfares of Positano were composed solely of stone steps; one soon mounted from the balmy air of the sea front to the rarified atmosphere of the mountains, and the sudden change of altitude made one's heart beat like a piston.

Mounting slowly, with frequent stops to enjoy the view, Ellen and I came suddenly to a doorway whose door stood slightly ajar. Inside, in an otherwise bare stone vault, stood some excellent modern sculptures.

This interesting sight prompted me to ring the bell, and in answer to my summons a head appeared over the terrace wall twenty feet above, and a pleasant voice said in perfect English: 'Won't you please come up?'

Two flights of stairs led from the vault to a wide terrace paved and bordered for several feet around the walls with beautiful *ceramica* tiles, designed in motifs of sienna, yellow, blue and black. On the tiles, and the ledge of the stone balustrade, fine specimens of exotic cacti were growing in large vases of terracotta and *ceramica* urns, glazed in blue and orange.

On one side of the terrace a magnificent growth of bougainvillia grew over an arched doorway, and on the other the thorny arms of a 'Queen of the Night' were festooned on wires in queenly solitude.

Odd pieces of wrought iron added a further note of elegance, and in a deep recess in the rear wall an aperture looked into a concealed well of clean, fresh water.

The whole place breathed an aura of perfect taste and fastidious living.

'I see at once that you are artists,' said our hostess, with a charming smile.

For half an hour we talked about art.

'I suppose that really, you are wondering who we are and why we have come here?' I said at length.

'No, not at all,' was the reply. 'I think it perfectly natural that one artist should wish to meet and talk to another.'

We explained our problem. How we wished to find a villa in which to work in freedom.

'Well,' she said when we had finished, 'I am alone. If you would care to come and live here, I have a whole floor of my house unoccupied. Come, I will show you the rooms.'

She led the way through two long glass doors, through a charming room and thence up a broad marble staircase.

The rooms upstairs were furnished principally with pieces of Venetian walnut, each piece a priceless antique, the walls were hung with Italian silks, three or four hundred years old, and the lovely *ceramica* tiles of the floors were warmed by the the addition of rugs and mats.

Off the hall two doors opened on to an upper terrace, decorated like its counterpart on the floor below, with cacti and terra-cotta.

In odd places were the stone and wood carvings of our sculptress.

'What a heavenly place,' said Ellen, 'but we could never afford to pay anything like it's worth in rent.'

'As for that,' said the sculptress, 'we will share expenses, and I think we will be very happy together.'

And that was how we came to live in the most exquisite house in Positano.

And that was how we made one of the best friends we have ever made in our lives.

Trial by Tandem (1950)

1948

Peter Pinney in Istanbul

The grandson of Sir Hubert Murray, long-time administrator of Papua, travel writer Peter Pinney (1922–92) began his life of adventure with the 2nd AIF in New Guinea where he won the Military Medal. His postwar life might be described as that of a professional traveller who moved around the world, sometimes without money, luggage, visas or passport. For Pinney, 'travel in new places, preferably strange places' was the principal way to enjoy life. His adventures have produced a number of travel books. The first and best known was Dust on My Shoes *(1952), his account of his overland journey (1948–1950) by foot, hitchhiking, local buses and train jumping, from Greece through the Middle East to India. His wanderings in Africa provided the material for two other travel books,* Who Wanders Alone *(1954) and* Anywhere But Here *(1956). Pinney told the last of his traveller's tales in* The Lawless and the Lotus *(1962), including his adventures as a stowaway and his job as a stand-in for Marlon Brando in* Mutiny on the Bounty. *In the 1960s he skippered a cray boat in the Torres Strait, marrying his cook, Estelle Runcie, with whom he wrote* Too Many Spears *(1978). By the 1980s, Pinney had settled in Brisbane where he worked on television scripts and on a trilogy based on his wartime experiences. An anthology of his travel writing,* The Road to Anywhere, *was published in 1993.*

By the street of brothels below Pera Palas we walked down to the Turkish baths.

The street was lined with steel and wooden doors equipped with sliding peep-holes, but most of the doors were open. Soldiers, sailors, and civilians paraded up and down, exchanging merry obscenities with the gross whore-mummas and scrawny harlots. Girls of all nations and descriptions lounged in the doorways and sat on the steps, clad in brief garments that laid accent on what they concealed, and smiling or scowling at passers-by.

Two policemen blew their whistles and the girls all moved inside, pushing the doors half closed. But when the police passed the girls came out again. As Marchand remarked with disgust *'Tiens!* One's mind and soul need a Turkish bath after seeing such things. It is worse than Algiers.'

The Turkish baths were built in spreading superannuated cellars under arched stone roofs supported by immense stone pillars. We undressed in perfumed and carpeted cabinets, and clad only in generous towels walked fifty metres in clapping wooden clogs over flagstoned floors to the sweating-chamber; here, under a great stone dome, was a circular steam-heated marble slab about fourteen feet in diameter.

We lay on the slab to cook. The ceiling was hidden by clouds of steam which congealed and trickled down the concave walls. The walls were lined by a score of marble basins, and here sat flabby Turks with fat tyres of excess flesh, sluicing, scrubbing, soaping, and sweating.

When we perspired freely an attendant led us to marble basins in a wing of the chamber, and we bathed with scented soap and hot water. A masseur rubbed and rolled and pummelled us, as if intent on moulding us to a more perfect design, then we washed and sluiced, and our ears, noses, and nails were cleaned.

In a cooling chamber we drank glasses of tea and lemon: and the cost was a lira apiece, a quarter of a black-market dollar.

High on a hill above the Golden Horn there is a broad promenade running by a dance palace, and by the roadside in a gay *lokanta*, or café, we sat at wine. The sun had set, stars glittered brightly in the sky, and the slopes of the hills were spangled with lights.

Hilltops near and far were crowned with constellations where strings of coloured lights were threaded from mosque to minaret in celebration of the Bayyram.

There was no moon yet, and the waters of the Golden Horn below were a black expanse touched here and there by the shimmer and flash of reflected lights from the farther shore. Powerful lights illumined the massive Mosque of Suleiman on the heights of old Stamboul, and made a wedding cake display of the modern university. Wood-smoke hung like incense in the air, the bazaars were closed, the first soft breath of the evening breeze brought the scent of flowers and the tang of the smoke to our eyrie.

The city was at peace, resting before the night's excursions.

Sachide and Murvecht sat with us on the balcony. There are many kinds of Turks, some dark and others fair, but these two girls were dark-haired, brown-eyed, fair-skinned, and generously endowed with Nature's gifts. Sachide was a sweet and naïve child with petal-pink lips and soulful eyes which even now were gazing with melancholy absorption on the river lights. She was a pretty creature of gentle breeding, with the charm of frank simplicity and a sentimental nature.

Murvecht, who taught dancing at Bulbul Dere in Usküdar, a league away in Asia, on the distant bank of the Bosporous, was more sophisticated and self-possessed. Her figure was a poem of lissom symmetry, and she moved with the poise and casual grace of a sylph; the creamy quality of her skin was comparable with that of Sachide's [...]

Sachide came back from her reverie on the river, and her sad thoughts had flown when she lifted her soft-brown eyes to mine and queried, half smiling, 'Dance?'

Sachide's English was not perfect. She had mastered some of the basic phrases and could carry on a curious conversation of nouns and verbs, but thought was a troublesome thing to her and she stumbled through life with a quaint and appealing helplessness. Her thirst for knowledge was limited and she shunned reality.

'Would you like to dance?'

'You, me, dance?' […]

Little Sachide danced well enough, and clung tightly to me with her head upon my breast. For a time she hummed to the tune of the music, then for a time she was quiet, and looking up at me she murmured, '*Seni chok sevurum.*'

'What is that?'

But she shook her head and would not answer. We danced on, as we had danced the nights before in various cabarets, and then found that Marchand and Murvecht danced alone in the midst of an admiring circle. Even in old and travelled clothes he cut a dashing figure, and she who knew men and dancing equally well led him expertly through a classical routine. With flawless grace and timing they held the floor, debonair blond gallant and dark-haired dancing girl, and when they ceased the crowd clapped their hands and shouted '*Encore!*'

The moon was rising.

Pools of white light shimmered on the sea, the pines were frosted with silver, and when the two of us stood on the unlit balcony it softly sheened her hair with argent. The tide was washing the rocks below; a ferry passed in a blaze of lights, its wake sparkling with moonlight and phosphorescence. A mild sea breeze washed us with the cool night air, and stirred her hair. She was very beautiful.

She moved restlessly, then turning she put one hand lightly on my arm, and gazing earnestly into my face said softly, '*Seni chok sevurum.*'

I smiled, and asked again, 'Tell me what that means.'

Her face was bathed in the pale glow of the moon.

'I love you,' she said simply.

Bending down I kissed her hair.

Even in the waning afternoon the sun was hot.

The sherbet-sellers and sweet-vendors lounged in the shade, and the ice-cream men with their *dondulmag* slept by their wagons while their ice melted and dripped away. A *pomah* dozed beside his drowsy dancing-bear in a covered alley leading to the wood-turners' street, and the *kafedjis* nodded sleepily, for there were few alive enough to order coffee.

We wandered hand in hand through shaded streets towards the spice bazaar, Sachide and I. We talked little, for the day had been long and we had already talked tenderly and to good purpose. We had gambled with dice by the Heavenly Waters under chenah-trees, and lunched in a tavern at Seriyet farther along the Bosporous. She had pillowed her head on my shoulder and slept on the ferry coming back, and together we explored the Blue Mosque and the Mosque of Suleiman.

She had purchases to make in the spice bazaar.

The Missir Tcharchi is a dark, roofed-over bazaar of heady perfumes and tantalizing smells, where all the spices of the East, and many of the drugs, are freely bought and sold. In shadowed cells and by colourful spreads of mustard and myrrh, rouge, white honey-comb from Ankara, and multi-coloured bottles sat fat Turks and Armenian merchants, weighing out ounces of this and that with slender balances of brass. Musk, patchouli, jasmine and rose-oils, hair-dyes and charms, rejuvenating tonics and love-potions and quack cures: all these things and many more threw their heavy scent into the air. Sachide bought seraglio pastilles and frankincense, and rose-essence from Bulgaria.

When we emerged from the bazaar dusk was at hand, and we walked behind the old Galata mosque amid the evening scramble of traffic.

'Where are we going?' I queried.

She indicated the packets I carried, and said, 'Oteli?'

Yes, I could leave them at my hotel; she had seen it days before in passing and knew of its shabby nature. At the hotel the manager refused to permit her to enter the premises, even to his office, and misunderstanding our intention he waxed indignant, no doubt wanting baksheesh.

A wretched policeman who haunted the premises, a sallow individual clad in a drab wool uniform of chocolate brown, challenged us offensively and demanded her papers. She had none with her. He heckled her for some moments, then indicated a police-station at the end of the street. With mounting ire I argued, and denounced him as a fool, and he grasped my arm. I whirled and knocked down his hand with force. He stepped back, drew his gun, and blew four blasts on his whistle.

They came running like fowls at feeding time. Twelve of them, from half a dozen different directions, civil and military police. Out of coffee-houses and alleys, from traffic duty and the main street; two leapt from a passing tram. They closed in and formed a ring about us, and Sachide stood tearful and downcast amid a great noise of squabbling and argument. No one spoke English and they all barked questions at once and in vain.

Two common soldiers of brutish aspect barged roughly into the group and one seized my collar, but I tripped him over backwards and thrust him savagely into the gutter.

Police held me fast, but a captain appeared, and he and I had a coffee-house acquaintance. I slipped him money and he ordered his colleagues to disperse.

'Do not bring ladies here,' he admonished me. 'It is not a good place.'

Sachide was weeping quietly, the rose-essence lay spilt on the cobbles and filled the street with unaccustomed sweetness. A passing taxi picked us up and she gave the driver some address not far from the Blue Mosque.

We alighted from the taxi in a curious side-street and went by dim arched doors into a grand covered bazaar, filled with the riches of the East. By the glittering avenue of goldsmiths we made our way to the silk market, where a gramophone ground out a harsh jangling discord and women felt and fingered their way among a wealth of splendid silks, satins, and heavy brocades.

There was a covered courtyard, dimly lit by smoking oil lamps which stood in brackets on the walls. Rolls of carpets lay about on the flagstones, and in narrow cells on all sides sat merchants amid a luxury of rich tamals and carpets, antiques, and elegant tapestries. It was the carpet bazaar, where the finest Turkish carpets are to be found.

Sachide led me to one of these narrow cells, where an old man sat in flowing robes on a plush carpet of exotic design; he wore a red fez upon his head, his face was lean and shrunken and tufted by a wispy white beard. On either side the walls were hung with tapestries and antiques: armour and chain-mail, silverware, and swords from Mongol, Turk, Tartar, Crusader, Saracen, and Arab, blazing and gleaming with the flickering light of the oil lamp.

Overhead was a sparkling crystal chandelier of Louis Quatorze; scrolls of calf-skin parchment yellow-brown as the old man's face lay neglected in a corner.

The old one smoked an ebony narghile, or hookah, embossed with silver and having a long tasselled tube and ebony mouthpiece. When Sachide stood before him, smiling, he made no movement, but peered closely at me through his gold-rimmed spectacles. She spoke quietly to him, and when he nodded slightly she removed his fez, kissed his bald pate and replaced the fez, and beckoned me to come with her through the narrow shop.

She took a candle from the wall and lit it from an oil lamp, and holding my hand she led me through a narrow stone arch behind a hanging rug. By a short but crooked corridor of stone, past small doors and a flight of mossed steps leading to a well, we felt our way by the feeble light until we came upon a door with two heavy bolts and a padlock. She unlocked this, slid the bolts back, and grasping my hand again led the way inside.

It was a strange room, well furnished with rugs, tapestries, enamelled vases, and a broad divan; yet there were no windows, only niches in the walls between the tapestries which seemed to lead upwards to the air. The atmosphere was musty, but when she set one of the seraglio pastilles on a silver tray and lit it, the air was spiced with a subtle fragrance. She brought dishes of sweet sutlasch and some pleasant drink, and after we sat on the divan. She put her hand up and listened intently.

Far away, from the bazaar or one of the streets above, came the haunting melody of a gipsy's flute. It was so distant we had to strain our ears to catch it, and then it stopped, and we heard it no more.

'G'zel?'

She smiled, and kicked off her slippers, nestling contentedly. But after a little while she murmured, 'I am sick.'

'Sick?'

'Appendix.'

One could not but smile at this unwarranted interruption.

'Tomorrow, hospital.'

But then I remembered a sunny morning during the previous week when we lay on the sand at Florya Beach. She had been giving me lessons in Turkish, and when she lay back stretching her arms, and yawning, I had noticed the tip of her appendix scar, above her swimming trunks.

'Your appendix has finished,' I chided her. 'So what is it that makes you sick?'

For a moment she searched for words, and then: 'Tomorrow, penicillin. Some bad man gave me sickness. I don't know...'

I stared at her aghast. The girl was indeed ill. How could she be so sweet and seem so innocent?

Disengaging her arms I rose, snuffed out the smouldering pastille, took the candle and went out of the door without a backward glance.

Dust on My Shoes (1952)

<u>1949</u>

Jill Ker Conway shipboard and in Ceylon

Born in the far west of New South Wales, Jill Ker Conway (1934–) evoked the arid land of her childhood in her autobiography, The Road from Coorain *(1989). After graduating from the University of Sydney in history, Ker left for North America in 1960 where she married John Conway and has since lived. Graduate work at Radcliffe College was followed by a period of teaching at universities in Toronto and then, in 1975, by her appointment as president of Smith College. Now a writer and public intellectual in the United States, with twenty honorary degrees and on the boards of giant corporations, Ker Conway is still engaged in a love–hate relationship with the land of her birth. This extract re-creates her first trip overseas, a ten-week family cruise to Ceylon when she was fifteen. Her life in North America is the subject of the second volume of her autobiography,* True North *(1994).*

Shortly after the household returned to normal following Eva's death, my mother began to worry that we would soon face another hollow celebration of Christmas, another season preoccupied with the awareness of loss, and with our inability to disguise the sadly shrunken size of the family gathering. A woman who knew no half measures, her eye was caught by an advertisement for an eight-week Christmas cruise to Ceylon by P. and O. liner. She quickly calculated that the cruise combined with three weeks of exploration on the island of Ceylon would nicely straddle the Christmas and New Year's holidays, returning us in time for me to prepare for school in early February. Mindful of her promise to Eva to care for her motherless daughter, she added her to the party. Before I knew what was happening, I was being taken on a euphoric shopping spree designed to clothe my unstylish fifteen-year-old form with cruise clothes and evening dresses suitable for dressing for dinner in the first-class P. and O. dining room. Hitherto I had been forbidden to attend my classmates' dances, and I was usually barred from parties where alcohol might be served. Now I was suddenly being prepared for a much more sophisticated adult world. My choices in clothes betrayed my lack of experience and introduced me to the discomforts of whalebone and strapless evening dresses. I was five feet six, overweight, and tormented by blotchy skin. Severe tailoring and careful choice of colors might have helped to camouflage this predicament, but I settled on pink tulle, white piqué and lace, and pale green organdy with rosebuds. The result was predictably awkward, but I knew no better. Barry, happy up to now with a tweed jacket and tie for formal occasions, was dispatched to acquire a dinner jacket and evening shoes. We became possessors of passports along with our fine clothes and began unaccustomed reading about the mysterious East. Suddenly, when I rode across the Harbor Bridge and looked down at the glittering white ocean liners lying at their moorings below, I saw them no longer as unattainable romantic symbols of a glamorous international world, but as a form of transport that I would shortly use.

My mother could not have decided upon any experience better calculated to banish our daily routine and superimpose startling new experiences on the troublesome memories of the year. They began the day our ship, the MV *Strathnaver*, sailed. Before the days of regular air travel, the departures of ocean liners were major events in Australia. Encouraged by postwar prosperity, thousands of Australians flocked aboard the P. and O. fleet of liners to make their ritual journey 'home' to England before settling down in their real homeland. Each vessel was farewelled by an alcoholic crowd, its members cheering and weeping by turns, shouting advice (much of it crude references to the ways of foreigners), remembering last messages, singing sentimental songs, and waiting at the docks until the last paper streamer thrown to friends aboard had broken. The *Strathnaver* was going 'through to Tilbury,' having picked up almost a full complement of passengers in Sydney. It sailed for eight days around the coast of Australia, stopping at Melbourne, Adelaide, and Fremantle, before setting out for seventeen days across the Indian Ocean to Ceylon.

Many passengers were made seasick by the swell going across the Great Australian Bight, and some were troubled by the pitching of a storm a day or so out from Perth, but we were entranced; exploring the ship, seeing our first flying fish, watching the other passengers. In the beginning, I was intimidated by the first-class dining room. The menus were enormous, remnants of an Edwardian style of dining. I was uncomfortable in my unaccustomed finery, and totally inexperienced in polite dinner table conversation. Gradually I learned the delights of choosing between caviar and smoked salmon for a first course, sampling grouse and other English game, eating my first Stilton cheese, and entering into serious discussions with our steward about what kind of soufflé would be best for dessert. I set to so heartily as a trencherwoman that no amount of pacing the deck could atone for my appetite, and the whalebone supporting the pink tulle began to be very confining indeed.

The evenings lived up to every movie I had seen about ocean voyages. The wake glowed with phosphorescence, the sea breeze blew gently, the band played sedate dance music, and a wonderful array of older people disported themselves on the dance floor. It was fascinating to work out with my mother which couples belonged together, who was having an affair, what widow was setting her cap at what retired major. My mother was as diverted as we were by the change of environment, but she was puzzled by her children's behavior. We were agog to find our place among the other young people on the ship, whereas she, still grieving, wanted to retire early and expected us to accompany her. My determination not to remain dutifully by her side was reinforced by our traveling companion, Eva's daughter, a few years my senior. She was understandably determined to enjoy a shipboard romance, and more than ready to argue about my mother's expectation that we would retire when she did. My mother could not require our presence to avert anxiety about road accidents so, reluctantly, she gave approval for us to retire when we chose. As soon as she went down to her cabin, we broke most of her carefully prescribed rules. I danced clumsily with strangers, Barry sampled more than the beer at the bar, and we began to get to know some of the other passengers.

Besides the usual Australian tourists, the ship carried Indian and Pakistani army and air force officers, families from the former Indian and Ceylonese Civil Service, the children of tea and rubber planters en route home from school and university for the summer holidays, and numerous retired English couples who made the journey out to Australia and back to escape the English winter. Some of the passengers must have been aware that India and Pakistan had just endured two years of murderous racial strife following Independence, and that British rule in Ceylon had ended less than a year ago. But we lived on shipboard as though the great British navy and merchant marine still controlled the globe. I became enamored of the son of one British planter family from Ceylon, and freed from my mother's supervision, I saw in the New Year at a particularly bibulous party in his cabin, where Barry came upon me, cheerfully tipsy at 1:00 a.m. This united us in a happy conspiracy of silence about our secret misdemeanors. My host and his friends seemed unaware that their world was about to collapse. Instead they gave me experienced advice about how to manage the 'natives.'

Elderly men and women told me romantic stories about the glamorous Northwest Frontier of the old British Raj; Barry and I listened enthralled to the war tales told by colorfully dressed Pakistani Air Force officers; all of us were regularly regaled with lengthy sea chronicles told by the petty officer who looked after passenger entertainment. His most memorable stories were of the wild behavior of the Australian troops the *Strathnaver* had carried to the Middle East in 1940, and brought home again in 1942 to defend their homeland from the threat of Japanese invasion. For me, he was the star of all the characters gathered on our voyage. More than six feet tall, he carried an enormous beer-inflated belly with stately dignity. His talk was always slipping toward profanity, and his language was peppered with vivid imagery. He ran the horse races and bingo games expertly, calling the numbers in rhyming cockney slang with a voice more gravelly than any I had ever heard. His dissipated eyes looked as though they had seen every form of human depravity and his demeanor of barely controlled scorn softened only when he talked about his adored ship. He liked instructing me, and never let fact stand in the way of a striking story. Ceylon, he told me, was an island so beautiful and so laden with spice trees and gardens that the perfume told one to expect landfall many miles out to sea. He had a gift for language. When he described Aden, the next port after Colombo, with its blue-grey mountains ringing the harbor and the sails of the Arab dhows reflecting the sunset, it seemed as though my life would be incomplete without seeing it with him to identify the forts and the British naval vessels lying at anchor in the roadstead. I began to understand the wonders of travel.

Once we disembarked in Ceylon, this understanding changed quickly to ambivalence. The Australia of my childhood contained only a minuscule population of non-British descent, so that I had never really seen another culture. Reading could carry me in imagination beyond the confines of Coorain or Sydney, but it could never make me experience a non-British world, let alone test the usual British imperial attitudes of superiority toward other peoples. Schooled as I was in all Australia's class sensitivities, I was unprepared for a society of caste. Colombo was a teeming Asian city where begging was a way of life. At the Grand Oriental Hotel, an ancient 'punkah boy' slept on a mat outside my bedroom door in case I called for anything in the night. I was troubled by having to beat the beggars away on the street, and by the instruction to ignore the tugging hands of the children who grabbed my skirts crying for money. I felt so disoriented by the extremes of poverty and by my uncertainty about how to behave that I could not relax and enjoy the color, the vitality, and the richness of the new sights and sounds. People told me that the children with stumps for legs, or holes where their eyes had been, were that way because they had been deliberately deformed so as to be more effective beggars. That did not help me sort out how to behave to them or what I thought about this new society.

The Grand Oriental Hotel, our base for a week in Colombo, lived up to its name. Its Edwardian splendor was fading in 1949, but its vast white marble lounge, sprinkled with cane tables and chairs, cooled with potted palms and soporific ceiling fans, seemed very grand to me. In the afternoons, there was a thé dansant, when the band played Strauss waltzes and Hungarian gypsy music. This was the hour when the white-clad young men who worked for the British banks or insurance companies came to sip cool drinks and dance away the afternoons with women whose toilette and elegant silk dresses had clearly commanded the attention of skilled servants. One of our shipboard friendships had been with a family traveling to the wedding of their eldest daughter to a young English bank officer, so we were soon introduced to this society. Its members brooded every afternoon over gin and tonic about the decline of the British Empire and the mess the Sinhalese would make of ruling themselves. Such expectations of nonwhite people had been one of the unquestioned verities of my world, but after my first actual encounter with the way a multiracial imperial society worked, I began to be less sure about everything. I could feel the hostility of the street crowds and the ever-present watchfulness of the hotel servants. They made me uneasy.

A new view of history began to shape my perceptions as soon as we left Colombo. The city itself, with its fragrant gardens, white-galleried buildings, and thriving commerce, registered only vaguely through my jumble of emotions about the poverty and the thinly veiled resentment of British-looking people. Our first visits to Buddhist temples and sacred sites gave me what then seemed the astonishing information that this great religious figure had existed nearly six hundred years before Christ. Each great temple contained relics of the Buddha, objects of veneration, just like Christian relics. Why had no one taught me more about this earlier faith so similar to Christianity in so many respects? Moreover, why had I been taught to date everything from the birth of Christ and the emergence of the Christian West, when great capitals like Anuradhapura, among whose white, gold, and grey ruins we climbed, had been thriving three hundred years before Christ's birth? Seeing these remains was an unexpected culture shock which meant that Europe could never again seem 'old.' After that, ancient remains always conjured up for me the greying rocks of Anuradhapura, the outline of its temples and palaces in perfect scale, clearly visible despite the encroaching jungle. Hitherto I had dated my understanding of political life with the development of the British parliament. As our guide talked about the thriving empire ruled from Anuradhapura and the political conflicts which had flourished there, the picture captured my imagination and made me realize that there were other political traditions about which I knew nothing. Military history also took on a new aspect after the scorching day when Barry and I climbed the hill fortress of Sigirya, dating from the sixteenth century. At the top, surveying the plains below, one could picture the ruling monarch whose armies had ridden elephants and had controlled the exuberant fertility of the irrigated plains below. One entered the pathway to the fortress through the fierce mouth of a lion carved in the mountainside, as large and commanding a monument as an Egyptian pyramid. Away from the massed population of the city, I could take in the beauty of the island and register such vivid new sights as the outline of the Temple of the Tooth in Kandy. Nearby, a patch of rain forest of breathtaking beauty, containing an undreamed-of profusion of exotic vegetation, had been preserved. The avenue of palm trees in the gardens of Kandy along which processions mounted on elephants had once paraded became a symbol for other kinds of grandeur than the photographs of England I had been taught to revere.

Despite the fact that such powerful and enduring subversive perceptions were being etched on my mind, I was not a happy traveler. I had been raised in a household of such precise regularity, governed by such an obsession with cleanliness, that I shared my mother's fears about whether our rooms were really clean, and I joined her in rejecting the unfamiliar-tasting food. Along with this low-level anxiety, I was puzzled about how to understand and organize the daily flood of new images. My first sight of a Hindu wedding procession outside a small village looked like such fun. The bright colors, the flowers, the music, and the energy expressed in the procession as it flowed sinuously along captured my imagination. My mother remarked that the bride was a child, and that village people often sent themselves into bankruptcy for such festivities. I knew this was true, but when I contrasted the scene with my mental picture of the kind of wedding I and my classmates would likely have, I wondered for the first time whether ours might be a little stuffy. It was disturbing to be prompted to such thoughts, and I was not certain I enjoyed it. So much of the culture we were viewing in our journey round the island was the product of religion. This was a Buddhist and Hindu country. I wondered idly what Australia was. Did people in Ceylon believe in karma and a cyclical view of history to explain away the terrible inequities between classes and castes? This set me wondering what beliefs we had at home to justify our inequities. Such ideas were unheard of. I began to look forward to going home and settling into a familiar routine.

As our return voyage drew to its close, it was clear that my mother was also relishing the thought of home. She had set about the journey impulsively and had given us an expensive and luxurious vacation, hoping to ease the sadness of Christmas without Bob. She had managed that wonderfully for Barry and me, and for Eva's daughter, but she had not reckoned with what her actions would mean. She had introduced us to the very world of fashionable luxury she had previously ruled out of bounds. Her action was prompted in part by guilt at the thrift which had prevented her from gratifying some of Bob's much simpler wishes. While she recognized this, she felt, childishly, that we should be more visibly grateful for the largess than we were. Our journey together made clear that she was no longer the center of our world, and that we were poised to search for new adventures on our own.

The Road from Coorain (1992 edition; first published 1989)

1953

Marie Byles in India

Born in England, Marie Byles (1900–79) came to Australia with her family when she was 12. She studied law at the University of Sydney and in 1924 was the first woman solicitor admitted to practice in New South Wales. An ardent bushwalker, mountaineer and conservationist, Byles travelled 'to ramble, tramp, hike and climb mountains, learn about boats and simply enjoy life'. What Australia lacked for Byles was 'real mountains', and in the late 1920s she left Australia to climb mountains in New Zealand, Scotland, Norway, Sweden and the United States. She wrote about her experiences in By Cargo Boat & Mountain: The Unconventional Experiences of a Woman on a Tramp Around the World *(1931). Travelling in Burma and Tibet in 1938, Marie Byles encountered Buddhism and in 1952 became a founding member of the Buddhist Society of New South Wales. In the following year she visited the holy sites of Buddhism in Burma, northern India and Nepal, and lived for a time as a hermit on the lower Himalayas. The trials of a Western pilgrim to Benares (Varanasi), the holy city on the Ganges sacred to Hindus, Jains, Sikhs and Buddhists, are recorded in this extract from* The Lotus and the Spinning Wheel *(1963), in which Byles interweaves her own travels with those of Buddha. She wrote about her experiences in meditation centres in Burma and later in Japan in* Journey into Burmese Silence *(1962) and* Paths to Inner Calm *(1965). Byles bequeathed her house in Beecroft with its bushland setting to the National Trust.*

During that long and wearisome bus trip through barren lands that had once been fertile, it had been gradually dawning upon me that the young man, to whom I had been entrusted, so far from being able to take care of someone else, was in need of being taken care of himself. On arrival at Gaya, the bus dumped us in the dust in front of a screeching picture theatre, and it was only after super-human efforts that I was able to get the young man to procure trishaws (bicycle rickshaws) to take us to a taxi stand and get us a taxi to Buddha Gaya about six miles out of town. It was late in the evening when we were put down at the rather dirty dak bungalow there. It was only later still that I realized how right Mr Hughes had been in insisting that I stay at a dharmasala and that the Maha Bodhi Society should not send European pilgrims to dak bungalows when it would not send Indians. The Bhikkhu in charge at Buddha Gaya did put in an appearance, but seeing the young man, he very naturally presumed I was being properly catered for, and at once departed. There seemed no means of getting supper except from my thermos! I parked my sleeping bag on the verandah while the young man occupied 'our' room. It is taken for granted in India that people in a party share the same room regardless of sex, and hence the wise rule of the Vinaya made by the Buddha that monks should not sleep under the same roof, that is to say, in the same room, as a woman. Of course when one is old enough to be a young man's mother, even a Brahmacharini should feel no embarrassment; but it was pleasanter in the cool night air and all would have been well had not the young man bolted and barred himself in so securely that it was a little awkward in the morning when one required to visit the bathroom.

[...]

There were mango groves near Buddha Gaya jutting out into the river bed, cool and shady, where one might meditate upon these things and let the Dhamma take possession of one's life and govern it. Yes, Buddha Gaya would be a good place to stay, especially if one lodged in one of the dharmasalas there. But for me there was that unfortunate young man. The prospect of having him hanging around my neck either here or during the rest of the Buddhist pilgrimage, was truly alarming, even though I knew I should have only loving kindness for the unfortunate. However, the Good Law provided the escape though it meant leaving Buddha Gaya immediately. A Ceylonese party drove up. They suggested my joining them for the rest of the pilgrimage. I seized the opportunity to give the young man enough money to take himself home. It turned out that the Ceylon party was making a kind of lightning-speed Cook's tour, which was not my line either and we did not in fact travel together. However, I was grateful to them for having provided me with the excuse for disposing of my attendant without hurting his feelings.

It turned out that the hasty departure to Gaya was out of the frying-pan into the fire. It was a six-hour railway journey from Gaya to Banaras. The carriage designed by its makers to hold eight, was soon overflowing with twenty-five plus their luggage, and Indian luggage resembles that of our great-grandparents, except that there are at least half a dozen small articles in addition to the bed roll and the huge trunk. There was no room to move an inch. The Indian women and children fell asleep happily on top of each other and the men yarned and spat. If only the spirit could transcend the body's pains, I thought wistfully. But it did not. All except two men tumbled out at the station before Banaras. Those that got out, it seemed, had had no right to be there at all, having only third or inter-tickets. At Banaras my unhappy body was fought over by coolies. It was late in the evening and I was exhausted. I gave up the idea of going out that night to Sarnath, which was Isipatana Deer Park, and instead got a trishaw to take me to Clarke's Hotel. And so ended the second stage of the Buddhist Pilgrimage — in a European hotel! And the memories of the Buddha's Enlightenment became submerged under a nostalgia for a peaceful little hillside cottage among the scented gum trees of Australia.

[...]

The pilgrims who came to Sarnath dharmasala usually stayed only a couple of days, long enough to worship at the temple and the stupa and to visit the places of interest. A few of them cooked their food on primuses in their rooms, and a few like me, ate with the resident bhikkhus in the little dining-room, for doing which a fixed charge was made (otherwise lodging at dharmasalas is free; you merely give such donation towards expenses as you can afford). Most had servants to cook for them. Some of the Tibetans cooked on little fires under the spreading mango tree in the quadrangle. The very poorest of these Tibetans walked all the way from Sarnath with packs on their backs and slept out under the bamboos in the park near the temple, spreading their voluminous gowns over them by way of covering at night. Once again it was the Tibetans who won the heart with their ready smiles. There was a lass from Lhasa, who went to a convent school in Kalimpong and spoke a little English. She had to attend mass every morning; when the teacher prayed to Christ, she prayed to Buddha. For what did she pray? 'The happiness of all beings, animals and insects as well as humans. If you have an enemy, you do good things for him. A Buddhist cannot have an enemy. You pray that everyone may be reborn among the angels, for all is suffering here, but among the angels, all is happiness.' It was not exactly a form of Buddhism my friends would consider orthodox. But it produced a people who seemed to show forth the teaching of the Buddha, more than a very great many of the orthodox. She introduced me to her lame uncle, a lama, or monk, and the light that shone from his eyes surely revealed the Deathless.

The only Europeans there, and they had been there for some months, were the Swedish couple. They came with me to take a boat along the shores of the sacred Ganges. It was both horrible and funny to see the temples sliding into the water half turned over — symbol of the transience of all, even of that thrice sacred city of Banaras. Little girls were placing tiny lights on bamboo mats to float away upon the waters; naked yogis with beautiful bodies were doing hatha yoga exercises on platforms by the holy waters, and the dead were being burned and their ashes scattered to the same sacred bosom.

Was the holy city Benares (or Banaras as it was then called or Baranasa as it is now called) anything like this in the Buddha's day? Probably not, for there were apparently no temples in his day, nor hatha yogis doing their exercises nor burning ghats where the dead were burned and their ashes committed to the river. But it is hard to say, for the city figures so little in the Texts. Sariputta the chief disciple of the Buddha, is mentioned as being there from time to time. Probably, being a Brahmin himself by birth, his teaching was more acceptable in this stronghold of Brahminism than was that of his Master who was sprung from the nobility. But even though we hear a little of what Sariputta taught there, we hear nothing of the life of its people, not even of the spinning and weaving of the fine Banaras muslin for which the city was renowned, nor of the growing of the cotton from which it was made.

The most distressing feature of Sarnath were the mangy dogs with their ribs sticking out like skeletons. With the avidity of the starved they snatched for and fought over the scraps that were thrown to them. And there was an aged cow which lay sick and dying for many days. Before we westerners condemn the Buddhist refusal to take life to save pain, let us remember that we condemn the aged and diseased men and women to the same misery that Buddhists condemn animals. They at least are consistent. We are not.

I dutifully 'did' the ruins of former Buddhist monasteries. They were much later than the Buddha's day. What most struck me was how small they were, the largest housing not more than about twenty-eight. I also 'did' the museum and the school and the other temples. But except in so far as such places show something of the teaching of the Buddha in practical living, I find it hard to work up any enthusiasm. From this angle Sarnath was not an inspiring place. Moreover, my body which had been badly run down before leaving Australia began to get poorly again. But, headaches or bodyaches or weariness, there was the rest of the Buddhist pilgrimage to complete. I decided it was time to depart.

The Ven. Sangharatana Thera would have put me on board the train, but that evening he had to entertain some VIP, so he committed me to the care of the trishaw driver. I was strangely at peace as we treddled along the smooth road in the misty moonlight to the Cantonment station at Banaras, though I knew there would be difficulties ahead, for it is not easy to travel alone in India, where luggage left unprotected may be stolen. Swamiji at Rajgir had predicted that before I left India I should have such trust and confidence in the care of the Lord that I should not even bother looking up trains! That time had not arrived! I have not the usual Buddhist complex against the personification of natural laws as 'the Lord', but after it had taken an hour and a half to find my reservation and after the train had departed forty minutes behind schedule, the loving care of the Lord was not in the least apparent to my unfortunate body, though perhaps the wisdom of not looking up time-tables was becoming apparent to the mind! In India most people know that the things of eternity are more important than the things of time. Until you absorb this obvious fact into your being, Indian ways do not seem to reveal the workings of Providence to the least degree. But when you do get it into your being, you realize that India has taught you the greatest lesson on how to live life happily.

The Lotus and the Spinning Wheel (1963)

1955

Christopher Koch in London

Novelist Christopher Koch (1932–), who was born in Tasmania, was an early participant in the postwar pilgrimage of young Australians to Europe, which carried them 'to the world, out of youth and into adulthood'. Named after A. A. Milne's Christopher Robin, Koch belonged to the last generation whose imaginations were formed by Britain. In 1955, a year after his graduation from university, he set out for the 'home we had never seen', for 'the cultural Blessed Isles'. Fragmented identity was to be a continuing theme in Koch's writing and life. Koch's trip deviated from the norm of the time in that he and his travelling companion left their ship at Colombo spending several months in Sri Lanka and India before proceeding on to disembark at Naples and hitchhike across the Continent to London. His arrival there is recalled in these extracts from his book of essays, Crossing the Gap *(1987). 'There was no other city that mattered … London was both the city of cities, and the all-wise, half-forbidding friend.' Koch learnt that the land of dreams was also postwar Britain, a grim, poor place compared with the carefree, prosperous Australia that he had left. His exploration of a part of Asia, if still unusual in the 1950s, was to become part of the conventional travel of the young from the mid-1960s. Asia was to be an important theme in Koch's essays, and in his novels such as* The Year of Living Dangerously *(1978) and* Highways to a War *(1995). He has now settled in England.*

Like many another child of the Empire in the thirties, I had been named after Christopher Robin; *When We Were Very Young* had been read to me when I was three. My brother and I had Dickens read to us when we were seven and nine years old, and Oliver Twist and Pip and Little Nell and Mr Bumble were famous figures we might some day meet: our parents and relatives spoke of them as though they were real, and I can still see my mother pursing her lips over Uriah Heep. 'Give us a child until the age of seven.' It wasn't the Jesuits who had us until that age, it was Christopher Robin, Buckingham Palace, Little Pig Robinson, Mr Toad, Sherlock Holmes, and a school called Clemes College. Our teachers made us keep scrapbooks on the doings of 'the little princesses', Elizabeth and Margaret Rose. What chance did we have? [...]

Those who have not been subjects of a global empire, who have not been made aware from infancy of what were then called 'ties of blood', will never understand these far-off things. No English man or woman will ever be able to experience what a colonial Australian or New Zealander of British or part-British descent felt about England. We were subjects of no mortal country; hidden in our unconscious was a kingdom of Faery: a Britain that could never exist outside the pages of Hardy, Kenneth Grahame, Dickens and Beatrix Potter; and yet it was a country we confidently set out to discover. We sailed, as soon as we reached our twenties, for isles of the Hesperides we never doubted were real. What no native of the 'mother country' could ever understand — what no one but overseas children of the Empire could ever experience, in fact — was the unique emotion summoned up by the first sight of a country known at one remove from birth, and waited for as an adolescent waits for love. We really did stare at the white cliffs of Dover with beating hearts; we really did survey London (familiar yet unfamiliar, in a dreamlike, paradoxical mix), with a surge of intoxication. This quickly wore off, as the cold realities of bedsitters and jobs descended on us; but nothing could rob us of those first hours and weeks.

These are archaic emotions, now. No doubt citizens of the imperial Roman possessions once experienced them, on coming into Rome for the first time. Possibly they will never be felt again. But those who dismiss them as a sentimental absurdity have no conception of their intensity, and fail to understand the central convictions and fantasies that history can brew up, shaking whole generations with their poignancy; making them willing to die for such fancies. Afterwards, as a joke, they are made to be merely quaint.

For me, the London of fancy became the London of fact at the age of twenty-two; and by pure chance, my entry was made via the Strand.

Robert Brain and I, penniless after hitch-hiking about Europe, had landed in England at Harwich, having come across by ferry from the Hook of Holland. We caught the train to London, and entered the tube system, to emerge into the city's open air at Charing Cross Station.

Here was the Strand then, on a fine summer's morning, carrying its human streams towards the Aldwych, St Clement Danes and the Inns of Court and Chancery where Dickens's Lord High Chancellor had sat at the heart of the fog, and no doubt sat still. Here were men actually wearing black morning-coats, pin-striped trousers and bowler hats, wielding furled umbrellas, whom we examined with joy, until one of them glared at us. Here was a real copy of *The Times*, bought from an actual, cloth-capped Cockney at the entrance of the station, who called Robert 'Guv'nor'. A man passed us now clad in a suit of green silk, wearing a green top hat and talking to himself. He was an unusual sight to young Tasmanians in 1955, but no one else in the crowd even glanced at him: here was the famous British tolerance of eccentricity. We entered Forte's café across the road, where we drank without complaint a grey liquid called coffee which was certainly not coffee; then, in a daze of delight, we wandered on under the promised porticoes and pinnacles of filigreed stone. There was Villiers Street, running down to the Embankment, where we might well have to sleep out, we knew, if we didn't find jobs immediately. And here, reassuringly, was Tasmania House, where we went in to the desk and found our mail awaiting us. This was our club, and London was already our home.

But if it was home, it was a stern and tight-fisted one. For the first time, we understood our good fortune simply in being born Australian. Post-war Australia was carefree and prosperous; post-war Britain was grim and poor; these facts were soon borne in on us, as we contemplated weekly wages which at home would barely have satisfied us as pocket money, and nearly half of which would be needed to rent a single bedsitting room. London was still marked by the Blitz: war-damaged buildings were being repaired, and flowers grew on the gaping bomb-sites. An air of austerity persisted, and people had the manner of cheerfulness in adversity: that style we had become familiar with in wartime British films. Faced with these realities, we soon separated. Robert landed a job in one of the counties, teaching in a summer school; and I found myself alone in London.

At that time, the new Welfare State didn't pay unemployment benefits which made survival possible; nor did one think of applying for them. I must quickly find work or starve; I had five pounds borrowed from Robert to stave off that eventuality, and my search began. Tramping the streets, gazing up at lighted windows in Charing Cross Road, Piccadilly and the Bayswater Road, peering through the doorways of buildings whose intimidating neo-Greek façades forbade entry to any shabby young colonial, I began to understand what the American writer Thomas Wolfe had discovered here before me: that there were two races in England, the Big People and the Little People.

These were the days before large-scale immigration from India and the West Indies, and the island's two indigenous races were very clearly recognisable; I was seeing, although I didn't know it, the last of the frozen old England which the post-imperial era was dissolving. The Big People, who ate in restaurants in Mayfair and Soho where the prices terrified me, were conveyed past in Jaguars and Rovers and Rolls Royces, and lived in another London than the one I was discovering. My London was the London of the tiny bedsitter in Bayswater or Earl's Court or Notting Hill Gate, with its gas-ring for cooking, gas-meter to pay coins into, aged washbasin and shared, freezing bathroom down the passage. 'Your bath will be on Tuesdays and Thursdays,' my first landlady informed me. 'Mr Drummond has his on Mondays and Wednesdays, and Miss Appleby has hers the other days.' My London was the London of the cheap caf, with sausages, eggs and chips for two and sixpence, and tea for fourpence. It was a London whose streets were the grey of old overcoats, its buildings of that liver-coloured brick whose hue seems the essence of despair; the districts of *Little Dorrit*:

> Wildernesses of corner houses, with barbarous old porticoes and appurtenances, horrors that came into existence under some wrong-headed person in some wrong-headed time... Rickety dwellings... like the last results of the great mansions breeding in-and-in...

This London, into which I was descending like so many other young Australians, was the London of the Little People: Cockneys and working-class Londoners who received us with the friendliness of fellow-spirits. Cockneys in particular assumed that an Australian was a sort of lost tribal brother, and one felt that this was so. The Little People existed with few creature comforts, keeping their clothes neat and maintaining an unaccountable jauntiness. They didn't own the houses they lived in; they had no cars; they could afford no holidays, except for a few days at Brighton; their only pleasures were a few pints of bitter in the evenings and a seat in the cinema or the music hall once a week. And this life was soon to be mine.

Crossing the Gap (1987)

1956

Malcolm Oram shipboard in the Persian Gulf

Malcolm Oram (1931–) was born in Sydney, the son of an English naval officer whose occupation gave his son varied experience but a disrupted education. Supported by factory jobs, Oram began studying engineering at night school. In 1953 he married Anna Bramley, an art student, and the beatnik couple dropped out of their studies and set off for Europe where they survived by peddling paintings, washing dishes and enduring the occasional regular job. After three years 'tramping around Europe', London winters and the '8.15 routine' palled, and they 'yearned for the company of our friends, for the pounding surf that rolled in from the Pacific, and for the smell of the bush'. However, there was an eight-month wait for tourist passages because of the shipping crisis and the pressure of the postwar immigration program: 'I thought how small I was, and how incapable I was of ever escaping from this technical society that squeezes us all into its pigeon-holes. I thought with distaste of the little pigeon-hole on the ship, and of Suburbia that waited us back home'. They decided instead to return overland, 'not just for adventure, not alone to see the world, but mostly for the chance to escape'. Equipped with a guitar and a Vespa motor scooter picked up in Italy, the couple joined the increasing number of Australians who took the overland route between Australia and Europe — the 'long brown path' — and lived to publish the story. This extract describes their journey on a pilgrim ship sailing from Basra to Bombay, on which their request to take a cheap deck passage together was refused, and Anna was forced to take a cabin.

The steamer was moored at the pier, just beyond the Customs shed. When we arrived the derricks were whining and clanging as cargo was perked upward and swung inboard. Coolies and porters were swarming over the decks, and up and down the gangplanks to deposit their enormous loads. The ship wasn't very big. Not much bigger than a channel ferry.

We were herded into the Customs House amongst the mustering crowd of prospective passengers. There were Pakistanis, Indians, Arabs and Negroids, and the air was full of an insistent babble, angry and pleading. The indolent police and Customs expressed their power and contempt in every movement and gesture, pushing and shouting and ordering. The people were old, young, ragged and poor. There were children a few months old, screaming and bawling in rag bundles, clutched by their mothers. There were old men, withered bone and parchment skin, feeble and shaky like rag-draped scarecrows. There were Arab women, shapeless black blobs, totally shrouded by abeya and veil. There were younger men and teenagers, who fought and argued, and managed for the old.

They had hungry eyes, these people, eyes pencil-sharp, sharpened by the war of existence. There was fear in those eyes, and there was cruelty. Black eyes darting to and fro, on guard for enemies, in search of prey.

There was an old man on a stretcher. The withered skin on his bones looked dead, but his eyes were alive, alive like an eagle. He would wear the green turban before he died.

When the Customs men spied us we were pushed through ahead of the others. We tried to protest, but the mere fact that we were Europeans, ragged as we were, rated us as superior beings. The incredible thing was that the people, too, stood aside with no word of protest. While the Customs were treating us with swami-politeness, an old Arab behind us was cuffed, shoved and abused.

We wheeled the scooter up the gangplank, and with the aid of the crew, lashed it securely to the rail. As I was checked on board I was branded like an animal, a purple ink stamp was pressed against my wrist. Anna almost collapsed laughing, but there was a touch of hysteria in her laughter. This would be the first time in eight months that we had been separated. She didn't stay long with me on deck amidst the cargo and the shouting. A crew member spied her, and led her aft to her cabin. An iron, barred door now separated us.

Meanwhile, the long stream of pilgrims was pouring into the narrow space between decks, a dark gloomy area that stretched almost from stem to stern, dodging around the engine-room with its scorching smell of heat and oil, broken up with cargo holds, steaming galleys, and companionways. The boards had been scrubbed, the soaking of water was still on them, yet they remained black and grimy. Overhead the low ceiling was an intestine mass of pipes, rusty flanges and chalky insulation.

The people were staking their claims, proclaiming a space as theirs by laying a mat, or fencing off an area with their gear and baggage. A few had erected harem quarters for the women by stringing up rugs from the pipes above. Some made walls of their gaily-painted tin trunks, or wooden chests, and before long the family coffee pot was simmering over a tray of charcoal. They brought livestock with them, too, ducks and chickens which they tethered to pipes and companionways.

I found a space for myself as far removed from the engine-room as possible, and spread my sleeping bag to claim it as mine. I kept the small rucksack with me containing things I may need on the voyage. The rest of the gear I had left with Anna for safe keeping in her cabin.

It was almost dark when the last passenger came aboard. I swathed myself in the sleeping bag and before long fell asleep. It was a chilly fitful sleep from which I awoke early to find the ship slowly slipping into the stream. I lit a cigarette and gazed around me. The pilgrims were already astir. The sun was rising and the faithful had spread their mats pointing towards Mecca. Beside me an old bearded Moslem was kneeling, softly chanting the morning prayer. Others were washing at the taps over the scuppers, blowing their noses and rinsing their mouths with noise and gusto.

The family groups had the coffee pots simmering, and children were bawling. Most of these people had made the pilgrimage to Mecca or Kadhimain, some perhaps to the Great Mosque in Damascus. They were poor and ragged, and had probably been travelling for months. The sick and aged could die content, for they had made the journey that every good Moslem should make once in his life. Others were Arabs seeking work, or business in the Gulf ports and India.

When I arrived on deck Anna was standing at the rail, waiting for me. The iron-barred gate that had separated us last night was open, and in fact remained so throughout the voyage, although policed by crew members to make certain that none of the deck passengers invaded the sanctum. However, no objections were raised about Anna coming to see me.

By late afternoon we were approaching the oil city of Abadan. Long lines of fish traps were spread along the river's bank, wooden piles driven in the mud to fence the tidal waters. Slowly round the bend Abadan came into view. There were tankers and tramps and all manner of shipping floating in the stream; amongst them darted a variety of small craft.

We nosed our way in amongst the anchored ships and came to rest. Spread over the barren shoreline was a frightening mass of steel organisms. Miles of intestine pipes burning bright with silver paint; squat silver storage tanks; cigar-shaped columns and cylinders; ladders and alleyways. Tons of steel, all bright, and brand new-looking, incongruous in an aged-worn land.

Lighters and canoes began to collect around the ship, attracted like moths to a lamp bulb. Wooden barges brought cargo and passengers. More Arabs, and Persians, destined for the Gulf ports where there is the smell of oil. They came clattering up the gangplank bearing their luggage and livestock, with their women, imprisoned in black shrouds, scurrying behind clutching infants and bundles [...]

Another day dawned. Below decks the morning prayer mats were spread, and the smell of cooking permeated the air. The engines throbbed and groaned, vibrating and drumming the deck beneath me. The women were preparing breakfast. I lay in my sleeping bag and watched life awaken the bowels of the ship.

The woman opposite was plucking a hen alive. The poor creature squawked and struggled in her grip, but the shrouded woman was unconcerned, or unaware of the creature's suffering. She just plucked methodically, with the same abstract movements of one plucking flowers. Other hens, poor unsuspecting things, were squatting miserably, with their legs tethered to pipes and companionways. There were some ducks making merry in the flooded scuppers, splashing and preening and shaking the water from their wings.

There were men hacking and spitting into the scuppers, and others were sitting round smoking the hookah. A group beside me, three men, were squatting round the water pipe, waiting for their turn with the stem. The tobacco was in the bowl, with a glowing coal of charcoal on top, and the smoker was sucking like a bellows through the long stem, coaxing the smoke, which bubbled through the water, whilst one of his friends fanned the coal with a fluttering hand.

A nauseating smell drifted from close by me. A smell of burning fat and kerosine. Two women were frying bread, flat cakes of dough, over a hissing primus. They were still veiled and shrouded, and in all the time I spent down below I didn't see one of these women lift her veil, even to eat. They simply tucked the food under the black folds, and there it disappeared into an invisible maw.

There were other black-draped women squatting around. There were two, still squatting where I had seen them last night. It seemed they hadn't even moved. Black blobs, impassive amongst possessions, dumped by their menfolk like any other article of baggage. Pathetic blobs of total black. One of them clutched a howling infant, and with a tired movement she bared her breast to meet its screeching demands.

The ship had stopped, and was slowly swinging on the tide from its moorings outside the port of Kuwait. The shoreline was as flat and misty as the early morning sea, just a long cluster of close-packed buildings, inscribing a line between sea and sky. This forlorn city is one of the richest spots on earth, yet the majority of its inhabitants live in rags. This is oil-rich Kuwait.

Lanteen-sailed lighters set sail from the port to cover the long shallow distance to the ship. The cargo of dates was swung over and more passengers swarmed up the sides. Some of them were Indians. Their contracts with the oil companies expired, they were on their way home. They came excitedly up the gangplank, full of gusto and self-importance as they shouted orders to the coolies bearing their luggage behind them. They were rich men now, by their standards, and carried out a bossy scramble to set up an exclusive colony by themselves on the deck. Most of them wore a hotch-potch of European clothing, loud American-type jackets and baseball caps, and were only too pleased to display their twentieth-century trinkets — key rings and watches, cigarette lighters and fountain pens. They spoke together in the rapid clipped tones of semi-English, and obviously counted themselves as superior beings [...]

We were already at anchor when I awoke next morning. The water was blue and shimmering, and the sun was hot, although it had not long appeared above the horizon. On the flat hazy shoreline there was a strange cluster of tall buildings. It was the city of Dibai. The buildings almost had the effect of skyscrapers. They were of parched mud brick, slender with two separate tiers. I found out later that the top tier, a high rectangle with long vertical slits, is, in fact, a ventilation tower. The light desert breezes flow through the slits and are sucked by partial vacuum to the hot void below.

The city looked forlorn and desolate, clustered so tightly together, with an endless expanse of desert stretching on either side. There were several dhows floating at anchor near us, and the craft from the shore were beginning to cluster around. More passengers were crammed in one of the boats below, shouting and arguing as they dragged their baggage on board. They were wild bearded men, with kufias wound turban-wise round their heads, some of them distinctly Negroid in appearance. They looked fierce and ragged, but even more alarming were their women. I encountered a physical shock when I saw them, so sinister and repellent were they at first glance. Perhaps it was calculated so. They were shrouded from head to foot in the black abeya, as were the other Arab women, but on their faces they wore a mask, a hideous hawk-like mask of purple leather, not unlike the visor of a Grecian warrior.

On deck they scrambled and argued with the men to claim a space. They seemed to exert more authority than the other women. One in particular, squatting amongst a pile of rag bundles, shouted instructions to her husband with domineering gestures, whilst a gluttonous infant gnawed at her breast [...]

Late that night there was a commotion downstairs, up towards the bow. From the open companionway we could hear the sound of excited voices, and the drone of music above.

'Let's go down and see what it's all about,' says Anna, throwing away her cigarette, and watching the red point drift towards the sea.

We climbed down the ladder, and made our way over the sleeping bodies, past the stalls where the merchants were playing cards, to the group of animated people clustered up for'ard. They made room for us to join them, with the bonhomie of party exuberance. Bottles were clinking and the blue haze of smoke clouded the animated and chattering cluster. A bottle of arrack was thrust into my hands, and we were invited to sit down, pushed forward to the circle of squatting and clapping figures.

The centre of attraction was a group of Omani women, still in their hawk-like masks, but with the black cloak cast aside to reveal their dresses. What a garish riot of colour! Their robes were embroidered to shame a peacock, and clustered with pendulant ornaments of silver and gold. Necklaces of coins, and chunky armlets of beaten metal. They had rings on their fingers and rings on their toes.

Music was wailing and scratching from an ancient bell-mouthed gramophone, modern Arabic music, an import from streamlined Egypt, hardly discernible above the chatter of voices. The onlookers were all men, all the oil-rich Indians were there, and the rest were Arabs. They clapped and joked with the women with the eagerness of schoolboys, and one of the girls, responding coquettishly with a toss of her head and a wiggle of her bottom, commenced to dance.

The boys began to howl and clap to the rhythm, pushing and shoving backwards to give the dancer room. With her arms stretched out like wings she wriggled her body, her breasts and hips and stomach bouncing as she stamped with her bare, ringed feet. The sex-starved men howled even louder with the blood pulsing through their excited veins. It was not a graceful dance, nor particularly intricate, yet the males were preening like turkeys.

One spurred by his comrades would reach out and pinch the wiggling bottom, and the roar of laughter would be drowned by the shrill, animated abuse. These women commanded a desire, a respect, a rivalry that no other Arab women, the purdah-draped blobs that we saw, remotely obtained. They were sitting in the throne. They were dancing girls, prostitutes, managed by the idiot-faced Arab with the bleak eyes, who was sitting behind, quietly puffing his hookah, his sharp eyes appraising the wealth of the drunken Indians.

The dancer retired, and engaged in a flippant banter with a bunch of cocky, almost bursting, excited Indians. There were shouts for another dancer. Everyone was acting big. Cigarettes were given generously and the clink of arrack bottles rang amongst the music. A group of the girls invited some of the men to share the hookah with them, flaunting their charms with laughter and raillery. Look at my wristwatch, honey! The boastful Indians displayed their wealth and trinkets.

The shouts for another dancer reached their peak, and a slightly plump prima donna rose to perform. She gave the impression of a bored sneer behind her mask as she tossed her head and began the first slow, stamping steps. She feigned unresponsiveness to the mounting applause. The record wailed, the men howled and joked and boasted. The dance tempo mounted. Her feet were stamping within the circle of the audience, swaying her buttocks, her belly was wiggling with abandon, and she issued the invitation with outstretched arms and bouncing breasts. The men were almost berserk with excitement, on their feet, stamping and clapping and howling. The bravest, urged by their comrades, hurled coarse remarks, and the dancer responded, jerking her body to and fro with suggestive motions, and wobbling her breasts with outstretched arms.

The proud Indian snapped off his wristwatch and placed it on her head. It disappeared with a swift motion, a movement of her hand in the dance, without recognition or a break in the tempo. Rupee notes followed and disappeared just as fast into the folds of her dress, and the air vibrated to stamping and clapping, and howls and shrieks of appreciation and delight. The excitement was tension taut. The whole five of the women were on their feet dancing now, wiggling and shuffling, clapping and singing. One of them, jealous of the others, snatched off her mask and revealed her face, and what restraint there had been was broken. The men clutched and grabbed at the girls. Some were dancing, others searching with their hands. But the women were the masters, and they called the tune. Soon they had order, and the men obeyed. The business commenced, an excited, breathless bartering for the price. The procurer in the background still sucked his hookah, and with his free hand was impassively changing the gramophone records.

The girl who had snatched off her mask was flaunting her power to the extent of donning the kufia of a man. Another snatched off her mask. They were both Negroid in feature, and wore a makeup of black charcoal, used like rouge on their cheeks and on the palms of their hands. For the first time I noticed the blood-red lacquer on the nails. Their teeth were badly stained, and their faces were coarse and ugly, but the men obviously didn't think so. They were in a state of almost exalted submission as the hookah was passed from hand to hand and the bargaining continued.

I had worked towards the front, trying to see everything that went on, and an Indian, more stolid than the rest, made room for me to squat beside him. The plump girl spied me, and began to ogle in an embarrassing manner. She took the hookah from her mouth and handed it to me, and not wanting to be impolite I took the stem and lightly inhaled the acrid smoke. The Indian nudged me so hard that the tube almost stuck down my throat.

'You're a bloody fool, man,' he exploded as I coughed and spluttered. 'She has syphilis, man. Look at her leg.'

I followed his gaze with my tear-filled eyes to look at the purposely-exposed leg. It was covered with ugly sores. The prostitute leered at me, a vulgar, hideous leer, and I crawled backwards as politely as I could to rejoin Anna. I was pale around the gills, and viewed my future with apprehension. I was beginning to feel a little revolted and wanted to get away to where the air was fresh, so Anna and I wedged our way out of the mob, back past the hatches and engine room and hot-smelling gal-leys, where the turbines thumped and the mass of humanity sighed and groaned and slept.

There was the old man they had carried on board, still alive, asleep near the engine room, with the stifling heat scorching the air around him, and the boards vibrating beneath his sleeping mat. He was like a stick swathed in rags, hardly moving as he faintly breathed.

You could almost feel the movement of the mass of breathing, sleep-ing bodies. There were the rug-draped harems where the women, used and cast aside, were in the land of deep slumber. There was the snoring of the old men, grey and withered, curled on their mats. There were women, still black and veiled, stretched asleep amongst their rags and utensils. There were children, too, burrowed close to their mothers, legs curled up under naked little brown bottoms.

There were Indian women, necks stretched back, big black eyes closed, their copper skins shiny in the faint light from the shuttered engine room, like sleeping butterflies in their coloured saris.

Outside the black sea hissed, parting in a shower of phosphorous at the knife-sharp bows. We sat smoking in the clear black night, watch-ing the Star of the East that shone brightly in front, beckoning us with a luminous streamer across the water. We didn't speak, we just sat and thought. This was no ordinary ship, this ship with its human cargo. It was a floating purgatory, the careworn faithful with their pilgrimage complete, knocking at the gates of heaven, but still floating in the anguish of life. And what of us, Anna and myself. We sat looking at the Star of the East, the star we had followed for so long. Now we were longing for another star, a cluster of stars, the Southern Cross that shone above our home.

The Long Brown Path (1957)

c. 1956

Shirley Deane in Spain

Teacher, Melbourne University lecturer in literature, broadcaster and travel writer, Shirley Deane (1920–) left Australia in 1948. From the early 1950s she lived in the Mediterranean with her artist husband and children. Her experiences of life in villages in southern Italy, Andalusia, Andorra, the Balearic Islands and Corsica were recorded in a number of travel books: Rocks and Olives: Portrait of an Italian Village *(1954),* The Road to Andorra *(1960), and* Feet in the Clouds: In the Mountains of Corsica *(1965). A sailing voyage that the pregnant Deane made with her husband*

and two young sons along the Mediterranean coast of Italy and around Corsica is recorded in The Expectant Mariner *(1962). In her travel books, Deane describes with wit and amusement her adventures in remote villages and observes local life and popular culture in intimate and affectionate detail. However, as in this extract from* Tomorrow is Mañana: An Andalusian Village *(1957), she could also be sensitive to the political nuances of ordinary village life under a conservative church and a military dictatorship. Her criticisms of Franco's Spain in this book led to her expulsion from the country.*

So we came to Pueblo with twenty pieces of luggage, two sons, and a brand-new cook. And, until our house was ready, we settled down to wait for it in the heart of the village, in the Street of Christ.

But 'settled down' is hardly the phrase to describe life in that narrow, noisy, fascinating, dynamic little street. There were cats and goats and donkeys everywhere, and children — an incredible number of children erupting from the doorways, making the street ring and echo with their games. There was singing and laughter, but never a sound in winter before 9 or 10 a.m. The people of Pueblo and their children go to bed after midnight, and get up late; they are not fond of hard work, and besides, there is too little work to do.

We, too, lay late in bed each morning, and listened to the village tuning up for the day, slowly waking to a confusion of musical sounds — the rhythmical beat of castanets clicking in the accomplished hands of little girls as they danced their way to school, the clattering of the donkeys' dainty feet, and the call of the milkman as he drove his herd of goats from door to door, their heavy udders swinging low to the cobbles, to squirt milk expertly into each waiting dish. For the housewives of this hot land have a sensible passion for freshness in food. They buy their milk on the hoof, their rabbits and hens still nibbling and pecking, and their fish on the beach as the boats come in, still gleaming and wriggling and smelling of the sea.

But now in winter the sea was often too rough for fishing, and there were no crops to be picked. There were always men idling at the street corners, proud, ragged, hungry men, standing or squatting, talking or dreaming, turning their heads in unison to watch each passing donkey, or the occasional bumpy progress of a bicycle.

And there were always women watching from their doorways, dressed in sombre black. For hours each day they stood there, looking up and down the street — like the men in winter, they had nothing else to do. Their houses are bare and tiny, and almost keep themselves clean, and there is little cooking, for the staple diet is bread. Their chief function is child-bearing, which occupies their full attention only once a year. For the rest of the time they stand and watch. They play no active part in the life of the street — that is left to the men, the children and the chattering girls. The women are the onlookers, the chorus who comment on the action, and all day long the street buzzes with their comment. They see everything, they hear everything, and the gossip swirls and hisses from one doorway to the next.

So life followed its leisurely, endlessly repetitive pattern, but it was never dull. On the contrary, it was a perpetually stimulating mixture of indolence and frenzy. A new village drama boiled up every day, and there was always something to celebrate — a procession or a wedding, a feast-day or a funeral [...]

A week or so after we arrived at Pueblo, the Mission began — eleven long days of religious observance, with services from dawn till midnight, and a cluster of visiting priests. The Mission is an annual event to renew the people's fervour, to coax the wandering flock back to the fold. Every morning during the Mission we were woken while it was still dark, but our sleepy rage was blown away by the incredibly sweet sound of chanting as the procession passed our window — the girls in white, the women in black, lanterns and incense swinging, and candles flickering in the cold, dawn breeze. There were few men's voices mingling with the clear, sweet voices of the women, for the men preferred the comfort of their beds. The women of Pueblo, having less to occupy their minds, are more devout.

Other processions passed at intervals throughout the day, and sometimes noisy groups of children with a priest, boys in one group, girls in another — for the whole social system is rigid and suspicious, and the sexes do not mingle, except by accident or skilful and surreptitious design, till they meet at the altar. Now came a disorderly procession of little girls, fluttering past in their clean white frocks. Two harassed priests walked backwards at the head of the procession, glaring helplessly at their charges. As they walked, they catechised the little girls, who chanted the responses sweetly in unison.

'How many gods are there?'

'There is one God.'

'Where do good little girls go?'

'They go to Heaven.'

'Where do bad little girls go?'

'They go to Hell.'

At the mention of Hell, all the little girls doubled up with laughter. They seemed to have no awful fear of hell-fire. Either they didn't believe a word of it, or they were young enough to be convinced of their own life-long virtue. The priests glanced at each other, cleared their throats, and quickly started again.

'How many gods are there?'

'There is one God.'

Precariously the priests negotiated a corner, and the responses drifted away along the next street.

The climax of the Mission was timed to coincide with the feast-day of *Santa Rosario*. Hermosa told us that there would be a grand procession through the village at nine o'clock sharp, and she organised us carefully for the occasion. She made me change my dress — everyone would be there, she said, and every woman in the village would examine me for flaws. She did nothing about Malcolm — already she despaired of parting him from his disreputable series of paint-bespattered pants — but she bustled off a shy village boy we had asked in for a drink, and served dinner an hour early. There was no time for coffee, she explained — we could have it, if we liked, when we returned. Then, all done up in her best black, she pushed us into the street, and linking arms with me in the inevitable Pueblo fashion, she swept us straight up to the market place, and into a bar. She collapsed on the nearest chair, panting with her exertions.

'There's plenty of time,' she gasped blandly. 'We might as well have some coffee while we wait.'

In a flash coffee appeared on the table, the proprietor's wife beamed and nodded behind the counter, and Hermosa beamed back triumphantly. It would have been clear to a baby that our visit was no surprise to either of them. The backroom girls, it appeared, had been at work to improve our drinking habits. The other bar in the market place was a Bar of the Poor — the fishermen drank there, and peasants from the mountains. We had wandered in the first week we arrived, found it clean and cheap and friendly, and saw no reason to change. But this bar of Hermosa's was the Bar of the Rich — the élite drank here, the mayor and the notary and the chemist and the Captain of the *Guardia Civil*. It was, explained Hermosa when we accused her of plotting, more suitable to our eminence as the only foreigners in Pueblo. It was, she said, more upper class, more gentlemanly — *mas señorito*.

'And besides,' she added practically, 'the coffee's better.'

It was, of course. Hermosa, we discovered, is always right — it is one of the most maddening things about her. (Months later someone told us that the *señorito* bar runs a small brothel on the side for the convenience of commercial travellers. It is not available to the men of Pueblo, who are watched night and day by their neighbours, but we enjoyed telling Hermosa about it. She is still recovering from the shock.)

On the night of *Santa Rosario*, however, we sipped our coffee suitably with the élite.

'Cognac,' said Hermosa wistfully at the top of her voice, 'is good with coffee.'

In a flash it was cognacs all round.

'Where's the procession?' we asked at half-past nine.

'What procession?' asked the proprietor tactlessly.

The efforts of the visiting priests to renew religious fervour had obviously been wasted on him.

'It will come,' said Hermosa, relaxing now after the effort of getting us dressed and out. 'Enjoy yourselves.'

After an hour or so, and several more cognacs, the procession slowly turned into the market place. First came the boys and men, then the image of *Santa Rosario* borne high on her canopy, and after a long and decent interval, the girls and women. Before each group a priest walked backwards, miraculously avoiding pot-holes and small boulders in the road. The priests chanted prayers, and led the singing.

Hermosa insisted that we join the end of the procession, along with the rabble of fathers and daughters who followed it together arm in arm. The singing, as always, sounded glorious to me, but Hermosa didn't think much of it.

After a faltering response, owing to the fact that the slowly-backing priest had turned a corner, and couldn't be clearly heard, she said in her hearty, penetrating voice, '*Santa Rosario* won't be interested in saving the souls of these characters — they don't sing well enough.'

The procession ended in the square by the Church, overlooking the sea. Here the whole crowd gathered, still neatly divided into males and females — several hundred people altogether, as visitors had come crowding in from all the farms and villages nearby. It was an impressive but not an impressed assembly. Everyone whispered and giggled, the men and boys lounged with their hands in their pockets, the girls, eyes sparkling with amusement, peeped out from their becoming black lace veils. When the leading priest made a personal appearance on the balcony of the Police Headquarters opposite the Church, a gust of laughter rustled across the square, like wind in sugar-cane.

There was a microphone on the balcony attached to a loudspeaker system which ran right through the village. As the fat priest's voice began to boom and crackle, the gust of laughter rose to hurricane force. He addressed the people of Pueblo for an hour, but it was impossible to understand one word. The loudspeaker mechanism, which was also attached to a microphone in the Church, was old and worn, but it was new to the village — the visiting priests had brought it with them. It caused a lot of amusement and caustic comment during the Mission. For every one of the eleven days, services were continually booming at us through the system, as we woke in the morning, as we undressed at night.

'The Word of God is all very fine,' grumbled the people, 'but we can do without it in our bedrooms.'

One night Malcolm and I went for a walk to avoid the Word of God. We walked across the fields of volcanic rock to the mountains, which were transfigured by patches of white moonlight, and dark, dramatic shadows. We walked for miles, but every inch of the way the sound of the Mission followed us on the still, clear air. We couldn't escape. It was all around us, following us behind, and echoing back to us from the mountains in front. The priest's voice rattled on, staccato, distorted, unintelligible. The responses of a hundred voices in the Church roared like infernal laughter in the mountains. They couldn't have been so disturbed, so shaken with sound — these mountains — since they erupted countless centuries ago. It was a monstrous, tinny, artificial sound — juke-box religion, canned religion, the religion of a Brave New World. It was unnerving and blasphemous.

But at last the Mission was over, and the visiting priests packed up their loudspeaker system, and departed. Once more the mountains were wrapped in their ancient dignity and silence. Once more the people settled back into the leisurely pattern of their lives, till the next village drama came to disturb it.

Tomorrow is Mañana (1957)

1959

Alan Moorehead in Kenya and Tanganyika

Born in Melbourne and educated at Scotch College and the University of Melbourne, Alan Moorehead (1910–83) was a journalist for the Melbourne Herald *for five years before 'escaping' to Europe in 1936: 'I yearned to go abroad, to get to the centre of things and events that I had been hearing about at secondhand all my life'. Joining the London* Daily Express, *he was sent to Gibraltar in 1937 and then to the Middle East after the outbreak of war. Moorehead became the best-known war correspondent in the North African campaign. The popularity of his three books on the war in North Africa, published together as* African Trilogy *in 1944, allowed him to move from journalism to full-time writing, and after 1946 he lived mostly in Tuscany. Moorehead won international acclaim for his biographies of Churchill and Montgomery, his travel writing, including* The Villa Diana *(1951) and* Rum Jungle *(1953), and his histories, notably* Gallipoli *(1956),* The White Nile *(1960),* The Blue Nile *(1962) and* The Fatal Impact *(1966), all of which drew on his ability to evoke a sense of place. His autobiography,* A Late Education, *appeared in 1970. Moorehead's interest in environmental matters is reflected in* No Room in the Ark *(1959), from which this extract is taken.*

Nairobi is the safari capital of Africa. This is the base where most of the hunters, the photographers and the ordinary run-of-the-mill sightseers assemble their vehicles and their equipment before they set off into the blue. You can travel very simply if you like, driving your own car and stopping for the night at country inns along the way. Camping, on the other hand, is more complicated and expensive and involves problems over petrol, water and food. Quite a number of people, however, get about with caravans or hunting cars that are fitted with beds, tents and cooking gear, and usually they take a couple of African boys along with them. Finally, you can go to one of the safari companies and travel *en grand luxe* complete with a white hunter and a regular entourage of servants [...]

In normal circumstances I do not think that my wife and I, on our journey through Africa, would have dreamed of going on a full-dress safari of this kind; we usually travelled by train or by ourselves in hired cars, and in any case we were not interested in shooting. In Nairobi, however, one of the best-known white hunters, Donald Ker, invited us to go out with him on a month's trip as his guests. Ker, a small compact man now in his early fifties, is an interesting case. Having spent half a lifetime hunting in the bush — at the age of sixteen he was already out on his own, sometimes for months at a time, shooting elephant — he cannot now bear to destroy a wild animal of any description, except for food; and even that he does with reluctance. His chief interest now is the study of wild life in its natural surroundings, and with this end in view he proposed a fascinating trip to the extreme south-western corner of Kenya. Here is an area of some six thousand square miles which for a long time has been a kind of island in the centre of the continent [...] Ker and my wife and I rode in front in a hunting car with Saidi, his head boy, and a five-ton lorry followed on behind. The lorry was loaded with sleeping and dining tents, food and fuel supplies for a month, a good deal of heavy equipment for making repairs and getting across rivers and swamps, and of course a medicine chest. Such of the ten boys who could not get into the cabin of the lorry were perched on top of the baggage. The sun was shining and morale was high.

It was Ker's idea to take a roundabout route to our objective, travelling southwards first to the Tanganyika border and then moving westward across the Serengeti Plains towards Lake Victoria. We were to stop just short of the lake at a place called Ikoma, on the Grumeti River, and then strike northwards into the unmapped and uninhabited country. All this first part of the journey has been pretty well known to travellers for the past thirty years, and the roads and the well-worn tracks give you a sense of familiarity and security. It is a vast space, but space that has been tamed and civilized. Yet it is impossible to travel far in this part of Africa without something outlandish happening. On our first night, for instance, when we were camping under Kilimanjaro, I was introduced to a special breed of leather-eating hyenas. Hyenas, heaven knows, are capable of anything, and their own flesh is said to be so repulsive that even vultures will reject it if they can get anything else. Hyenas prey upon the young, the weak, and the dying, and no carcass is too rotten for their taste. Here around this camp there was no shortage of food; we had seen a dozen different varieties of antelope moving around the waterholes just as the daylight was fading, and the baboons were in hundreds. Yet this particular breed of hyenas around our camp was said to have a special predilection for good solid tanned boot leather. I did not altogether believe this, but when I went to my tent that night I tucked my own shoes (a thick-soled pair bought just a month before in London) well under my camp-bed.

Sleeping under canvas in the African bush is a special experience until you get used to it. The leopard coughs in the darkness. The hyenas grunt and snarl and whoop as they prowl about. A faint flicker of rose light from the camp-fire strikes the canvas above your head, and you hear, or think you hear, the first distant throaty roar of a hunting lion — though of this you cannot be quite sure because the noise is very similar to the deep voices of the African boys who sit on, hour after hour, around the fire telling endless stories to one another, and pausing only, when the leopard comes near, to throw another log on the flames. One thing at least is tolerably certain: wild animals loathe and fear the human smell, and although they may approach quite close out of sheer curiosity they will not come into the camp itself. Often in the morning you will see the tracks of some large animal, a rhinoceros perhaps, not fifty yards from your tent. The tracks, a series of large rosettes in the dust, come on very steadily until suddenly the animal has picked up the hateful scent in the air, and you can see where he has wheeled sharply away into the bush.

It seemed therefore incomprehensible to me on this night that I should have been woken by a strange presence in the tent. It was not so much a presence as a smell; a smell so vile, so absolutely sickening, it appeared for an instant to be an imaginary thing, part of a particularly bad dream perhaps. I groped for a flashlight and something an inch or two away from my face vanished into the darkness. All this was a great joke in the morning when the boys searched everywhere and found not so much as a trace of a hobnail from my shoes. Even the rubber heels had been eaten. After that I slept with my second pair of shoes inside my bed.

Hyenas have amazing savagery and determination. One alone will drive away a cheetah, the great spotted cat which is the fastest thing alive. (When some years ago cheetahs were raced against greyhounds in England the cheetahs jumped clean over the greyhounds' backs to get to the front.) Two hyenas will force a leopard to abandon a kill; a dozen of them will defeat a lion. Once Ker and I in our car headed off a hyena that was about to pounce on a baby Thomson's gazelle, and we chased it for upwards of six miles at twenty miles an hour, round and round in circles on open ground. It was not even breathing hard when we stopped at last. And when it turned its dark muzzle over its shoulder towards us, looking at us without rage or fear, simply accepting, as wild animals do, the instant prospect of death, we were a little ashamed.

Part of Ker's aversion to shooting is tied up with this matter of pursuing animals in cars. In earlier times — and not so far back as Roosevelt either — you tracked your quarry sometimes for scores of miles and for days or weeks on end. In a certain sense you earned the trophy. Now you drive along in comfort until you find your buffalo or your rhinoceros and the law requires you to walk only five hundred yards away from your car before you shoot. Very little exertion and not much danger is involved. Neither hunger nor any great skill in tracking brings you to the kill; and somewhere in all this the true excitement dies away.

I began to see Ker's point quite unexpectedly a day or two after we had left Kilimanjaro behind us and were moving west through cultivated country on the edge of the Great Rift Valley. We were six thousand feet up and a cold rain was falling. Across the muddy soil a stray gazelle buck came running, and a young African tribesman, naked except for a cloth around his waist, started up in pursuit. Normally the man would never have had a ghost of a chance of catching the buck, but perhaps he thought the mud would slow it up and anyway this meant a month's supply of meat. Man and animal went flying across the skyline at tremendous speed, bounding from one tussock to another, and they must have gone half a mile or more when the buck took an unlucky turn towards a group of native huts. A woman came out with a spear in her hand, and as he rushed past the young man grabbed it out of her hand like a runner in a relay race. He disappeared finally, his spear held high and a barking dog at his heels, over the curve of the hill. The buck was still going well and I don't think the young man ever caught up. Yet he was a real hunter, almost a figure from a classical frieze with that straining back, and one wished him luck, one would have liked to have seen him launch the spear and the kill would have been a good kill at the peak of a concentrated excitement.

No Room in the Ark (1959)

1962

Cynthia Nolan in Ethiopia

Cynthia Reed (1913–76) was born in Tasmania into a wealthy pastoral family with artistic interests. She made her first trip to Europe in the 1920s where she was greatly attracted by the theatre, the Diaghilev ballet and modern art. She returned to Australia but left again in the early 1930s, travelling through North America to England where she trained as a nurse at St Thomas Hospital in London. This experience became the basis for her later novel, A Bride for St Thomas *(1970). From London Cynthia Reed went to the New York Medical Center to further her nursing studies. When war broke out she came back to Australia. Through her brother, John Reed, an art patron and prominent member of the Angry Penguins group, she moved in the circles of modernist writing and painting, and in 1948 married Sidney Nolan. The journeys they embarked on together provided the material for her travel books,* Outback *(1962),* One Traveller's Africa *(1965),* Open Negative: An American Memoir *(1967),* A Sight of China *(1969) and* Paradise and Yet *(1971). The Africa that Nolan describes is one seen through the lens of European art and literature as is illustrated in her wry account of their pilgrimage by plane and bus to find Rimbaud's house in Harar. In her later years Cynthia Nolan was tormented by tuberculosis and she committed suicide in London. She was remembered with fondness and affection in Patrick White's autobiography,* Flaws in the Glass *(1981).*

'Just look at it, will you,' Sidney muttered. 'You can see why, apart from all the other reasons, Rimbaud lived around here. It's all so like something I latched on to when I was a youth. A part of my life, those poems were, when I was eighteen in Melbourne and was starting off to try to say my own say, and finding out all the difficulties in a town that had the same sort of closed mind that Charleville had in 1870. Reading Rimbaud was an enlightening experience for me. Well, he produced that great revolutionary body of work and then he quit. He came to Africa and he didn't pretend, it wasn't a stunt. He quit.' [...]

We were over a vast, brown, speckled plain where dry river beds were the only tree-lined roads. The land melted into the distance, the greys and browns becoming ever more delicate until they were whispers, shadows of colour, or echoes which were not so much colours as afterglows. And even glow was too strong a word; they were rather aureoles of colour already reflected from some far-off world.

Sidney was photographing at top speed, excited by having one area after another isolated, concentrated in a round or square.

'The only difference from Australia is that there's no horizon line here, remember that,' he told me, not taking his eyes away from the telephoto lens. We flew on. Soon there were bare, uneven summits beneath us and the colour was very much stronger. Beaming, he turned to say that this was 'the complete recipe'. Soft sooty specks were thrown from slight clouds to move over ground which looked as though it had been fired, but was in fact black basalt formation through which ran ochre channels dotted with new-green bushes [...]

A taxi was waiting. It tore over the rough country road, into the market square, and through the companionable crowd exchanging gossip round the door of a ramshackle bus. As soon as we appeared the seats immediately behind the driver and his friend were vacated and we were thrust into them. Then we sat for three quarters of an hour and waited for the bus to fill up. The seats were of remarkably hard wood and had uncomfortable backs which left a space just where one needed support.

A woman heavily veiled and draped got in. Was she really able to see from behind that strip of white lace that covered her eyes and ran like a crack in the dead black bundle? As our crowded conveyance moved out of the town she took off this mask and let the enveloping folds of her cloak fall back to reveal a plump bare-armed girl in a floral frock.

The asphalted road mounted gently, winding through scrubby hills. Along a dry watercourse a train of camels undulated. Several tall slim girls, dressed only in a brown piece of loosely girdled cloth passed over one shoulder and falling to their feet, walked, with surging gypsy strides, beside them.

'They must belong to the same tribe as the girl Rimbaud brought to live with him in Aden,' Sidney said. 'She looked just like that, I know she did.'

The women who got in or out at every village, on the other hand, seemed another race or mixture and were inclined to buck teeth. One no longer saw fresco-faces but Muslim women, sometimes heavily veiled. Many flies clustered round their babies' eyes and the unmistakable smell of discharge competed with new-mown hay, for at every stop the bus became more crowded with chat.

On the left was a lake, on the right a large grove of eucalypts among whose trunks a busy market was in progress. We had only 30 kilometres to travel, but they seemed interminable. At last, stopping at the outskirts of Harar, on a corner of the large main road which has been driven right through the heart of this old Islamic town, we were set down.

Feeling slightly sea-sick I walked over ground that appeared to be rushing to meet me and followed Sidney up the stairs to our room. The hotel had been built, well enough, by Italians, but the present management left just about everything to be desired. We longed for baths but there was no hot water and no soap, both bathroom and lavatory smelt like a *pissoir*, and we could not get anything but coca-cola to drink. However, as we had found so often, there was a rewarding view from the lavatory window which framed a wire pen surrounded by oleanders, poinsettias, geraniums, and an ostrich savagely pecking at pebbles.

On the other side of the netting a bullock hide had been spread under a flowering oleander; its very recent inhabitant was being divided up by a muscular and skilled man. He was a carver on the grand scale and would have put any surgeon to shame. Small boys placed great portions of ruddy meat in a wheelbarrow hazed with flies and trundled them away.

It was four o'clock. We had eaten nothing since an early slice of breakfast toast but in spite of this and of being so near the equator, the altitude prevented any feeling of exhaustion. Sidney could not wait.

'I know where Rimbaud's house is,' he confidently told me. 'It's near a Czech church —'

'A Czech church? What's that look like?'

'What do I care. It's a church with a tree growing in front of it and the house is two-storey and overlooking the town. Rimbaud could see the white twin-minarets of the Turkish mosque rising above the flat mud-roofs of the houses.'

We were already walking away from the hotel up a slowly curving dusty road; soon there was a church with a tree growing before the entrance.

'Damn, I remember now, it wasn't a Czech church, it was a Czech hospital.'

But he soon located a two-storey house. 'Just as I have so often, and for so long, imagined. And Rimbaud would sit in one of those upper rooms, looking on to the brown-baked walled town and across to those blue mountains.'

It did not matter that this house was not, as we had been told it should be, a Muslim school. Sidney was on another plane of reality. He went a little way off, by himself, and I sat down on the dry grass and closed my eyes, knowing he would remain here for some time.

The minutes went by and perhaps I dozed a little. Daylight began to fade, allowing the first stars to shine weakly out. Suddenly there was the sound of pounding hooves. Two horses raced past, their riders young men bending low, their shamahs flying. One horse was snow-white. Sidney ran to keep them in sight but already those thundering beats were away around the next bend — fading — leaving only a blur of disturbed dust. He turned to me then, his eyes sharp as ice. 'The one on the white horse, it was Rimbaud.' His voice squeaked with excitement and conviction.

There was another path back towards the town, downhill and across a boulder-strewn stream. A man who was stooping washing his feet straightened and stood upright. Surely this was where the photograph, 'Rimbaud at Harar', was taken? Stained, faded and spotted, it lies in the files kept at the library in Charleville, the town the poet so detested, where he suffered so abominably — and whose citizens now honour his fame. But a group of children who had been following us began to chant *ferrenge*, foreigners, and Sidney, looking round in surprise, realized for the first time that we were not alone. To hold his thoughts intact he walked off briskly, soon outpacing me. I was left crossly trotting a hundred yards behind him, a perfect victim for teasing infants.

At 8 a.m. next morning there were grunts and shouts, typical of the noises one sometimes hears on the acutely disturbed floor of a mental hospital. But the hotel was near a military school and this was the hour for inspection and a change of guards. The shadows of gum-trees striped khaki shoulders, providing Sidney with an immediate flashback to his army camp-life outside a country town in Victoria.

The soldier on guard saluted and went through a great deal of music-hall business with his rifle. 'Poor bloody mug, learning to dig your own grave.' With a sigh Sidney turned from this aspect of warfare to remember his own experiences. 'I enjoyed some of it, terrifically. Being out in the Australian country and having time to think did a lot to my painting, got me to see the Australian thing away from anything else — from people and talk and reproductions in books — got me to see what I had to do and say.'

A soldier on horseback trotted past, leading another horse by the bridle. 'I'd like to have a horse and really learn to ride. Just think of those riders last night, racing their horses. Rimbaud,' he said, 'Pierre Chardin, Livingstone and all the others. Africa is a magnet that attracts steel filings from all over the world.'

Last night I had looked up Enid Starkie's *Arthur Rimbaud* and read, 'The chief place in the city (Harar) was the principal market square; it was surrounded by a high wall and one whole side was taken up by Raouf Pasha's palace which he built when he conquered the city in 1874. It was the only large building in the town, the only building with a second storey, and this was the house rented...' It was *here* that Rimbaud lived, above the store, trading cheap European goods for musk, coffee, hides, ivory, guns and gold, or bargaining for them at the cheapest rates he could get. He was trader, gun-runner, explorer and probably slave dealer. But although obsessed by making money he was exploited by his employers and the local inhabitants. In Harar he continued to think out plans that were to make him rich but that never succeeded, for the good reason that he was not a businessman.

Egyptians held Harar for ten years; Rimbaud was here under their jurisdiction and again later after its conquest by Menelek, King of Tigre. When Ras Makonnen lived in the palace as governor he became a close friend of the Frenchman who no longer wrote poetry and had by then endured years of frustration, hardship, disappointment and terrible intellectual loneliness. He had changed, or rather his 'merciless clarity of vision', his charity and his capacity for affection, had triumphed. 'The people of Harar,' he wrote, 'are neither more stupid nor greater scoundrels than the white niggers of countries alleged to be civilized. They are merely of another breed, that is all. They are, if anything, less nasty…' There is no life more infinitely pathetic than that of this great poet; his was a genius exploited and betrayed, first and last, by his mother.

The drilling figures in khaki marched down the road and out of sight. 'Let's go,' Sidney exclaimed, suddenly back from Dimboola where he too had lived in khaki. He began to collect cameras.

'This palace,' I said, my finger between the pages of the book marking the place, 'this palace where Rimbaud lived must be the one we saw last night when we were overlooking the town. Do you remember, it stood above all the other houses?'

Sidney was not interested, the other house had been good enough for his visions. But after we had gone along the wide new main boulevard and were nearer the old city, walking past shops that were little more than booths selling odds and ends of clothing and soft drinks or coffee, he once again began looking for a 'two-storey house that is now a school'.

And soon there was a church with a tree before it, then a Czechoslovakian hospital with a newly-built wing. A white-coated, golden-haired woman, a stethoscope dangling from one hand, walked through a small group of out-patients waiting in the courtyard and crossed the road. She looked pleased and content and I would have liked to stop and talk with this happy doctor. But now Sidney quickened his pace. In front of us was a tumble-down wall surrounding an area of trampled earth and a slightly decrepit two-storey building. Some children had again been following us. They were now joined by others who had been playing among the stones.

'Ask them if this is a Muslim school.'

'Yes, yes, Muslim,' chanted the crowd of boys. 'Come on, come on.' It was the Pied Piper in reverse. Tugged and pulled, danced in front of and beckoned, we followed them up rickety stairs. Avoiding holes where veranda boards had rotted through, we went round the back of the house and again gazed upon the far semi-circle of mountain tiers.

The children pointed boastfully down into the smelly yard explaining to us, unnecessarily, that they had lavatories. They grabbed at Sidney's arms when he began to photograph, clamouring that he point the camera in directions they found more interesting, chiefly, for once, themselves. Others were continually joining them. They were beginning to grow slightly menacing. Soon stones were likely to be thrown. We were relieved when some youths yelled at them to leave us alone and chased them away, allowing us to wander up and down the narrow, maze-like, rain-corroded tracks between high stone walls. An occasional door ajar revealed life going on in dusty earth courtyards. Sometimes it was the rubble and mud walls of the square houses themselves that lined the way; then there would be a foot-square opening high up under the flat mud-and-lath roof. There was something both secret and alluring about these quiet walled pathways and the hidden simple life that went on either side of them. Hararis no longer placed their sick in these alleys, there to recover or be devoured by the hyenas and other wild animals who managed to slip through holes in the city's walls or past one of the five huge fortified gates, but apart from a few changes in customs this part of the town was exactly as it had been when Rimbaud listened, at night, to the 'baying of the wild dogs on the ramparts'.

We had been walking unthinkingly and found ourselves suddenly back on the main street. A passer-by stopped to tell us that if we wished to photograph, we would find a good view from the second storey of a house nearby and slightly set back from the pavement. He pointed towards stairs, on the outside of the building, that led straight to the veranda.

'No,' said Sidney, suspecting foul play. But I was already half-way up for I wanted to look down into the town, to see from above what had been standing for so long. Sidney, unwilling to be left alone on the pavement, chose the other evil and followed me, muttering. But once upstairs he was pleased for not only could he again see the house (Muslim school) where Rimbaud had lived, but also the old mosque which although now roofed in corrugated iron still carried its two minarets, dazzling in whitewash. Men in flowing robes paced across the courtyard, left their sandals by a doorway and entered the building for prayer. Others were pounding, with small pestles, what looked to be the leaves of chat. Sidney could photograph undisturbed. Already he had screwed the telephoto lens into one of the cameras and was gazing through it.

Long slim pigeons with red eyes and snow-speckled wings stood on the wooden veranda struts. Stepping carefully, I explored round the corner — to come slap up, face to face, with what most certainly was the old palace of Raouf Pasha. What an example of serendipity! The tall building was crumbling in places but inhabited, for behind the barred groundfloor windows, where Rimbaud had stored the goods he purchased and those he used for bargaining, a boldly printed frock moved as though possessing a life of its own. Upstairs there were wrought-iron gratings too, but only over the lower half of the windows. Before the wide arched doorway two sheep, white but for black heads and necks, bleated as if from habit.

Between the house on whose veranda we stood, and the palace, was a large open space, certainly once part of the great market-place which was thronged daily by noisy merchants bargaining over their cattle, hides, guns, ivory, musk and coffee. A single pomegranate tree was in flower; there were a few tall inky cypresses which sent meagre shadows across the bare ground. A soldier in khaki, taking a short cut, led a reluctant goat by a leather thong. They disappeared between the rows of cube-houses directly below us. There were bicycle wheels and a broken chamber pot lying on rusting iron roofs; in a beaten earth yard a mother bathed her baby in a red-and-pink enamel basin. Sidney, slung about with cameras, called out that he was finished here and wanted to go to the open market outside the city's remaining walls.

'I've found the real Rimbaud house,' I told him.

'I don't care, either of the other two will do me.'

Once again in the back lanes of the town we lost our way in a small square where open booths were selling underclothes, coloured soft drinks, rolls of flowered or plain cotton and strings of glass, plastic, and amber beads. A girl knelt on the ground before a basketwork tray on which she was neatly arranging plain rounds of silver and of brass, bracelets for women and children. While looking at an amber necklace and in spite of all our efforts to refuse his services, we were picked up by a very dubious looking man who spoke French. He told us he was unemployed and would gladly take us to a house where men were making jewellery from silver.

'No, thank you.'

A girl, gaily dressed in a red and orange shamah and coloured skirt, now began to talk vehemently to our self-appointed guide. She had a round pretty face and was herself wearing a string of beads.

'She says, "What do they want with amber, that's our thing, that belongs to our country. What do they want with it?"'

She was very young and in quite a temper.

'She reminds me of our daughter, who must be just her age. Tell her we have a daughter and want to bring her a present from Harar.'

The girl looked thoughtful, then nodded her head. We hoped this was an acceptable answer; it had been a truthful one.

'Do you know anything of Rimbaud?' The guide became ecstatic. Monsieur Rimbaud the French poet? Yes, of course he knew about him. Did we want to see the little house where he lived when he came back to Harar after the governor Ras Mokannen had taken over the palace? Where he lived with the girl?

'That house was pulled down,' I said coldly.

'But it's been built up again.' He laughed triumphantly.

I would have gone with him. I would have spent weeks talking about Rimbaud, here where he had lived for so many years. Sidney was carrying a letter of introduction written to a doctor who was the local authority and knew whatever was to be known of the stones and land-marks, the facts and fiction, the comings and goings — to Cairo, Aden, Tajoura, Ankober and the plains of Danakil — of the tragic French-man. But Sidney also knew exactly what he wanted from this town which he had first dreamed about when, as a boy, he was reading both the translations of the poems and those terrible cries of boredom, frus-tration and pain, Rimbaud's letters to his mother.

'You would rather go to the market? I'll show you. This way please.' We were then shepherded along until we were outside the city walls but about a mile from where we wanted to go. 'The market will begin this evening,' our guide smiled.

Sidney suddenly pushed me into a passing gherri and in a whirl of dust we left the man standing with his mouth open. He was so aghast that the cupidity was completely wiped from his face.

One Traveller's Africa (1965)

1965

Dymphna Cusack in Albania

Dymphna Cusack (1902–81) wrote in her autobiographical notes that she started on her 'nomadic career' at the age of 3 when she moved from Wya-long where she had been born to Cooma. After graduating in arts from the University of Sydney, Cusack worked as a schoolteacher until crippling neu-ralgia forced her retirement. Although told that she would never work again, her capacity to dictate allowed Cusack to become a prolific writer, now best known for her novel, Come in Spinner *(1951), co-authored with Florence James. Cusack, as well as writing some thirteen novels, worked for*

*women's rights, the peace movement and the socialist cause. Her first over-
seas trip in 1930 took her to Ceylon where she was utterly repelled by British
racist attitudes to indigenous people. With her husband, Norman Freehill,
Cusack spent most of the years from 1949 to 1972 overseas, living mainly in
the Eastern Bloc where she could support herself with the royalties from the
sales of translations of her books, which went into the millions in Russia.
Her time abroad produced three travel books,* Chinese Women Speak
(1958), Holidays Among the Russians *(1964) and* Illyria Reborn
*(1966), her account of her visit to Albania, which begins with an evocation
of the Illyria of Shakespeare. Appropriately, her official guide was a poet.*

A dream come true at last, I said to myself as the plane took off from
the Budapest aerodrome into the driving sleet. Here I was flying southward to that romantic land which had haunted me ever since my
schooldays when I asked on my first entrance as Viola in *Twelfth Night*,

'What country, friends, is this?'

and the answer came,

'This is Illyria, lady.'

Far off in that Australian country town the word glowed in my
mind along with Samarkand and Rome, Isphahan and Peking, all
seemingly unattainable as dreams. And now with Rome and Peking
and Samarkand already in my world of reality another dream was to be
realized.

To get so far I had flown across a Siberia blanketed in snow and ice;
to an England muffled in fog; back to a snowy Paris; southward over
Europe, an abstract painting in white and black and grey. And now
below me on a bitter morning stretched a vast snow-covered plain with
wind-driven patterns, cobalt blue shadows, and the Danube looping
across it like a ribbon of steel.

I lost myself in a dream. All my life I had read everything I could
find about Illyria, a land whose history goes back into the mists of
time, on whose soil all the ancient civilizations of the Mediterranean
have left indelible traces, of whose past so much is written; of whose
present so little is known.

'One hour and we are in Albania,' my travelling companion, a
young engineer returning from the University in Warsaw, told me in a
mixture of Italian and a lingua franca we had invented to fill our linguistic gaps. On the map he traced with a loving forefinger the outline
of his tiny homeland embedded like a jewel in the matrix of the
Balkans: Jugoslavia closing round it in the north and east, Greece on

the south-east and south, on the west an improbably blue Adriatic with the heel of Italy less than fifty miles away at its closest.

Albania! That jolted me out of my Illyrian sentimentalities. What did I know of Albania except that the tourist office had guaranteed that there would be sunshine?

[...]

Here, I was to find, Yesterday and To-day are always close together. Everything reminds one, too, that here East and West met and mingled. Western clothes, baggy Turkish-type trousers (prekushe), voluminous pantaloons (citjane) tight to the ankle, worn by Musulman women of all ages topped usually by a black waistcoat, the whole surmounted by a triangular white veil of fine muslin drawn nun-like across the brow, one point hanging down the back, the others loosely crossed in front.

Others wear a black chachaf, a black shawl worn much the same way, its corners covering the ears and chin, sometimes even the mouth, and falling cape-like to the waist above a shapeless black skirt.

The Poet explained that not so long ago the skirt reached to the ankles and over the chachaf went the mask-like perché that hid the face entirely, as the yashmak does.

Life flows by, placid and unhurried in the clean streets. Housewives shopping; a kindergarten in short white smocks above long pants taking its morning walk, girl and boy hand in hand; a tall old man walking by with slow dignified steps, in jodphur-like homespun trousers, a long brown sheepskin cape swinging from his shoulders, a weathered cheleshe on his head, the Albanian fez-like, high white felt hat.

Two old women, their heads swathed in black, billowing black capes falling to their heels turned into the gateway of a Greek church.

From the minaret, the Muezzin called the Faithful to prayer while the Angelus pealed out from the Roman Catholic Church.

There was much to delight the romantic eye, particularly in the ancient market-place with its narrow cobbled streets lined with the tiny shops of artisans, 'soon to give way to a House of Culture,' my Poet said proudly, showing me the plans of a fine building. In a way, I regret it, for here is a picture for which the maker of travelogues would give much, an island of life as it must have been for all the city's three and a half centuries.

We made our way through the tangle of alleys, the scene new and strange to me, the extraordinary variety of folk costumes rivalling the standardized tailored clothes of Western fashion, peasant women in richly embroidered costumes, some fresh and new, others very much the worse for wear; striped aprons in a harmony of vivid colours; baggy brown trousers; full skirts topped with embroidered jackets;

embroidered veils of white and yellow; headkerchiefs; knitted stockings of an infinite variety of intricate designs — everything homespun, every pattern with its own significance.

The greater number of the sellers in the market are women, in itself a new thing. In the 'old' days (so close!) it would have been thought not only a shame, but a crime for a man to let his wife go to market.

They are as curious about my clothes as I am about theirs, and many eyes go to my slacks. Nowhere in the world have I seen women wearing such an astounding variety of pantaloons as I saw in the next six months — voluminous, stove-pipe, frilled and striped. Yet my very ordinary slacks always caused excited comment, obviously not all approving.

A handsome people, these. Haughty faces. High-prowed noses, flashing dark eyes, luxuriant black hair: an amalgam of ancient stock and countless invaders that time has subtly moulded into a distinctive racial type.

A high degree of artistry is shown in the hand-knitted socks with traditional complicated patterns of purple and red and yellow and black, the woven brez men wind around their waists like a cummerbund. Cheleshes in every degree of newness and oldness, some encircled with red scarves, others with yellow. Embroidered waistcoats above white felt chideke — the tight Balkan-type trousers that suspend themselves miraculously from the hip and cling like a second skin to thigh and calf. Braided in black there is nothing more picturesque particularly when topped with a cape-type coatee with woollen pompons on the shoulders and a long fringe swinging with every movement.

'There is a legend that long ago that cape was worn in colours,' my Poet said, 'but after the death of our national hero, Skanderbeg, it was changed to black in sign of mourning and it has been black ever since.'

Village-made, pointed, upturned opingas (the peasant footwear of the Balkans) step side by side with factory-made shoes.

I had a feeling that Yesterday was very close, a feeling that deepened as we entered a low dark shop selling ancient costumes richly and beautifully embroidered in gold and silver, their designs quite different from the peasant costumes.

'They were once worn by the beys and pashas and their wives. Before the peasants could not afford anything so beautiful, to-day they wear them on festive occasions.'

I was only half-attentive; I wanted only to look and to listen.

Incessant, deep-tone chatter. Somewhere a radio playing a tune in an Eastern mode: the Poet hummed a few bars. 'A Tirana wedding song.' The quacking of ducks, the gobble of turkeys, the braying of donkeys, the clop-clop of wooden sandals. The tinkle of a stringed instrument they call the cheftele. Chickens to sell, eggs to sell, fodder to sell.

In shops men carving long wooden pipes and cigarette holders and colouring them dexterously.

A forge where a smith beats out on a primitive anvil an axe of the shape that was found in Illyrian tombs.

Gaily dressed gipsies peddling home-made tinware. A maker of cheleshes and pantoufles (white felt slippers) working the soapy wool on a sloping table whose ribs have been worn bare, taking pinch after pinch of wool and felting it into the soapy mass.

Shops with foodstuffs I have not seen elsewhere. Sellers of llokum (that in my childhood we called Turkish Delight), the most delicious I have ever tasted. Halva one eats with a spoon from a minute saucer. Coffee shops where café turq — black, thick, syrupy — is drunk in tiny cups.

The smell of baking; trays of large brown loaves withdrawn from deep brick ovens.

An old woman in a black citjane, a large dish of corn bread balanced on her head, wrapped in a white veil from which looks out a weathered face with sunken tragic eyes.

Homespun carpets sway in the breeze, royal blue and crimson and an exciting green, their traditional designs older even than the city. (One finds them also in Bulgaria and Roumania.) Shops with cheese and kos (the Albanian yoghourt); black olives and green olives (they have no equal anywhere in the world); piles of red pimentos; oranges and lemons from the Albanian Riviera.

The new food market across the square is conducted with full regard for the science of hygiene and is consequently more frequented but less picturesque!

In the Street of The Goldsmiths the craftsmen turn out exquisite silver filigree work of a great variety of designs. Witness to the old world so short a time away was an antique shop with a display of superbly engraved guns and pistols.

A photographer with a waiting queue and, on his list of samples, a picturesquely caparisoned male with a gun in his hand, and a miniature arsenal of outsize pistols in his brez. To what period did such an anachronism belong?

The Poet shrugged: 'Zogu's time. The Vendetta raged, the gun was always at the ready. Only twenty years ago in this market two of his followers fought and two innocent people were killed.'

Illyria Reborn (1966)

1969

Nancy Phelan in Chile

Writer Nancy Phelan (1913–) was born in Sydney to a family with literary leanings. The niece of writers Louise and Amy Mack, she attended the Sydney Conservatorium and the University of Sydney, and first went abroad in 1938. She married in England and lived there until the end of the war. Her autobiographical work, The Swift Foot of Time *(1983), recalls her time in England in the 1930s and 1940s. After her return to Australia, Phelan continued to travel widely and has told the story of her travels in a number of books:* Atoll Holiday *(1958), about her experiences with the South Pacific Commission Social Development Section from 1951 to 1956,* Welcome to the Wayfarer: A Traveller in Modern Turkey *(1965),* The Chilean Way *(1973) and* Morocco is a Lion *(1982). Phelan visited Chile in the period leading up to the 1970 presidential election, which returned Salvador Allende as the world's first democratically elected Marxist head of state. Her reporting on the democratic tradition of 'the Chilean way' reflected common opinion at the time, but it was crushed by the CIA-backed military coup of General Pinochet in 1973.*

The first Chilean soil I landed on was Easter Island, *Isla de Pascua*, a great triangular island over 2000 miles west of the mainland. The Santiago–Tahiti plane stops there for two days on its flight across the Pacific.

The native name is Rapa Nui; it was called Easter Island by the Dutch admiral, Roggeveen, who discovered it on Easter Sunday, 1722, and it became Chilean in 1886. In the past, Spanish, French and British expeditions called there, but until the Lan-Chile airline service began, the only regular communication with the world was a Chilean naval ship bringing supplies once a year. The only white residents were Chilean officials and a Capuchin priest, the only visitors stray anthropologists or archaeologists.

Between planes it is still very lonely. Huge long-headed stone figures stand staring out to sea or fallen flat on their backs. Some have pitched forward upon their faces, others lie still unfinished in caverns, rigid, half-formed, as though melting into the stone. On the high rocks overlooking the ocean are carvings of bird-men and below are subterranean caves where youths of the island went into retreat before undergoing tests of endurance. These included swimming out to a group of rocks, to collect the egg of a sea-bird.

At each end of the island are extinct volcanoes. On blue days the wide grassy slopes of the saddle between them are golden like grain and the sea is the colour of cornflowers, but with a grey sky and bitter winds there is a feeling of absolute isolation. Silent, motionless, the crocodile-coloured crater lake in the mountain evokes a sense of foreboding.

Some of the islanders, who are friendly and poor, work at the airways transit camp and sell wooden figures and shell necklaces to tourists. They are organised to dance for the tourists, but even when put into *pareus* and grass skirts with flowers behind the ear they are not really gay like the Polynesians further west. There is something sad about them, something sombre about Rapa Nui, as though past sufferings ... the ravages of smallpox, the raids of Peruvian slave-traders ... have left an intangible cloud.

On this remote and lonely island you may now meet transient groups of North American Moms with blue hair and bejewelled glasses. They come on Package Tours — 'Mysterious Easter Island' — from the U.S.A. via Santiago, the Chilean capital, and are prone to beat down local souvenir merchants and complain about lavatories, meals and having to sleep in tents.

Santiago lies inland, at the foot of the Andes. It is a cheerful city which looks more French than Spanish. Though it is over four hundred years old, it has been destroyed so many times by earthquakes and other disasters that very few Colonial buildings are left.

When I arrived it was crowded, hot and untidy. I had come into the midst of a garbage strike which made me feel at home, since I had just left one in Sydney. The heat was also familiar, though in Sydney a breeze may come from the harbour during the day and at night there may be a cool change from the south. In Santiago you swelter all day without relief, but after dark the temperature always drops. On the terrace you need a stole, even a cardigan, and at first I felt cold in the night. This cooling-off, which is due to the Andes, allows you to pull yourself together for the next day [...]

Street stalls were set up wherever there was room, selling plastic monstrosities, books, ball-point pens, novelties. There was a long line under the trees in the Alameda where the crowds promenaded, chatting and pausing to look and buy.

The Alameda de las Delicias is the central section of a very long avenue, named after Bernardo O'Higgins, the Chilean Liberator. It runs like a ribbon across the map of Santiago, from the Alameda Station, where trains leave for the south, at one end, to Providencia, where the smart shops are, at the other end. It follows a dry river-bed, an arm of the Mapocho River on which Santiago is built.

Looking up from different parts of the city you see the Andes, pale and bare against the sky, with far-off peaks of eternal snow. In the hills and slopes on the outskirts of town are restaurants and night-clubs where people go to forget their worries in drinking, singing and dancing. In winter there are magnificent ski-slopes within easy reach.

Between Avenida O'Higgins and the Mapocho River is a Japanese garden, now called Parque Gran Bretana. If you ask why, you are told that the name was changed during World War II when 'Japanese Gardens' sounded unpatriotic. You may also be told that technically Chile is still at war with Japan, since no separate peace treaty was ever signed.

On the far side of the river is the hill of San Cristobal. From the top, which is reached by funicular, is a fine view out over Santiago and up to the mountains. At night, a floodlit figure of the Virgin floats above the city. It is charming to see, but has not been very effective against destruction.

From time to time the earth shakes, just to remind you. One day, at the Crillon Hotel, the crockery began to rattle. Olga leapt up, but the gentleman at the next table leant across and said soothingly, 'Do not disturb yourself, senora; it is only a little *terremoto.*'

Perhaps this unpredictable background has helped form the Chilean national character, the mixture of stubborn philosophical endurance and ability to snatch enjoyment from very little. The people are of European descent, often with a decreasing Indian strain. Spanish blood has been mixed with French, German, English, Irish, Italian, Scandinavian and Yugoslav. The aristocracy and landowning families were mainly Basque.

The mixture of bloods, their geographical conditions have made the Chileans different from their neighbours. They are more balanced, less explosive. They also have a large steady middle class. They have been called the English of Latin America.

For most Chileans, life has never been easy; there have always been wars with Indians or earthquakes, or tidal waves, floods or fires, and now, among other things, unemployment and years of shocking inflation, going up annually. Yet so far there has been no great bloody revolution, apart from the War of Independence. People tell you with pride that that is not the Chilean way; that they have always tried to solve their problems by politics rather than shooting, that in their national motto, *By Reason or by Force*, reason comes first.

They are proud of their reputation as the most democratic, the most politically mature South Americans. Bolivar himself considered them more suitable for a republican form of government than any other peoples in the continent, but in fact the democratic tradition goes back even further, to pre-Conquest times. The Araucanians were dedicated to freedom and their chiefs were elected by the people.

Everyone in Chile talks politics, even the children. It is part of daily life, almost an obsession. In November, city and countryside were already plastered with names of candidates for the September elections, and discussions raged in buses and streets. Chilean politics are unspeakably complicated, but everyone has opinions.

[...]

One night I went with Juan and Yvette to the Pena de los Parra, an old house in an old part of Santiago. When we arrived, several *carabineros* were out in the dark street by the front door. They looked both homely and sinister, with chubby faces but business-like rifles. We wondered if they were expecting a protest or demonstration of some sort, for students and left-wing supporters come here for the music.

Inside, we passed through a couple of rooms where records and hand-made copper jewellery were displayed for sale, and entered a smoke-filled darkness. People were sitting quietly round tables, waiting peacefully, not even talking. We edged into a bench against the wall and a carafe of red wine was brought.

Through an opening into a second room I gradually discerned more figures on chairs, on stools, on the floor. Between the rooms a kitchen chair stood on a dais. In the background, high up, bars of yellow light shone through a fanlight.

Presently a weak lamp was switched on above the kitchen chair and a boy appeared with a guitar. He seemed very young and the shadows thrown down on his face gave an impression of sadness. He began to play gently, almost to himself, then to sing in the same meditative, absent way, as though a particular note had brought something back to his mind. He sang beautifully; his voice was warm and rich, it had strength and fire without harshness. The songs were nostalgic, melodious, going down into the far depths of memory and human experience. Their essence was universal, their words were of love, heart-break, protest, gaiety underlined with sadness, but the rhythm, the music, could only be Latin American.

What makes this music so unmistakably different? Is it the Indian strain? The haunting element in Spanish music is there, but the harsh Arab touch is replaced by something softer, more wistful and vulnerable. Sometimes it is terribly human, sometimes not quite of this world. It does not have the detachment, the elusiveness of the East, nor the faint undertones of self-pity of Russian and Irish melancholy. It is deeply tragic and lost, unaffected by bursts of high spirits.

The next singer was Isabel Parra, a thin girl with a beautiful-ugly face. She sang with a guitar, then with a strange little instrument covered with fur, made from an animal's body. It was shaped like a tiny mandolin and had a tone of extraordinary sweetness.

Her voice was small but pure. She sang quietly, with intensity, of the hills, of the sadness of separation, of love and loneliness, of mothers weeping because their babies were dying of hunger. She asked why men were so cruel to each other and life so full of bitterness. She bent over her little fur instrument as though nursing an animal, her face half-lit, half in shadow.

When her songs were done, she slipped away, and people quietly drank their wine and ate *shaslik*. No one talked.

The Chilean Way (1973)

5

1970 to present

Travels in postmodernity

T he arrival of the jumbo jet in 1970 produced as profound a change in the meaning of the overseas trip for Australians as the development of the steamship a century before. No longer was overseas travel necessarily a time-consuming 'once in a lifetime' experience. Suddenly Australians had physical access to the outside world as never before. Despite this, the Grand Tour tradition of a year in Europe accompanied by copious diary-writing continued for many Australians on completion of their formal education. The difference was that they could expect to revisit highlights of their Grand Tour on many later trips during their lifetime, and they could diverge considerably from the beaten track, along with their families, when they returned overseas as businesspeople, conference-goers, sportspeople, shoppers, and holiday-makers. Australians felt at home in the world as never before, a confidence reflected in contemporary fiction as well as the emergence of Australian-based tour guides such as the Lonely Planet publications. A surprising number of writers represented in this section maintain homes in more than one country. Another critical transformation came when postwar migrants and their children returned to countries of origin scattered throughout the world. Through their travels they developed a whole new set of meanings for words like 'Home' and 'Australia' and 'Return', and added considerably to the Australian stock of emotional attachments to place.

But this is also the era of the 'post-tourist',[1] the tourist who bears no animosity to other tourists and embraces the unauthentic with relish and irony, the modern nomad who knows no settled attachment to place. Just at the time when Australia was released from its burden of provinciality, when Australians were confident in their cosmopolitanism, when Australian fiction seemed as at home in Europe or Asia or America as Australia, when Australians could confidently claim a seat in the intellectual republic of the West — at the very time that process was taking place, postmodernity decided to revalue the margins. Australia was condemned to a metropolitan status just as the centrifugal rush off to the periphery began.

1975

Suzanne Falkiner in Central America

Born into one of Australia's best-known sheep-breeding dynasties, Suzanne Falkiner (1952–) not only travels and writes about her travels, but has also reflected on the travel experience of that generation of Australians who came of age in the 1960s and 1970s. At 21, having finished a university education that had failed her expectations, she packed a canvas bag and with cheap champagne in paper cups was seen off by friends at Central Railway Station on the first stage of her overland trip to Paris. She spent three years travelling in Asia, Europe and South America. On her return in 1977, Falkiner worked in publishing and as a freelance writer, writing up her travel experiences and weaving them into her first novel, Rain in the Distance *(1986), in which the boundary between fiction and travel writing disappears. She has speculated on the readiness of young Australians to 'lightly get up and go, sojourning for years in another country before equally lightly returning home'. For herself at least, travel was the means to inhabit a greater psychological territory. Yet she has asked whether Eveleigh Street, Redfern, might not be further away and more threatening to white middle-class Australians than Bond Street, London. In* Writers' Landscape *(1992), Falkiner explores the sense of place in the imagination of Australian writers, while her interest in psychological transgression is found in her 'faction' work,* Eugenia: a Man *(1988), based on the life of an Italian woman who lived as a man in Australia for over twenty years. Falkiner now lives in Sydney, but spends some months each year at her house in Italy.*

It took a long time to get to Buenos Aires from Mexico city, some five or six months, travelling by local bus and trucks. We came down off the plateau and over the Rio Grande, leaving the suburban ratlands. Further south the country became less fertile. Cactus grew on the hillsides like small trees, the houses grew more primitive.

We stopped for a while in Oaxaca, where the streets were full of cowboys and children peddling chewing gum and cigarettes. There were no buses, so from there Jane and I picked up a ride with a rubber thong salesman in a small yellow Volkswagen. With him we voyaged through green mountains with eagles drifting in high circles above the forest, past valleys filled with floating cloud, past mud-brick huts with plastic Coca Cola signs displayed proudly.

At one point we stopped at a dusty plaster village with a blazing hot central square full of untenanted soft drink stalls and football game machines left over from some fiesta. The plaza was dominated by a huge old white-washed church. The shoe salesman disappeared with his neat briefcase into the local *zapateria*, a rectangle of darkness in a white wall where only a few pairs of second-hand shoes and plastic sandals hung outside, and while we waited for him we sat at an outdoor table and drank warm Coca Cola from bottles scratched and opaque from recycling. I remember thinking then that I was going a long way from the things I knew.

At Tehuantapec we sat in the market and waited for the bus south among dried maize leaves and political posters and wooden-handled knives from China laid out on sheets of plastic and watched over by squatting, silent Indian women.

At San Cristobal de Las Casas we again stopped for a few days, feeling a little ill from the height, resting and drinking camomile tea. I remember spending mornings in a white and turquoise courtyard, mending my clothes, while the old man who ran the hotel sunned himself on a plastic chair, drowsing, seemingly immobilized by the powerful light. San Cristobal was a clean white town with white-paved streets and a church on a hill where the bishop blessed the *campesinos'* trucks and bicycles for twenty pesos apiece.

Approaching Guatemala the highway was again lined with thick green rainforest. Bright yellow butterflies floated above the lantana. I caught glimpses of a marshy water covered with duckweed; the atmosphere was hot and sticky. We caught a bus full of *campesinos* to the border; the driver blew us a kiss and then turned the bus around and churned back into Mexico. We started walking with our bags on our backs through No-Man's Land towards the Guatemalan side. Three kilometres. There were no more buses that day, perhaps because it was Sunday. I walked for half an hour, my bag hanging heavier all the time on its leather strap, until Jane drew gradually ahead, and I was alone.

I don't know what happened after that. The air became thick and oppressive, and suddenly it was so quiet that I could hear a ringing in my head. My shirt was soaking wet. I put my bag down carefully on the road. Everything — the pebbles on the roadside — seemed strangely close and distinct. I sat with my forehead on my knees, resting against my bag. I do not know how much time passed like this. I felt nauseated, my head was too heavy to lift, and Jane had disappeared.

When the wave of dizziness passed, I looked up and saw in the distance two Guatemalans approaching. Small men, in woven shirts and calf-length white trousers. The sun flashed on the silver machetes they carried. The idea came into my mind that they were going to kill me, take my money belt and passport, and throw my body in the jungle. There was only the empty road in either direction, and the ringing in my head. I could already see my body lying there, flies buzzing, the rib cage split open like a melon.

They seemed to be approaching very slowly. When they were alongside me, on the other side of the road, they stopped, and held a short conversation. One of them approached me, where I was still squatting on the ground, the glittering machete swinging loosely in his hand. He looked down at me and spoke.

'*Perdone?*'

He spoke again, patiently.

I suddenly realized that he was offering to carry my bag.

[…]

Guatemala. The name painted on the back of the bus, so far as I could translate, was 'Nobody's Sister'.

In the front a fat man, part-Indian, part-Latin, talked loudly in Spanish, holding up plastic pop-out packets of dirty-green pills. The bus was full, mainly with Indian women sitting two or three to a seat. Jane and I found seats towards the back. The women watched the *mestizo* over the heads of their babies, bound closely to the bodies with shawls, with calm, enigmatic expressions. The babies were silent. It was twenty minutes after the scheduled time of departure.

'... *viente-cinco para uno solamente, cinquante para dos, uno quezal para quatro completo ...*'

Talking continuously, the man fanned the packets expertly in one hand and with the other held up paper charts. These were protected from the dust in plastic bags, and represented lungs and intestines. His brown thumb looked dirty against the lurid illustrations. The day was hot, and the bus filled with the acrid smell of the *campesino* women dressed in layers of sweat-stained cloth. The monologue showed no signs of ending; the women stared in silence. We also waited.

Then, quite suddenly, just as the bus was about to move and the driver was tapping the hawker impatiently on the shoulder, one woman pulled out a little roll of twisted cloth from her woven *yuipil* and handed over a small amount of money. Another did the same. Soon half a dozen women in the bus were counting out coins from meagre supplies hidden around their bodies and examining the little folders of pills, which at a distance appeared to be vitamins. The *mestizo* got off, grinning, and the bus started.

Time passes slowly on buses.

The man sitting next to me filled in his time by systematically pulling his broken watch to pieces, and then one by one losing all the cogs and sprockets from his outspread handkerchief as the bus progressed over the rutted road.

The sun changed position in the sky, and then, suddenly, hours had passed.

In Salvador we sat in a shack beside the black sand beach on wooden chairs eating oysters and *conchas*, shellfish soaked in their own blood-red juice. The stalls sold turtle eggs like dented ping-pong balls, soiled with the sticky black sand, and delicate shell necklaces of translucent sunset pink. The Salvadoreans on the beach, skinny adolescent boys mainly, swam in their underwear; collected empty beer bottles on their rickety tables; and hissed quietly at us when we passed. Although not when we were with Gustavo.

As evening approached, fluorescent tubes made hard white patches in the fading afternoon light, illuminating the shacks. The musicians wandered from restaurant to restaurant, table to table, playing sad, romantic songs, looking bored. Gustavo beckoned them over and paid for a song.

On the beach a mottled brown pig scuttled around on the black sand, staying well away from the waves that crashed on the rock-strewn waterline.

Gustavo said, 'At this time of the year there are rocks. You should have come at a different time.' He seemed embarrassed by the presence of the rocks, which made swimming uncomfortable.

I didn't understand. I said, 'You mean at other times there aren't any rocks?'

'No.'

'Where do they go?'

Gustavo didn't know. The tides. He shrugged. It was one of those mysteries into which he had not inquired.

When we met Gustavo he was wearing a Daytona Beach Tee-shirt and strolling tentatively along the shore beside the volcanic lake. He was gentle-looking, verging on plump, with the inevitable little Latin-American moustache and soft brown eyes, and he had very bad breath. We had caught a bus away from the city's dirty buildings and roaring traffic and found ourselves in a shanty-town of fried chicken and fried-fish houses, little shacks among the trees overflowing with children and dogs, men in singlets, broken-down vehicles. We were nervous, trying to get away from the half-naked boys who walked on our heels repeating in a monotone the few English phrases they knew. The older men sat back in their chairs in the café-shacks, hissing from a distance with slow, amused grins on their faces.

'Are you American?' I had asked him. Meaning, North American. The company of an American might have saved us from the attention of the men.

He looked confused. Said that he spoke English but was not American. We asked him if it was safe to eat the little fried fish from the stalls. Then he laughed.

'For me, yes', he said. 'For you, no.'

He took us to lunch. When we had finished, he asked us if we would be offended if he paid. Then he drove us to the beach in his car, to swim and listen to the bored musicians.

A few days later he arrived at our hotel with a small, dark man with long hair and startling blue eyes. This was Enrico, who was partly

Indian, he said. They had come to take us to another beach, a private one, owned by the blue-eyed Indian's family.

We drove seventy kilometres in a battered truck through the rain-forest, parallel with the coastline, until we turned off the highway to a dirt track that wound down a valley towards the sea. In the front of the truck Gustavo concentrated on his driving, while, bouncing in the ruts, we held onto the dashboard and door frames for support. I thought uneasily, We don't know these men.

The track continued for about eight kilometres, steadily deteriorating, taking us further from the psychological safety of the asphalt road. I looked at Jane and she looked back, widening her eyes a little. She shrugged almost imperceptibly. Outside the left-hand window the ground appeared to fall away into a steep gully. It was six o'clock, and I estimated that we had only an hour of daylight left. Then we reached the beach.

The house Enrico had spoken of had been partly destroyed by a rockslide, and the thatched roof was a bare wooden skeleton in places, letting in the sky. It balanced precariously on a huge rock. In front was a platform of tiles, some brightly coloured, some cracked, the edges falling away into the eroded gully. From its broken rim, steps descended a cliff-face of sheer black rock to the black sand of the beach. The light was already fading.

We had come here to swim. We were governed by the conventions of the invitation. So, in spite of the gathering dusk, amid the twisted trees, we shyly and carefully took off our outer clothes and laid them on the rocks. We picked our way into the ocean, feeling naked. The two men followed.

We swam in a natural pool formed by an enclave in a jumble of volcanic rocks, which had been patched with concrete in the larger gaps. In the dimness our bodies seemed too pale in the transparent water. Except for Enrico, whose dark skin blended chameleon-like with the black rocks. The men watched us as we swam, and were in turn buffeted by the turbulent water within the pool, but mostly they seemed concerned with their own activities.

Afterwards, we sat on the rocks, smoking cigarettes, holding them carefully in our wet hands. It was now almost completely dark. Bats swooped out of the vegetation, flickering in the corner of the eye. The waves looked silver. The blue-eyed Indian sat down next to me, having composed a careful sentence in English.

'What kind,' he asked slowly, 'what kind of physique does a man have to have to please you?'

Gustavo had obviously told him that I had turned him down the night before.

The man's long black hair fell over his face, and he appeared only as a dark shadow beside me. I remembered, earlier in the evening, watching a tiny crab that he had allowed to run over the knotted muscles of his upper arm. Its claws were too small to grip the nuggety flesh. He reminded me then of Antonio. Now he was waiting for an answer. I tried to think out a sentence in Spanish. I looked at him, and then suddenly all my accumulated tension left me. It didn't matter. I laughed, sitting on my rock. He looked puzzled, but said nothing.

That was all, really. Nothing happened. I don't know what I had expected. What was important was to overcome the fear of the *cul de sac*. Enrico and Gustavo drove us back to the hotel, out of the storm, to safety, and left us there, smiling, apparently happy with the day.

Rain in the Distance (1986)

1978

Gerard Lee in Indonesia

Born in Melbourne, the son of a bank manager, Gerard Lee (1951–) moved with his family to Brisbane when he was 14. After a Christian Brothers education, he entered the University of Queensland, leaving with an arts degree in 1974. Lee embarked on a career as a primary teacher until a prac teaching experience in Fortitude Valley changed his mind. He has worked as a clerk, salesman, house-painter and journalist, including four years on the Bundaberg News-Mail *and the Brisbane* Telegraph, *interspersed with bouts of travelling. His stories, mostly satirical pieces set in Queensland, caused some offence among the locals. His work includes novels, collections of short stories and film scripts, including* Sweetie *(1989) with Jane Campion; and in 1995 he wrote and directed his first solo feature,* All Men are Liars. Troppo Man *(1990) concerns Australian travellers in Bali.* Eating Dog *(1993) is a self-deprecating collection of travel stories from the age of the jumbo jet depicting the insecurities and vulnerability of the young Australian abroad. In Sulawesi on his twenty-seventh birthday he is prepared to admit he is not in control of the situation.*

You catch a bemo in the main street of Rantepao. If you're smart you'll sit in front so you don't have to share your seat, for six hours, with squealing pigs or a bag of sweet potatoes. You'll sit with the driver and another passenger and you'll keep winding the windows down because it's 100 in the shade, 120 in the sun and 200 in the front cabin. You'll keep winding them down, and they'll keep winding them up because they're cold or scared of devils or some other thing you wouldn't even begin to understand. (Ask one question, get fifteen answers.)

After about the second hour you'll start to smell, really badly, and so will they. They'll sweat and smoke cheroots, you'll sweat and fart dog-meat farts. The ducks at your feet, pissed off with being tied up so long, will start to shit carbon monoxide. And the odours will mix together in the cabin and cook so that as you pass over the mountains on the worst dirt road you've ever seen, as you skirt cave-ins and fallen rocks and 300 metre drops at 90 K, as you ford streams and chug up impossible grades and swish around hair-raising bends, you'll be on the verge of puking, but you won't let it happen, you'll hold back somehow, because you know, deep down, that that's what they want you to do. They're doing all this so they can watch a white man puke.

And then, suddenly, just as you're on the verge of giving in, just as you're about to heave all over the windscreen and the guy next to you and the ducks at your feet and top off the stench you've spent the last six hours creating, you'll see it down below, nestled in between azure sea and jungle mountain — the little wooden houses of Palopo, cuddling in together under the coconut palms and above it all in the pinking evening sky, a soft moon. You'll think it looks like paradise, you'll think it's been worth it, you'll almost cry at its beauty, and when you get down there, amongst it all, you'll change your mind.

I thought it was paradise. It looked like the kind of place you could live on fresh fish and coconut milk and sweet fruit drinks and be happily attended by simple young girls. It looked untouched, like a freshly opened box of chocolates with none missing.

The bus pulled into a gravelly area about the size of a football field. There was a market going on at one end and near the bus stop, a kiosk.

[...]

At the nearest cab rank, the becak drivers watched as I tried to make a deal with various members of their fraternity. I walked from one end of the line to the other — about thirty men — offering what I believed to be a fair price for a lift down to the sea. They wanted about ten times the usual price. Eventually, I decided to walk it but two of them followed me down the road for about a hundred metres, hassling and baying, trying to get me aboard. Nasty guys.

The birthday boy then entered the Street of Hell. I could see the ocean at the end of this long street lined with coconut palms and cute wooden houses. It was dusk and I hoped to sit on the beach for a while and calm down. As I entered the street a woman's voice from a house on the right called out to me: 'Hello mister.' And then she laughed. I didn't look, I kept my eyes on the soft sea.

Then som one on the left called out, the same thing. I shot quick glances to ei er side and saw women's faces appearing in windows, laughing, call ıg out, obscured by the tropical dusk.

In a few m ıutes I was in the thick of it. Those behind were still calling after me, nd from either side the laughter seemed to be coming from deep wi ıin the trees. '*Hello mister, hello mister, he he he he.*'

Up ahead, could hear them being aroused. They were coming out onto their ver ndas in groups of five and six. A schoolgirl's laughter is hard to take b t two hundred metres of grown women laughing is like being beaten o death. Simone de Beauvoir says girls laugh at men almost involu tarily because of their fear of the erect penis. I tried to keep that thou ;ht to the fore.

This was t e paradise I'd seen from the mountaintop, these were those elegant alms, these, the sweet wooden houses and these, the simple, young girls. I was losing my grip. I slipped into a cargo cult state of mind Why didn't the Australian Government have a long-range helicopt r to fly in and save lost Aussie boys like myself trapped in a dusty Ind nesian street? I was so close to home. More than anything, I wante to see that helicopter appear in the sky, above red light flashing, the c able pilot in dark shades with a tiny mike, pressing the button, letting lown a skyhook to winch me up and spirit me away. He didn't have to ıke me into the bubble with him, he could just let me hang there, or the end of the line as we fled south across the watery straits, speedir ; through the night … It would only take a couple of hours and I'd e home. There below me, the wonderfully deserted moonlit plains of my own beloved country, spreading out. He could drop me anyw ere on Cape York, anywhere in the Gulf Country, any wild place, any crocodile-infested river, I could walk it from there. I'd be safe. Anywh re in Australia.

But the laug ing kept on … *hah ha haha ha ha ha haa haaa ha ha.*

Somehow I ma e it to the beach which was another severe body blow. Mudflats stretc ed for more than a kilometre before any suggestion of water.

I walked alo ; the esplanade — a few shops and huts, most of them deserted, and f ally found a place with a light on, a shipping office. When I say offi e, I use the term loosely. It was also a storage shed for drums of petrol nd plastic tubing. A fellow was working at a desk. He was chubby-fac l with a bulging nose, a sheen of sweat across his features. Were the any boats to Australia or Nuigini? I asked. He told me, no.

I tried to ask bout planes but I didn't know the word. The diction-ary would have ome in handy. There was a blackboard behind his desk. I mumbled and fumbled my way over there with him looking at me in growing unease, and tried to draw an aeroplane. He was mildly amused, but put out that I had the cheek to use his chalk. My first attempt wasn't good enough. On the third go I managed something recognisable. He shook his head, no planes.

'Where do the boats go?' I asked.

'Malili,' he said, bored with me now. 'Canadian boat leave Malili,' (he pointed south) 'Cape York.'

'Cape York? In Australia?'

'Yes, on Thursdays.'

Thursdays! If I got on that boat I'd be in Australia by the weekend. I could hitch home from Cape York! I could walk it. Home and hosed. The huge steel hull of that Canadian vessel loomed up in my mind. It was my saviour. I pictured it at the dockside in Malili. I talked to the captain; I mixed it with the crew, played cards in the canteen and got dropped off on the Cape. I was going to get on that ship.

'Where's Malili?'

He pointed to it on the map. It was just across the water from Palopo on one of the many peninsulas in Sulawesi. He explained I could buy a ticket and leave on a boat tonight at 9 p.m.

'Tonight?!'

He nodded.

On my way to the jetty, I reminded myself I was on holiday and although I'd had food poisoning, intestinal worms, ring worm, skin parasites, moles, tropical ulcers, diarrhoea, dysentery and Bali Belly and had eaten everything from dog meat to pigs' bowels, it was all part of the adventure. I should be glad and not want to rush home to be among familiar trees and houses. I looked around me, this place was Paradise — coconut palms, white beach (under the mud), silken sea, a full moon rising. I'd think of all this later with longing. Already, I was starting to miss the place. Good old Palopo.

There seemed to be nowhere to eat but I wasn't interested in looking either. My presence would have turned any cafe into a theatre restaurant. I needed to be alone, to look over the water for a while. I decided the best place was out along the jetty, past where the boat was docked.

As I walked out along the jetty I saw the boat, about twenty metres long, and low in the water, was being loaded with cargo. Workmen were carrying bags and lengths of wood down a narrow bending gangplank. A few weak globes lit their way. Getting nearer, I put a sarong around my head to avoid attracting attention. An old man roasting peanuts on a small fire noticed me, but showed no sign of excitement.

I continued further out along the jetty into the dark and sat, staring back across the water on the trees, the soft lights of the town. I was even starting to relax and enjoy it when a pair of powerful lights flashed across me and the sound of a four-wheel drive approached. My first instinct was to jump into the water but I stayed cool; perhaps they'd drive by.

The vehicle stopped directly behind me. I glanced around as they cut the engine and turned on the emergency lights. It looked like the police. Jumping into the water would mean I'd be gunned to death. 'Hello mister,' the driver said, climbing out. I turned back to the water ignoring him. He was the worst kind of Indonesian — a Michael Jackson look-alike. And his friend was the same, I saw, from the corner of my eye as they both squatted down on either side of me.

'Hello mister,' the driver tried again, now a little uncertain.

'Do you speak English?' asked the other.

I didn't answer. They tried a number of languages — French, German, Italian. I made absolutely no response, no movement and slowly it dawned on them that I was weird and probably dangerous. They climbed back into the car and drove away.

Towards nine o'clock, when the boat was supposed to leave, I wandered down and walked on board. The place was crowded: people standing around on the jetty, saying goodbye and others on board settling down for the night on deck. A sailor came up and asked me to follow him. He led me down a ladder through the lower deck and up another ladder to a plywood box that looked like a dog kennel. I understood, this was a locker and threw my pack through the door. He asked me for the equivalent of three bucks which I paid and then he pointed to the kennel again. He wanted me to get into it.

'Why?' I said.

'You sleep here.' I looked around. A crowd had already gathered on the outer deck watching our transaction. Was the white boy actually going to get in to the box? Yes, he was.

I bent down and climbed through the door. It would have been a great arrangement if I was the kind of pervert who'd always wanted to have sex with a backpack.

Using an ancient yoga technique, I rolled over and looked out the opening through which no breeze was forthcoming. It was blocked by a group of twenty or so girls who were very interested in what I was doing in the box. They weren't being cute about it either, they were pointing and jeering. A little family squeezed in in front of the girls and started making themselves at home. The wife watched me intently as she put down mats, set water to boil on a stove, wrapped and unwrapped parcels of food, chopped vegetables and cared for the baby.

I rolled over foetally and faced the wall feeling like a lyger.

Ten o'clock came round and we still hadn't budged but I'd spent a useful hour holed up there while every one of the two hundred passengers plus their relatives and friends who came to see them off, filed past my box to look in or greet me. Then, the engine started up and something within me broke forever. My 'cabin' was directly on top of the engine room and directly beside the exhaust pipe. Within seconds it was about ten degrees hotter. A normal man would have cut his wrists at this point or dived overboard and fed himself to sharks. But the writer always has an out. Everything the writer does, everything that happens, and especially everything that goes wrong, is grist for the mill, I thought.

I take up pen and begin to jot down notes in the back of my exercise book. Once I do this, the girls start giggling.

'Molls,' I mutter to myself.

'Hot mister? *Panas*?'

I've undone a couple of buttons on my shirt; can't control themselves.

> Just hit the road, be cool, let the flow take you, go anywhere, trust the people stream, yeah, and wind up in a dog kennel being perved at by Palopo harbour molls.
> Gabriela.
> God! This dieseline's so bad.
> 'Go to Sulawesi!' Boyle said. 'It's really something.' I'll kill him. I'll shoot him six times in the heart on the beach at Bondi, then walk up, gun in hand, to the Gelato Bar and eat a dish of ice-cream while I wait for the police to come. It will be early. The air will be clear and fresh, the sea quiet. Six shots will ring out between the headlands.
> But Gabriela, where are you tonight? What country, what cabin, what hotel, motel, what bedroom, what bed has the luck to surround you?

And so we sailed away, into the night of my twenty-seventh birthday and I felt the sea, sliding like grease under the hull as we headed out toward my hope and my salvation. Malili.

[...]

Since childhood, I'd wanted to wander off the map into some dark territory. And here I was, on the edge of darkness and chickening out already. I hadn't even started. The petty privations, the gut aches, the discomfort of being under observation, they'd worn me down. I'd caved in.

Within fifteen minutes I was in the air on my way back to the tourist traps.

Reality had been too much for me.

Then Bali was below with all its charms laid out — the volcanic peaks, the tropical sea, the shoreline, the verdurous carpet stretching away — all of it like a huge sickly-sweet birthday cake that says EAT ME.

Eating Dog (1993)

1979

Clive James in Los Angeles

Writer, literary and television critic, and media personality, Clive James (1939–) is one of a long line of Australian writers who have chosen to live in Britain. After studying at the University of Sydney, where he edited Honi Soit, *James joined the 1960s rush to Europe on New Year's Eve of 1961, boasting that he would be gone for five years. He took another degree at Cambridge, where he was president of Footlights. If the origins of the expatriation of Clive James are common to that 'lucky' generation, his subsequent path was exceptional as he became one of Britain's most prominent critics, columnists, broadcasters and public intellectuals. His publications embrace mock-heroic epics, rock lyrics, literary criticism, autobiography, television journalism and fiction, and his literary and television style delights in playing on the borderlands between high and popular culture. James traces his sense of being at home in the postmodern world of airports and airlines to his childhood in the suburb of Kogarah, under the flightpath of Sydney's Kingsford-Smith 'aerodrome'. A born 'post-tourist', elaborating the ironies of travel for travel's sake, he suggests that the real story of mass jet travel is that of 'the world opening up to people who have no qualification for exploring it except the price of a ticket'. Yet Sydney, he claims, remains so real in his recollection he can taste it, and it was his first trip back, after fifteen years, that produced the first of his 'postcards', which became an irregular feature in the* Observer *from 1976 to 1984: 'Now that first impressions were common currency, they counted more than ever. Get them down and bring them home'. This postcard from Los Angeles was first published in 1979.*

Surfing in the jet stream created by the polar wind as it curved down across the Atlantic, my Pan Am Boeing 747 made landfall somewhere over Newfoundland, crossed into the United States over Minnesota and found clear air above the snowfields of Colorado. A storm took back the half-hour we had gained. We landed at Los Angeles just ahead of the rain.

I didn't really want to get off. The in-flight movie had been *California Suite*, in which there is a scene where Maggie Smith, playing an English actress flying to Los Angeles for the Academy Award ceremonies in which she will find out whether she has won the Oscar for Best Supporting Actress, watches an in-flight movie about herself flying in an aircraft through a raging storm. For this very role, the real-life Maggie Smith had just been nominated for Best Supporting Actress. Flying along with earphones plugged into my head while watching Maggie Smith flying along with earphones plugged into her head watching herself flying along, I had suffered a partial collapse of the will to live. The twentieth century was getting too complicated for a simple soul to cope with.

When I finally staggered off the plane and claimed my luggage, it seemed only natural that Bruce Forsyth should come running towards me in the reception area. I couldn't remember what I had written about him that had been so bad, but in these days of instant travel there was no reason why he should not have chosen LA airport as the site of my execution. I shut my eyes and waited for the blow. When I opened them again, it was to discover that he had run past me and was embracing somebody else.

Los Angeles had been coming to me all my life, but this was the first time I had come to it. Prejudices are useless. Call Los Angeles any dirty name you like — Six Suburbs in Search of a City, Paradise with a Lobotomy, anything — but the fact remains that you are already living in it before you get there.

The city's layout is a tangle of circumferences which have lost contact with their centres. It all makes sense as long as you can drive. Unfortunately I can't. Or rather I can, but nobody believes in my ability enough to give me a licence. So instead of hiring a car I had to head for my motel by cab. On the San Diego freeway it was like stock-car racing. Pick-ups with flambeau paint-jobs, fat back tyres and bulges on their bonnets went past on either side like bullets, nose down with a gear to spare. Painted like one of Altdorfer's blue night skies fretted with flames, a customised van overtook us, paused long enough for us to absorb the fact that we were looking at the back end of the MIKE VANCE CREATIVE THINKING CENTER MOBILE PLANNING UNIT, and then zoomed away. Despite the comparatively low speed-limit, nobody seemed capable of going slowly. A minatory billboard loomed. 'I TRIED FOUR MORTUARIES — FOREST LAWN WAS LOWER.' MRS JACKIE MULLINS.

My motel, which I shall call the Casa Nervosa because I wouldn't want you to come crashing in and spoil its exclusive atmosphere, lay on Santa Monica Boulevard, near where it bends towards Hollywood. Somebody had tried to make contact with the previous occupant of my room by kicking in the door. There was a swimming pool which by some fluke did not contain a floating body. This was the very motel in which Andy Warhol had filmed one of his nerveless epics. Not even the rain could completely eliminate the lingering aroma of Joe Dallesandro's hair oil. As the sudden night fell, I waited alertly for the scream of Robert having his nipple pierced.

But there was no time to waste. Barely pausing to change, shave and order another cab on a telephone still hot from Sylvia Miles's breath, I raced to Outpost Drive in Hollywood. Here I was to attend the small buffet supper marking the opening night of Gore Vidal's newly decorated house. The concrete footpath was still drying when I arrived. Hysterical with jet-lag, I narrowly avoided falling into it and thus becoming the first total nonentity to have his entire body immortalised in Hollywood cement.

Ushered politely in, I leant weakly against the wall while vainly searching the magnificent interior for an unfamiliar face. Joanne Woodward, Paul Newman, James Coburn, Stefanie Powers, Anthony Perkins, Mia Farrow, Jean-Pierre Aumont and William Holden were all present. I was introduced to Paul Newman. Well, how else do you expect me to say it? That I was introduced to Paul Klutz? Newman looked at me with eyes like chips of frozen sky. He was fascinated. It had probably been twenty years since a face he didn't recognise had got close enough to him for him to realise that he didn't recognise it.

Desperately I hunted for someone obscure enough to talk to. There was nobody. Finally I settled for George Segal. Momentarily diverted by the novel experience of conversing with somebody he had never heard of, Segal listened amiably while I told him how the film on the plane had been about Maggie Smith watching a film on a plane and in this film on the plane she was watching a film about herself on another plane. Segal looked very interested, as if he were rediscovering something. Success had cut him off from this kind of boredom. Stardom can be limiting.

Next morning I was bowling along the freeway under a clear sky in a 1964 drop-head Cadillac chauffeured by Hector and Alphonse, two young men who until the day before had been working as carpenters in Vidal's house but had now decided to start a new career as assistant journalists. Brilliantly overqualified for the task — Hector was a botany student and Alphonse a marine architect — they knew everything about LA [...]

Beyond Santa Monica the Beach starts curving left at Pacific Palisades. By the time it gets to Malibu it is no longer for the general public, since the beach houses of the wealthy shut it off from easy access. But Pacific Palisades is also the place where Sunset Boulevard starts its long run inland. Now you are in amongst the hills and canyons where those who have really made it have their principal houses. In Bel Air and Beverly Hills those houses which are not completely screened by trees look like illustrations from a freshly printed encyclopaedia of every architectural style since the Minoan civilisation. Factory-fresh limousines and replicars are parked in the open, so that the sun can light them up.

Even the most visible of these houses, however, is equipped to resist uninvited entry. Here the name Charles Manson is no joke. Gates have guard-houses and electric locks. There is closed-circuit television in the shrubbery. Lawns have spring-up spikes like a Vietcong ambush. These defensive measures should be kept in mind when you lay out two dollars for MAP AND GUIDE TO THE FABULOUS HOMES OF THE STARS and discover that ELKE SUMMER lives at 510 N BEVERLY GLEN, BEL AIR. Try walking in on her unannounced and you are likely to be greeted by an anti-tank missile coming down the driveway at chest height.

By now it was time to stop, before I became like the dazed heroine of Joan Didion's marvellous novel *Play It As It Lays* — the girl who drives on the freeways endlessly. We came home to Hollywood along Sunset Strip, which is really just a stretch of Sunset Boulevard that has let down its hair, not to say trousers. For a few strident blocks, THE ONLY TOTALLY NUDE LIVE STAGE SHOW ON THE STRIP vies for custom with MALE EXOTIC DANCERS. As S.J. Perelman deathlessly put it, De Gustibus Ain't What Dey Used To Be [...]

Despite rumours to the contrary, the studios have never stopped growing. Most of the television programmes that stop people going to the movies are made in the movie studios. All television ever did was shrink the demand for ordinary movies. The demand for extraordinary movies increased. If any one thing is wrong with the movie industry today, it is the unrelenting effort to astonish.

The standard tour of Universal Studios is well worth the trouble. The place was a chicken farm when Carl Laemmle took it over in 1912. Now Universal City has 470 acres of tight-packed production facilities, including a back lot through which your tour tram climbs, dives and tunnels, while houses burn around you and bridges collapse beneath you. The tour is unflaggingly cute. I would have liked to have spent more time in the props warehouse, where five million props are classified in racks and shelves. Instead we had to watch a demonstration of the superhuman powers allegedly wielded by Six Million Dollar Man and Bionic Woman, both of whom stem from Universal. So does the Incredible Hulk.

So, once, did the Creature from the Black Lagoon, who used to emerge from one of the ponds on the back lot and press his rubberised attentions on Julie Adams. From *Frankenstein* and *Dracula* through to *Jaws* and *Battlestar Galactica*, Universal has always been a hot studio for monsters and special effects. I enjoyed my tour but often felt that I might as well have gone to Disneyland.

So I went to Disneyland. Fleeing south-east on the Santa Ana freeway, the Cadillac ate the miles. The sun was bright and once again there was stock-car racing taking place all around us. A topless Volkswagen Beetle with a Chevrolet V-8 motor and wheels off an F1 racing car went past us like a low-flying aircraft, its driver scanning the sky for police helicopters. The freeways distort time and space to the point where Disneyland, when you arrive, seems like reality. Hector and

Alphonse knew the place inside out. They pronounced Pirates of the Caribbean to be the best ride.

Bobbing in a boat through tunnels and caves, you pass through mock sea-battles and watch mock towns being mock sacked. Mock pirates chase mock wenches. What will happen to the wenches when they are caught? The question is never asked. Totally innocent purpose is combined with infinitely elaborate execution. In the Haunted Mansion the hologram ghosts sing and dance around the graveyard while a hologram severed head speaks to you from inside a crystal ball. The technology is post-Einstein, the psychology pre-teen. There is a connection: only a thumb-sucker could ever have dreamed such things were possible.

Hector and Alphonse persuaded me that without a ride on the Matterhorn my life would be incomplete. The Matterhorn is a high-speed switchback that loops around, when not hurtling through, an artificial mountain. Strapped into a drop-tank capsule I tried to think of other things while the G-force successively pushed my head through my collar-bone, pulled it out again, and turned it back to front. Miraculously my Mickey Mouse ears stayed on, but I didn't dare open my eyes, lest something worse than what I was imagining was taking place. When I finally drummed up the courage to take a look, we were heading back in the Cadillac for dinner at Carlos and Charlie's on Sunset Strip. Plastic ears humming in the wind, I was ready for the heavy action.

Flying Visits (1984)

1980

Gillian Bouras in Greece

Melbourne-born teacher Gillian Bouras (1945–) married her Greek-born husband in Australia. In 1980 she went with her husband and two sons to his village in the Peloponnese. The trip was intended as a six-month trial to decide whether the family would settle in Greece or Australia. Her account of the experience was published as A Foreign Wife *(1986). They remained in Greece where Bouras faced all the differences in language, culture and customs that the hundreds of thousands of European migrants to Australia have undergone. Her Greece differs from the romanticised constructions preferred by Australian expatriates and island-hoppers. She relates the everyday events of her life in a new country with vivacity and warmth and occasional exasperation. Greece also provides the story lines in* Fair Exchange *(1991) and* Aphrodite and the Others *(1994).*

We arrived in Greece, George, Dimitrios, Nikolaos and I, on 23 July 1980. The Ancona ferry, oddly but appropriately named *Kangaroo*, docked at Patras in the early morning. Our two previous family holidays in Greece had been winter holidays, defined, limited and safe, bound by the opening and closing dates of the Australian summer school holidays.

This time it was different. We were to have six months in Greece, a time of evaluation and discovery. At the end of that time we had to decide between Australia and Greece.

'You've got to make up your mind,' I remember remarking somewhat bitterly to George. 'Get this Greek thing out of your system one way or another.' Now I think of all the remarks or incidents that come back to haunt human beings at various times, most often at three o'clock in the morning, and this one of mine returns constantly. Now I, too, have the 'Greek thing' in my system, and I know I'll never be free of it, not even if I leave Greece tomorrow and stay away for fifty years. Most Greeks know George Drosinis' famous poem, 'The Soil of Greece', in which the poet pleads with his native country:

And should it be my fate — a black and desolate fate — to leave and never to return, I will finally ask you to forgive me...

I understand those lines now, finally. For me, too, it would be a black and desolate fate to leave and never to return.

I viewed Patras through a blur of fatigue and apprehension, and though I have passed through the city several times since, the initial faint memories are the ones which linger. Patras spreads along the sea in cubes of grey. The land is flat and the water scarcely moves; between water and buildings lies a no-man's land of stony beach, low walls and eddies of rubbish. But St Andrew's Church rises grandly on the skyline and its domes and tiles relieve the monotony of concrete.

I was unprepared for the heat and the dust of the Peloponnese. We stopped at Pirgos and I fell victim to a lightning-strike fit of depression. This uninteresting market town lay baking in the heat. Dust swirled in a hot wind which blew down the main street; everywhere there seemed to be only the signs of decay: broken gutters, holes in the footpaths, paint peeling off doors, downpipes hanging loose, scraps of paper blowing, neglected cats and dogs prowling.

The boys stood drinking flat lemonade and sweating slightly under their Aussie towelling hats. What was I doing here? What was I letting myself in for? I really did not know. Assailed by doubt, I sucked on my bent straw, self-dramatizing madly, an Antipodean Jamesian heroine, come to the Old World from the New. It was my father's fifty-ninth birthday. Nine days before, he had said, standing at six a.m. in a chill Tullamarine: 'Mind you come back in six months.'

I felt like returning immediately.

I felt better when I saw the sea again, a sparkling blue expanse this time, separated from the road by greenery of all shades, stalwart trees, slender pines, scrubby bush. Just before we reached Kiparissia we swung away from the sea, and the oleanders, pink, rose and white, changing colours for miles, dazzled from both sides of the highway.

'The Colonels planted them,' said George.

'H'm,' I replied, grudgingly. 'I suppose that's something.' And there were the mountains, always the mountains, looming through the summer haze.

Along the Athens–Kalamata road, the names of the villages sound like music: Parathisia, Paradise, and Allagi, which means *change* and which became a village with a sense of mission during Mr Papandreou's election campaign in 1981. His motto played on the names of the village: Allagi; Hristofileika, Aghios Floros, Aghios Konstantinos. At Aghios Konstantinos we turned off the main road to drive the winding mile and a half to the village. Olive-groves stretched away on either side of the road. It was one o'clock in the afternoon. Heat pressed like a weight and the cicadas shrilled incessantly. Nothing stirred; I felt adrift in time and space. Nothing seemed familiar, because I could remember only the greyness and dampness of winter, the squelch of mud, and rolling mist, not baked clay, tinder-dry stalks of grass and fiery sun.

But then I saw the colours of summer, white walls, grey walls, the blaze of bougainvillea, red and mauve, the glow of geraniums, the white stars of jasmine, the bursts of roses and carnations. Carnations, redolent of cinnamon and cloves, virtually grow themselves in Greece, and bloom even in December. Once upon a time there were few flowers in the village. Well-water and precious energy were not to be expended on such frivolous trifles. Flowers bloomed once the water was laid on during the fifties. Some old women, however, still think it is a waste to cultivate flowers; after all, *paithaki mou*, there are plenty of wild ones. You should be growing vegetables instead, they tell me, as I direct an unwilling, low-pressure, evening squirt of water at sunflowers, morning-glories, marigolds, and my annual crop of vulgarly ostentatious zinnias. But *Yiayia* loves flowers and her terrace boasts pots of purple fuchsias, fringed fern (under the grape-vine away from the heat), green bushy basil, and assorted splashes of geraniums.

We pulled up opposite the gate. There seemed to be no sign of life, save the cacophony of the cicadas. The air continued heavy. Then the gate scraped open, and George's sister, Vaso, eldest child of the family, stood watching us clamber out of the car, sticky and sweat stained, on to the road.

'You came,' she said, simply. 'Welcome.' *Yiayia* hovered in the back-ground, snuffling quietly into her handkerchief. And so George came home, and although I did not realise it at the time, he had come home to stay.

Dimitrios and Nikolaos took to village life immediately. They remembered, vaguely, their winter holidays, but this was high summer. After being cooped up in suburban Melbourne, they viewed the free-dom of country living as unadulterated bliss. Whenever I sent them on an errand to the shops in Camberwell Road, Melbourne, I would reit-erate the instructions 'Go straight there, come straight back, and don't speak to any strangers on the way.' I would be tense until the ten-minute excursion was over. In the village they roamed everywhere and talked exuberantly to everybody, right from the start. Wearing only shorts and thongs, they climbed trees, picked fruit, played in the dust, turning browner all the time, and all the time serving their apprentice-ship with the neighbourhood children, trying to learn new games, wrestling with the unfamiliar argot. Although George has always spo-ken Greek to them, he had made a conscientious effort to speak stan-dard Greek and had avoided village speech patterns, colloquialisms and slang. Language was a crucial area of adjustment. It was just as well we had arrived seven weeks before school started; even so, both boys found classroom Greek very difficult at first [...]

Another major area of adjustment was, naturally, that of mother-in-law and daughter-in-law relations. This, I quickly realised, resembled a minefield: the dangers, very real ones, were there, but they were hid-den, and I was often unaware of the form they took. Conscious that I should not usurp *Yiayia*'s place in her own home and kitchen, I was bewildered when she expected me to act as hostess to people I did not even know. When visitors came I was expected to wait on everybody, even though I still felt a visitor myself. I was totally ignorant of her expectations, while she, I think, thought that daughters-in-law are, or ought to be, the same the world over. We did not, and do not, com-municate well. The difficulties which rapidly emerged in the first month developed into problems during the sixteen months we lived in her house.

I cannot live, especially in Greece, without books, paper, pens and ink. *Yiayia* can sign her name: I saw her do it once. She took a dim view of my paper invasion. The day a trunk containing eighty of my books arrived from the customs house, she paled visibly, while I was almost prancing with excitement. '*Panagia mou*,' she exclaimed, greatly moved, 'So many books! Can't you sell some of them?' I could not believe my ears.

I was a sad disappointment to her. I know that now. The day she asked me to help her plant garlic was a turning-point, in that it proved to her, once and for all, that I was a dead loss. I came to garlic fairly late in life: I had certainly never tasted it before I met George, and I had never seen it growing. She handed me the tiny bulbs, which were inscrutably smooth all over. There was nothing for it but to ask. 'Which end goes in the ground?' I enquired, quaking. The silence was thunderous. Other foreign wives have had similar experiences; one friend of mine firmly believed that peanuts grew on trees. Her mother-in-law could not conceive of such ignorance.

I am still not sure what *Yiayia* wants in a daughter-in-law, but I often feel I am not it. I can cook, knit, crochet and garden, but they are not my all-consuming interests. I do not lose sleep if the house is untidy; I have a lamentable tendency to pine for other places, city sights, even other countries; the local church almost creaks in disbelief whenever I darken its door. It is obvious that I fall short, but I cannot change, and I do not want to.

Recently I had occasion to look up the word *privacy* in my Greek–English dictionary, which is an Oxford publication, and of good repute. I should have known that I would not find a direct equivalent. It takes time, suffering and patience to realise that privacy is a privilege of affluence. George and his five siblings slept in a row in the passage, right outside their parents' door. Houses in the village are often attached: normal conversations, let alone quarrels, can be heard at all hours. As well, for the illiterate, other people's lives take the place of newspapers, magazines and novels and are a never-ending serial or soap opera. *Yiayia* would wait, breathlessly, for George to come home from work to tell her everything that had been happening in the outside world. Everywhere you go, people ask, '*Pou pas?*': 'Where are you going?' 'What are you doing now?' It takes a real effort to construe these enquiries as genuine interest, rather than nosiness, but the effort must be made. Two English friends of mine have stated that their most critical moments concerned their threatened privacy. One was aghast when old women patted her tummy as a matter of course and asked whether she was pregnant. The other nearly exploded with rage one day when she turned to go upstairs and her mother-in-law routinely inquired '*Pou pas?*'

A Foreign Wife (1986)

1981

Vincent Buckley in Ireland

Vincent Buckley (1925–88) was a poet, editor, critic, and professor of English at the University of Melbourne from 1967 to 1987. Born in Romsey, Victoria, and educated at the Universities of Melbourne and Cambridge, he brought a Catholic perspective to Australian intellectual life. His early cultural formation was the Irish Australia of the Church, republicanism, politics and horses. With seven Irish-born great-grandparents, Buckley developed a strong sense of identity with Irish culture and politics as well as a deep love for the land of his ancestors. His negotiations with his Irish–Australian identity are the subject of his autobiography, Cutting Green Hay *(1983).* Memory Ireland *(1985) relates a visit to Ireland and carries the imprint of the New World's fascination with the antiquity of the Old, and the divided identity of someone who 'regards himself on one level as Irish but knows that on another level he is not' and who kept going back 'to learn more of myself and my people'. The central section of* Memory Ireland *is devoted to one prolonged episode in the struggles of Ireland, the Republican hunger-strike in The Maze Prison in 1981. Buckley was in Ireland during the first weeks of the hunger-strike in which ten men were to die, and was profoundly moved by the fortitude, emotional resources and intense mutual fellowship of the prisoners.*

I cannot imagine that there is any country in which you are as close as you are in rural Ireland to the prehistorical and the transhistorical: for this is not, as is often said, a land obsessed with history, but a land of largely forgotten pre- and posthistory. People there inhabit their historical past like a dreamtime. They don't care to get dates or timescales into perspective; the dimension of the not-to-be-spoken-of is so close. By this I do not mean that the country is primitive in a raw way; it has a brooding, mannered soft quality which bespeaks the long-folded corners of a civilization. It is not primitive force, but pre-human presence that meets you here. The force just stands there, as it were, half-way between light and enclosing twilight.

Local Kildare people have generally shouldered it away, for it is not signposted, is seldom asked after, and its importance is not validated by its being the object of visible international attention. On the road from Athy to Portlaoise you round a curve, and there on your right is a ruined rock fortress looming out of the fields, for all the world like a smaller Rock of Cashel. It is called Dunamase, a fortress for many hundred of years, contested over and over by kings, armies and adventurers. When I mentioned it to Mark Wright, a local strong farmer (and the 'luckiest man with a racehorse in Kildare', so they all said in Kilcullen), it turned out that his relations came from near there, and he was astonished by my interest in it. Sure hadn't it always been there. Always the same. Never enquired after. When you grew up you'd never notice it.

Mark did not say these things, but they do represent a common attitude. Ireland has grown up, to EEC height and with a Brussels haircut, and it did not need to notice those earthy old rocks any more. It is understandable; such an outcrop, centaur-like, part rock and part building, is a solitary and inexplicable thing; what is there to say about it? You might think of it as a pre-poetic gift of time, but what use is that either? Personally, I could never write poetry about such places. As Michael Hartnett the poet said to me, 'Cut out everything that rattles. No history, no myth, no politics, no piety.' I think that was the list; and in a way I agree with him; there has been too much 'myth', which is often a fancy name for fanciful pretending, and poetic 'history' is often mere tourism in time. The actual past is too tense for such fancifulness; each historical act took place in a land drenched in prehistory; and how do you get the multiple effects of that? [...]

Once you realize that there are 'antiquities' in some nearby places, you quickly find that they are everywhere. On top of Brewel Hill, just behind our place, are the Pipers Stones, a group of heavy white quartz stones arranged in some obscure but beguiling pattern. Everything about this site is enigmatic, although the stones clearly signify something ceremonial. You climb to it across the usual hilly paddocks, richly covered in cowdung; but indeed you will not know where to start the climb unless you ask a near neighbour, for there are no signs of any kind to tell you. The 'stones' are hidden away inside an enclosure which is fenced and planted with prickly small trees; cow-dung is everywhere, and so are cows, browsing paranoiacally away beneath the branches. The enclosure may have been a fortified rath in pagan times, and seems to have had a specific sacred significance; the view from its edges is magnificent in all directions. Is it worth seeing? It is neither an historical antiquity nor a legendary matrix; for nothing of any importance is thought to have happened here, nor is it said to be 'owned' by any of the legendary heroes, by Dairmuid and Grainne, or Finn, or the Wizard Earl of Kildare. It is a slate, a *tabula rasa;* but it is clearly an important site, much more gripping to an observer like myself than Mullaghmast of the Hosting, however important its inscribed stone, or Ardscull of the Shouts and Battles [...]

Further down the Carlow road is the beautiful high cross of Moone. Again, it is set in a monastic graveyard, a few yards from the back wall of an ugly Georgian house on the one side, and fifty yards from the busy farmyard of a dairy farm on another. Again, it is unobtrusively set, but this one is a recognized national monument, and is signposted and supervised as such. What is interesting and characteristic about it is that it is one more example of culture's not being removed from nature. This is the secret and the problem of ancient Ireland as it survives in the present: it is not easy to find, it is not usually made much of, it is small-scale, it is likely to be drab or damaged; but, above all, no strict lines of reverential demarcation are drawn around it so that you focus on this one thing, are encouraged to be preoccupied with it, are led to set it in your mind's retina as still and perfected as a fly in amber. That may be an English habit, the way of an imperial conqueror, freed by conquest and its riches to contemplate things both as possessions and as objects of deliberately heightened aesthetic attention. Irish remains are not objects in that sense, unless you are seeing them in the national museum in Dublin. The high cross of Moone, which half the time is trickling with rain as the crack across its middle grows imperceptibly wider, which is perennially damp, which cannot preserve and highlight the contours of its own carvings in the face of the weather, is not isolated in that way. You take it in its context, of house, cowyard, grass, grave-stones, ruined chapel. You are not looking at, you are inside this gestalt. You are not sure when and how its component parts have come together, but you are aware of the stone buildings and crosses not as things set aside from nature but as things planted in nature, to be features of its growth. This adds to the damp, but also to the antique calm. It is very hard to take a satisfying photograph of Moone; you cannot photograph the smell of cow-shit and grass.

Irish antiquity, then, is like the country itself; it is not squeaky clean, and it is not homogenized. It is seldom spectacular, and it does not often lay claim to unusual beauty as an object-self. Moone is in any case part of a larger whole in the immediate vicinity, the lorries which speed through Castledermot on their way to the south-west or to Dublin would not be worried about the ancientness of its foundations, with their still trailing enigmas. They would be more conscious of the accident black spot near Ballitore, at which there were at least five accident deaths while we were living nearby [...]

Recounting this detail in sober prose, I feel very far from the 'ancient Ireland' of Yeats's romantic dreaming, which is full of marvellous doings and short on objects which just stay there, encapsulating their secret. Aristocratic dashers, crazed peasants and warty ramblers are nowhere in evidence — although they may, of course, lie in this very clay. Nor does anyone keep the graveyard in tourist condition, for no tourists know about it; and although I had been looking for it, I did not know it when I found it.

Given these facts, ancient Ireland, which 'knew it all', is safe from foreigners, for it sure as hell is hidden from the Irish; perhaps the endlessly draining weather will open up its secret.

Antiquity in Ireland exists, then, not as a spectacle, a sight, within a clearly defined social frame; it is, instead, a site from which the country can be seen, as presumably it was used *ab origine*. It is not an object, or a society; it is a place, often barely distinguished from the places around it. It is seldom the organizing centre of a city; usually, it exists outside cities entirely, it is not and never has been part of a city civilization, and it reveals nothing of city economy or gods. It is part of an open world, in which the sacred node does not gather things around it, but grows downward and up, to the beings of the netherworld or those of light and air. Like Tara, Dun Ailinne, or the Curragh, it was once a place of periodical gathering. The Hill of Allen, Dun Firinne, and Mullaghmast are thought to be the abode of sleeping gods or dead heroes. Others were, in effect, open air temples. Others were defensive enclosures. If we think of the great forts of Dun Aengus, on Inismore, and the Grianan of Ailech, in northern Donegal, we are seeing ancient Ireland in its military aspect: large, commanding, defensive, perhaps built by slaves.

To me the most extraordinary scene of all is the great and mysterious complex in Sligo, of which the foci are the solitary mountains of Ben Bulben and Knocknarea, much hymned by Yeats, and the solitary prehistoric mountain graveyards of Carrowkeel and Carrowmore. Ben Bulben now has a mine on its cold top, and the poisonous muck is being drained off into Lough Gill, to sink beside Yeats's isle of Innisfree. And just as investigators are about to discover something crucial and exciting about the megaliths of Carrowmore, they also discover that the miners of gravel have been before them.

Irish antiquities, then, while free of the museum atmosphere, suffer from the paddock condition. In the fields they may be unobtrusive, even insouciant, but those fields are likely to 'belong' to someone who has little care for them, and that makes them vulnerable. If they are not capital assets themselves, they very likely lie next to resources which are; these are mined, and they are undermined. The pastoral condition of the country has preserved many of them from that fate; at the same time, the climate which creates that condition is apt to preserve them by burial; a high proportion of the artefacts in the museums have been uncovered from boglands. Metal, stone and wood become lost, or flake, or crumble in the delicate full damp of the country; if they go into the deeper dampness of the bogs, they will be preserved from erosion as well as commercial exploitation, but at the risk of staying unrecovered forever.

This climate has led to a peculiar fatalism both in the inhabitants and in commentators on Irish history; the Irish are felt, even by themselves, to be peculiarly fated by their weather patterns. This feeling, in turn, suggests that the Irish climate is in some way extreme, inhospitable, unlivable; but it is not; on the contrary, it is temperate, even equable; the trouble is that it is persistently damp, and it is changeable. So the Irish, their herds and their buildings and their towns, have been shaped by a climate which is damp, but moderate; predictable, yet changeable to the point of volatility; not dramatic so much as broody; its mean is strikingly temperate; you might feel that you need to let your bones be gathered and absorbed by a nature so beautiful; if it induces discontent (and it does), it is not because it is threatening but because it is by turns enlivening and depressing; it is a country in which the pathetic fallacy is easy to indulge.

[...]

The tower, or castle, was flanked by a house; nobody knew the age of either. One authority says the tower is thirteenth century; Mr M, during his attempt to sell it, said sixteenth; but he was almost certainly selling it short, unless of course he regarded that as a particularly dashing century. Its roots have been down certainly since the thirteenth century. You don't call that ancient? I don't myself, exactly. But it had one ancient feature, a sheela-na-gig set into its south wall, at about breast height, where the sun in winter and spring would fall fully on it and change its lichen grey to a rust-rose glow. And it was the sheela which made me fall so immediately in love with the whole place the day I first saw it.

Sheela-na-gigs are figures carved or incised in stone, and found in many parts of Ireland, England, France and Scotland. They are more numerous in Ireland, where they are to be found in the walls of church or castle. Often it seems that a figure on or in a castle wall has been brought from some neighbouring church, which was its original site. The figure may be set beside or above the door, beside or above a window, above or within an arch; it may be set vertically or horizontally. The figure is always female, and is always characterized by an enlarged vulva, which her posture is arranged to display. She is often said to be a 'fertility figure', but whether her posture asserts fertility or fends off sterilizing agencies is a matter of opinion; she may be, as some others say, a figure to ward off evil, or to warn: 'erotic display as a means of warding off evil'; she may have some further function; she may have a variety of functions.

Then again, is she a survival from pre-Christian times, a witch-figure, or a representation of a pagan goddess from the times when Celtic civilization gave great power to the female? The leading authority, Jørgen Andersen, thinks the most numerous images come from the twelfth century, are part of a medieval or romanesque fascination with and fear of female sexuality, female being, the grotesqueness coming from the ambivalence which the period felt for what was becoming central to it. On this account, sheelas would be a diversionary minor art-form within the medieval Christian complex.

But why has Ireland so many of them? Nobody seems to know. The sheela-na-gig, despite her Gaelic name, may be one more thing imposed by the Norman adventurers of the late twelfth century on the soft, pro-tean, assimilative fabric of Irish life; and she may have frightened hell out of the clansmen; or she may have given them a good laugh.

Anyway, Blackhall Castle has one, a relatively mild, relatively sym-metrical one. I don't see how anyone could regard this sheela as a figure designed to frighten, warn, or create an impression of the potency of evil. Her facial expression is faint and vague, her hands are not pulling the lips of her vulva apart (as so may sheelas do), and she is carved sym-metrically, with aesthetic rather than obsessive care. She is one of the two or three sheelas known to exist within Kildare. I found her a warm, domestic *genius loci*, for even in winter the afternoon sun bathed her whole figure. But such feelings are very subjective, and whatever any-one else may have felt about her, surely she has scarcity value. Surely an owner or a tenant would see to her preservation.

My landlord showed little interest in her; she was probably too 'early' for his sense of relevance; she was not manorial. One horse-owner, a civilized man though not, I think, of very deep Irish prove-nance, hustled his sons away from looking at her; his view was succinctly expressed, 'Too much fertility in Ireland.' Though he was always keen on more fertility among horses.

Trinity College Dublin sent experts to take a cast of her for an exhi-bition which has still not been held. The experts were from Belfast, and surprisingly vague in their answers to my questions, about sheelas. The owner made moves to sell the property, and as I listened to prospective buyers indulging their fantasies I became worried. None of them talked of re-roofing the castle; more than one said he found it unsightly. Grandiose plans were voiced for pulling out all the trees and planting grass, for making productive use of the space occupied by the castle, which will certainly fall down in the foreseeable future unless someone literally grasps the actual nettle. I tried ringing the guardians of culture. I will not try to remember who they were, or what authority they rep-resented; for each was nicer and more concerned than the one before, each offered to come and see the object with the idea of putting a restraining order on it. None came. Before leaving Kildare, I said to Larry and Mary Mulryan, 'Well, you have some influence in Fianna Fail. Will you make sure that, if there is any project to pull down the castle, the question of the sheela-na-gig will be raised in Dail Eireann?' They said they would do their best. I fear they will get no thanks for it.

Irish obsessed with history, indeed.

Memory Ireland (1985)

1981

Robyn Davidson in the United States

Born on a Queensland cattle station, Robyn Davidson (1950–) was educated in Brisbane before going on to study biology at the University of Queensland and music in Sydney. In 1977, after she moved to Alice Springs, Davidson set out to walk across the desert to the Western Australian coast, accompanied only by camels and a dog. Her best-selling account of the journey, Tracks *(1980), was the Thomas Cook Travel Book of the Year and recalled a Victorian tradition of adventurous solo travel by women.* Travelling Light *(1989) describes various more conventional travels in Australia and overseas, including a crossing of the United States on the back of a motor-bike, 'a gleaming black and silver sin machine', which she had no intention of learning to ride. Riding for Davidson 'always meant a relationship with an animal'. She currently divides her life between London, New York and Alice Springs.*

There is no stretch of highway in the world more boring than Route 75 through Ohio. After hours of staring at soggy flat farmland, from the back of a Harley-Davidson, through billowing truck fumes and drizzle, my first glimpse of the truck stop cafe was a welcome, if surreal, relief. The American mid-west breakfast of two eggs, bacon, sausages, hominy grits, french fries, pancakes, carcinogens and sodium nitrite was to keep us alive until we reached California, where, miraculously, as soon as you crossed the border, you began eating beansprouts, whole-wheat bread and spinach salad with blue cheese dressing.

There were at least 200 trucks parked outside this three-acre extravaganza. Truck drivers who wore ten-gallon hats, T-shirts ('I'd rather push my Harley than ride a rice-burner'), turquoise and silver belt buckles, and snakeskin boots with toes so pointed they could open envelopes, jostled for position at the food counter, or crowded into the space-invader rooms, or riffled through back-copies of *Easyrider* in the reading rooms, or quaffed beer in the bars, or filled their tanks at the forest of gas pumps. Everything a truckie ever wanted or needed was there, including cowboy-booted squaw-tasselled truck-groupies hanging provocatively and vacantly around the doors. Our breakfast neighbour eyed us suspiciously until he found out we were from Australia. 'What's it like livin' in one of them goddamn socialist countries? I hear tell you can't even carry guns there. Man, I couldn't live without mah guns.'

Since leaving New York, three weeks before, we'd been living out a 'Leave it to Beaver' re-run. I don't think I could have tackled it without my genuine, padded, press-studded, black leather Harley-Davidson motorcycle jacket. Not only did I walk taller when I had it on, and feel meaner and look tougher, but the human sea in the streets of Manhattan parted before me. It was, as a leftie journalist had said when the first space shuttle went up, 'biblical, man'.

And after the torment of a three-week publicity tour, I needed any props I could get. When I wasn't collapsing in Hyatt hotel rooms, or being powdered up for chat shows, or fearing for my life on aeroplanes, I was holed up in the cavernous splendour of a white, well-appointed loft in Soho, where chemically fed pot-plants watched my back; where subdued jazz played on the FM; where endless replays of Reagan getting shot (his theatrical *pièce de résistance*), interspersed with doctors' reports and static, played on the TV; where sirens played on the streets; where there were two phones with buttons and dials and red flashing lights, neither of which I knew how to work; where the taps required an IQ of 500 to be turned on; where rows of fumbly security locks on the front door, lift buttons, lift door and apartment door did nothing for my paranoia because any thug could climb up the fire escape and break a window; and where there were only frozen orange juice, Best Foods mayonnaise and fifty rolls of film in the fridge, because everyone ate out. Except me.

So I rang Steve, who joined me from London a week later. When he suggested we buy a motorcycle and ride from New York to California, where he was born and raised, but hadn't seen for ten years, I barely put up a struggle. The thought of wind in my hair, the freedom of the open road, and dying instantly under the wheels of a Mack truck seemed almost appealing. The only things I had against the idea were the possibilities of either spending the rest of my life feeding mashed bananas to a quadriplegic or waking up in some mid-west hospital, unable to remember my own name. There was also in me a deep resistance to being second in command. If Isabelle Eberhardt — that eccentric Victorian wanderer — hit the nail on the head with 'life on the open road is the essence of freedom', she qualified that with 'no one is free who is not alone'. Quite.

And I was ignorant of bikes. I didn't like them. I had no intention of ever learning to ride one. I didn't even understand bikie language. Riding to me has always meant a relationship with an animal — horse, donkey, camel even. You don't ride a machine, you sit on it. Nor was I good 'bikie moll' material. Good bikie molls sit on the back and keep their traps shut. They don't whinge. They aren't back-seat drivers. When the bike breaks down, they don't blame the driver, er, rider. There was a lot I had to learn.

It was raining when we went to pick up the gleaming black and silver sin machine. It sat at the back of the shop like a poisonous insect. While Steve talked with the proprietors about teflon sprockets and eighty-cubic-inch shovelheads, I strolled around the accessories. Was this an S and M outfitters or what? I picked out the most expensive helmet (I like my brains where they are) and then my gaze alighted on the leather jackets. I took one out, tried it on and, hey presto, transmogrification. I placed my fag between my lips, squinted through the smoke, put my thumbs in my pockets and ambled back to the guys. They spoke to me! I now understood how the invisible man felt when he put his bandages on. 'Great deeds and great thoughts,' as Camus said, 'all have a ridiculous beginning.'

Ah, the intoxication of speed as we hurtled from beneath the broken teeth of Manhattan's skyline and onto the freeway. After the first thirty miles, I started loosening up. Enjoying it even. There was, after all, some pleasure in not being the one in control. My limpet-like clutchings, the involuntary shutting of the eyes when we leaned into a corner, were being replaced by stunts: the standing up on the pegs to give fist salutes to other bikers, the leaning back on the sissy bar to roll a smoke, and the moving from cheek to cheek to relieve the growing numbness in my bottom. After a hundred miles the discomfort was intense, the grumbling loud. Harley-Davidsons are not designed for the comfort of the bit-of-rag on the back, they are designed for the comfort of the rider, and for style. I was hunched on a stylish vibrating fence-post and feeling resentful.

I tapped Stevie on the shoulder (he was singing 'I just wanna ride on my motorcyyyyy-cle'. Could this regressed maniac be the man who had seen me through thick and thin in London?) and asked him to stop at the next sports shop. We were bound for Vermont, and there were no sports shops. There were drug stores, which sold invalids' inflatable toilet seats. I had no shame; I bought one. I was willing to risk my credibility with the bike fraternity, but my buttocks, never. I grew very attached to that cushion over the next three months. If Flann O'Brien was right about molecular transference, then Steve was becoming more like a bike, and I was turning into…

We rode ten hours that day, across the Adirondacks, around the swooping bends of Lake Champlain, through the first sweet hints of spring — polluted only by those totems to the American Dream: the omnipresent cars and billboards, the gas stations, the baseball caps and the fast-food franchises. America is a car culture, constantly travelling to greener pastures. Americans do not see the horror, junk and pain littering the way. There is always a new frontier to head for, so how much you bugger up the one you're on is irrelevant. This faith in the future at the expense of the present comes from moving fast with the windows wound up.

By the time we arrived at our friends' country house just outside Hinesburg, we were exhausted. We couldn't talk. We drooled. They put us to bed. I was too tired to attack Steve for bringing me on this tor-turous and pointless journey. But after three days with them, during which we gum-booted our way through Vermont's mud season (appar-ently not its finest) and stuffed ourselves with home-made apple pies, and swapped vitriolic reminiscences of book tours and reviewers, the desire to be off hunting for new frontiers began to infect me too. The first burst of acceleration as you leave somewhere in the early morning is almost worth the increasing tedium of the following miles.

[...]

There are many good reasons for visiting the States, but, to my mind, the two that stand out like Manhattan's twin towers are tasting, for the first time in your life — in a down-at-heel roadside restaurant on the outskirts of a ghost town whose name you will never remember — real Mexican food and real Margaritas, and seeing, also for the first time in your life, the astonishing wonderland of the south-western deserts. Put them together, add a bike and good weather, a soupçon of snow-capped mountains in the distance, and you've a recipe for hedo-nistic joy.

Perhaps it was the sudden injection of chilli rellenos, tequila and vit-amins, perhaps it was the high altitude, piney-woods country of Ari-zona, perhaps it was the sniff of the arid zone that made my spirits soar but, whatever it was, by the time we flew through those vistas of limit-less forest, rolling green into grey into blue, I was feeling on top of the world. By now I had replaced my helmet with a scarf — had become a convert, in fact, to the anti-helmet-law lobby (because, let's face it, if you do bounce off your bike at eighty miles per hour, no feat of engi-neering ever designed is going to keep your grey matter from spilling). You feel better with it off, you see more, you don't suffer from neck strain, you can hear birdcalls distorted by Doppler effect, and if you're going to be mad enough to ride a bike in the first place, you may as well go the whole hog.

Enough has been written about the marvels of the Grand Canyon, and all of it under-statement. The place is magnificent. But the tourists and the prices began to grate, so we headed for Monument Valley — John Ford country; home of what's left of the Navajo. It was, if any-thing, even more awesome than the canyon, and to which no film or photograph could do justice. Mile after mile the endless flatness stretched on, interrupted only by towering monoliths of bare rock and the occasional eagle wheeling through the wall of silvery heat shimmer, rising up into blue-black sky. This was what I'd been looking for. This was where the heart was.

While Australian deserts have a more unearthly, prehistoric, mytho-logical quality, while they demand more depth of feeling, the American deserts take the cake for sheer brazen grandiosity and impact. They don't grow on you, they hit you in the back of the head like a mallet. Away from the reservation itself, where we were required to stay on the roads, I was able, for the first time, to sleep in the sand dunes, and to walk out into the desert as far as I could and not see a fence, or a path, or a soul.

Coming from Australia, I had considered this privilege a right. But in America nature was fenced in — under glass. For most people the pleasure of being alone in the wilderness was a thing of the past. The bush had become an alien, dangerous and distant thing. Control is the name of the game, and I wonder how Australia will deal with the same problem, which it eventually must, as all the wild places are taken over by multinationals and tourism. Our extraordinary freedom to move where we like will become the privilege of a select few. This recurring theme, of seeing Australia's future in America's present, was what disturbed me most. That Australia is learning nothing from American mistakes, that we are swallowing all the worst aspects of the dross and spillage of the American Dream.

We strolled along the well-graded National Park paths, and read plaques informing us in large print that some European explorer had discovered the place, and then in small print at the bottom that an unnamed Indian guide had taken him there. Some things are the same the world over.

Two days later we were surrounded by the chintz and tinsel of Las Vegas. (If you can possibly wean yourself off the silly notion of including Las Vegas in your tour of the south-west, do so.) We drove down the main street and headed right on out of town. Death Valley was far more appealing.

The temperature on the road now was up to 130 degrees. We put wet clothes under our jackets and wrapped wet turbans around our heads. Driving for hours in such heat, even with interruptions for swims in tepid canyons, or for tinkering with a sick and overheated Harley, or for praying for your life as the bike lunges from side to side in the turbulent winds of mountain passes, has a debilitating effect on mind and body. It begins to bend you a little. It rakes at your flesh like claws. It passes out of the realms of mere scorching into some uncharted territory of pain. Camping out that night didn't appeal; I wanted crispy sheets and air-conditioning.

We pulled into a motel on the shores of Lake Mead — a tinpot joint with a bar and gaming room across the street which, like all bars in Nevada, contained perpetual night for the benefit of gamblers. We soaked for hours in hot water (high velocity grime takes weeks to shift), then turned the telly on to the local news. An atomic bomb had been tested 150 miles north that day. 'What????' I was anxious enough about contracting cancer in this region, what with all the uranium tailings left on Indian reservations for the kids to play in, and what with actors dropping like flies because they'd been on location in this country, without having to contend with fallout.

After a sleepless night, during which I imagined I was being penetrated by deadly and invisible beams, we packed up at dawn. The cleaning lady arrived. I grabbed her arm and, with alarm in my voice, asked her if she'd heard the dreadful news. She smiled indulgently at this poor stupid foreigner and, with a certain pride, said, 'Goodness, honey, there's nothin' to worry about. They go off all the time. Sometimes they're so big the walls shake. I think it affects the pot-plants a little, you know, but we're used to it around here... and it's better than being overrun by them I-ranians.'

'Steve, get me *out* of here.'

Travelling Light (1989)

1982

David Malouf in Italy

Born in Brisbane of Lebanese and English parents, writer David Malouf (1934–), like Christopher Koch, was part of the postwar diaspora of middle-class young. He lived, taught and travelled in Europe from 1959 until 1968 when he returned to teach English literature at the University of Sydney. In the late 1970s, Malouf left the university to become a full-time writer and to live part of each year in a village in southern Tuscany. Italy seized Malouf's imagination when he first disembarked in Naples in 1959. Two of his novels are set in the Italian peninsula, An Imaginary Life *(1978) in the ancient Italy of Rome, and* Child's Play *(1981) in the modern Italy of terrorism. In his response to Italy, Malouf delicately articulates a common new world theme, a sense of harmony between the people and the landscape, a harmony reaching across generations and centuries, a heritage unavailable to immigrant societies. Malouf's Italy is one that is fast disappearing and his evocations are tinged with romanticism and nostalgia. The questions of place, of borders, of exile and belonging, and of identity remain constant themes in Malouf's writing.*

A vast jigsaw of spaces that fit one into another, the village piles century on century and is still in the process of being made. Built of a mixture of granite boulders and tufa, it is grim in winter, but when the stone is touched with sunlight it mellows to a soft gold. Roofs are flat and projecting, and are of corrugated terracotta, blotched with grey-green or yellow lichen and held down against the wind with stones. Every house has dark-green slatted shutters, long windows with varnished frames and inner shutters of solid white. Under each window are rings for flowerpots and a smaller ring for a flag.

One side of the village faces north-east into the wild country towards Siena. It gets no sun after mid-morning and bears the full blast in winter of the *tramontana*. The other faces the sea. Protected from chill winds, it gets the sun in winter, the sea breeze at five o'clock every summer evening and on clear days the sea itself is a glowing band between the hills. It appears so suddenly at times, when the late sun strikes it, as to make a flash at the corner of my eye as I sit working, as if out there somewhere a match had been struck.

At such times the whole plain comes alive in all its detail of fields, pasture, vineyards, olive groves, and the mountains as ridge after ridge of impenetrable *macchia*.

What are the characteristic sights of this landscape?

In high summer, when the earth is baked hard and everything is yellow-brown after the harvest, gabled 'houses', sometimes fifty metres long, appear in the fields. They look like primitive temples and are made of great blocks of hay. Other fields are lined with the giant mill-wheels turned out by another brand of harvester. Only small landholders make hay in the old way, as a round stack with a conical roof, that is gradually sliced away till it resembles a waisted hourglass.

Very strange they look in late summer moonlight, these impermanent structures — megalithic temples, mill-wheels, hourglasses in the flat fields.

In autumn, when the hills have been ploughed and show their original colours from blond, through all the ochres to black, the strangest sight here, especially on days of frost, is the bare-boughed persimmon with its orange fruit, each one more brilliant than the sun. They look sinister; like witches' apples, turning transparent as they ripen and rot. Below them, chrysanthemums — white, yellow, pink, rust. They are grown here not as house-flowers, but to be carried, first at All Souls, then each Sunday afterwards, to the cemetery, where every grave has its pot. These are the extravagant, abundant, wonderfully fleshy and long-lasting flowers of the dead.

Spring. Elaborately dressed plastic dolls appear in the boughs of cherry trees, all bows and bonnets like hanged babies. They are meant to scare off birds.

In May, great swarms of fireflies, in such brilliant drifts that on moonless nights you can see your way by them. Nightingales. And from the vineyards the regular boom of the automatic cannon that are used to keep off boar. All night they go boom boom. In poorer vineyards, sleepy children beat saucepans, and all the way into the distance the dogs bark.

Easy to see here how a cuisine comes into existence. It has nothing to do with the refinements of art.

For one whole month there are only artichokes and broad beans; in another tomatoes, runner-beans, zucchini; cherries till you cannot bear the sight of them; later strawberries. Everyone has a brief surplus of everything, to be eaten, given away, pickled, or dried and preserved under oil. There are no luxuries. A luxury is an ordinary commodity available at the wrong time or in the wrong place. Here everything is ordinary and has, prepared in as many different ways as possible, to be eaten till it is used up and the next thing appears. Cuisine makes the necessary palatable.

Every family here eats out of its own *orto* — seldom bigger than the kitchen, often the size of a kitchen table — where half a dozen artichokes, a row of broad beans, lettuce, tomato, and various kinds of spinach keep a household going throughout the year. Basil and sage grow on windowsills, capers in the crevices of walls, and rosemary, with its pretty blue flower, in unruly six-foot hedges.

All of this speaks for the abundance but also the frugality of Tuscan living. Nothing is wasted. Mealtimes are serious social occasions, prolonged and formal both in shape and in the rituals they follow, but the fare is simple, healthy, boring; coarse unsalted bread is the staple, oil instead of butter, and everything is cooked on top of the stove. My friend Agatina, I notice, uses her oven for storing crockery, and when it is empty and open the cats sleep there.

When I acquired Agatina's house (as it is still called in the village) I also acquired Agatina, her husband, Ugo, eighty-two, and her sister, Celeste, who died last month at eighty-six. I go to Sunday lunch and sometimes in the late afternoon as well, to sit in the kitchen with the women; drinking sweet tea, watching them do their needlework, and listening to Agatina's stories. Over the years I have also acquired the history of this family of intelligent, well-to-do *contadini* (our word, peasant, won't quite do) who own several houses in the village and many small pieces of land with olives, vines, cherries and figs.

Agatina's parents and all four of her brothers and sisters once lived in my house. The father, who was lazy and fond of drink, died of a fall at the bottom of my inner staircase; Agatina never fails to sigh over the spot and to warn me against coming down in the dark. (She is too polite to mention drunkenness.) [...]

Her husband, Ugo, comes from a rival place on the other side of the valley. Very tall and handsome, an ex-gamekeeper, he is entirely his own man, but inside the house Agatina rules. He is paid the traditional deference of being asked whether the *pasta* is cooked, and is always served first: but he suffers, I think, from being an outsider and from having married above himself; Agatina still uses, as many local women do, her family name. The house, both in fact and spirit, is hers. Only in these last days, when he has been too weak to go into the fields, has Ugo ever spent time in the big kitchen, which is the one room of the house in general use. It is sad to see him sitting on a little chair by the window with his stick in his hand and the three cats at his feet.

The kitchen in these houses is the women's room; men, if they are not eating or sleeping, are expected to be either in the fields or at the bar. It is the largest and warmest room in the house. Here the television stands, playing all through every mealtime — an awesome experience at Agatina's since, as she often says, 'two of the three people in this house, and one of the cats, are stone deaf'. Here too, the women gather at the kitchen table, which is spread between meals with a good lace cloth, to gossip, knit, or do their elaborate fancy-work — Agatina with a little wooden footstool because her feet do not reach the floor. This footstool is a relic of the days when, in my tiny sitting-room, she made her living by minding children, thirty at a time, while their mothers were in the fields. It is of thick walnut, about nine inches long and six high, and belonged, forty years ago, to an orphan, now the husband of her favourite niece [...]

But all the dead are still living here. They are living in the *campo santo* beyond the church, a large walled area, a rectangle very like the one C. itself makes on ancient maps, with its own chapels and funerary monuments and a great wall of slabs, each with an electric candle. The whole place glows at night like an alternative village, which is what it is; a neighbouring, utterly ordinary and unfrightening 'village of the dead'. Sunday visits are made there; there is continuous traffic on the road.

Death here is a commonplace and sociable occurrence. Black-edged notices appear in the square beside the daily headlines. The bell tolls — a single long stroke for a man, a two-note broken one for a woman. Everyone hears and knows.

But if not shocking, or even shameful as it sometimes is with us, death always comes unexpectedly and too soon. She was only eighty-six, Agatina says of Celeste, why her? There are others so much older. (It is true: half the village seems to be over eighty.) She wasn't *old*.

Once, when I had a fever, Agatina came and insisted that I call a doctor. These fevers, she told me, are dangerous. There was a girl here died of such a fever last week. Terrible! Absolutely overnight. Which girl? I asked. You know her — Carlina. Died overnight. But Agatina, I protested, she was eighty-three! Precisely. So you see you can't be too careful. Call the doctor and make sure he gives you a suppository. (Italians are addicted to all sorts of drugs and the pharmacy in any village is a wonder of wonders. But suppositories are, for quite primitive reasons I suspect, the favourite of all remedies, and indispensable to any serious cure.)

Sunday at Agatina's: In the summer, when the clock has been put forward, we eat early enough for our meal to coincide with the Pope's mass on television.

Time in Agatina's house is a sacred commodity, not to be interfered with. She despises the 'legal' hour. All her clocks keep the real one, and she felt magnificently justified last year when a workman (*poveretto!*) fell to his death in a nearby village while changing the hands of the clock.

So all through lunch in summer we eat with the Pope's Mass at full volume, and Celeste and Agatina, between sips of soup and bursts of gossip, participate in all the responses, spoken and sung.

'That Eglantina, I tell you, is a perfect viper — Hear us O Lord,' says Agatina. 'This pasta is not my best,' says Celeste. 'I apologise, *Professore* — Hallelujah, hallelujah, blessed be he who comes.' The three cats, which climb over the backs of our chairs and leap up to sniff at saucepans, are driven off with swipes and a holy, holy, holy. Papa Woytila's health is commented on from week to week: 'He looks worse — he's failing. And he's not even sixty!'

Mass is followed by the news bulletin with its lists of newly arrested terrorists and the death-toll in the gang wars in Naples (357 since the beginning of the year) and Palermo (116). It all seems very distant, like news from another country or from a century we have not yet reached.

It is. Italy is a misty, metaphysical concept here. 'Look at that cat,' says Agatina, 'she understands every word! Just like a Christian.' She means just like a human being. On another occasion, when I have brought, say, a Dutchman and two Australians to see her, she will say, 'Oh well, we're all Italians here.' She is speaking of our common humanity.

The truth is that the village is its own world, as complete and self-enclosed, even without its walls, as it was 100 or 900 years ago. Its months are measured by the work that is appropriate to them, as in old sculptures: ploughing and harrowing, seeding, harvesting, grape-picking, the olives; and its years by who was born there. 'I am from '96,' Celeste would say, reckoning in the Italian manner. Time is concrete or it has no meaning. The dead go on forever in a new place at the bottom of the hill and their lights burn long after the village itself goes dark. As for geography, that gives out at the first horizon.

'Australia,' Agatina says, as she might say Saturn or Paradise. It is a continent she has now acquired, in the sense in which I have acquired her family history; she locates it in some empty area of her experience between Poland, where Papa Woytila comes from, and New York, where a grand-niece recently spent the summer. It is the place I exist in, in her thoughts, when I am not fifty metres away in 'her' house. Time is too continuous, too present, too large to be thought about, and space too small. Such are the conditions of this world!

12 Edmonstone Street (1985)

1984

Germaine Greer in Brazil

One of Australia's best-known contemporary expatriates, Germaine Greer (1939–) became an international public figure after the publication of The Female Eunuch *(1970), now a classic of 1970s feminism. She sees her early life in Melbourne as dominated by the desire to escape, riding her bicycle to Port Melbourne 'to stand watching the streamers breaking as lucky people sailed away'. She wanted to 'transcend suburbia', become a cosmopolitan intellectual, a wandering scholar, in the manner of Erasmus of Rotterdam. For Greer, as for so many of her generation, life seemed to be a party that was happening somewhere else. After attending the Universities of both Melbourne and Sydney she left Australia to continue her education at Cambridge, and to begin her life as an expatriate. Writer, academic, columnist, broadcaster, Greer, like Clive James and Barry Humphries, has thrived on the British need for Australians to play the role of intellectual larrikins. Greer's journey by paddle-steamer up the River São Francisco through the arid north-east of Brazil was made as part of a BBC television series on river journeys. Her steamer, tarted up for television, was on its final working trip before being turned over to the tourist industry. In her record of the journey, Greer was aware of the ironies of television tourism and its staged authenticity, supremely confident of her own grasp of what was really authentic. She saw the demise of the river and its life as a bigger issue than the fate of the picturesque paddle-steamer.*

The car crashed from pothole to pothole, as the old cobbled roads gave way to sluices of sand in which it yawed and slewed and slid, the motor coughing as the carburettor breathed in more sand to add to what already swirled up and down the fuel line. The lycra glamour and commercial cacophony of the centre were soon left behind. The ruins of grandiose town-planning schemes lay all about. Grids of paved street stood up above the seas of sand, while the traffic wove itself through the breaks in the tumbledown ramparts. Broad carriageways led their rows of empty lamp-standards slap into blank walls. Scrawny cattle of mixed race, mostly zebu, picked their way daintily through the mess on their way to graze on the river-flats. A huge bus station with quays and platforms and shelters and even a snack-bar stood cut off from the roadway by a 10-foot drop. Up by the tarmac sat a small crowd of hopeful passengers under an improvised tarpaulin. Although their bundles of bedding and smoky cooking fires betokened a long stay they all gazed fixedly up the road as if a bus was due in five minutes.

Makeshift shelters began to proliferate. The driver was puzzled by my insistence that he plough farther and farther from the paved road, where there was no sign of regular streets and he had to navigate by following vague tyre-tracks in the sand. The people crammed into the tiny shanties stared out at us. Pigs rooted in the human excrement in the road. We passed files of women with kerosene tins of water on their heads. We saw other women too, sitting open-legged by the roadside, gazing expectantly as we dragged our dust trail towards them. Even at a quarter to seven in the morning their demeanour was unmistakable. The Bishop of Juàzeiro was to tell me three times in a single conversation (and I myself had not brought up the subject) that there were 2000 prostitutes in Juàzeiro. If by prostitute he meant any woman struggling to live any way she can, including offering sexual services for money, the estimate was a conservative one. If he meant women actually making a living by prostitution, the estimate was fantastic. Juàzeiro was a town of would-be prostitutes without clients. The manners of the younger leotard-wearers in town were as free as those of their role models from the Avenida Paulista in São Paulo, which they studied continually on television and in the glossy gossip magazines. The men they rubbed up against under the trees along the river quays were the ones who might have brought a few cruzeiros to the desperate women in the mud huts out on the vast fringes of the city. Wherever the men in our film crew went, girls called out to them, ogled them, accosted them, hid amorous notes in their baggage. The men preened, correctly interpreting the lovesick chorus as a tribute to their conspicuous success in being rich, employed, healthy and white, and did nothing beyond a little mild showing off. For all the atmosphere of extravagant willingness, sex is still a serious matter in the Nordeste, if only because contraception in any form is practically unknown. First births occur early and most unions are informal, in the pattern familiar to us from other post-slavery societies. Some of the priests struggling against this sexual chaos refuse to baptise children unless their parents agree to marry at the same time. The threat is toothless because Nordestino religion is only partly based on Catholicism. Given the real magnitude of the problem, the humanitarian enterprise of the Diocese of Juàzeiro, which undertakes to teach 'prostitutes' needlework as a better way of making a living, is simply ludicrous.

We began our river journey at Juàzeiro in the middle of the river rather than at the source or the mouth because we had to rendezvous with our paddle-steamer for the journey upstream to Pirapora. The boat, the *São Francisco*, was the star of our show, and the film crew, understandably, were very keen to get to know her. From my hotel balcony I could see her yellow-painted funnel and her upper storey as she rode, or rather sat, at anchor beside the basalt-paved slipway, part of the elegant system of quays built in an earlier era, when the river carried goods and passengers and some of the wealth generated by sugar and leather percolated to the river towns. There was little or no activity on the river now. It flowed full, fast and turbid towards the rapids below Santa Maria da Boa Vista. I was not to learn for some time that this high level was artificially maintained, or that the exigencies of feeding the six hydroelectric stations 350 kilometres downstream at Paulo Afonso had caused devastating floods in Juàzeiro for three years in succession. The São Francisco had never been a sleepy, silty river, but a swift and sandy one. Fifty years ago when the *remeiros* poled their long boats down it, the voyage back upstream was a terrible ordeal, for they had to force the boats against the strong current by jamming the punt-pole hard against their breastbones until their chests were laid open. These fearful wounds were cauterised with boiling tallow in an agonising ritual.

The *São Francisco* had begun life on the Missouri River in 1913; to ply the São Francisco she needed a special piece of equipment, a large anchor hanging from the prow. When her flat bottom ground to a halt on the shifting sand-bars of the 'Velho Chico', as the river was affectionately called, a sailor would wade out with the anchor, to which a winch-cable was attached, until he found deeper water. He would drop the anchor and the steamer would pull herself across the bar by winching in the cable. Apart from our boat, and another hulk rotting beside her, the only paddle-steamer doing business in Juàzeiro was working high and dry in one of the town squares as a restaurant. We had been told that there was a monthly boat carrying general passengers upstream and crossing another on the journey down, but, although the people who told us this appeared to believe it, and many citizens repeated the information, no such boats existed. When our paddle-steamer, or *gaiola*, came in sight of the river towns, she was the first they had seen in three years. What we eventually came to realise, as she panted and waddled ever more slowly, making a bare 5 or 6 knots and burning whole forests to make even that, was that she was also the last they would ever see. She had been refurbished to make a last voyage upriver, which is to say that the rust had been given a few coats of silver stove paint and the woodwork brightened up and the BBC had subsidised the cost of passage so that real people could travel with us. She seemed to me as trumpery as any stage set.

I was afraid that once we were borne away from the confusion and the squalor on the broad, cool river, sipping *caipirinhas* (wonderful drinks made with *cachaça*, whole limes and sugar) on her shaded upper deck, the reality of the Nordeste would slip beyond my grasp. Once the *São Francisco* arrived in Pirapora she would make short day-trips for the tourists staying at the hotel there, if indeed she would do so much. Despite frantic attempts to maximise the tourism potential of the valley of the São Francisco, and the determined exploitation of anything even faintly picturesque, the tourist industry has failed to take off [...]

So, while the crew investigated the boat and gauged the level of its picturesqueness, I haunted the less salubrious purlieus of the city, peeping in at doorways where dozens of sweating people sat entranced by the soap operas 'Pane, Pane, Beijo, Beijo' or 'Louco Amor' in rooms not 10 feet square, peering through the gate at the exclusive country club, so exclusive indeed that it appeared to be derelict, always coming back to the market, where it seemed to me I could see athwart the economic reality of life in the interior. There was not much buying and selling going on. The vendors waited, and crowds of small boys waited by their wheelbarrows, hoping that someone would pay them to push her purchases home. Occasionally a matron resplendent in leotard and curlers sailed by, with a barrow-boy in her wake, struggling to keep his barrow with its towering load of watermelons and yams from tipping its costly cargo into the maggoty muck underfoot. The sinews on their little arms stood out like bowstrings.

It would have been surprising if the Brazilian government and most of the functionaries we met had not assumed that we had come to Brazil to make a tourist film. Brazilians, even the poorest and most isolated, are intensely aware of the media. We had only to let our eyes, let alone the camera's eye, rest for an instant on any individual for him to start performing, even if all he was doing was washing his car or scratching his crotch. Everyone we met had his own idea of what we would want to see, and no scruple whatsoever in rigging it up whether we encouraged him or not, and then demanding a fee for doing it. When I began asking about infant mortality rates, or parasitic infestation, or the resurgence of malaria, or the unrestricted sale of dangerous drugs and baby foods or antibiotic abuse, everyone lost interest. As I was a woman, it was difficult for any Nordestino to imagine that what I thought about anything was of any interest to anybody. At times I despaired of ever putting together an intelligent film, and never more than in those early days in Juàzeiro. The chief cause of my misery was that ghastliest of all the ghastly manifestations of fake folk art, the *carranca*.

In the days when cargo-boats plied the river, some were decorated with grotesque figureheads, which no one found particularly remarkable. When the river trade languished, the boats rotted and the figureheads rotted with them, until an enterprising collector realised that they were eminently collectable. In the time-honoured fashion of the art impresario he began a systematic study of them, pointing out correspondences (of a fairly inevitable kind) with figureheads from Phoenicia and medieval Turkey. Amidst all the brouhaha there emerges one *carranqueiro* of genius, Francisco Guarany, who began making *carrancas* in 1901 at the age of seventeen, and by 1940 had made about eighty of them. When the *carranca* cult developed he was persuaded to parody himself and made figureheads for boats which no longer existed. A tribe of *carranqueiros* who had never seen the genuine article began to produce thousands of *carrancas* which may be seen in every curio shop in Brazil, hideous perfunctory things made of unseasoned wood crudely lacquered in red, white and black and of all sizes, some tiny enough to fit on pencils, others huge. One, outside Juàzeiro, stands $3\frac{1}{2}$ metres tall. Almost all these objects are crude, soulless and utterly spurious; the common prejudice against the Nordestino people can only be reinforced by them.

The thought of being forced by circumstances to treat these objects seriously in our film produced in me a sensation not unlike panic. We were committed to struggle out into the *sertão* in the blinding heat in a VW Kombi, which boiled and threatened to leave us stranded on the blistering macadam at any moment, to pay homage to a *carranqueiro* called Xuri. His *carrancas* were only half a notch better than the usual rubbish, but still I was not sorry that we were there, or that the director of the film had commissioned a huge *carranca* (although I prayed that we would not actually have to show it in the finished film). The beautiful thing about Xuri was not his spurious craft activity but his whole life. He lived in a tiny house, with two tiny rooms and one larger one with door fore and aft. The whitewashed adobe was velvety cool to the touch, and the mild draught through the tiles and the gaps between walls and roof kept the air fresh. In a miniature fenced compound before the house his wife grew a few four-o'clocks and African marigolds, lovingly cosseted with used water. She was tall, upright, smooth-haired and brown-skinned with that quality of stillness in her repose that comes with Indian blood. One daughter was away at school. Another sat in a beautifully made folding chair, the design of which has not changed since its European original was made in the mid-sixteenth century, trailing delicate fingertips over the armrests with all the aplomb of an infanta. The littlest was feverish. Her hacking cough had been around for too many weeks.

In their vegetable garden, corn, melons, marrows and cucumbers struggled against the looming drought. Already the growing season was almost over. As the cruel sun slid down the sky, and Xuri's trees began to cast long, violet shadows towards the little house, and his wife slipped out with a dish of something for the green parrots that Nordestinos love so well, it seemed a good and dignified life. The cattle and goats clanked past on their way to their stalls. An occasional *vaqueiro* tipped his fringed hat as he rode past. We were the false note, encouraging Xuri to chip away at a *carranca* for the camera. Xuri obeyed silently, but in his eyes I thought I saw the look. His lady patroness, who had led us to him, told us loudly how one *carranqueiro* whom she had rescued from destitution took his first pay-cheque and spent it on drink and drugs, abandoning his hungry family. 'Amazing. These people.' Her house was full of the worst bad art it would ever be possible to see, debased embroideries, abominable carvings, gross daubs of sentimental subjects. Clearly she could see no reason why a man reduced to making a coarse fool of himself in lieu of making an honest living should throw up everything and embrace a slow death. I thought if Xuri did not do such a thing, it was largely because of something I saw in his wife's eyes, a wise, disabused, mischievous twinkle.

As Xuri's patroness could not be prevailed upon to hold her tongue during the filming, she was sent off to take me to visit others of her protégés, a family of lace-makers. Once again I was reluctant, for I had seen the lace, which was a meagre remnant of European tradition, uninteresting and irrelevant to everyday life. The old women, all without men for one reason or another, were supposed to live by their lace-making, but with a metre of lace, a week's work, selling at 300 cruzeiros (about 15p) they clearly did not. Their house was rather grander than Xuri's, for it was faced with brick, and had rooms opening on both sides of the main one, but the beds of the three sisters were all to be found in one room. Another served as a store for their family possessions, and the other two were empty. In the fenced compound behind the house was a low, round mound, about 4 metres across, of smooth quartz pebbles, where washing would be thrown to dry and bleach in the sun, but if the gentle ladies were forced to survive by taking in washing no one mentioned it and I didn't like to ask. It was not until my second visit that I realised how close to going under the old ladies were. Chronic malnutrition is not so easy to detect among the elderly. In their calm and lovely house floored with silver sand brushed every day into a fan pattern, the nunlike sisters with their charming manners were practically starving.

Russell Braddon et al., *River Journeys* (1984)

1987

Kate Jennings in New York

Poet and essayist, Kate Jennings (1948–) was born in Temora, grew up in south-western New South Wales, graduated in arts from the University of Sydney and now lives in New York. In the late 1960s and early 1970s, she was heavily involved in student and left-wing politics and in the feminist movement. In 1975 she edited Mother I'm Rooted, *'an eccentric if democratic collection of poems by Australian women, a big, thick book full of the female experience'. In the same year she published the first volume of her own poetry,* Come to Me My Melancholy Baby *(1975), and moved to New York where she works as a writer and editor. Her latest volume of poetry,* Cats, Dogs and Pitchforks, *was published in 1993. Place, both that of childhood memory and present moment, is a central issue when the settled expatriate recalls the newcomer's first impressions of New York in* Save Me, Joe Louis *(1988).*

Winter in New York. It has been snowing. The sky, what I can see of it, is a dirty yellow, the colour of a sweat-stained singlet. Lexington Avenue is ankle-deep in brown slush. As I step off the curb to cross at Seventy-First Street, a station wagon stops at the traffic light next to a brand new black BMW. Apparently the station wagon is too near the BMW for the driver's liking because he leans across and yells, 'That's too damn close!' The lights change. As the two cars proceed up Lexington, the driver of the BMW swerves and bounces his shiny car off the side of the station wagon. The people in the station wagon are a picture of astonishment. Again the BMW bounces off the station wagon. And again. The cars jitterbug slowly up Lexington. Then the BMW speeds away, spurting slurried snow into the air.

What am I doing here?, I say to myself, not for the first time. What am I doing here, daughter of Edna and Laurie, granddaughter of Madge and George, Phyllis and James?, as if this litany of familiar names will ward off New York's deranged nastiness.

[…]

The windows of our apartment on East Seventy-Second Street face north, so the light is milky and dreamlike. My desk is at a window which looks out over carriage houses, ailanthus and ginkgo trees, the green copper dome of St Jean Baptiste, and apartment houses of pre-war vintage topped by homey wooden water tanks, none of them very high by New York standards, a human cityscape unmarred by the monstrous towers that cast their doomsday shadows all over town.

To the west is Park Avenue with its dowager apartment buildings and ever-present doormen, Madison Avenue and merchandise guaranteed to give you an immediate attack of acquisitiveness, and Central Park. A short walk from the Seventy-Second Street entrance to the park is an esplanade sheltered by long rows of oaks, and at the end of the esplanade, a bandshell. The last time I walked by *Peter and the Wolf* was being performed with a full orchestra and Dustin Hoffman as one of the readers. Beyond the bandshell, the newly restored Bethesda Fountain terrace. This stately area attracts lone violinists and flautists as well as jam groups of blacks playing African music.

Next to the terrace is a small lake, where families and lovers take the air in rowboats. Early one recent Sunday morning, my friend Bob and I, addled by work and the porridge-like humidity for which New York is notorious, hired one ourselves. Our oars kept slipping out of the rowlocks and snagging on slimy aquatic weeds, but we felt better for it. In the middle of all this ersatz pastorality, we came across a scene totally unexpected in the middle of New York and one of heart-warming optimism: a fellow fishing.

To the east are modern apartment buildings honeycombed with studio apartments for singles. These young people, so jaundiced they refer to love as the 'L word', hang out in Second Avenue restaurants with names like Ciaobella, Tuba City Truck Stop, and Camelback and Central.

There are sights and faces worthy of Breughel in this neighbourhood. Most of all I love to watch the dog walkers, the professional ones, who at any given time have upward of fourteen dogs on leashes that fan out around them like streamers on a maypole. You name it, there are poodles, pugs, beagles, spaniels, collies, terriers, huskies, Labradors, Egyptian salukis, even mutts, all trim and well groomed. The walkers seem to be in telepathic communication with their charges, who sail by like a miniature armada, impervious to distractions and lesser dogs.

I used to think being a dog walker would be an idyllic occupation, a naive notion. Many of them, apparently, are martinets, impatient of interruptions and delays, sympathetic only to the dogs, and even those are exercised at such a brisk pace they fall over when they get home and sleep all day. To make matters worse, the world of dog walkers is rife with more feuds than an English department. 'See that?' said one dog walker of a rival's pack. 'Terrible. No rhythm and no regard.' In retaliation, the rival accused his critic of the most heinous dogwalking crime of all. He said, down his nose, 'She drops her leashes.'

Late one summer afternoon, Bob and I set out for Central Park. We kept passing festive Puerto Ricans instead of the usual button-upped burghers. What were they doing here? The reason soon became apparent. A jubilant parade to celebrate Puerto Rico Day was proceeding up Fifth Avenue, turning the decorum of the neighborhood on its head. The first float we saw, sponsored by the Hotel Tropicana, was a knockout — a dozen cha-cha-ing big-bosomed showgirls in gold lamé swimsuits. There was applause but surprisingly no catcalls or wolf whistles. I looked around. The men in the crowd were in a seventh heaven, a mixture of awe and lust on their faces. They stood quite still, feasting their eyes, shaking their heads as if the sight of these beauties was almost more than they could bear. Then, after the float had gone by, their faces broke into big, lazy, cat-got-the-cream smiles.

The Tropicana float was followed by a contingent of women from the garment workers' union. They carried placards announcing 'A Woman's Place is in the Union'. Much cheering. Behind them, the longest stretch limousine I have ever seen, the kind that is rumoured to have a swimming pool. Loudspeakers affixed to the roof of the limo blasted out that corny Frank Sinatra favourite, 'New York, New York'. In Spanish, of course. *Si triunfas aquí, triunfas en cualquier parte.* If you can make it here, you can make it anywhere. The crowd joined in at the top of their lungs. I wouldn't like much to be a Puerto Rican trying to *triunfas* in this city.

On our way back we joined pleasure-weary Puerto Ricans on their way home. As they passed the new Ralph Lauren Polo store on Madison Avenue, normally a magnet for window-shoppers, none of them so much as glanced at the wares displayed there. They were completely oblivious to the charms of safari jackets, blue blazers with brass naval buttons, spectator shoes, straw boaters, duck pants, silk foulard shirtwaists, and alligator pumps.

The upwardly mobile of New York flock to Ralph Lauren like pilgrims to a shrine. Limos two-deep line the curb. Lauren has made millions out of creating clothes that bestow an instant pedigree on the wearer. Ironically, Ralph Lauren was born Ralph Lifschitz, son of Frank and Freida. He grew up in the Moshulu Parkway section of the Bronx, the same area that spawned Calvin Klein. 'There are always people who will say, and not nicely, that I changed my name for business reasons,' said Lauren, hurt by accusations that he had taken on a more Waspish moniker to suit his clobber. 'It was changed by my father for his reasons, whatever they were.'

I am not beyond looking in the windows of the Polo store myself. Early in the spring, a pair of shoes caught my fancy. On Madison Avenue, if you have to ask the price of something, you probably can't afford it. I'd had to ask the price of these shoes, so for months I pondered the foolishness of buying them. My covetousness got the better of me. A week after I bought the shoes, I received a letter in the mail. The thick, creamy envelope was hand-addressed. 'Dear Miss Jennings,' read the note inside. 'Thank you for stopping by Polo last week. It was a pleasure to work with you! I hope you enjoy your woven flats — they are great all year round. Thanks again and have a lovely summer. Sincerely, Connaught Meagher.' Golly. I had to restrain myself from writing a chatty little note back pointing out that handing over a credit card is not exactly 'work'. I wonder if Connaught's father changed his surname too. For his own reasons. Whatever they were [...]

I haven't always shopped at Ralph Lauren, dined at Petrossian, and danced at Doubles. When I first came to New York, I had no money, no prospects, few friends, and an inflated sense of my own worth. 'There are too many women with ambitions beyond their talents, experiences beyond their capacity, with romantic daydreams of glory and fame as the center of attention — we have too many of their sad histories,' wrote Katherine Anne Porter, who was not known for charity toward members of her own sex. She did not include herself, of course, in their number. Unfortunately, it was close to the truth in my case.

I found a third-floor tenement apartment on the West Side of Manhattan, in a neighborhood known as Hell's Kitchen. These tenements started to crumble as soon as they were built at the turn of the century; eighty years later, patched like perished bicycle tyres, they were in danger of collapsing altogether. I didn't have north light; I had hardly any light at all. The floors sloped so badly that the furniture had to be placed against one wall. The bathroom was so small, I had to step into the tub from the end. But I considered myself lucky: other people I knew in the neighborhood had to make do with a tub in the kitchen. And the rent was reasonable. I could just afford it.

My apartment, with its fire escapes zig-zagging across the windows, could have been a set for *West Side Story*. In fact, one son of the Puerto Rican family who lived there for thirty years before I moved in was killed in a 'rumble'. I found some lethal-looking handmade weapons in the rubbish left behind. I also found a shoe box filled with papers documenting some girl's life. There were baby photos and other mementos, report cards, confirmation scroll, social security card, and death certificate. I couldn't bring myself to throw it away, so I took the box next door to the Pentecostal Church, which my Puerto Rican family had attended, and left it on the doorstep.

Hell's Kitchen earned its name because it was, in a tough city, one of the roughest neighborhoods. I asked Kathy Clark, a friend who had lived there all her life, what Hell's Kitchen was like when she was a child. 'It wasn't as bad as people make out,' she said. 'There were drunken brawls and gang warfare — the Irish mafia went after each other with shotguns — but the streets were safe. The Catholic church kept everyone in line. The priests didn't hesitate to knock two heads together to put some sense into them.'

To Kathy, the drug traffic and the crime it brings in its wake is worse, far worse, than the gang warfare of her youth. Muggings by junkies are an everyday occurrence. Police shakedowns are a neighborhood attraction. (They are shakedowns in the literal sense of the word because the junkies have to be brought down from the rooftops where they hide. Sometimes I would look out my window only to catch a view of a stream of pee splashing to the ground.) I have seen people shot, stabbed, and brained by two-by-fours. I was standing outside the corner bodega when a man next to me was knifed. He keeled over like a felled tree. What is that liquid? I thought, as blood bubbled out of him.

I was burgled twice in Hell's Kitchen. The second time they took my pride and joy, a warm winter coat and a pair of boots for which I'd saved for months. In a murderous mood myself, I waded through the books and clothes that had been strewn on the floor to call the police. When one came, he stood in the middle of the chaos and asked, 'Are you sure you've been robbed?' I hated to think what the interiors of some apartments must be like if he didn't find this unusual, and then I remembered the old woman who had died on the top floor. The police broke down the door to find not only her corpse but the neatly packaged bodies of eight cats in various stages of decomposition.

To add to the violence, landlords, eager to get rid of rent-control tenants, had arsonists set fires. When the building opposite me went up in flames in the middle of the night, I set a pillow on the windowsill so I could watch the spectacle in comfort. People came pouring out in their pyjamas and nightgowns, clutching pets and treasured belongings. The landlords, looking like undertakers, arrived the next morning to survey the 'damage'. The building had been handily gutted and could now be tarted up for the gentry.

Of all the violence I saw in Hell's Kitchen, the episode that sticks in my mind was probably accidental. Early one morning, I came across the chalked outline of a body on the road. There was a small pool of blood. Nearby, a crumpled tie. Some fellow on his way to work had met his maker. Soon the chalk mark would be obliterated by the rush-hour traffic.

I took a job on a magazine, not the *New Yorker* or *Harper's* or the *Atlantic*, the kind of magazines I read and admire, but one of the many publications that service the American travel industry. Although I didn't think so, I was lucky to get the job because all I had in the way of marketable skills was a dime-a-dozen Arts degree. Of the many problems I had in adapting to office routine, not the least of which was my resentment at even being there, was my sense of humour. Or my co-workers' perception of my sense of humour. Cecil Day Lewis has observed that one of the basic rules of American conversation is that you can be serious or frivolous, but never in the same paragraph. In true Australian fashion, I was in the habit of being irreverent about even the most weighty matters. Worse still, and again in true Australian fashion, I usually did this with a straight face. My co-workers didn't get it. Instead of praising my wit, they found me insulting.

People do come to New York to seek fame and fortune, but many more come to hide. I dearly wanted to return to Australia, but I was too proud to go home with my tail between my legs. Instead I crawled into the woodwork along with millions of others. Filled with self-loathing, I took refuge in the gin mills on Seventh and Eighth Avenues. Nobody cares who you are or where you come from in these dives. In Australia, among my set, this would have been deemed romantic. 'Slumming it' we called it. Doing our bit to break down class barriers. We liked to think of ourselves as déclassé, when actually we were being as middle class as Madame Bovary. Anaesthetizing myself at four o'clock in the morning with cheap gin in the company of a whole lot of other deadbeats wasn't romantic. It was pathetic.

Save Me, Joe Louis (1988)

1990

Peter Conrad in four places

Peter Conrad (1948–) was born in Tasmania; his sense of its oppressive provinciality is described in Down Home: Revisiting Tasmania *(1988). As soon as possible after graduating in arts from the University of Tasmania, he headed for Oxford, where he has taught English since 1973. Thus he fulfilled the ultimate dream of a childhood spent 'reading about what my life would be like when I was reborn in the Northern Hemisphere', of a sensibility in which the imagination was English and the routine reality Australian. He has published books on English literature, American art and Italian opera,*

and writes and teaches in the United States as well as England. Where I Fell
to Earth *(1990) explores the accidental yet deep-felt sense of place for a postmodern transatlantic global villager whose quadruple life in Oxford, London, Lisbon and New York means he can still avoid calling Australia home.*

The window has four panes of glass, each of them containing a different scene: a wall of grimy brick and a tree shyly uncurling leaves like
croziers; next to it the quadrangle with the Greek god, who today is
wearing a clown's red nose, strapped in place by a rubber band; the garden buzzing with heat, the lemons aglow, the birds cross-hatching the
air; beside that the ballet of cabs, trucks, dogs, gestures and attitudes
choreographing itself on the street corner.

A different person wanders through each of the panes. In Oxford there
is a figure availing himself of his ancient right to take short-cuts across the
barbered grass. The porters once used to shoo him off it, mistaking him
for a student; no longer. He is on his way to dinner, in a gown speckled
with specimens of institutional meals eaten during the last fifteen years.
The gown serves as a black all-over napkin. It is also beginning to come
apart at the seams, its threads tangling and frazzling like distracted
thoughts. Pathetically, it is the wrong gown: it denotes the rank of BA, not
the MA which you are automatically awarded a few years later. The MA
gown is a swishier item, with flaps which trail under the arms modelled on
some late medieval fashion. I could not avoid getting the degree, but I
never acquired the gown. This counted as Peter Pan's refusal to graduate.

The London space is occupied by someone else, reluctantly grown-
up whether he likes it or not: the householder who wonders whether he
dares to trust this shelter, hears a creak in the floor boards as if it were a
snapped bone, treats a pipe which chugs and grumbles as a digestive
upset, and transfers all his mortal anxieties to brick, wood and plaster.
If it rains will the roof leak, and if it doesn't will the tree die? Sometimes
he tries to convince himself not to care: we acquire this need for
domestic protection, after all, just at the age when we begin to perceive
that it will not last and therefore does not matter. The obsession with
permanence accompanies the knowledge of temporariness.

In New York this housebound pot-plant of a person sheds such cares
and, having dropped off his bag, loses himself at once in the street.
Though I know I have to wait for the elevator and catch up with the
doorman's maladies on the way out, I always want to dive directly from
the fire-escape and feel the liveliness down there slap and splash and
cleave in front of my face like water. I understand why baptism requires
total immersion. People gush, flood, cascade along the sidewalk in a
flotsam of ripped jeans, gelled hair, power shoulders and aloof, appraising shades; transistors dispense rap, the bell on a fire-engine clangs, and

the self-proclaimed psychic lounging on the vinyl banquette in her basement shrills, 'Hey, come get a reading today'. Why not let her invent a future for me?

After all in Lisbon I can reinvent a past for myself. The person I see in that frame of glass is tracking a rabbit through the flowerbeds with the inducement of a carrot and the threat of a broomstick. He seems to be wearing short pants.

Each character in this quadruple life has his own identity, even his own name. To multiply the self is one way of wriggling free from it, suggesting that it is a facet not a face. Remember the adolescent delight in experimenting with signatures? Every twiddle or loop or staccato jerk of the pen sketches a character you might become. What I most favoured at that age was a scrawl which rendered me illegible. It was the announcement, to myself if to no one else, of a mystery [...]

Each of the window panes contains someone different. Changing longitudes, I move between times or ages. I can recover childhood at will in Lisbon, for the price of a ticket there. Conversely, going back to England means the resumption of responsibilities, of adult cares — sealing the roof, feeding the birds, fertilising the tree, teaching the young, listening to the church clock dole out time. England longs to turn everything into an antique. I groan inwardly each year as I edge further up the seniority league in Oxford. When I was first taken to see the rooms set aside for me at Christ Church, the colleague in charge of such things explained that they had been cunningly manoeuvred away from their former clerical use, and I need not fear eviction by some incoming chaplain. 'They're yours until the retiring age,' he said. He meant to please me, but my heart sank to hear it. I was twenty-five at the time: so *this* was to be it?

But in America the first job/house/wife/nose is not necessarily the last. There was always the chance of exit in that direction, to New York with its adolescent faith that you can be anything or anyone you wish, so long — to quote Miss America — as you feel good about yourself. 'I'm changing my life' is the national creed. It is what the country means, after all. New York keeps alive in me the sense of potentiality.

Returning once to Oxford after a year on leave, I asked one of the college secretaries what had happened while I was away. 'Nothing' she almost snapped, and looked affronted by the very thought of something happening. Then, having got over her irritation, she added, 'Oh, the Queen came to dinner' — though this was a ritual, and therefore did not constitute a happening. It reaffirmed the past; nothing could be less of a novelty. In my rooms, the owl still nodded sagely on its rickety perch.

My first outing in New York is always a survey of what's new: most things are. The city has reconstructed or redefined itself in my absence. The Tex-Mex restaurant across the park is now Burmese, the florist who serenaded his blooms with baroque music has given way to a store selling cowboy boots with a window display of bleached steer skulls, the deli has lunged further down-market and now stocks only the tabloids and not *The New York Times*, the tenement has been reclad as a condominium with post-modern portholes to conceal its wooden water-tank. The dancer across the street has moved on, or is dead. His blinds are pulled up on a bared box which awaits its next transformation. There is a brisk turnover in lives here. The future is always arriving prematurely. The clothes shop dummies wear Bermuda shorts while the last blizzard of winter is scourging the street, and have already adopted flannels in broiling August. After a while, the American acceleration of time alarms me. Can't they see that it is an anticipation of the end? Hence the comfort of retreating to my various safe pasts: Oxford with its gathering dust, Lisbon with the hare-brained rabbit.

They are different pasts. Oxford, like Highgate Cemetery, is the voluminous history we come from and return to. I spend the year there working chronologically through English literature, as the bell clangs above me and the seasons rotate in the meadow. Shakespeare, Sidney and Spenser occupy the autumn. We cough our way through Milton in the winter. The romantic poets arrive in time for the summer — skylarks, nightingales, daffodils, splendour in the grass. In October it all begins over again. The young pass through and are annually replaced. They and the texts remain the same age. Only I get older.

Lisbon is a personal past, a childhood I can live out of sequence, squeezed into vacations from adult existence. However many years pass, I will stay the youngest member of this family. Rosalina, pleading for permission to kill and cook the rabbit, regularly offers to replace it with a new one. It will look just the same, she promises; there are plenty at the market. Perhaps she does just this while I am away. It could be a different rabbit each time, and therefore younger than it was when I last saw it. So long as it is white, would I notice the difference?

Flight was always my ambition, my motive and my motor. Not so much flying as the idea of fugitiveness. During my first trips out of Tasmania to the mainland, I used to watch the plane's propeller jerk, spin, whirl and then vanish into a blur of energy. When it revolved fast enough, it became invisible. As far as I understood it, that was the meaning of flight: it conferred disincarnation [...]

It is just because the fall to earth is so unpredictable and undesigned, like the person falling, that we make a cult of the place where the faller crash-lands. Each spot has its anthem, its boast of centrality. The Londoners after hours in the pub next door to me rowdily warble that maybe it's because they're Londoners that they love London so. Maybe they are right: what other reason could there be? From the *fado* dens in Lisbon you can hear the singers hoarsely chanting the praises of their melancholy Lisboa. In New York, New York, the jingle asserts that it's such a wonderful town they had to name it twice.

These are our noisy protests against coincidence and happenstance, our dreams of predestination. Life is a long exercise in turning chance into choice, accident into design. Hence those windows which act as frames, pretending that what travels across them is a picture. Hence too the notion of home, with its wishful rearrangement of geography. It decrees a centre, and thus an anchorage. Every love — whether personal or civic — subscribes to the idea of necessity, and entails an illusion of permanence [...]

A summer evening in Oxford, the usual walk around Christ Church meadow. The wind shaking an earlier rain from the trees, and a sunset which opened across the washed sky like a flower; Magdalen tower streaked with gold; the playing fields across the river waiting unruffled for the next consignment of larking lives to spill onto them; the river itself almost forgetting to flow. It was one of those occasions when you can quite happily deduct yourself from the world, simply because you realise your extreme good fortune in being in it.

In a panel beside this, a stifling April afternoon in New York, another year. I am slogging up Bleecker Street. Between one block and the next, the temperature plunges. Clouds roll in to close over the city. The sun, plummeting faster than usual to hide in New Jersey, lights them from underneath: they are green, swollen, about to burst. A gust of grit slaps my face. Somewhere to the north, a powdery flash detonates in the sky. Then a drum-roll batters the street. A Latino kid with a feather in his hair, worried about the water-tightness of his boom box, says to his friend 'Hey man, is the world gonna end?' It didn't. Not that time.

Or I am crossing Waterloo Bridge at night in a winter gale, wondering whether this is the same city I first saw from here all those years before, and whether I am the same person who saw it then. A skyline of cranes instead of churches, floodlights like banners on the façade of the Savoy, sapphire arcs on top of the Lloyd's Building. The water below is black and choppy. A shamefaced youth asks for money to buy a cup of tea. He came over from Ireland to work on a building site, had his tools stolen, lost his job, couldn't pay his rent, and now dosses down beneath the bridge. 'I'm saving up to go home,' he says, to cover my fussing as I try to calculate how much I need to keep for my bus fare. 'I've been here three years, and I'd like to go back if I could. The way I look at it is, I've seen London.' I walked on, a fellow pilgrim. The city lures us, jumbles us up, and then — accepting no responsibility for the dreams it excites in us — sends us briskly off to our different destinations or destinies. Perhaps it was dangerous to want more than a single life. The city abounded in people you had only just escaped having to be.

And the first time I was asked a question in the street in Lisbon. It must have been ten years ago, at a bus stop. An old woman in the queue — all in black, scarf knotted under her chin, a professional widow — asked me if the bus which was pulling in went to Santos. I understood the question but did not know the answer. At least I was able to tell her in Portuguese that I didn't know. She looked embarrassed, bewildered at having approached a foreigner. Evidence of mental frailty on her part, she probably thought. The strangers, the blow-ins from out there, were supposed to be instantly recognisable. They wore bright colours, carried cameras, and did not travel by bus. What was this one doing in camouflage? Another passenger told her what she wanted to know, and she hauled herself onto the bus with her flagon of olive oil and her strip of dried cod. I was so taken aback at being mistaken for someone who was not a stranger that I didn't realise it was my bus too.

All these days recur, with the aid of a few verbal clues. Representation promises to make what is absent present again, but the reach of words is longer than their grasp. All they can do is catch the trace a body has left in departing.

Where I Fell to Earth (1990)

1991

Andrew Riemer in Austria and Hungary

For the first 150 years of white Australia's history, the journey to the place of family memory took travellers back to Britain, and only a few, such as Nathan Spielvogel, to other parts. Since the mass migration of the postwar era, the Australian population has included hundreds of thousands of people for whom 'Home', memory and ancestral sites mean somewhere else. Writer, academic and literary critic Andrew Riemer (1936–) was born in Budapest and came to Australia with his parents at the age of 10. The Australia in which Riemer landed was determined on the assimilation of its immigrants, and Riemer assimilated. He became a teacher of English literature at the University of Sydney. Riemer has told the story of his early years in Australia, of the making of a new identity while both losing and retaining the old, in his memoir, Inside Outside *(1992). His childhood was not only suburban Sydney but also the stories — more romantic and alluring with the passage of time — of his parents. His memory was a carefully nurtured myth of a past Europe, of a paradise from which he had been expelled, a Europe now only experienced in fragments in sidestreets and alleys, when mood, moment and memory converge. In 1991, Riemer embarked on a journey of time and place to Sopron in Hungary and Vienna in Austria, the province and the metropolis of his childhood and family memory. In* The Habsburg Café *(1993), the coffee and cakes of Vienna collapsed adult memory and childhood experience.*

It is as a legacy, no doubt, of such an obsession with food among members of my family and the society they had inhabited that for many years I have been visited without warning by a sensation that must have had its origin in the rituals of this world. It is a potently visual and olfactory sensation, and it has remained remarkably consistent even though months or years sometimes separate its sudden and inexplicable visitations. It always comes in the same form: I am looking at the junction of two narrow cobbled streets on a wintry afternoon. There is still some light in a leaden sky but a gaslight attached to the corner building by a sturdy bracket is already alight. The conjunction of the two streets forms an acute angle, so that my gaze travels down each, allowing the buildings on either side of both streets to be seen. They are low structures with steeply pitched roofs. The large arched gates are secured by heavy wooden doors. Many of the windows are barred. A light snowfall leaves a thin layer of greyish-white ice on the cobblestones, which extend to the walls of the buildings, for there are no footpaths in these narrow streets. A little way up one of the streets, a warm orange-yellow light filters through the curtained window of a shop.

It is a banal image, culled perhaps from a painting, an illustration or even from one of those realistic stage settings that I saw as a child on outings to the theatre in one of these towns or cities. Yet its effect on me is very peculiar. I experience a sensation of great peace and contentment, mixed with an acute sense of loss, whenever the image pops into my consciousness from a recess of my personality where it has been dormant. It is accompanied, moreover, by its most curious attribute, a powerful scent, bringing to the nostrils of my imagination the characteristic odour of an Austro-Hungarian café, a heady amalgam of aromas, among which vanilla and coffee are dominant.

I can attach no precise source to this sensation, nor am I able to find any explanation for its unheralded appearances. But I have felt, as the years pass and as it insists on returning, that it represents something fundamentally important — whatever it might be. It speaks to me of something that demands to be recovered but is perhaps no longer recoverable: innocence, the clarity of childhood, a world that has been compromised by experience and lost in time.

I have often thought that this image, sensation, or visitation is merely a trick provoked by the literary disposition, a consequence, perhaps, of reading too much Proust. Yet as it returns with its haunting insistence, sometimes in broad daylight, sometimes in a vividly remembered dream, I realise that it first struck me during my early adolescence, in the first years of my life in Australia, long before I had heard Proust's name, or read even a page of *Remembrance of Things Past*. Rather, I am convinced, it must emerge from a private vocabulary of images and memories. It is a visual and olfactory emblem of the lost fantasy-world of Kakania: the characteristic appearance of its streets in some city or town, mixed with a whiff of its equally characteristic and perhaps most significant institution — a café where the sweet odour of vanilla mingles with the pungent scent of highly roasted coffee. In my imagination, this café of the Habsburg world — in some unknown city or town of my early childhood when that Empire and realm, though no longer a political reality, still exerted an influence throughout its former territories — has assumed a position of undisputed centrality. It has become a distillation, a compact, fleeting yet powerful image of a world irrecoverably lost, a world compromised by hatred and brutality, a world which must be approached with the armour of irony fully in place, and yet a world of irresistible allure. And it provides, no matter how tenuously, or how contingently, some signs of the survival of that world in dreams, in the imagination or in visions imprinted on my memory many years ago, a time when all experiences and sensations were new, fresh and shiningly clear.

[...]

Walking along a narrow cobbled street — more alley than street — behind the cathedral, I am pulled up short by that most evocative aroma: sweet vanilla and pungent coffee. It is a commonplace scent, perhaps the characteristic smell of Kakania; it floods over you every time you walk through the glass doors of one of the great cafés of Vienna or Budapest. Rarely, however, is it as enticing as it is now, flowing through the open door of a small café on this autumn afternoon. My dream-sensation of melancholic wellbeing returns with almost urgent immediacy. I cannot resist walking into the café, even though I've only just had a sandwich at the buffet of the art gallery, having been wearied by endless rows of bulbous women, eviscerated martyrs and dead pheasants.

This is a very modest café. Half-a-dozen small marble-topped tables are ranged along one wall of the narrow room. The wall opposite is occupied almost entirely by a glass-fronted counter, displaying on mirror-backed shelves a variety of cakes, gâteaux and pastries. These have an invitingly homely look, very different from the sculpted extravaganzas offered for the delectation of their patrons by the great cafés of this city. If those establishments emulate the salons of aristocratic mansions — marble halls, Chinese rooms, wintergardens — this small café resembles the drawing rooms of bourgeois apartments seventy or a hundred years ago. The fierce though faded flocked wallpaper certainly looks old enough to be considered antique, while the lace curtain draped over the window at the front has lost most of its pattern through repeated darning. The crystal chandelier hanging from the ceiling has been rendered opaque by decades of steam, coffee fumes and tobacco smoke.

At this early hour of the afternoon, the place is practically deserted, though in an hour or two it will no doubt be jam-packed, as all Viennese cafés, large and small, are crowded at the appropriate and traditional time of five o'clock. Now there are only two customers, *habituées*, it would seem. They are elderly ladies of indeterminate age, for both of them are heavily made up, with obviously dyed hair or perhaps wigs. Their gnarled and knobby fingers suggest that they are very old indeed. The waitress, who is probably the proprietor, stands beside their table, one hand resting on the back of one of those spindly chairs which provide the usual furnishing for such establishments. As a concession to the season, no doubt — though the day is warm, even oppressive — she wears fur-lined felt boots over black stockings.

The three women are deep in conversation. I sit down at one of the tables at a discreet distance from them. The waitress acknowledges my presence and resumes the briefly interrupted discussion. There is, of course, no hurry — everyone in this part of the world seems to have ample time. The rhythms of café-life admit no haste. I have learnt to accept this convention, even though I live in a country where people are usually impatient and often in a hurry. I have not yet learnt, however, the art of staring vacantly into the middle distance, at which Europeans seem so adept as they sit in cafés, hanging on every word spoken at the next table. I know that it is quite proper to listen to these conversations as long as you maintain the fiction that eavesdropping would never enter your mind. Lacking that skill, I now do what I always do in such circumstances: I become wholly absorbed by the pages of my address book.

The ladies' conversation is hard to follow. They speak in the slurred and mellifluous Viennese dialect which almost constitutes a distinct language. All I am able to catch is a few words. They are sufficient, nevertheless, to give some indication of what they are talking about. It seems that they have been occupied by this topic for some time; it may indeed be that I have strayed into an instalment of a long-running, real-life serial. Certainly, what I glean from their rapid and largely incomprehensible conversation seems to have the ingredients of a conventional soap opera. The centre of attention is a young woman, the daughter of one of the customers. Her husband seems to be an out-and-out rotter. I understanding nothing of the long litany of his crimes and outrages, but the exclamations of the lamenting mother's companions clearly indicate their gravity. I begin to wonder whether this is a tale of marital infidelity — but it could just as easily be a matter of money, for I am able to catch the words 'twenty thousand schillings' which form a sort of leitmotif throughout these lamentations. Perhaps it's both, for now I begin to hear sneering references to 'that kind of woman'. Even if feminist theory has penetrated this most conservative society, it has obviously made no impact whatever on these elderly members of the Viennese middle class.

Now, after what has obviously been the proper lapse of time, the waitress excuses herself and shuffles over to take my order. I ask for coffee, knowing that you mustn't immediately specify which of the many kinds of coffee available in these establishments you would prefer. Instead, it is necessary to engage in an elaborate ceremony of negotiations, eliminating one by one the various options — iced or hot, long black or short, with warm milk or cold, with whipped cream or with brandy or rum, or perhaps that peculiar mixture of coffee and drinking chocolate that some people in this part of the world seem to enjoy so much.

Having satisfactorily concluded these negotiations, she now asks me, with a formal smile, what I would like to eat. Nothing, I reply, only coffee. The disappointment on her face is unmistakable. She gestures towards the glass-fronted counter. Can't she tempt me with one of her wonderful cakes or pastries? And, lowering her head, dropping her voice to a whisper, she suggests a piece of her *Sachertorte*. This, she assures me, is *echt*, the real thing, the genuine article, made in the house — I won't find any better in all of Vienna. It seems churlish to refuse. As she disappears behind the counter to draw the coffee and to dispense the cake, I fancy that I detect a look of triumph on the faces of her customers, who had suspended their litany of woes to observe our negotiations. This foreigner will now find out what a real *Sachertorte* tastes like, their expressions seem to suggest.

Every café in Vienna serves a chocolate cake of that name. Yet not many years ago the world's press carried reports of a complicated court battle between the owners of Demel's, the most sumptuous of Vienna's cafés, and the management of the Hotel Sacher over their respective rights to use that most distinguished appellation. Commonsense would have suggested, of course, that the hotel's richly brocaded and outrageously expensive café should have the sole right to that name. The litigation was concerned, however, not with commonsense but with the complicated toing-and-froing many years ago of pastrycooks between café and hotel. Who invented *Sachertorte?* the learned judges were asked to determine. Further, does the inventor retain the right to the name, or does it rest with the place of invention? I cannot remember the outcome of this complex legal process, which amused the international press for a week or two before some other quaint and trivial story came to occupy its attention. Perhaps, it occurs to me, the case is still *sub judice*, pending a determination which could well establish a precedent of great culinary import.

What is perhaps most surprising is the ordinariness of that disputed delicacy. Wherever *Sachertorte* is served in Vienna, it is always the same: a dense chocolate-flavoured cake, with a trickle of jam in the middle, glazed with a thin layer of shiny chocolate. To my possibly unrefined palate, this fabled confection seems indistinguishable from the products of those packets of cake-mix that crowd the shelves of supermarkets. Can this be the cause of such heated litigation? Is it for this that cafés all over the city risk goodness-knows-what fines and penalties as they continue to tempt you with their own *echt* version of the famous confection? Perhaps *Sachertorte* is charged with a mystic significance that we outsiders cannot comprehend. That may be the reason for the fierce rivalry between Demel's and Sacher's, why countless establishments flout legal restraints, finding a characteristically Kakanian way around the 'Hands Off!' sign.

The waitress returns with my coffee and a slice of cake. She places these offerings on the marble table-top with ceremonial deference, and, as though this were one of those vast crowded cafés where once in a blue moon even the best of waiters might get into a muddle, announces one black coffee and one piece of *Sachertorte* — with cream, she adds. I lift the fork to taste a morsel. The elderly ladies have stopped talking again, and are looking at me with almost coquettish smiles in anticipation of the sensation I am about to experience. The taste is indeed wonderful, a rich, nutty, chocolate substance, much more moist and aromatic than such cakes usually are. It is, moreover, quite unlike any *Sachertorte* I have ever been served in the cafés of this city.

It would be inaccurate to say, though, that I had never tasted anything like it in my life — as the coy smiles of those ladies seem to be suggesting. This confection seems identical to a cake my mother used to bake, the recipe for which was lost when she died, consisting, I recall, of eggs, chocolate, ground hazelnuts but containing no flour. She always insisted that this was the real *Sachertorte*, a recipe given to her by the Ursuline nuns of Sopron who had educated her. She couldn't remember how those supposedly devout and otherworldly women came by that closely guarded secret — which even the two warring establishments, Sacher's and Demel's, seem to have lost judging by their contemporary offerings — but she maintained, to the end of her life, that the wonderful cake she used to serve in Sydney, in a world seemingly light-years removed from Sopron and Vienna, was the only real, genuine, indeed *echt*, version of the celebrated delicacy. Sitting in this homely café in a sidestreet of the old city, savouring the wonders of what is (I am persuaded) obviously the genuine article, smiling at the two ladies who look as if they are about to burst into applause, I experience a wonderful sense of contentment, even perhaps of peace.

The afternoon is wearing on. More customers arrive, all elderly, stocky and short, overweight because they have indulged no doubt in too much genuine *Sachertorte*. They greet everyone politely, smiling, sometimes shaking hands, and dispose themselves at the remaining unoccupied tables. The place is positively buzzing: the waitress is obviously going to be rushed off her fur-clad feet for the next hour or two.

[…]

Around the next corner we come upon a sign placed in the gateway of one of the few freshly painted houses. We step inside a surprisingly spacious courtyard where, at its far end, another sign over a doorway identifies the location of a café. The place resembles — and once it probably was — a ground-floor apartment. The first room we come upon contains the obligatory glass-fronted and mirror-backed counter displaying a selection of homely cakes and pastries. One of the two doors in this hallway leads to the café itself — a series of interconnected small rooms, each with two or three marble-topped tables and plush chairs. The second door obviously leads to the kitchen.

All the tables in the first room are occupied. At one, a pair of elderly ladies are scraping the last bits of a creamy confection from shallow glass dishes. We find a table in the second room. The only other occupant is a middle-aged gentleman in a baggy suit. His briefcase has been placed on the chair opposite him. He is reading a newspaper while finishing a cup of coffee. An untouched glass of water stands on a small saucer on top of a paper doily.

The suspicion that this café had once been a dwelling is even stronger in this room. Two sash windows with lace curtains look onto the courtyard — an undesirable aspect according to the domestic hierarchies of this world. A large winged door on the opposite wall leads to another room, perhaps the owner's apartment. The walls are papered with a pattern known in English as Regency. A chandelier of Bohemian glass hangs from the moulded ceiling.

It would be easy to imagine this place as it would have looked when it housed some worthy citizen of Sopron. As we wait for our order to be taken, I begin to spin fantasies about this place. Who lived here in the 1920s, the years in which my mother was growing up in this tight little town? Since this was a courtyard flat on the edge of the old town, it is unlikely that its occupants were grandees. It is much more likely that they were relatively hard-up, like my mother's people, though no doubt able to aspire to some measure of bourgeois propriety and comfort. Did they know my mother? Were they parts of the rumour mill that spread the news of her scandalous conduct around the town? Did my mother visit friends or acquaintances here? Perhaps this was where the not-very-accomplished portrait painter executed a likeness of her on a large oval board — commissioned to commemorate her first ball — which she always detested and took some pleasure in chopping up to provide fire-wood in the bitter winter of 1945, as Budapest lay in ruins around us.

The atmosphere of the café is comfortably somnolent. The tiled stove in the corner sends out a mellow heat. We are silent, each lost in his thoughts. Perhaps my acquaintance is thinking about what he must do in his three or four days in Austria. I, for my part, looking around at the comfortable furnishings of this little café on the border of what used to be the two great nations of the Habsburg realm, am struck by a sense of curious appropriateness. It seems to me entirely fitting, indeed inevitable, that these months of wandering around the territories of what used to be Kakania, that world which gave the various members of my family many of their dreams and preoccupations, their fantasies and also their fears, should come to an end here, in a café, perhaps the most characteristic and poignant image of that world's communal dreams.

It also strikes me with particular force that the anomalies and para-doxes of this world are beyond resolution, just as my own confused and ambiguous responses to the tinsel pomp of Austria and the turmoil of contemporary Hungary must always remain balanced on a knife-edge between scorn and attachment, fear and indifference. Yet in this little town, rich with images of a mythic world, and in this unassuming café, there may remain a few echoes of a former life, of a lost world, capable of being cherished and recaptured, briefly and provisionally, in this fos-sil of the Dual Monarchy, the bitter-sweet, serio-comic dream of Kaka-nia, which once, in the distant past, beguiled so many members of my family, seducing them with its siren-song of the good life.

As my eyes travel around this warm, comfortable, slightly dowdy place, I notice the faded etchings and lithographs decorating its walls. They show perspectives of this city, always dominated by its watch-tower, some executed with great skill, others with a charmingly naïve ineptitude. In each of them, whether accomplished or amateurish, the engravers and draughtsmen have managed to include, somewhere in the elaborate designs framing these views of the town, a curiously-shaped crown, the emblem of the Kings of Hungary, and the proud double-headed eagle of the Habsburgs.

The waitress arrives to take our order. Only coffee? Nothing to eat? Could she perhaps recommend her *Sachertorte*, homemade, according to the original recipe, far superior to anything we'd find in Vienna?

The Habsburg Café (1993)

6

Returning home

C. H. Bertie ended his story with the words: 'The two supreme days of voyage abroad are: the day you leave port and the day you reach home'.[1] Departure and return adapted the rhythms of the journey abroad to the narrative requirements of the travel writer. The whole point of travel was to return home. Not all those represented here returned to Australia after their travels, but all made an imaginative return during their travels, just as they had arrived imaginatively at their destinations long before they ever left home. They have all reflected in their many different ways on what 'Home' means. But whether or not that 'Home' had changed while they had been away, the experience of the outside world meant that it would never be the same again.

1904

Nathan Spielvogel in the Mallee

The days go quietly along, 'Skat' fills in the time, but I am tired of doing nothing. I want to get on my bike and go riding up the red metal road to my little school on the hillside once more. Ten days from Colombo to Fremantle, but every day brought us closer. Came the 1st day of June, and we watched eagerly for the lighthouse. Some are looking for the new land where they hope to begin life afresh; some are looking for wives, or husbands, or children; I am looking for the pure atmosphere of my native land. Towards even a sharp eye notes light, and there was Rottnest Island. Two hours later we were at the wharf, and I stepped ashore once more on my home land. How sweet and clean everything seemed after Colombo and Aden and Port Said.

The first thing I heard on landing was, 'Bli'me, blokes, where did he get that hat?' referring to my German head gear. This is Australian. The Australian is a different type to the Englishman. These men at Fremantle pier were not the same as those at Southampton. The Australian is longer and thinner. His pockets were made at the same time as his hands, and he has a slouching walk. Here is the independence that is the delightful trait in the Australian. The obsequiousness of the Continental and English workmen is missing. This man doesn't touch his hat and 'Sir' one every three words. Likewise his hand isn't constantly itching for the tip. He gets a decent wage from his employer, and that satisfies him. One of our first class English passengers said, 'Take this parcel, my man!' 'Excuse me, I am not your man,' was the reply.

I have come back to Australia feeling proud that I have come back to a country where freedom is more than a name. We wandered up and had supper. Fresh bread from Australian flour, sweet butter, and, best of all, some Australian whiting. I did enjoy it. Our German friends are amazed and delighted with Fremantle. 'Verandahs,' said one. 'Who put these up?' 'The shopkeeper.' 'What for?' He can't understand it. And the Australian girls completely amazed them. 'Why! your housemaids and shop girls dress and behave like ladies of nobility. Look at that!' And my eyes followed a pretty little Australian draper's assistant tripping to work. She was good to look at. I felt proud of her. We took train to Perth. What a surprise awaited me! It is a great business city; in fact, more up-to-date than even Melbourne, though, of course, not nearly so large. We travelled by one of the 60 feet electric trams to the beautiful gardens. We climbed the hill and gazed on one of the loveliest views my eyes had ever seen. Perth is a beauty. Back to Fremantle, and on board to receive welcome letters from home, papers, news from friends and relations. Off again; round Cape Leeuwin; rough seas; my troubles! I'm coming home. How long the days seem; Thursday, Friday, Saturday, Sunday, and Monday comes. We are in Largs Bay. I count up my cash. I have 3s. 4d. Just nicely managed.

Off once more; the roughest night I had on the whole voyage; many thrown out of bed; bruises common. I sat up and watched the Heads' lighthouse and Sorrento and Queenscliff. Town lights. When we arose Thursday morning we were at anchor at Port Melbourne, and dear familiar faces were waiting to greet me on the pier.

Good-bye was said to all the friends I had made during the month spent together, and tips paid to the stewards, who that day were particularly attentive. A few days in Melbourne and Ballarat among friends, and I am once more back in Dimboola, delighted to feel that I have my work to do, perfectly satisfied that notwithstanding all the beauties, the treasures, and grandeur of the whole world, I prefer to live here my simple life with its few pleasures and still fewer pains.

I mounted my bike this morning and rode off, up the old red winding road, through the long avenue of perfumed wattles, now all tenderly bending under their burden of blossom, past the strip of nodding mallee bushes. The air was fresh and mellow. The sky was serenely blue. An old Jack sat on a dead limb and laughed merrily. Around the bend and past the little bridge, and there was the school on the hill, set in its little bower of gum trees. The little ones, with excited faces, and the true welcome gleaming from their eyes, were there lined up awaiting to greet me once more. Ah! This is better than the Tower of London, Unter den Linden, and the Vatican. This little room with its fifty little folk has given me more pleasure than all the wonders I have seen. London has its Abbeys and Museums; but it has its awful, grinding misery. Berlin, its palaces and galleries; but it has its Militarism. Italy has its historic past; but also its filth and beggars. But here, the blue sky above, the spreading gums around, the innocence and the simple faith of my little people — all these have no 'but.'

And so I drop back into the old groove—into the once disliked, but now appreciated, routine—perfectly contented. My own land is the best land. Adieu.

A Gumsucker on the Tramp (1905)

1928

Nina Murdoch in Melbourne

It is the conventional thing for an Australian who has been abroad to declare that Australia has no peer. As one sets foot again on Australian soil, one may tell of the wonders of the old world only if the peroration of the description is: 'But Australia's good enough for me!' Set to music, that might easily become the Australian national anthem.

The stranger, if he has any criticism to make, must sugar-coat it with references to sunshine and hospitality and the youthfulness of Australia as a nation. The truth is that as a nation we are on the way toward emulating the baby of the family who has grown so accustomed to being indulged and considered bright for his age, that he cannot bear criticism or correction, and goes on considering himself bright for an infant, long after he has arrived at school age. I must confess to suspecting the flattering stranger of insincerity, and the Australian who can see no fault in Australia, either of insensibility or a cowardly assumption of blindness.

If Australia wants to be self-satisfied she has as yet only her climate for complacent contemplation — and even that is no more wonderful than Italy's. Physically, she is not beautiful except with the beauty of familiarity to those who are her sons. In Switzerland I was asked: 'Australia is very beautiful, is she not?' But within sight of Jungfrau's dazzling brow I could not answer 'Yes.' I replied that my country was more interesting than lovely. One would like to be able to boast of one's native land, but to do so without truth does more harm than good in the end. I met young men in Europe who had been led to believe that Australia was a land of Canaan into which they might walk penniless and unskilled, and from her generous hands pluck an immediate fortune.

I met, on the other hand, a well-educated woman, a writer from Lithuania, who cried out with excitement at discovering me to be an Australian. She excused herself for that involuntary exclamation by explaining that 'she had never seen one before.' All she knew of Australia was what she had learnt from a geography book twenty years ago.

We had white crows, and cherries whose stones grew on the outside, and the dogs of Australia did not drink like European dogs. Was that not so? She had always been curious to know just how our dogs did drink. And what was the official language of Australia? Had we a speech of our own?

I was often asked that. A friend of mine had the same question put to her by a Devonshireman, and with difficulty restrained the wicked desire to tell him 'Nulla nulla.' My little Parisian dressmaker was surprised to know that we did not habitually speak French. Oh! So Australia belonged to the English! The lift-boy at my Florentine hotel, an otherwise well-informed young person, had an idea that Australia was part of India. And the hotel-porter at Hastings was proud to own himself familiar with the name. It was somewhere in Canada he knew. At St Ives, a resident asked if I had met some relatives of his who were living in Australia in Charles Street, not far from the pier.

One understood why our soldiers during the Great War yielded to the temptation of inventing ostrich ranches at Woolloomooloo and kangaroo farms at Footscray. Yet the faintly insulting ignorance concerning Australia of people overseas ought to be a tonic for us. From it we should realize that we have yet to achieve something more than being the biggest island in the world; something more than a sunny climate; something more than sporting records and a heavy wool-clip and an easy swinging of broad shoulders. To the English even we are little more than a curious antipodean people with nice eyes and appalling voices, and an amusing habit of expecting people to be impressed when we say we come from Australia. Compatriots I met abroad were stung to indignation by the polite disinterest in Australia of the average English man and woman. For my part I found it stimulating. That and the determined politeness of the French, which could find nothing more to remark about us than the sturdy build of the soldiers we sent to the Great War. On such occasions I experienced a secret joy at the thought of what we have yet to do. What creative delight awaits us who have yet made little or nothing! How splendid to be a nation in the making with all romance ahead of us!

I could not, with my fellow-Australians, feel insulted because the world was hardly aware of our existence. Why should it be aware of us — yet? What have we done — yet?

When English people said in flat tones: 'You come from Australia? How interesting!' and gazed at me to see what mark of savagery I bore, some spirit of adventure in me hugged itself with delight. I thought of Michelangelo before a shapeless block of stone. I thought of Rembrandt facing an empty canvas. I thought of a mother watching the gaucherie of her adolescent son and reading through it to the ultimate splendour of his manhood. I thought of all the glory and beauty of the world, that men who were once awkward youths had made from bare and shapeless things. I thought of form and colour starting and glowing and taking on an immortal beauty at their bidding. And a great excitement and exaltation filled me at the thought of what we may achieve in nationhood if we but go about it with the combined humility and vanity of true artists.

When I came home I was able a little to see ourselves as others see us. No one but an imbecile would be able to travel without afterwards seeing himself and his native land from a new and more critical angle. (That perhaps may explain why there is no more charming Englishman than the one who has lived out of England!)

On returning to Australia, the first thing that struck me was our lack of graciousness. As I have said before, we are afraid to be charming for fear our courteousness be mistaken for servility. While we imagine ourselves pure democrats we remain as jealous of our dignity as Spanish grandees. And so we conduct ourselves (especially in business affairs) with a 'Take-it-or-leave-it!' air designed to express independence, but achieving only a depressing ungraciousness that robs us of the very dignity we aim at. Our isolation no doubt breeds in us ungraciousness and self-complacency.

It is difficult to say from what arises our dread of betraying sentiment. But because of it, conversation between Australians is mere camouflage. When the joyous purpose of conversation is revelation! Because the Latins realize this instinctively their everyday life is enriched with a vivacious charm of which we do not dream. Your Parisian market vendor philosophizing over her weighing-scales, sends you away with a fresh thought as well as a kilo of apples. Your Venetian chambermaid, your Ticinese boatman, your French concierge are charming and stimulating conversationalists because they do not fear sentiment, and will express the joy and sorrow, the dread and amusement and surprise of life without shame.

Who in Australia departs a hair's breadth from the commonplace in conversation runs the immediate risk of uneasiness on the part of his vis-à-vis. If by chance an Australian feels anything so deeply as to be led into a momentary expression of emotion, he interpolates as soon as possible some facetiousness with which he hopes to wipe out the shameful memory of his lapse. One slides one's eyes away from any sign of deep feeling here, as if it were an indecency. And so, beauty languishes. For beauty, I do believe, has emotion both for cause and effect, springing like a plant from the seed of sentiment and flinging up a flower of loveliness that in its turn breeds in the beholder an emotion which begets more beauty, in an endless cycle of beauty and emotion, emotion and beauty.

I am not of those who can contentedly say: 'Australia's good enough for me!' I heard that assertion with its terrifying avowal of myopia, in the magnificence of the Doge's Palace; before the exquisiteness of the vistas in the grounds at Versailles; in the splendour of the great Roman squares. It echoed among the Swiss Alps and down the corridors of the great Dutch galleries, and along the historic streets of London. I heard it again and again, yet it never failed to depress, like meeting a blind man on a perfect day.

When aviation makes it possible for the school holidays of Australian children, and the annual leave of many a small-salaried man and woman to be spent overseas, please God complacency which is paralysis will give place in us to vanity which is a motive power.

Australia is not good enough for me!
She is as yet no more than the matrix of the glorious opal the world will wear when the hands of her true lovers have done their work.

There was a day when Venice was but a few scattered islands in a lagoon. Her lovers, seeing what she lacked, ransacked the world and laid its riches at her feet. They were not blind because they were her lovers. Nor should we be who love Australia. It is no treachery to the beloved to be aware of her shortcomings and eager for her to win the things she lacks. Much nearer to treachery is the complacency which declares she is already perfect. And they most truly love Australia who return to her with minds like argosies, full-freighted with memories of the best things of the world and the desire to see her reproduce them for her own embellishment.

Seventh Heaven (1930)

1988

Gerard Lee at Bondi

Late in the afternoon, I walked along the foreshore at Bondi Beach with a Scotsman who like myself had lived for some time in Paris. He'd only recently arrived in Australia and I wanted to show him the famous beach. We started at the north end, Ramsgate Avenue, and walked around to the south headland till we had a view of Tamarama.

It was that time of day when, if you're lucky enough to have a thin cloud covering, the sky goes pink and the water goes pink and azure, and a kind of green-pink and there's even some cream in there, if you give yourself time to see it. We stood on the cliffs in a slightly uncomfortable breeze looking down into the breakers and further out into the green water. All this colour was disappearing fast, draining out of the landscape.

Billy seemed to like it, though with people from the UK you can never tell. I was anxious in a cultural-cringe kind of way that he should like Bondi. I wanted him to say it was better than the Scottish Coast, and the Irish and the English Coast. What would have satisfied me was if he'd said it was the best coast he'd ever seen in the whole world. I waited but he didn't speak. He just stood there looking out and smoking, the wind flicking the hair off his Scottish brow.

'There's always women around here,' I said, 'with romantic looks on their faces. They wear PLO scarves and those guerrilla pants — the ones you can hide grenades and bayonets in.' He smiled, but made no comment.

'And they're always talking about men, you can tell.'

'Ah, how you can tell?'

'They stop talking when they see you coming.'

He let out what seemed to be an 'ach' of annoyance.

But just then, a woman, alone, in designer-guerrilla clothes and bare feet (shoes in hand) came along the path toward us.

'See,' I murmured.

'I cain't hear her talkin' about men.'

She walked out to the edge of the cliff, stood about a centimetre from the drop, lifted her arms and closed her eyes. Slowly she leaned out into the air. Billy shook his head and looked away, but had to look back.

'What's she doin'?'

He didn't know?

'She's being romantic, she's holding hands with death.'

'Ah, you're a smartarse.'

'She's not going to jump, Billy. If you're going to jump, your eyes are popping out of your head, your knees are rattling and you're not wearing Najee pants.'

I wished I was as unselfconscious as she was.

On the way home the sky was darkening and we stopped at the north end to look back.

The lights from the shops along the esplanade had come on, blues (from the Nirvana Liquor Store and The Ruins); yellows (New Zealand Ice Cream); the white loops from the hotel roof; pinks, everything. Behind them the sky was a peachy colour and above that, a light blue with a great airy depth to it.

'Look at thart,' Billy said, as a final word on the discussion we'd been having, Sydney versus Paris. 'It's so much better than Paris. How could you want Paris when you've seen the lights o' Bondi.'

'Billy,' I said, 'I was talking about the Seine and the beach here. Aquatically, there is no comparison.'

'Ah, Gerard.' He belted the tip of a new cigarette against the packet and put it in his mouth. 'Of course, there's no comparison. Why would anybody want to compare it? We're in Australia for Christ's sake, Paris is in France.'

'What? Have I been going on about this?'

He smiled: 'Just a wee bit.'

But I don't think he understood. When the winter westerly whips into the waves, making them choppy but rideable, and you're out with the grommets desperate for anything, and darkness begins to fall till you only know the good ones by the sound they make, and you're happy and wet, waiting out there, rocking on the evening sea, for the last big one to take you in, and you happen to glance inland and suddenly, there they are, the lights of Bondi, the soft colours growing brighter, and behind them, the twinkling suburbs up to Bellevue Hill, you think, My God, how can I be so lucky — and you do tend to go on about it a 'wee bit'.

Eating Dog (1993)

NOTES

Introduction

1 Ann McGrath, *'Born in the Cattle': Aborigines in Cattle Country*, Allen & Unwin, Sydney, 1987, pp. 4–5; see also Krim Benterrak, Stephen Muecke & Paddy Roe, *Reading the Country: Introduction to Nomadology*, Fremantle Arts Centre Press, Fremantle, 1984.

2 D. J. Mulvaney & J. Peter White, *Australians to 1788*, Fairfax Syme & Weldon, Sydney, 1987, pp. 94–101; Geoffrey Blainey, *Triumph of the Nomads: A History of Ancient Australia*, Macmillan, Melbourne, 1975, pp. 238–9, 246–51.

3 Russel Ward, *The Australian Legend*, Oxford University Press, Melbourne, 1966, especially pp. 1–6.

4 David Walker, 'Travellers to the Orient', *Asian Studies Association of Australia Review*, vol. 12, no. 1, 1988, pp. 12-17; David Walker & John Ingleson, 'The impacts of Asia', in *Under New Heavens*, Neville Meaney (ed.), Heinemann, Melbourne, 1989; Alison Broinowski, *The Yellow Lady: Australian Impressions of Asia*, Oxford University Press, Melbourne, 1992.

5 N. D. McLachlan, '"The future America": Some Bicentennial reflections', *Historical Studies*, vol. 17, no. 68, 1977, pp. 361–83; L. G. Churchward, *Australia & America 1788–1972: An Alternative History*, Alternative Publishing Cooperative, Sydney, 1979; Richard White, *Inventing Australia: Images and Identity 1688–1980*, Allen & Unwin, Sydney, 1981, ch. 4.

6 R. C. Thompson, *Australian Imperialism in the Pacific: The Expansionist Era 1820–1920*, Melbourne University Press, Melbourne, 1980; Ann Stephen (ed.), *Pirating the Pacific: Images of Travel, Trade and Tourism*, Powerhouse Museum, Sydney, 1993.

7 For statistics see *Year Book Australia 1995*, Australian Bureau of Statistics, Canberra, 1994, pp. 68, 430–3, and other editions; *Overseas Arrivals and Departures*, Australian Bureau of Statistics, Canberra, annual publication.

8 See Ros Pesman, David Walker & Richard White (eds), *An Annotated Bibliography of Australian Overseas Travel Writing*, compiled by Terri McCormack, ALIA Bibliographies on Disk, Canberra, 1996.

9 Charles Higham & Michael Wilding (eds), *Australians Abroad: An Anthology*, Cheshire, Melbourne, 1967; John Hammond Moore (ed.), *Australians*

in America, 1876–1976, University of Queensland Press, Brisbane, 1977; Robyn Lucas & Clare Foster (eds), *Wilder Shores: Women's Travel Stories of Australia and Beyond,* University of Queensland Press, Brisbane, 1992; Geoff Page (ed.), *On the Move: Australian Poets in Europe,* Butterfly Books, Springwood, NSW, 1992; Robin Gerster (ed.), *Hotel Asia,* Penguin, Melbourne, 1995; John Borthwick (ed.), *The Road to Anywhere: The Travel Writings of Peter Pinney,* University of Queensland Press, Brisbane, 1993; Laurie Hergenhan & Irmtraud Petersson (eds), *Changing Places: Australian Writers in Europe 1960s–1990s,* University of Queensland Press, Brisbane, 1994; Rosemary Creswell (ed.), *Home and Away: Travel Stories,* Penguin, Melbourne, 1987.

10 Note however two issues of *Australian Cultural History,* 'Australian perceptions of Asia', no. 9, 1990, and 'Travellers, journeys, tourists', no. 10, 1991; *Meanjin,* vol. 43, no. 9, 1990, special issue titled 'Unsentimental journeys'; Gaetano Prampolini & Marie-Christine Hubert (eds), *An Antipodean Connection: Australian Writers, Artists and Travellers in Tuscany,* Slatkine, Geneva, 1993.

11 As, for example, in Paul Fussell, *Abroad: British Literary Traveling Between the Wars,* Oxford University Press, New York, 1980.

12 Richard White, 'The outsider's gaze and the representation of Australia', in *Australia in the World: Perceptions and Possibilities,* Don Grant & Graham Seal (eds), Black Swan Press, Curtin University of Technology, Perth, 1994, pp. 22–8.

13 Dorothy Green, *Ulysses Bound: Henry Handel Richardson and Her Fiction,* Australian National University Press, Canberra, 1973; Brenda Niall, *Martin Boyd: A Life,* Melbourne University Press, Melbourne, 1988; Hazel Rowley, *Christina Stead: A Biography,* Heinemann, Melbourne, 1993; Garry Kinnane, *George Johnston: A Biography,* Nelson, Melbourne, 1986.

14 Donald Denoon, 'The isolation of Australian history', *Historical Studies,* vol. 22, no. 87, 1986, pp. 252–60.

15 Two recent examples are Judith Brett, *Robert Menzies' Forgotten People,* Pan Macmillan, Sydney, 1992, and Janet McCalman, *Journeyings: The Biography of a Middle-Class Generation 1920–1990,* Melbourne University Press, Melbourne, 1993.

16 Rana Kabbani, *Imperial Fictions: Europe's Myths of Orient,* Pandora, London, 1994, p. 10; see also Edward Said, *Orientalism,* Routledge & Kegan Paul, London, 1978.

17 Ethel Turner, *Ports and Happy Havens,* Hodder & Stoughton, London, 1912, p. 73. Turner might have been reading the latest novels rather than talking to acquaintances. In 1905 E. M. Forster's rather conventional Italophile, Philip Herriton, on the first page of *Where Angels Fear to Tread* was advising 'that it is only by going off the track that you get to know the country', Penguin, Harmondsworth, 1976, p. 19.

18 Randolph Bedford, *Explorations in Civilization,* S. Day, Sydney, 1914.

19 John Forbes, 'Europe: A guide', in his collection *The Stunned Mullet,* Hale & Iremonger, Sydney, 1989.

20 Interestingly, Australian autobiography, unlike travel writing, has been recognised as a significant genre. See Richard Coe, *When the Grass was Greener: Autobiography and the Experience of Childhood*, Yale University Press, New Haven, 1984; John & Dorothy Colmer (eds), *The Penguin Book of Australian Autobiography*, Penguin, Melbourne, 1987; John Colmer, *Australian Autobiography: The Personal Quest*, Oxford University Press, Melbourne, 1989; Joy Hooton, *Stories of Herself When Young: Autobiographies of Childhood by Australian Women*, Oxford University Press, Melbourne, 1990.

21 Patrick White, *Flaws in the Glass: A Self-Portrait*, Jonathan Cape, London, 1981, pp. 100, 116.

22 Manning Clark, *The Quest for Grace*, Penguin, Melbourne, 1990, pp. 66, 219.

23 Martin Boyd, *A Single Flame*, Dent, London, 1939, p. 167.

24 Christina Stead, *For Love Alone*, Collins/Angus & Robertson, Sydney, 1990 (1945), p. 343.

25 Henry Handel Richardson, *Myself When Young*, W. W. Norton, New York, 1948, p. 98.

26 Cited in Roslyn Pesman Cooper, 'Majestic nature — squalid humanity: Naples and the Australian tourist 1870–1930', *Australian Cultural History*, 10, 1991, p. 55.

27 Clive James, *Unreliable Memoirs*, Picador, London, 1980, p. 168.

28 Peter Conrad, *Where I Fell to Earth*, Chatto & Windus, London, 1990, p. 25.

29 Richard White, 'The soldier as tourist: The Australian experience of the Great War', *War & Society*, vol. 5, no. 1, 1987, pp. 63–77.

30 Cited in Eric Leed, *The Mind of the Traveler: From Gilgamesh to Global Tourism*, Basic Books, New York, 1991, p. 107.

31 Leed, p. 106; see also Percy Adams, *Travel Literature and the Evolution of the Novel*, University Press of Kentucky, Lexington, 1983.

32 Frank Graham, *Man's Dominion: The Story of Conservation in America*, M. Evans & Company, New York, 1971, p. 76.

33 Norman Lindsay, *Hyperborea: Two Fantastic Travel Essays*, Fanfrolico Press, London, 1928; John Docker, *The Nervous Nineties: Australian Cultural Life in the 1890s*, Oxford University Press, Melbourne, 1991; Van Ikin (ed.), *Australian Science Fiction*, University of Queensland Press, Brisbane, 1982.

34 Richard White, 'Bluebells and Fogtown: Australians' first impressions of England, 1860–1940', *Australian Cultural History*, no. 5, 1986, pp. 44–59.

35 Roland Barthes, *Mythologies*, Hill & Wang, New York, 1972 (1957), pp. 74–7.

36 White, 'Bluebells and Fogtown', *Australian Cultural History*, pp. 54–6; Richard White, 'Sun, sand and syphilis: Australian soldiers and the Orient, Egypt 1914', *Australian Cultural History*, no. 9, 1990, pp. 57–60; Pesman Cooper, *Australian Cultural History*, pp. 49–50.

37 Ambrose Pratt, *Magical Malaya*, Robertson & Mullens, Melbourne, 1931, p. 268.

38 C. E. W. Bean, *What to Know in Egypt: A Guide for Australian Soldiers*, Cairo, 1915, pp. 11–13.

39 A. W. Dobbie, *Rough Notes of a Traveller*, 2nd series, Simpkin, Marshall, Hamilton, Kent & Co., London, 1890, p. 44.

40 John Stanley James ('The Vagabond'), *Occident and Orient*, George Robertson, Melbourne, 1882, p. 124.

41 Frank Moorhouse (ed.), *The State of the Art: The Mood of Contemporary Australia in Short Stories*, Penguin, Melbourne, 1983, p. 2.

42 Among many examples, Fussell; Leed; Dean MacCannell, *The Tourist: A New Theory of the Leisure Class*, Schocken Books, New York, 1976; Dennis Porter, *Haunted Journeys: Desire and Transgression in European Travel Writing*, Princeton University Press, Princeton, 1991; Michael Kowalewski (ed.), *Temperamental Journeys: Essays on the Modern Literature of Travel*, University of Georgia Press, Athens, 1992; Mary Louise Pratt, *Imperial Eyes: Travel Writing and Transculturation*, Routledge, London, 1992; James Buzzard, *The Beaten Track: European Tourism, Literature, and the Ways to 'Culture' 1800–1918*, Oxford University Press, Oxford, 1993; John Urry, *The Tourist Gaze: Leisure and Travel in Contemporary Societies*, Sage, London, 1990; Sara Mills, *Discourses of Difference: An Analysis of Women's Travel Writing and Colonialism*, Routledge, London, 1991; see also the journal *Annals of Tourism Research*.

43 Ros Pesman, *Duty Free: Australian Women Abroad*, Oxford University Press, Melbourne, 1996, p. 4; Victor Turner, *Dramas, Fields and Metaphors: Symbolic Action in Human Society*, Cornell University Press, Ithaca, 1974, pp. 166–230.

44 G. C. Dixon, *From Melbourne to Moscow*, Geoffrey Bles, London, 1925, p. 12.

45 Australians are not the only nationality to have constructed their travels as pilgrimage: see Ian Reader & Tony Walter (eds), *Pilgrimage in Popular Culture*, Macmillan, London, 1993.

46 Pesman, *Duty Free*, p. 140; see also Michael Davidson, *Leningrad: American Writers in the Soviet Union*, Mercury House, San Francisco, 1991; Sylvia Margulies, *The Pilgrimage to Russia: The Soviet Union and the Treatment of Foreigners 1924–1937*, University of Wisconsin Press, Madison, 1968; Paul Hollander, *Political Pilgrims: Travels of Western Intellectuals to the Soviet Union, China and Cuba 1928–1978*, Oxford University Press, New York, 1981.

47 A. W. Martin, *Robert Menzies: A Life*, vol. 1, Melbourne University Press, Melbourne, 1993, p. 148; Nancy Phelan, *Swift Foot of Time: An Australian in England 1938–1945*, Quartet Books, Melbourne, 1983, p. 5. For a brilliant analysis of the meaning of England for Menzies, see Brett.

48 Peter Cochrane, The love of England, unpublished paper, 1995.

49 George Johnston, *Clean Straw for Nothing*, World Books, Sydney, 1970, p. 83. See also White, 'Bluebells and Fogtown', *Australian Cultural History*, pp. 50–1.

50 Turner, *Ports and Happy Havens*, pp. 24, 72.

51 Cited in Pesman, *Duty Free*, p. 5.

52 Christopher Koch, *Crossing the Gap: A Novelist's Essays*, Chatto & Windus, London, 1987, p. 1. For Koch, ironically, it was the beginning of a sustained examination of Asia in the Australian imagination.

53 See Buzzard, ch. 1. For the Grand Tour see Jeremy Black, *The British Abroad: The Grand Tour in the Eighteenth Century*, Sutton St Martin's Press, New York, 1992; John Towner, 'The Grand Tour: A key phase in the history of tourism', *Annals of Tourism Research*, vol. 12, 1985.

54 Kevin D. S. Murray, 'A life in the world in Australia', *Australian Cultural History*, no. 10, 1991, pp. 32–45.

55 Buzzard, pp. 130ff.

56 Richard White, 'Overseas', in *Australians 1938*, Bill Gammage & Peter Spearritt (eds), Fairfax, Syme & Weldon, Sydney, 1987, p. 441; K. S. Inglis, 'Going Home: Australians in England 1870–1900', in *Home or Away? Immigrants in Colonial Australia*, David Fitzpatrick (ed.), Division of Historical Studies and Centre for Immigration and Multicultural Studies, Australian National University, Canberra, 1992, pp. 105–6.

57 Pesman, *Duty Free*, pp. 24–7.

58 J. M. Ward, *James Macarthur: Colonial Conservative 1798–1867*, Sydney University Press, Sydney, 1981, pp. 12–20, 41–5; Margaret Kiddle, *Men of Yesterday: A Social History of the Western District of Victoria 1834–1890*, Melbourne University Press, Melbourne, 1961, pp. 489–98.

59 John Hirst, 'Egalitarianism', in *Pastiche I: Reflections on Nineteenth Century Australia*, Penny Russell & Richard White (eds), Allen & Unwin, Sydney, 1994; Penny Russell, *'A Wish of Distinction': Colonial Gentility and Femininity*, Melbourne University Press, Melbourne, 1994.

60 Cited in Pesman, *Duty Free*, p. 26.

61 White, *War & Society*, pp. 63–77.

62 James Hingston, *The Australian Abroad*, 2nd edn, William Inglis & Company, Melbourne, 1885, Preface. See also Walker, *Asian Studies Association of Australia Review*, pp. 12–17.

63 Henry Lawson, 'Letters to Jack Cornstalk' (London, September 1900), in *Complete Works*, vol. 1, *A Camp-Fire Yarn*, Leonard Cronin (ed.), Lansdowne, Sydney, 1984, p. 784.

64 Florence M. Taylor, *A Pot-Pourri of Eastern Asia: With Comparisons and Reflections*, Building Publishing Company, Sydney, 1935, Foreword.

65 White, 'Bluebells and Fogtown', *Australian Cultural History*, p. 44.

66 G. H. Morrison, *An Australian in China: Being the Narrative of a Quiet Journey across China to British Burma*, Angus & Robertson, Sydney, 1972 (1895), pp. 35–6.

67 Clive James, *Flying Visits: Postcards from the* Observer *1976–1983*, Cape, London, 1984, Introduction.

68 Moorhouse, p. 2.

Nationalists

1 *Sydney Morning Herald*, June 1895, cited in *Constitutional Centenary*, vol. 4, no. 2, 1995, pp. 14–15.

2 Henry Lawson, '"Pursuing literature" in Australia', in *Henry Lawson: Autobiographical and Other Writings*, Colin Roderick (ed.), vol. 1, Angus & Robertson, Sydney, 1972, p. 115.

Travel and culture

1 Robin Gerster, *Big-Noting: The Heroic Theme in Australian War Writing*, Melbourne University Press, Melbourne, 1987.
2 *Picturesque Travel*, Burns, Philp & Company, Sydney, n.d., p. 7.

Travels in postmodernity

1 Buzzard, pp. 336–7; Urry, pp. 84ff; Maxine Feifer, *Tourism in History: From Imperial Rome to the Present*, Stein & Day, New York, 1986, pp. 259–71.

Returning home

1 C. H. Bertie, *For Pleasure*, Angus & Robertson, Sydney, 1937, p. 268.

SELECT BIBLIOGRAPHY

Reference works

Adelaide, Debra. *Australian Women Writers: A Bibliographic Guide*. Pandora, London, 1988.

Adelaide, Debra. *Bibliography of Australian Women's Literature 1795–1990*. Thorpe, Melbourne, 1991.

Australian Dictionary of Biography, vols 1–13. Melbourne University Press, Melbourne, 1966–93.

Ferguson, J. H. *Bibliography of Australia, 1881–1969*. Angus & Robertson, Sydney, 1949–69.

McCulloch, Alan. *Encyclopedia of Australian Art*, 3rd edn. Allen & Unwin, Sydney, 1994.

Miller, E. Morris & Frederick T. Macartney. *Australian Literature: A Bibliography*. Angus & Robertson, Sydney, 1956.

Pesman, Ros, David Walker & Richard White (eds). *An Annotated Bibliography of Australian Overseas Travel Writing*. Compiled by Terri McCormack, ALIA Bibliographies on Disk, Canberra, 1996.

Who's Who in Australia, vols 1–32, various publishers, 1908–1996.

Who's Who of Australian Writers, 2nd edn. Thorpe, Melbourne, 1995.

Wilde, W. H., Hooton, J. & Andrews, B. *Oxford Companion to Australian Literature*, 2nd edn. Oxford University Press, Melbourne, 1994.

Anthologies

Borthwick, John (ed.). *The Road to Anywhere: Peter Pinney's Travel Writing*. University of Queensland Press, Brisbane, 1993.

Gerster, Robin (ed.). *Hotel Asia*. Penguin, Melbourne, 1995.

Hergenhan, Laurie & Irmtraud Petersson (eds). *Changing Places: Australian Writers in Europe 1960s–1990s*. University of Queensland Press, Brisbane, 1994.

Higham, Charles & Michael Wilding (eds). *Australians Abroad: An Anthology*. Cheshire, Melbourne, 1967.

Lucas, Robyn & Clare Foster (eds). *Wilder Shores: Women's Travel Stories of Australia and Beyond*. University of Queensland Press, Brisbane, 1992.

Moore, John Hammond. *Australians in America, 1876–1976.* University of Queensland Press, Brisbane, 1977.

Studies on Australian travel and travel writing

'Australian perceptions of Asia' (thematic issue). *Australian Cultural History*, no. 9, 1990.

Broinowski, Alison. *The Yellow Lady: Australian Impressions of Asia.* Oxford University Press, Melbourne, 1992.

Horne, Donald. *The Intelligent Tourist.* Margaret Gee, Sydney, 1992.

Pesman, Ros. *Duty Free: Australian Women Abroad.* Oxford University Press, Melbourne, 1996.

Prampolini, G. & M-C. Hubert (eds). *An Antipodean Connection: Australian Writers, Artists and Travellers in Tuscany.* Slatkine, Geneva, 1993.

'Travellers, journeys, tourists' (thematic issue). *Australian Cultural History*, no. 10, 1991.

Autobiographies and biographies

Bedford, Randolph. *Naught to Thirty-Three.* Currency, Sydney, 1944.

Buckley, Vincent. *Cutting Green Hay: Friendships, Movements and Cultural Conflicts in Australia's Great Decades.* Allen Lane, Melbourne, 1983.

Capturing the Orient: Hilda Rix Nicholas & Ethel Carrick in the East. Catalogue, Waverley City Gallery, Melbourne, 1994.

Clune, Frank. *Try Anything Once: The Autobiography of a Wanderer.* Angus & Robertson, Sydney, 1933.

Conrad, Peter. *Down Home: Revisiting Tasmania.* Chatto & Windus, London, 1988.

Conway, Jill Ker. *The Road from Coorain.* Alfred Knopf, New York, 1987.

Conway, Jill Ker. *True North, A Memoir.* Alfred Knopf, New York, 1994.

Freehill, Norman with Dymphna Cusack. *Dymphna Cusack.* Nelson, Melbourne, 1975.

Grant, Bruce (ed.). *Arthur and Eric: An Anglo-Australian Story from the Journal of Arthur Hickman.* Heinemann, Melbourne, 1977. (For Eric Muspratt.)

Holman, Ada. *My Wander Year: Some Jottings in a Year's Travel.* William Brooks & Co., Sydney, 1914.

Indyk, Ivor. *David Malouf.* Oxford University Press, Melbourne, 1993.

James, Clive. *Falling Towards England: Unreliable Memoirs Continued.* Jonathan Cape, London, 1985.

James, Clive. *May Week Was in June: Unreliable Memoirs Continued.* Pan, London, 1991.

Koch, C. J. *Crossing the Gap: A Novelist's Essays.* Hogarth Press, London, 1987.

La Nauze, J. A. *Alfred Deakin: A Biography.* Melbourne University Press, Melbourne, 1965; reprinted by Angus & Robertson, Sydney, 1979.

Macleod, R. (ed.). *University and Community in Nineteenth Century Sydney. Professor John Smith, 1821–1885.* Sydney University Press, Sydney, 1988.

Magarey, Susan. *Unbridling the Tongues of Women: A Biography of Catherine Helen Spence.* Hale & Iremonger, Sydney, 1985.

Malouf, David. *Johnno.* University of Queensland Press, Brisbane, 1975.

Marr, David. *Patrick White: A Life.* Random House, Sydney, 1991.

Moorehead, Alan. *A Late Education: Episodes in a Life.* Penguin, Harmondsworth, 1976.

Moran, H. M. *Viewless Winds: Being the Recollections and Digressions of an Australian Surgeon.* Peter Daniels, London, 1939

Muspratt, Eric. *Ambition: An Autobiographical Novel.* Duckworth, London, 1934.

Niall, Brenda. *Martin Boyd: A Life.* Melbourne University Press, Melbourne, 1988.

Pearl, Cyril. *Morrison of Peking.* Angus & Robertson, Sydney, 1967.

Phelan, Nancy. *Kingdom by the Sea.* Angus & Robertson, Sydney, 1988.

Phelan, Nancy. *Swift Foot of Time: An Australian in England, 1938–45.* Quartet Books, Melbourne, 1983.

Pocock, Tom. *Alan Moorehead.* Bodley Head, London, 1990.

Prichard, Katharine Susannah. *Child of the Hurricane: An Autobiography.* Angus & Robertson, Sydney, 1963.

Riemer, Andrew. *Inside Outside.* Angus & Roberston, Sydney, 1992.

Roderick, Colin. *Henry Lawson: A Life.* Angus & Robertson, Sydney, 1991.

Taylor, Griffith. *Douglas Mawson.* Oxford University Press, Melbourne, 1962.

Throssell, Ric. *Wild Weeds and Wind Flowers: The Life of Katharine Susannah Prichard.* Angus & Robertson, Sydney, 1975.

White, Patrick. *Flaws in the Glass: A Self Portrait.* Penguin, Harmondsworth, 1983.

Yarwood, A. T. *From a Chair in the Sun: The Life of Ethel Turner.* Viking, Melbourne, 1994.

SOURCES AND ACKNOWLEDGMENTS

à Beckett, Sir William. *Out of Harness.* J. J. Guillaume, London, 1854, pp. 72–5, 78–85.

Becke, Louis. *Wild Life in Southern Seas.* Unwin, London, 1897, pp. 147–57.

Bedford, Randolph. *Explorations in Civilization.* S. Day, printer, Sydney, 1914, pp. 20–2, 24–5, 36–7, 168.

Blannin, Captain Alfred. *Hasty Notes of a Flying Trip with the Victorian Rifle Team in England and America in 1876.* George Robertson, Melbourne, 1877, pp. 133–7.

Bouras, Gillian. *A Foreign Wife.* McPhee Gribble/Penguin, Melbourne, 1986, pp. 22–6, 28–30.

Boyd, Martin. *A Single Flame.* Dent, London, 1939, pp. 72–9, 85–7.

Buckley, Vincent. *Memory Ireland: Insights into the Contemporary Irish Condition.* Penguin, Melbourne, 1985, pp. 93–4, 98–100, 103–5, 108–10.

Byles, Marie. *The Lotus and the Spinning Wheel.* Allen & Unwin, London, 1963, pp. 47, 55–6, 66–8.

Clune, Frank, *All Aboard for Singapore.* Angus & Robertson, Sydney, 1941, pp. 118–21, 123–6.

Conrad, Peter. *Where I Fell to Earth: A Life in Four Places.* Chatto & Windus, London, 1990, pp. 234–5, 239–41, 243–5.

Conway, Jill Ker. *The Road from Coorain.* First edition, Heinemann, Melbourne, 1989; Minerva, 1992, pp. 127–34.

Cusack, Dymphna. *Illyria Reborn.* Heinemann, London, 1966, pp. 1–2, 8–11.

Davidson, Robyn. *Travelling Light.* Collins, Sydney, 1989, pp. 76–9, 83–6.

Deakin, Alfred. *Temple and Tomb in India.* Melville, Mullen & Slade, Melbourne, 1893, pp. 64–73.

Deane, Shirley. *Tomorrow is Mañana: An Andalusian Village.* John Murray, London, 1957, pp. 6–7, 9–13.

Dinning, Hector. *By-ways on Service.* Constable, London, 1918, pp. 243–5.

Doull, David. *With the Anzacs in Egypt: Life and Scenes in the Land of the Pharaohs, as Seen through Australian Spectacles,* J. A. Packer, printer, Sydney, 1916, pp. 56–64.

Falkiner, Suzanne. *Rain in the Distance*. Penguin, Melbourne, 1986, pp. 117–19, 122–7.

Gaunt, Mary. *Alone in West Africa*. T. Werner Laurie, London, 1912, pp. 355–68.

Greer, Germaine. In *River Journeys*, Russell Braddon et al., BBC, London, 1984, pp. 122–30.

Hides, Jack. *Papuan Wonderland*. First edition, Blackie & Son, Glasgow, 1936; Arkon (Angus & Robertson), Sydney, 1973, pp. 77–81, 92–4, 115, 120–4.

Hingston, James. *The Australian Abroad*, vol. 2. Sampson, Low, Marston & Co., London, 1879, pp. 481–90.

Hogan, James F. *The Australian in London and America*. Ward & Downey, London, 1889, pp. 114–17.

Holman, Ada. *My Wander Year: Some Jottings in a Year's Travel*. William Brookes & Co., Sydney, 1913, pp.15–16, 44–7, 87–9.

James, Clive. *Flying Visits – Postcards from the* Observer *1979–1983*. Picador, London, 1984, pp. 81–4, 86–9.

Jennings, Kate. *Save Me, Joe Louis*. Penguin, Melbourne, 1988, pp. 1, 12–15, 18–21.

Koch, Christopher. *Crossing the Gap: A Novelist's Essays*. Chatto & Windus, London, 1987, pp. 28, 32–6.

Lawson, Henry. 'New Zealand from an Australian's Point of View'. *Fair Play*. In *A Camp-Fire Yarn: Henry Lawson Complete Works*, Leonard Cronin (ed.), Lansdowne, Sydney, 1984, pp. 344–6.

Lee, Gerard. *Eating Dog: Travel Stories*. University of Queensland Press, Brisbane, 1993, pp. 109–10, 114–19, 122; 153–5.

Malouf, David. *12 Edmonstone Street*. Chatto & Windus, London, 1985, pp. 69–76, 78–9.

Mawson, Sir Douglas. *Home of the Blizzard: Being the Story of the Australian Antarctic Expedition 1911–1914*. First edition, Heinemann, London, 1915; Revised popular edition, Hodder & Stoughton, London, 1934, pp. 186–93.

McCulloch, Alan. *Trial by Tandem*. Cheshire, Melbourne, 1950, pp. 161–2, 170–3, 178–82.

McGuire, Paul. *Westward the Course! The New World of Oceania*. Oxford University Press, Melbourne, 1942, pp. 190–5.

McLaren, Jack. *My Odyssey*. Cape, London, 1923, pp. 247–56.

Moorehead, Alan. *No Room in the Ark*. Hamilton, London, 1959, pp. 68–75.

Moran, H. M. *In My Fashion: An Autobiography of the Last Ten Years*. Peter Davies, London, 1946, pp. 10–15, 31–3.

Morrison, A. F. (A Rambling Victorian). *Sketches in Russia*. William Inglis & Co., Melbourne, 1886, pp. 26, 106–11.

Morrison, G. E. *An Australian in China*. Horace Cox, London, 1895, pp. 50–2, 80–7, 91–4.

Murdoch, Nina. *Seventh Heaven: A Joyous Discovery of Europe*. Angus & Robertson, Sydney, 1930, pp. 1–2, 5–10; 252–6.

Murray, J. B. *American Trails*. Melbourne University Press, Melbourne, 1944, pp. 35–42.

Muspratt, Eric. *The Journey Home*. Duckworth, London, 1933, pp. 136–41, 144–51.

Nolan, Cynthia. *One Traveller's Africa*. Methuen, London, 1965, pp. 226–36.

Oram, Malcolm. *The Long Brown Path*. Horwitz, Sydney, 1957, pp. 148–50, 152–3, 160–4.

Phelan, Nancy. *The Chilean Way: Travels in Chile*, Macmillan, London, 1973, pp. 31–41.

Pinney, Peter. *Dust on My Shoes*. Angus & Robertson, Sydney, 1952, pp. 52–9.

Pratt, Ambrose. *Magical Malaya*. Robertson & Mullens, Melbourne, 1931, pp. 259–65.

Prichard, Katharine Susannah. *The Real Russia*. Modern Publishers, Sydney, 1934, pp. 1–3, 6–9, 13–14, 23–5.

Riemer, Andrew. *The Habsburg Café*. Collins/Angus & Robertson, Sydney, 1993, pp. 18–19, 57–62, 276–9.

Rix Nicholas, Hilda. 'Sketching in Morocco'. *Studio*, vol. 63, no. 259, 1914, pp. 35–6, 39, 41.

Smith, John. *Wayfaring Notes (Second Series): Holiday Tour Round the World*. A. Browne & Co., Aberdeen, 1876, pp. 94–6, 158–9, 250–3.

Spence, Catherine Helen. 'An Australian's Impressions of England'. *Cornhill Magazine*, XIII, January–June 1866, pp. 110–20.

Spielvogel, Nathan. *A Gumsucker on the Tramp*. S. Spielvogel, printer, Ballarat, 1905; 2nd enlarged edn, G. Robertson, Melbourne, c. 1906, pp. 29–30, 32–6, 38–9; 105–7.

Stephens, A. G. *A Queenslander's Travel Notes*. Edwards, Dunlop & Co., Sydney, 1894, pp. 98–103.

Turner, Ethel. *Ports and Happy Havens*. Hodder & Stoughton, London, 1912, pp. 161–7, 171–5.

Vincent, Alf. 'Vagabonding in Asia'. *Lone Hand*, vol. 2, no. 8, 1907, pp. 133–8.

White, Patrick. *Flaws in the Glass*. Cape, London, 1981, pp. 115–23.

Wirth, George. *Round the World With a Circus*. Troedel & Cooper Printers, Melbourne, 1925, pp. 84–7.

INDEX